Group Dynamics in Exercise and Sport Psychology

How do group members influence each other's behaviour in sport and exercise settings?

Can a better understanding of group dynamics raise individual and team athletic performance or improve the outcomes of exercise interventions?

Much human behaviour in sport and exercise settings is embedded within groups where individuals' cognitions, emotions, and behaviours influence and are influenced by other group members. *Group Dynamics in Exercise and Sport Psychology: Contemporary Themes* explores the unique psychological dynamics that emerge in sport and exercise groups. It provides a clear and thorough guide to contemporary theory and research. Recommendations are also presented to inform applied psychology 'best practice'.

Drawing together the expertise of international specialists from sport and exercise psychology, the text covers core themes as well as emerging issues in group dynamics. The text is organised into four sections:

Part 1: The Self in Groups
Part 2: Leadership in Groups
Part 3: Group Environment
Part 4: Motivation in Groups

Group Dynamics in Exercise and Sport Psychology: Contemporary Themes will be of interest to psychology, kinesiology, sport and exercise science students and researchers, as well as consultants and coaches.

Mark R. Beauchamp is an Assistant Professor at the School of Human Kinetics, University of British Columbia, Canada. His research primarily focuses on the social psychology of Group Dynamics in sport and exercise contexts.

Mark A. Eys is an Assistant Professor at the School of Human Kinetics, Laurentian University, Canada. His research has focused on the sources and consequences of understanding role responsibilities in team environments as well as issues related to group cohesion in both sport and exercise.

Group Dynamics in Exercise and Sport Psychology

Contemporary themes

Edited by Mark R. Beauchamp and
Mark A. Eys

LONDON AND NEW YORK

First published 2007
by Routledge
2 Park Square, Milton Park, Abingdon, Oxon, OX14 4RN

Simultaneously published in the USA and Canada
by Routledge
270 Madison Avenue, New York, NY 10016

Routledge is an imprint of the Taylor and Francis Group, an informa business

Typeset in Goudy by
RefineCatch Limited, Bungay, Suffolk
Printed and bound in Great Britain
by TJ International Ltd, Padstow, Cornwall

British Library Cataloguing in Publication Data
A catalogue record for this book is available from the British Library

Library of Congress Cataloging in Publication Data
Group dynamics in exercise and sport psychology : contemporary themes /
    edited by Mark Beauchamp & Mark A. Eys.
        p. cm.
    Includes index.
    1. Sports—Sociological aspects.   2. Sports—Psychological aspects.
3. Exercise—Sociological aspects.   4. Exercise—Psychological aspects.
5. Social groups.   I. Beauchamp, Mark.   II. Eys, Mark A.
    GV706.4.G75 2007
    306.483—dc22
    2007024474

ISBN13: 978–0–415–42664–0 (hbk)
ISBN13: 978–0–415–42665–7 (pbk)
ISBN13: 978–0–203–93798–3 (ebk)

ISBN10: 0–415–42664–2 (hbk)
ISBN10: 0–415–42665–0 (pbk)
ISBN10: 0–203–93798–8 (ebk)

Contents

Biographies

Editors

Mark Beauchamp is an Assistant Professor in Exercise and Sport Psychology at the University of British Columbia, Canada. He received his undergraduate degree from the University of Exeter (UK), a Master's from Queen's University (Canada) and his PhD in sport and exercise psychology from the University of Birmingham (UK). His research primarily focuses on the social psychology of groups within sport and exercise settings. His research has been supported by funding agencies such as the Nuffield Foundation and the Social Sciences and Humanities Research Council of Canada. Mark has published in a variety of journals such as the *Annals of Behavioral Medicine*, *Journal of Sport and Exercise Psychology*, *Journal of Applied Social Psychology*, *Journal of Health Psychology* and *Group Dynamics: Theory, Research and Practice*. He is a Chartered Psychologist (British Psychological Society) and is also accredited by the British Association for Sport and Exercise Sciences (BASES). Mark has worked in a consulting capacity with athletes from a range of sports including amateur, professional and international competitors.

Mark Eys is an Assistant Professor of Sport and Exercise Psychology in the School of Human Kinetics at Laurentian University in Sudbury, Ontario, Canada. He received his undergraduate degree from the University of Waterloo and his Master's and PhD from The University of Western Ontario. His current research interests include role ambiguity and acceptance in sport and exercise groups, the measurement and correlates of cohesion and social influences in exercise. Mark's research related to cohesion in youth physical activity groups is supported by a 3-year standard research grant from the Social Sciences and Humanities Research Council of Canada. He has published his research in the *Journal of Sports Sciences*, *International Journal of Sport and Exercise Psychology*, *Journal of Applied Sport Psychology* and *Journal of Sport and Exercise Psychology* and is a co-author of the book *Group Dynamics in Sport* (2005; Fitness Information Technology). In 2001, he was awarded the Canadian Interuniversity Sport (CIS) Coach of the Year for his work with The University of Western Ontario women's soccer program.

Contributors

Julian Barling is Professor of Organizational Behavior and Psychology in the Queen's School of Business and Associate Dean with responsibility for the PhD, MSc and

Research programs in the School of Business. He is the author of several books, including *Employment, Stress and Family Functioning* (1990, Wiley and Sons), *The Union and its Members: A Psychological Approach* (with Clive Fullagar and Kevin Kelloway, 1992, Oxford University Press), *Changing Employment Relations: Behavioral and Social Perspectives* (with Lois Tetrick, 1995, American Psychological Association) and *Young Workers* (with Kevin Kelloway, 1999, American Psychological Association). He is currently editing *The Handbook of Organizational Behavior*, which will appear at the end of 2007. In addition, he is the author/editor of well over 125 research articles and book chapters and was the editor of the American Psychological Association's *Journal of Occupational Health Psychology* from 2000–2005. He serves on the editorial boards of the *Journal of Applied Psychology, Leadership and Organizational Development Journal* and *Stress Medicine*. He was formerly chair of the American Psychological Association's Task Force on Workplace Violence. The recipient of many accolades, in 2001 he received the National Post's 'Leaders in Business Education' award and in 2002, he was elected as a Fellow of the Royal Society of Canada and named as one of Queen's University's Queen's Research Chairs. He has worked with different organizations on leadership development and his current research focuses on how transformational leadership can enhance employee's psychological and physical well-being.

Marc Brackett is an Associate Research Scientist in the Department of Psychology at Yale University. He also is the Deputy Director of Yale's Health, Emotion and Behavior Laboratory and Faculty Fellow in the Edward Zigler Center in Child Development and Social Policy. Dr Brackett is the author, co-author, or editor of over 40 scholarly publications, including four educational curricula for school administrators, teachers and students, which focus on the role and importance of emotion-based skills training in school settings. His current research focuses on (a) the measurement of emotional intelligence, (b) the relation between perceived and actual emotional intelligence, (c) links between emotional intelligence and relationship quality, well-being, academic/work performance and (d) testing whether emotion-based skills training can improve the personal lives and academic/job performance of students and teachers. Most recently, Dr Brackett (with colleague, Dr Susan Rivers) developed the RULER model of emotional literacy which posits that teaching children the knowledge associated with Recognizing, Understanding, Labeling, Expressing and Regulating emotions contributes to positive youth development. Dr Brackett also has been the principal investigator on many grant-funded projects examining the effects of emotional literacy training in school children.

Steven Bray is an Associate Professor in the Department of Kinesiology at McMaster University in Hamilton, Canada. His research focus is on social perceptions that arise in interdependent contexts such as client–healthcare practitioner interactions and sport teams and how those perceptions relate to the thoughts, feelings and behaviors of the participants. Steven teaches courses in Health and Exercise Psychology as well as Research Methodologies. He is an Associate Editor for the *European Journal of Sport Science*.

Shauna Burke is an Assistant Professor in the Bachelor of Health Sciences Program at the University of Western Ontario in London, Ontario. Her research area is the psychology of sport and exercise with a primary focus on group dynamics and physical activity. In 2004, Shauna received the prestigious Canada Graduate Scholarship for Doctoral students, awarded by the Social Sciences and Humanities Research Council of Canada (SSHRC). In addition to frequent presentations at national and international scientific and professional conferences, Shauna has published her research in a number of peer-reviewed journals including *Journal of Applied Sport Psychology, Small Group Research, Psychology of Sport and Exercise* and *Sport and Exercise Psychology Review*. Shauna also serves as a Digest Compiler for the *Journal of Sport and Exercise Psychology*.

Bert Carron is a Professor in the School of Kinesiology at the University of Western Ontario. Carron has been an author/co-author of 14 books and monographs, 30 chapters in edited texts and 145 refereed publications. Professionally, he is a Fellow in the American Academy of Kinesiology and Physical Education, the Association for the Advancement of Applied Sport Psychology and the Canadian Psychomotor Learning and Sport Psychology Association. He is a Past President of the Canadian Association for Sport Sciences and a former member of the Board of Directors of the Sports Medicine Council of Canada. In 1998, Carron was a co-recipient of the International Council of Sport Science and Physical Education's 'Sport Science Award of the International Olympic Committee President'. Currently, Carron is a member of the Editorial Board of the *Journal of Sport and Exercise Psychology*, the *International Journal of Sport Psychology* and *Small Group Research*.

Graig Chow is a doctoral student in sport psychology at Michigan State University under the direction of Deborah Feltz. He received his BA in psychology from the University of CA, Los Angeles where he was involved in research on sport commitment among elite athletes. While he has conducted studies on self-efficacy and coaching efficacy, his recent work has focused on the relationship between group motivational processes and performance using multilevel frameworks. His research has been presented at the annual conferences for the Association for the Advancement of Applied Sport Psychology and the North American Society for the Psychology of Sport and Physical Activity. For 2004–2008, he is the recipient of the Michigan State University Enrichment Fellowship. He has taught sport psychology and sport sociology courses and is an occasional reviewer for refereed journals.

Paul Estabrooks is an Associate Professor in the Department of Human Nutrition, Foods and Exercise at Virginia Polytechnic Institute and State University and leads the Virginia Tech Obesity Dissemination and Implementation Research Center housed within the Carilion Biomedical Institute. Dr Estabrooks' research focuses on health promotion related to physical activity, healthy eating and weight management. He uses a participatory model that integrates research and medical or community personnel to develop and test practical behavior change interventions with the ultimate goal of translating effective interventions into practice. Dr Estabrooks has a strong interest in the potential of group dynamics and other socially based principles to be used to support healthful environments. He has received numerous awards for his work and is currently funded by the US Department of Health and Human Services to complete studies examining the process of physical activity behavior change and worksite weight management.

Deborah Feltz is Professor and chairperson, Department of Kinesiology, Michigan State University. She earned her PhD in physical education/sport psychology from the Pennsylvania State University under the direction of Daniel M. Landers. She has devoted more than 30 years to researching the relationship between efficacy beliefs and sport performance and has written over 75 publications on the topic, and a book, *Self-efficacy and Sport*. In 1986, while on sabbatical at Stanford University, she studied with Albert Bandura who triggered her interest in the concept of collective efficacy. Her most recent scholarship has focused on the development of a model of coaching efficacy and how coaching efficacy relates to a team's collective efficacy. She has received numerous awards for her research, including the Outstanding Dissertation Award of the Sport Psychology Academy of National Association of Sport and Physical Education; a Research Consortium Writing Award; the Mabel Lee Award Early Career Award from American Alliance for Health, Physical Education, Recreation and Dance; and the Early Career Distinguished Scholar Award from North American Society for the Study of Sport and Physical Activity. She was a member of the National Research Council's Committee on Techniques for the Enhancement of Human Performance and the sport psychology advisory and sport science advisory committees to the USOC. She is an American Psychological Association Fellow, former president of the American Academy of Kinesiology and Physical Education and president of the North American Society for the Study of Sport and Physical Activity.

Chris Harwood is a Senior Lecturer in Sport Psychology at Loughborough University, where he completed his PhD in 1997. His research, teaching and training interests lie in the areas of achievement motivation, motivational climate and psychological skill-related education for youth sport coaches, athletes and parents. He is a BASES High Performance Sport Accredited Psychologist and Chartered Psychologist with the BPS, serving both organizations with respect to their training and qualification programs. As an applied researcher and practitioner, Chris serves on the editorial board for the *Journal of Applied Sport Psychology* and *The Sport Psychologist* as well as serving on the Sony-Ericsson WTA tour professional advisory panel. He has consulted widely with national governing bodies and professional clubs over the past 12 years and currently works within junior and senior professional tennis, youth soccer and cricket.

Colette Hoption is a doctoral candidate in Management at Queen's University, specializing in Organizational Behavior with a minor in Marketing. She is under the supervision of Julian Barling. Prior to her doctoral studies, she completed a Master of Science in Management and undergraduate degrees in Psychology and French studies. Colette's research spans a variety of topics such as proactive behavior in the workplace, group decision-making and the need for uniqueness. Her primary research interests are in the areas of leadership and followership. Her research has been presented at conferences such as The International Association for Conflict Management Conference and Association for Psychological Science Annual Convention. Her work has also been published in the *Journal of Applied Psychology*.

Ben Jackson is a doctoral student at Leeds University (UK) investigating the psychological aspects of close sporting relationships, under the guidance of Mark Beauchamp. Ben received his BSc from Leeds University in 2004, focusing his studies on role perceptions in interdependent teams. In addition to his primary area of research, which examines efficacy beliefs in sporting dyads, Ben is also currently involved in research into collective clarity in sports teams. He has recently had his doctoral work published in the *Journal of Sport and Exercise Psychology* and has presented papers at the annual conference for the North American Society for the Psychology of Sport and Physical Activity, as well as the British Psychological Society's quinquennial conference. Ben has taught on a variety of undergraduate sport psychology modules and regularly facilitates mental skills workshops with a range of athletes and teams.

Sarah Jeffery is a Master's student in the Human Development program at Laurentian University in Sudbury, Ontario, Canada. Her general area of research interest is youth sport and physical activity. More specifically, Sarah is interested in how social psychological variables such as sport status and perceptions of cohesion affect exercise adherence among youth. Sarah is the recipient of an SSHRC Scholarship for work on her Master's thesis examining physical activity patterns across the academic transition from elementary to high school. Sarah has presented her undergraduate and Master's research at national and international conferences and also holds a position as an editorial assistant for *Athletic Insight*.

Sophia Jowett is currently a Senior Lecturer in Sport and Exercise Psychology at Loughborough University, UK. She received her PhD from the University of Exeter in 2001. Sophia's research examines the interpersonal content and functions of dyadic relationships in sport settings. A research emphasis is placed on understanding the interpersonal dynamics involved between the coach and the athlete from a theoretical, methodological and practical viewpoint. This research is funded by such institutions as Economic and Social Research Council, the British Academy and the Nuffield Foundation. The findings of her research have been published in a broad range of scientific journals and conference presentations. Sophia is on the editorial board of two peer reviewed journals. She is an accredited sport psychologist with the British Association of Sport and Exercise and chartered psychologist with the British Psychological Society.

Vikki Krane is the Director of the Women's Studies Program and a Professor in the School of Human Movement, Sport, and Leisure Studies at Bowling Green State University. Vikki teaches courses in the areas of sport psychology, sport and gender, and women's studies. Her research is grounded within an interdisciplinary framework combining feminist, queer, and cultural studies perspectives. Within this framework, she employs social identity perspective to investigate heterosexism in sport, specifically focusing on body image and the experiences of lesbians in sport. Additionally, Krane is a past-president, Fellow, and a Certified Consultant of the Association for Applied Sport Psychology. She is the former editor of *The Sport Psychologist* and the *Women in Sport and Physical Activity Journal*. Her PhD is from the University of North Carolina at Greensboro.

Amy Latimer is an Assistant Professor and Queen's National Scholar in the School of Kinesiology and Health Studies at Queen's University in Kingston, Ontario, Canada. She is also a Research Affiliate in the Health, Emotion and Behavior Laboratory at Yale University. Her research aims to understand and promote healthy lifestyle behaviors in the general population and among people with chronic disease and disability. Her research focuses specifically on (a) identifying the factors that motivate people to adopt healthy behaviors and (b) testing motivational interventions to encourage people to make healthy lifestyle choices. Dr Latimer's research has been published in journals spanning the fields of psychology, kinesiology, public health and rehabilitation.

David Lavallee is a Professor of Psychology of Sport in the School of Sport and Exercise Sciences at Loughborough University, UK. His educational qualifications include a Master's degree in Psychology from Harvard University and a PhD in Sport and Exercise Psychology from the University of Western Australia. He is Editor of *Sport and Exercise Psychology Review*, Associate Editor of *The Psychologist and International Review of Sport and Exercise Psychology* and Editorial Board Member of the *Journal of Clinical Sport Psychology* and *Psychology of Sport and Exercise*.

John Phelan is a Lecturer in the School of Business at Queen's University in the area of Organizational Behavior. Additionally, he has taught at Queen's School of Physical and Health Education in the area of Psychology of Coaching and Leadership (1989–1994). John is also a Mental Skills Coach for the New York Rangers of the NHL and from 1994 to 2004 worked for Ottawa Senators. He is in high demand for his approaches to leadership, coaching and team effectiveness. He has coached for over 25 years, including Men's and Women's Elite Rugby teams, Queen's University Men's Ice Hockey, English Professional Ice Hockey League, as well as the Prince Edward Island Senators of the American Hockey League. John has worked with many organizations such as Team Canada Men's Ice Hockey 2006 Olympics, Team Canada Fall 2004 (the Canadian World Cup winning hockey team), Canadian Olympic Sailors (Tornado Class – 2004, Greece Games) and the Canadian Men's Olympic Gold Medal winners in Salt Lake City. John has received numerous teaching accolades including Queen's School of Business Commerce Society President's Award, Class of 2006 and Class of 2005 which recognizes a professor's overall contribution to the graduating class. He has also been involved in the Queen's Executive Development program since 1989 and is well-known for his view on the importance of a personal philosophy of life and lifestyle balance: 'Life is a choice and I choose to be happy!'

Tara Rench is presently a PhD student at Michigan State University studying Industrial/Organizational Psychology. She graduated with honors in Psychology from Wright State University. Tara worked as a Research Assistant in the Health, Emotion and Behavior Laboratory at Yale University where she was involved in research examining effective strategies for communicating health messages. Her research aims to examine individual differences in motivational processes and to develop and validate selection tests for organizations.

Kim Shapcott is a PhD candidate in the School of Kinesiology at the University of Western Ontario. Her research interests focus on examining various group-related factors in sport teams and developing interventions based on group dynamic principles. Kim is also a certified Biofeedback and Neurofeedback clinician and has consulted with numerous elite level athletes from a variety of sports. Kim has published her research in peer-reviewed journals such as the *International Journal of Sport Psychology* and *Small Group Research*. She has also presented her work at several national and international conferences.

Christopher Shields is an Assistant Professor in the School of Recreation Management and Kinesiology at Acadia University. His research interests focus on the healthcare professional–client relationship and the impact this relationship has on an individual's exercise-related thoughts and behaviors. He is specifically interested in how this relationship can be used to promote independent activity among symptomatic and asymptomatic populations. Dr Shields teaches courses involving the application of social psychology to physical activity behaviors as well as courses focusing on broader issues of health promotion practices. In his down time he can be found enjoying outdoor activities with his family.

Robert Schinke is an Associate Professor of Sport Psychology in the School of Human Kinetics at Laurentian University in Sudbury, Ontario, Canada. A former Canadian Equestrian Team member, Rob completed a Masters with a specialization in Sport Psychology and a Doctorate in Education, where he researched the effects of support-system optimism on national team athlete performance during major international competitions. Rob has produced more than 100 academic and applied publications and presentations to this point in his career. Rob's research related to cultural sport psychology continues to be supported by several research grants from the Social Sciences and Humanities Research Council of Canada. In addition, Rob serves as editor and chief of *Athletic Insight*, and reviews for the *International Journal of Sport and Exercise Psychology*. As a certified practitioner with the Canadian Sport Psychology Registry, Rob has worked with national teams and professional athletes and management groups in Canada and abroad for more than 10 years.

Martyn Standage is a Lecturer in Sport and Exercise Psychology in the School for Health at the University of Bath. He received his PhD in 2003 from the University of Birmingham. Employing laboratory and field methods, the majority of his research examines issues pertaining to motivation, isolating key mechanisms and testing their application to sport, exercise, physical education and health settings. His research has been published in journals such as the *Journal of Educational Psychology, Motivation and Emotion, Health Education Research, Journal of Health Psychology, Journal of Sport and Exercise Psychology, Psychology of Sport and Exercise, Journal of Sports Sciences* and the *British Journal of Educational Psychology*. He has also authored several book chapters addressing the motivational processes of individuals in physical activity settings.

Robert Vallerand received his PhD from the Université de Montréal, and pursued postdoctoral studies in Experimental Social Psychology at the University of Waterloo. After a year at Guelph University, he joined the Université du Québec à Montréal where he is presently full professor of Psychology and Director of the Laboratoire de Recherche sur le Comportement Social in the Department of Psychology. Robert has written/edited four books and more than 165 articles and book chapters, mainly in the area of motivation. He has also been awarded numerous research grants. He has served as chair of the Psychology Department and President of both the Quebec Society for Research in Psychology and the Canadian Psychological Association. He also serves as Consulting Editor on a number of journals including the *Journal of Personality and Social Psychology, Personality and Social Psychology Bulletin, Motivation and Emotion, Psychology of Sport and Exercise, International Journal of Sport and Exercise Psychology* and the *Journal of Sport and*

Exercise Psychology. Robert's current research interests focus on the hierarchical model of intrinsic and extrinsic motivation, as well as on a new conceptualization on passion toward activities. He also received the Sport Science Award from the International Olympic Committee.

Preface

No one can whistle a symphony. It takes an orchestra to play it.

H. E. Luccock

Within exercise and sport environments, a considerable amount of psychological research has focused on examining group members' thoughts, feelings and actions and the manner in which they both influence and are influenced by other group members. Indeed, whether one is interested in getting sports teams to perform better, or bringing about improved adherence within exercise classes, it is essential to understand the psychological dynamics that operate in these group settings. *Group Dynamics in Exercise and Sport Psychology: Contemporary Themes* explores the unique psychological dynamics that emerge when people form and exist within, sport and exercise groups. Specifically, prominent international as well as emerging scholars have been brought together within this edited book, the first of its kind, in which group dynamics issues are covered in relation to both contexts.

Effective group functioning and teamwork requires an acute understanding of inter-personal processes (as well as hard work!). In order to foster this understanding, authors of each chapter have drawn from diverse theoretical perspectives as well as recent research findings, to cover a number of themes that are typically not found within sport and exercise psychology texts. With this in mind, one of the major objectives of this book is to promote further interest in the area of group processes in sport and exercise psychology, both in terms of stimulating exciting new research directions as well as informing evidence-based interventions.

The book is divided into four distinct, yet inter-related, parts. Part I focuses on the *self* within groups. Given that groups are comprised of individuals, it is logical that the first part of the book examines the role and influence of personal factors within group settings. Specifically, in Chapter 1, Amy Latimer, Tara Rench and Marc Brackett examine the construct of emotional intelligence. They comprehensively explain what is meant by emotional intelligence and explore how emotion-related capabilities can play a fundamental role within interpersonal physical activity settings. In Chapter 2, Mark Beauchamp, Ben Jackson and David Lavallee draw from recent trait-based and type-based approaches to understanding personality and present an integrated framework to inform team development interventions in sport.

Part II centers on *leadership*. Leaders are particularly influential in the lives of groups and group members and in this section, three distinct approaches are taken to explore the role of leadership within sport and exercise groups. In Chapter 3, Colette Hoption,

John Phelan and Julian Barling provide a review of transformational leadership theory and explore how transformational leadership research can be extended within the field of sport psychology. In Chapter 4, Sophia Jowett explores the nature of the coach–athlete relationship and provides a framework to suggest that when coaches have the interpersonal skills and resources to connect with every athlete on a team, close coach–athlete relations can in turn ignite a sense of togetherness among team members. In Chapter 5, Steven Bray and Chris Shields focus on the role of proxy agency within health and exercise contexts. Bray and Shields discuss some of the paradoxical implications of using third parties (e.g. exercise instructors, health professionals, etc.) and explore how confidence in these significant others can both help and hinder our physical activity and exercise efforts.

In Part III, four chapters are presented that relate to the *group environment*. In Chapter 6, Mark Eys, Robert Schinke and Sarah Jeffery review recent research advances related to roles and role-related perceptions within sport teams. Specifically, they explore how role perceptions potentially influence the ability of individual group members to operate effectively both *independently of* and *interdependently with* other group members. In Chapter 7, Albert Carron, Kim Shapcott and Shauna Burke provide a historical review of the development of cohesion research in sport and exercise psychology. They trace the conceptual and empirical developments of this highly researched psychological group construct and present an articulate framework for future research and application. In Chapter 8, Paul Estabrooks synthesizes theory and research corresponding to group-based interventions within public health and behavioral medicine contexts. In particular, a review is presented of group-integration interventions that specifically target the enhancement of physical activity behaviors. In Chapter 9, Vikki Krane presents an absorbing chapter on gendered dynamics that exist within sport teams. In this, she draws from a social identity perspective to explain how team norms and cohesion develop (both negatively and positively) and presents direction for alleviating divisiveness among and between teams related to gendered beliefs.

The final section of the book, Part IV, revolves around *motivation* in groups. Motivation represents one of the cornerstones of sport and exercise psychology research and in this part of the book three diverse approaches to the study of motivation are presented. In Chapter 10, Martyn Standage and Bob Vallerand discuss the application of self-determination theory to group-based settings in sport and exercise and explain how the environment can be structured to support athletes' and exercisers' basic psychological needs. In Chapter 11, Chris Harwood and Mark Beauchamp review achievement goal theory and explore how this popular theoretical framework can be extended to better understand the motives of athletes within sport team settings. In the last chapter of Part IV, Chapter 12, Graig Chow and Deb Feltz provide a systematic review of the construct of collective efficacy and map out how a team's sense of shared confidence emerges and influences other important team-oriented outcomes.

Group Dynamics in Exercise and Sport Psychology: Contemporary Themes has been written to appeal to a wide audience primarily involving upper-level undergraduate and postgraduate students, as well as researchers interested in conducting research within the area of sport and exercise psychology. However, it is anticipated that practitioners interested in applying the latest theory and research to inform 'best practice' will also find this book of interest. Indeed, we hope that this book will appeal to coaches, exercise instructors, sport and exercise psychology consultants, physical educators, as well as those involved in coach/teacher education. In short, it is our hope that this book will appeal to anyone interested in understanding what makes groups *work* (well) and what enables *good* teams to become *even better*.

Mark R. Beauchamp
Mark A. Eys

Part I
The self in groups

Photograph by Richard Lam/UBC Athletics. Reprinted courtesy of The University of British Columbia.

1 Emotional intelligence

A framework for examining emotions in sport and exercise groups

Amy E. Latimer, Tara A. Rench and Marc A. Brackett

Introduction

On November 19, 2004, the Detroit Pistons played the Indiana Pacers at home in a regular season game of the National Basketball Association (NBA). As a result of 'dysregulated emotions', this game has been described as one of the most infamous games in the history of the NBA. Following an altercation with a Detroit Pistons player, Indiana Pacer, Ron Artest, became outraged when he was struck in the face by a full beverage cup thrown from the crowd. Artest, joined by a team-mate, stormed into the stands and physically attacked several Detroit fans. Desperately, the Pacers' coach and players from both teams tried to intervene. However, after returning to the court, Artest and team-mates continued to battle with fans until being escorted to the locker room by security. The game was ended with 45.9 seconds left to play. Artest was suspended for the rest of the season (i.e. 85 games); several of his team-mates also served multi-game suspensions (Montieth, 2004).

As the above incident clearly demonstrates, emotions inherently influence behavior and relationships in sport and exercise (Vallerand and Blanchard, 1999). Anger may fuel a bench clearing brawl, whereas joy resulting from winning a playoff game may promote team cohesion and persistent effort in subsequent practices. The incident also emphasizes the role of emotion-related skills or abilities, including the *perception*, *use*, *understanding and management* of emotions on individual performance and team functioning. Artest and his team-mates' failure to *manage* their emotions led to a violent outburst which ultimately prevented the game from resuming and resulted in player suspension. In contrast, emotionally-skilled individuals and groups are likely to produce favorable outcomes. For example, in the exercise domain, an emotionally-skilled individual would most likely *understand* the guilt she is feeling due to a missed aerobics class and might *use* this guilt to motivate her to return to class the following week ('To avoid feeling guilty for missing class again, I am going to make sure I show up next week'). Furthermore, attending the class the following week and preventing an exercise lapse from turning into a bad habit may result in a sense of pride and continued class participation.

Emotions are short-term feeling states that have certain components including an elicitor (i.e. an internal/external trigger), a subjective experience, a physiological response and behavioral expression (Parrott, 2001). Research examining the inherent influence of emotions in the realm of sport and exercise has flourished in the past couple of decades (Crocker and Graham, 1995). Substantial knowledge has been gained regarding (1) the antecedents of an individual's emotion in sport and exercise (i.e. the causes of precompetition anxiety, the effects of exercise participation on emotion) and (2) the consequences of an individual's emotions on sport and exercise behavior (i.e. how certain emotions are facilitative for one athlete and debilitative for another, how social anxiety affects a novice exerciser's intention to sign up for a gym membership). Although scant, research also has examined the impact of individuals' emotion-related abilities on performance outcomes (e.g. Totterdell, 1999). With these research advances focusing largely on individual performance, the interpersonal aspects of emotion and emotion-related abilities in sport and exercise have been neglected for the most part (Vallerand and Blanchard, 1999).

Emotions play a fundamental role in interpersonal situations (Frijda and Mesquita, 1994; Keltner and Haidt, 2001) serving as a critical source of information that can evoke both emotional and behavioral responses from others (Frijda and Mesquita, 1994). Emotion-related abilities also are essential to group functioning (Brackett *et al.*, 2006). For example, accurately perceiving a person's emotions (type and intensity) facilitates the prediction and understanding of that person's subsequent actions (Elfenbein and Ambady, 2002). Managing emotions effectively also is critical to optimal interpersonal functioning as this skill enables one to express socially appropriate emotions, behave in socially acceptable ways and handle difficult situations skillfully. Within the sport and exercise domain, the interpersonal aspects of emotions and emotion-related abilities manifest in myriad situations, including interactions between athletes and coaches, officials and fans, personal trainers and clients and aerobics instructors and students. Furthermore, given their social nature, the interpersonal aspects of emotion are prominent particularly in sports teams and exercise groups.

Research on the role of emotions and emotion-related skills in the context of sport and exercise groups is limited. However, evidence from other subdisciplines in psychology, such as social and personality psychology and industrial/organizational psychology can inform the area. Sport and exercise psychology research examining emotions among individual athletes and exercisers is also relevant. In particular, the theory of emotional intelligence (EI) (Mayer and Salovey, 1997; Salovey and Mayer, 1990), which is rooted in social psychology, provides a useful framework to guide emotion research in sport and exercise groups. EI refers to an individual's capacity to process emotion-laden information in order to enhance cognitive processes and facilitate social functioning (Mayer and Salovey, 1997; Salovey and Mayer, 1990).

The purpose of this chapter is to demonstrate how EI theory may provide a useful framework to study the interpersonal aspects of emotion and emotion-related abilities in sport and exercise groups. First, the theory of EI and its measurement will be discussed. In this section, we review Mayer and Salovey's (1997) four-part theory of EI and briefly describe their performance-based measure of EI, the 'Mayer–Salovey–Caruso Emotional Intelligence Test' (MSCEIT; Mayer *et al.*, 2002). Second, the link between EI and group effectiveness will be reviewed. Due to the lack of research in the sport and exercise domain, we discuss findings from studies conducted on small groups in business and how they might apply to sport and exercise settings. Finally, potential implications and suggestions for future research on the role of EI in both sport and exercise settings will be addressed. In this section, we present research examining the relationship between leadership roles and EI. In this section, we focus on the extent to which EI impacts leadership effectiveness.

Theory and research: what is emotional intelligence?

The concept of EI was derived from early psychological research on the three components of the mind: cognition (thought), affect (feeling) and conation (motivation) (Mayer and Salovey, 1997; Salovey and Mayer, 1990). EI theory proposes to connect the first two components of the mind: cognition and affect. Intelligence belongs to the cognitive component of the mind and refers to how well one engages in tasks pertaining to memory, reasoning, judgment and abstract thought. Emotion belongs to the affective component which involves emotions themselves (e.g. sadness, anger and fear), moods, evaluations or preferences and feeling states (e.g. energy or fatigue). Thus, the theory of EI links cognition and affect by suggesting that emotions make cognitive processes more intelligent and that one can think intelligently about emotions.

Based on this notion, a model of EI was developed. Four interrelated emotion abilities emerged: perceiving, using, understanding and managing emotions. More specifically, EI is defined as 'the ability to perceive accurately, appraise and express emotion; the ability to access and/or generate feelings when they facilitate thought; the ability to understand emotion and emotional knowledge; and the ability to regulate emotions to promote emotional and intellectual growth' (Mayer and Salovey, 1997, p. 10). A brief summary of the four emotion-related skills that comprise EI follows; more detailed presentations can be found elsewhere (e.g. Brackett and Salovey, 2004; Mayer and Salovey, 1997; Mayer et al., 2004).

Perception of emotion pertains to the ability to discern emotions in oneself and others (i.e. facial expressions), as well as in other stimuli, including voices, stories, music and works of art. People who are aware of their own and others' emotions gain a large amount of information about themselves and their environment. For example, an athlete who is sensitive to her level of pre-game anxiety will know whether she needs to include relaxation exercises in her warm-up. In contrast, those who do not recognize their own and others' emotions are cut off from this useful information. The perception of emotion is the foundation of EI; without this ability, one cannot use the other three EI skills (Salovey et al., 2002).

Use of emotion involves the ability to generate emotions in oneself and others in order to focus attention, enhance cognitive processes and improve memory. This skill is based on the knowledge that emotions directly affect cognition. Happiness, for example, fosters creativity and acceptance (Fredrickson, 2001). Similarly, happiness leads to more optimistic thinking, while sadness leads to more pessimistic thinking (Mayer et al., 1992). Proficiency in this domain involves the ability to generate different emotions in different contexts in order to influence thoughts or behavior (Salovey et al., 2002).

Understanding of emotion involves knowledge of the language of emotion and of the causes and consequences of emotional experiences. People feel sadness, for example, after experiencing some sort of loss and feel happiness after experiencing a gain. This skill also involves comprehension of how emotions blend together (e.g. knowing that a feeling of contempt results from concurrent feelings of anger and disgust) and how they change over time in given situations (e.g. knowing that if a source of frustration is not removed, the frustration is likely to turn to anger and, eventually, to fury).

Management of emotion refers to the ability to regulate one's own emotions and those of other people. Research has shown that, while there are various techniques for managing emotions (e.g. exercising, relaxing, shopping, smoking cigarettes, drinking), some strategies work better than others (see Thayer *et al.*, 1994). Thus, this skill involves both knowing what strategies are most effective and executing them appropriately (Salovey *et al.*, 2002). Importantly, proper management of emotion does not entail ignoring or suppressing emotion. On the contrary, experiencing a range of emotions can be useful. Even 'negative' emotions such as sadness, anger and guilt can have positive effects. Intense grief, for example, may allow us to experience and appreciate joy (Salovey and Mayer, 1990; cf. Solomon, 1980).

Measuring EI as a set of abilities

There are two general methods used to measure EI: self-report inventories and performance-based tests. Self-report inventories ask participants to rate themselves on several dimensions of EI as well as on a number of other unrelated qualities, such as optimism and motivation (Bar-On, 1997; Petrides and Furnham, 2001; Schutte *et al.*, 1998). There are a number of problems with these inventories, however. Namely, they tend to (1) be contaminated by self-report bias, (2) correlate highly with existing personality measures, (3) lack incremental validity in the prediction of important life outcomes and (4) be mostly unrelated to performance-based measures of EI (Brackett and Geher, 2006; Brackett and Mayer, 2003; Brackett *et al.*, 2006).

Performance measures on the other hand attempt to assess EI objectively with tasks that require participants to solve emotion-laden problems. The predominant task-based measure of EI is the Mayer Salovey Caruso Emotional Intelligence Test (MSCEIT; Mayer *et al.*, 2002). The MSCEIT has answers that are objectively better than others. The MSCEIT measures EI using two separate tasks for each of the four domains. *Perception of emotion* is measured by having respondents rate the presence of an emotion in (a) photographs of people's faces and (b) landscapes and abstract pictures. *Use of emotion* is measured by having respondents (a) generate emotions in order to recognize descriptions of emotions and (b) report how useful various emotions would be while completing certain tasks. *Understanding of emotion* is measured by having respondents (a) recognize how simple emotions combine to form more complex emotions and (b) select the emotion that is most likely to occur when another becomes stronger or weaker. Finally, *management of emotion* is measured by having respondents read emotionally provocative vignettes and then rate the effectiveness of different emotion-regulation strategies in (a) private situations and (b) interpersonal situations (Mayer *et al.*, 2003).

The MSCEIT is considered an objective test of EI because answers are determined by reference to normative or expert samples and, accordingly, vary in terms of how correct they are vis-à-vis the norms generated by these samples. Consensus scores reflect the proportion of people in the normative sample (over 5,000 people from North America) who endorsed each MSCEIT test item alternative. Expert norms were obtained from a sample of twenty-one members of the International Society for Research on Emotions (ISRE).

The reliability and validity of the MSCEIT have been established using both consensus and expert norms across multiple studies (Mayer *et al.*, 2002; see also Mayer *et al.*, 2004). More information on the psychometric properties of the test can be found elsewhere (Brackett and Salovey, 2004; Rivers *et al.*, in press). In brief, scores on the MSCEIT predict a wide range of both self-rated (e.g. smoking, alcohol use, violence) and objective behavioral outcomes (e.g. social problem solving ability) beyond general intelligence and personality (see Brackett and Salovey, 2004; Mayer *et al.*, 2004). MSCEIT scores do not overlap meaningfully with measures of intelligence. In a study with 330 college students (Brackett *et al.*, 2004), MSCEIT scores were only modestly correlated with verbal intelligence measured with Verbal SAT scores. In another study, verbal intelligence, as assessed by the WAIS-III vocabulary subscale and Verbal SAT scores correlated modestly with the Understanding Emotions branch of the MSCEIT (which relies on knowledge of emotional vocabulary), but not with any of the other branches or with the total score (Lopes *et al.*, 2003). A modest correlation is consistent with the notion that EI abilities allow individuals both to garner emotions to facilitate thinking and regulate emotions in order to focus on important information but are not a central determinant of intelligence in other domains (Mayer and Salovey, 1997).

The MSCEIT was developed and is used primarily in adult samples. Examining EI in children has been limited by available measurement instruments. A youth version (YV) of the MSCEIT – the MSCEIT-YV – is now available from Multi-Health Systems (MHS; Mayer *et al.*, 2007). The MSCEIT-YV can be administered individually or in groups and is appropriate for children aged 11–17 years. The development of this measure allows researchers to test the developmental postulates of EI theory (i.e. that emotional intelligence develops with age and experience; Mayer *et al.*, 1999).

EI research in the context of groups

Because little research has examined the role of EI in sport and exercise groups, we rely primarily on evidence from work groups to exemplify how EI may affect group performance. Work groups serve as an appropriate model for sport and exercise groups because the social nature and factors (e.g. group dynamics including leadership, group cohesion and communication) related to performance and success are similar in both contexts (Jordan and Ashkanasy, 2006). Furthermore, given the limited research in the area, our discussion extends beyond emotions and encompasses other affective components including moods and feelings. Indeed, emotions, moods and feelings are distinct concepts. Moods are less event dependent (i.e. an elicitor is not a necessary component), less likely to be expressed and more persistent than emotions. Feelings are the private mental experience of an emotion (Damasio, 1994) whereas emotions are expressed overtly through facial expressions and other forms of non-verbal behavior. It is appropriate to discuss all three concepts in relation to EI because emotions, moods and feelings make-up the affective component of thought which EI encompasses. Thus, using EI theory as a framework, we review literature about emotions, moods and feelings which supports the view that overall EI and its component abilities, specifically *perceiving, using, understanding* and *managing* emotions, influence performance outcomes in work settings. We extend these findings from the literature to suggest how overall EI and each of the four EI abilities may affect functioning in sport and exercise psychology groups. Because a majority of studies on EI rely on self-report measures of the construct, the findings are limited to constraints discussed above.

Overall EI

The potential importance of EI for effective work group performance has been highlighted by several researchers (e.g. Cote and Miners, 2006; Daus and Ashkanasy, 2005; Lopes *et al.*, 2006a). Collectively, these researchers propose EI as an important group resource necessary for effectively navigating the inevitable social and emotional aspects of group work (Wolfe *et al.*, 2006). In turn, it is posited that EI is related to performance, organizational commitment and organizational citizenship. Empirical research examining the relationship between EI and group performance provide some support for these hypotheses.

A series of three studies (Jordan and Ashkanasy, 2006; Jordan *et al.*, 2002a; Jordan and Troth, 2004), examined the relationship between EI and performance in small work groups composed of 3–7 undergraduate students. In each study EI was assessed using the Workgroup Emotional Intelligence Profile (WEIP; Jordan *et al.*, 2002b). The WEIP is a self-report measure of emotion-related skills that was developed to conform to the Mayer and Salovey ability model and provide a situation-specific index of EI (i.e. the WEIP assesses EI displayed specifically when working in groups).

In two of the studies (Jordan and Ashkanasy, 2006; Jordan *et al.*, 2002a), group performance scores were based on three independent raters' evaluations of each groups' log sheets. The raters judged each log sheet for goal focus (the generation of appropriate goals and the team's focus on goal attainment) and team process (the quality, understanding and attention to goal achievement processes). The findings from the two studies were somewhat mixed. Whereas one study revealed that higher team average WEIP scores were associated with greater goal focus (Jordan *et al.*, 2002a), the second study failed to corroborate this finding (Jordan and Ashkanasy, 2006). Consistent across studies, however, was the finding that WEIP scores were not related to team process evaluations.

Supplemental findings from the second study provide some insight into the lack of significant findings across the studies. In addition to the self-reported WEIP, the second study included a peer report version of the WEIP in which team members rated the emotion-related skills and abilities of each individual in their work group. Using the peer report version of the WEIP a small but significant relationship emerged between EI and both group performance outcomes. Furthermore self-reported and peer-evaluation WEIP scores were only weakly correlated. Thus, the lack of findings across the first two studies might be the result of individuals' inability to evaluate accurately their EI (Brackett *et al.*, 2006) and not the lack of relationship between EI and group performance outcomes.

In the third study of this series (Jordan and Troth, 2004), group performance scores were based on the outcome of a problem solving task rather than subjective performance evaluations as in the first two studies. The problem-solving task was a survival situation exercise requiring participants to rank 15 items according to their importance for survival. Performance quality was determined by comparing participants' rankings to expert consensus rankings. A smaller differential between the participants' and expert rankings was indicative of greater performance. Participants first completed the task individually and then as a team composed of 4–5 members. As expected, team performance on the task exceeded performance of its individual members. Furthermore, higher average WEIP team scores were associated with better overall team performance. These findings suggest a link between self-reported EI and performance on a problem solving task. Although this finding holds promise for the proposed role of EI in group effectiveness, further research should be conducted to demonstrate whether EI, when measured with objective measures, predicts these outcomes.

Application to sport and exercise groups

Although research in the area is scant, the potential impact of EI in sport and exercise has been recognized (Botterill and Brown, 2002; Eckmann, 2004; Gordon, 2001; McCann, 1999; Zizzi et al., 2003). Undeniably, sporting events and exercise settings are environments replete with emotion. For example, in the description, which opened this chapter, of a brawl at an NBA game, anger, surprise, fear and disgust were among the spectrum of emotions displayed during the altercation. EI is a collection of mental abilities that athletes or exercisers may use in order to cope and succeed in situations charged with emotion. In the case of the NBA brawl, high EI was demonstrated by the athletes who evaluated the situation and reacted quickly but calmly, while attempting to remove their team-mates from danger. Emotionally intelligent athletes recognize the emotions that they and the people around them are feeling; use their emotions to respond appropriately to the situation; understand the impact their emotions are having on their behavior and manage their emotions in order to accomplish their goals.

To date, only one study (Zizzi et al., 2003) has explored the relationship between EI and performance in the sports domain. A total of 61 players drawn from 10 collegiate baseball teams completed a self-report EI test (SREIT; Schutte et al., 1998). Performance data included the season total hitting (hits, doubles, walks and strikeouts) and pitching statistics (earned runs, walks, hits allowed, strikeouts and wild pitches) for individual players. SREIT scores and pitching performance were correlated positively. However, only the relationship between SREIT scores and number of strikeouts pitched reached conventional levels of statistical significance. SREIT scores and hitting performance were unrelated. This study only examined the relationship between self-rated EI and individual performance statistics and it should be noted that the role of EI in group performance was not examined. Determining that EI is related to pitching performance but not hitting performance suggests that overall EI may be particularly important for certain roles within a team. More research is needed to examine this possibility.

EI also may be important for success in exercise groups. Consider an aerobics instructor who notices that her students are sluggish and falling behind in the aerobics sequences. To remedy the situation, she may change her music selection to include songs with a more upbeat tempo and begin demonstrating the exercise combinations with more vigor. The instructor's actions reflect her level of EI. She *perceives* that her students are lacking energy and *understands* that this lack of energy is hindering their perform-ance. By changing music and effectively *managing* her own emotions (i.e. becoming more enthused and energetic), she is *using* emotion and emotion-laden music to inspire improved performance among her students. Indeed, it has been suggested that with this example, fitness instructors with greater EI will have better client ratings (Eckmann, 2004), however, empirical research testing this hypothesis is lacking. To further under-stand the influence of EI on group performance, it is important to know how each ability (i.e. perceiving, using, understanding, and managing emotion) contributes to the EI-performance relationship. This is the topic of the following sections.

Perceiving emotions

With substantial evidence that people are sensitive to the emotional climate in a group and adjust their mood accordingly (i.e. mood linkage or mood contagion; Barsade, 2002;

Totterdell *et al.*, 1998) it is not surprising that of the four EI-abilities, perception of emotion is the ability that has garnered significant attention. Together this research provides evidence that perceiving emotions in oneself and others is related to better team outcomes.

For example, the study of undergraduate business students by Jordan and Ashkanasy (2006) that assessed both self-reported and peer-evaluated WEIP scores provides evidence that accurately perceiving emotion in oneself is related to group performance outcomes. A smaller discrepancy between self- and peer-ratings (a plausible indicator of greater perception of emotion in oneself) was significantly correlated with effective goal focus and team processes. The results of this study suggest that correctly identifying one's own feeling states may contribute to group success.

There also is evidence suggesting the importance of perceiving emotion in others within team-centered environments. Among a group of businessmen, more accurate recognition and identification of emotional content in voice samples and video clips was related to better work performance and increased advancement to higher positions (Rosenthal *et al.*, 1979). Participants' professional success was attributed in part to their ability to judge colleagues' reactions and preferences and, in turn, work productively with these individuals. Because the study outcomes were related to individual-centered performance, it is unclear as to whether the ability to perceive emotion affects team performance.

One investigation of individual and team performance on a problem solving task provides some insight, however. The members of 47 undergraduate work teams individually completed the MSCEIT, a performance measure of EI and a social problem solving task requiring them to rank the order in which they would lay off fictitious employees based on personal and professional attributes. The students then completed the same problem solving task with their team-mates. Results suggested that only the ability to perceive emotion was related to higher individual performance on the problem solving task. None of the EI abilities predicted group performance. It was posited that EI and its component abilities were not predictive of group performance due to the short-term nature of the work groups and problem solving task. Accordingly, further research is needed to elucidate the relationship between perception of emotion and group outcomes.

Application to sport and exercise

The ability to perceive emotion may have important implications for performance in sport and exercise groups. Being able to perceive emotions accurately might provide an athlete indication about when to help another team-mate get out of a troublesome situation. For example, an athlete who reads others' emotions with ease might recognize that his team-mate is angry and intervene before a fight with an opponent erupts. He also might act as an offensive outlet for a team-mate who is under defensive pressure from an opponent and becoming anxious. The ability to perceive emotion might also facilitate communication between team-mates and prevent conflict. An athlete with the ability to sense that her team-mate is upset might offer the second team-mate time to regain her composure before offering advice for the next game. Furthermore, the ability to perceive emotion in opponent teams may provide a competitive edge. Athletes who can sense fear or anxiety in opponents hold a substantial psychological advantage and may play more assertively than usual in order to capitalize on an opposing team's apprehension. With several ways in which the ability to perceive emotion might affect sport and exercise group performance, research is needed to test the numerous possibilities.

A study of professional cricket players provides some preliminary evidence that is consistent with the findings in business, demonstrating that perception of others' emotions may be important for individual performance in a team setting (Totterdell, 2000). The players from each team rated their own mood and their perception of their team-mates' moods over the course of a competitive match. The individual players' moods correlated strongly with their team-mates' moods. This player-team mood association is described as mood linkage which results from players perceiving the team's mood and adjusting their own mood accordingly. Interestingly, individuals' mood also predicted individual performance. Together these findings suggest that perception of team-mates' moods may influence a player's emotions which in turn may influence individual performance. Again, like most studies conducted thus far, actual ability to perceive emotion and team performance were not considered in this study. However, because individual performance is often integral to overall team success, it is likely that the effects of team mood on individual performance will manifest in team-related outcomes.

The ability to perceive emotion has potential implications for exercise groups as well. A personal trainer with the ability to perceive emotion will be able to use emotions as cues, indicating when to intervene in order to prevent a client from becoming frustrated with an exercise that is too difficult. An aerobics instructor who is adept at this skill will be able to identify whether a novice exerciser is feeling anxious about joining a new class and may make an effort to help the participant feel more comfortable. Research to date on exercise groups has not examined these possibilities using performance measures of EI.

Using emotions

Many of the cognitive skills necessary for effective teamwork (e.g. decision-making, creativity) are influenced by emotion. Positive emotions are related to an enhanced ability to make important decisions quickly (Isen, 2001), generate future plans (Mayer, 1986), organize thoughts (Isen and Daubman, 1984), solve problems using creative thinking (Isen *et al.*, 1987) and persist in the face of obstacles (Salovey and Birnbaum, 1989). Conversely, negative emotions help individuals to re-prioritize and focus their attention on important tasks (Salovey and Rodin, 1985). Thus, a team that can generate emotions to facilitate thinking in a manner consistent with their task will likely experience great success.

The findings from a series of laboratory studies provide preliminary support for this possibility (Lovaglia and Houser, 1996). Participants were paired with a virtual partner and assigned randomly to receive a positive or negative mood induction. In the positive mood induction condition, participants gave their partner a gift and received a similar gift. In the negative mood induction condition, participants gave their partner a gift but the partner did not reciprocate. Following the mood induction task, participants independently completed 25 trials of an ambiguous, binary-choice decision task. In 20 of the trials, participants received feedback that their partner preferred the alternate choice and were given the option of changing their decision to agree with their partner. The study demonstrated that negative emotion decreased the likelihood that participants would change their opinion to match that of their partner. Positive emotion increased the likelihood. Taken together, these findings provide empirical evidence to exemplify how emotions can be used to affect group processes (i.e. positive moods can be used to create improved group decision-making).

Application to sport and exercise groups

Emotions are widely used by individual athletes to prepare for optimal performance. Indeed, substantial anecdotal and empirical evidence suggests that increased arousal narrows attentional focus (Landers, 1981). Thus, athletes use their arousal levels to achieve an optimal level of focus. For example, a World Cup keeper who is playing in a stadium of 100,000 rowdy soccer fans may find that a heightened level of arousal helps him focus on relevant game cues (e.g. ball location, player positioning) and disregard irrelevant cues (e.g. the boisterous fans). Other athletes may use emotion to generate energy and persistence (Hanin, 1999). Consider a boxer in the final round of a title fight. He must overcome his fatigue and pain to continue throwing explosive and powerful punches. Given that anger is associated with forceful and vigorous behaviors (Maxwell, 2004), he might use anger to as a means of enhancing his performance in the final round.

As yet, there is no empirical evidence demonstrating the role of emotions to enhance team performance. Some evidence suggests that implementing a single emotion-based intervention for all members of a team would not be optimal for affecting team success (Raglin and Morris, 1994; Turner and Raglin, 1996). Within a team, substantial variability exists in the optimal level at which a certain emotion enhances performance. One athlete may use high levels of arousal to reach optimal performance states while her team-mate might perform best with a lower level of arousal (Hanin, 1999). Thus, while an arousal heightening intervention might be effective for the first athlete, the same intervention might be detrimental to her team-mate. It may be that individuals should be encouraged to use emotion within a team context. That is, players may be instructed to generate emotions that 'work' for him or her.

The use of emotion also may be important in exercise, particularly among exercise instructors. It has been established that exercise enjoyment is associated with increased exercise adherence (Sallis and Owen, 1998). An instructor might aim to foster enjoyment in his participants as a means of increasing their program adherence. An instructor also might use emotion to elicit greater effort from her students. Cuing participants to feelings of anger and frustration during a cardio kickboxing class might lead to more effortful punches and stronger kicks. Conversely, a yoga instructor could use positive emotions or emotion-related states such as compassion to get her students in the proper mindset for their practice. Evidently, there are a number of ways emotions could be used to enhance performance in sport and exercise. Research should continue to examine the efficacy of these strategies and consider how an individual's ability to use emotion may influence intervention effectiveness.

Understanding emotion

The ability to understand emotions – to have a diverse emotion vocabulary and to understand the causes and consequences of emotion – is particularly relevant in group settings (Elfenbein, 2006). Individuals who are skilled in this domain are able to express emotions, feelings and moods accurately and thus, may facilitate clear communication between co-workers. Furthermore, they may be more likely to act in ways that accommodate their own needs as well as the needs of others (i.e. cooperate). In a group conflict situation, for example, a member with a strong ability to understand emotion will be able to express how he feels about the problem and why he feels this way. He also should be able to take the perspective of the other group members and understand why they are reacting in a certain manner. Appreciation of differences creates an arena for open communication and promotes constructive conflict resolution (Ayoko *et al.*, 2002; Hobman *et al.*, 2003; Kay *et al.*, 2001) and improved group functioning. Moreover, because this ability also involves knowing that emotions can change or progress in intensity, an individual who is skilled in this area might be more apt to address problems as they occur rather than allowing them to escalate. Active conflict resolution strategies as such, foster positive group emotions and relationships (Desivilya and Yagil, 2005).

A study of 18 teams of Executive MBA students demonstrates the importance of understanding emotions for encouraging positive team relations (Rapisarda, 2002). Each team member completed the Self-Assessment Questionnaire/External Assessment Questionnaire (Boyatzis, 1982; Goleman, 1998), a self-report measure of emotional competencies and a brief questionnaire evaluating group performance and cohesion. Similar group performance and cohesion measures were completed by faculty members. Empathy (an emotional competency related to the ability to understand the causes of emotions in others) was correlated positively with group and faculty members' evaluations of group cohesion. Perceptions of group performance increased along with empathy. However the correlation between these two constructs did not reach a standard level of significance. Together these findings suggest that the ability to understand emotion in others may be particularly important for creating an environment conducive to teamwork (i.e. a cohesive team).

Research on mood linkage (see Barsade, 2002) suggests that understanding the consequences of emotion also may be important in fostering team relations. It is well established that moods can be transferred within groups (Barsade, 2002) and in turn can affect team processes. Thus, an individual with the ability to understand emotion will realize that their emotional state can influence group processes and may attempt to approach group tasks in hopes of inducing a similar mood among other group members. This possibility needs to be examined further.

Application to sport and exercise groups

It is well recognized that understanding the causes and consequences of emotions can impact performance in sport. In fact, a common individual-centered intervention technique involves having athletes recall a peak performance and describe the emotions associated with this performance (Hanin, 1999). The objective of this process is to have athletes develop an understanding of the cause–effect relationship of emotions and performance and subsequently implement strategies to elicit the emotions necessary to attain peak performance (i.e. use emotion to create conditions for optimal performance). Future research in the area might examine whether some athletes are more receptive to this type of intervention than others. Athletes high in EI might be better at describing their emotion experience during a peak performance and may make the link between emotion and performance more easily than athletes lacking the ability to understand emotions.

In addition to having an impact on individual performance, understanding emotion may be important in a team setting. For example, the ability to understand emotion may influence performance by affecting coaches' and players' pre-game preparations. A coach who understands that too much arousal will be detrimental to her players' performance and too little emotional stimulation may hamper performance could tailor her pre-game pep talk accordingly. Alternatively, a player who realizes that he is anxious and does not want his negative emotional state to spread to his team-mates may step aside and try to regulate his emotions (the fourth domain of EI) before interacting with his team-mates. Having an understanding of emotion also may influence behavior during a sporting event. A player who knows that emotions escalate may purposely antagonize an opposing player in hopes that frustration will lead to anger which in turn will result in an aggressive act warranting a penalty.

Among team-mates, good communication and conflict resolution may be enhanced when athletes have the ability to understand emotion. Similar to work groups, understanding emotion may promote open and accurate communication and active conflict resolution strategies. Athletes who understand emotions will know that emotions, especially negative ones, directed toward them by their team-mates during a game or practice situation were likely not intentional. They will realize that the sporting event and not their actions per se was likely the cause of their team-mate's emotional reaction. This realization should ensure that positive relationships are maintained off the field.

In the context of exercise groups, understanding others' emotions may help to create a positive class environment. For example, an experienced exerciser who understands the range of self-conscious emotions (e.g. shame, embarrassment) a new overweight exerciser may be experiencing on the first day of class may make an effort to welcome the newcomer and introduce him to other class participants. Similarly, a class instructor who knows that singling out a participant to correct his form could embarrass him and reduce the likelihood of him returning to the class might opt to provide feedback in a way that preserves the participant's pride (e.g. provide general class feedback, approach the participant after class). Although exercise leaders and participants with the ability to understand emotion likely contribute to the creation of a positive emotional environment in an exercise setting, research is still needed to establish this possibility.

Managing emotion

Given that group work is laden with emotional events (e.g. finishing a project results in pride and then sadness because the group will no longer be working together), the ability to regulate emotion optimally in both the self and other people is a critical skill for effective group functioning. In a group feedback session, an individual with high ability to regulate emotions will accept feedback readily, hold back from criticizing others opinions and try to maintain a relaxed atmosphere to ease others' anxiety related to the feedback process. Conversely, an individual with low ability in this area may become obviously upset when he is given critical feedback and may fail to consider how his emotional outburst may be affecting the emotional status of others in his group.

As depicted in these examples, emotion management seems particularly important for creating positive interactions between group members. In a study of 44 employees in a *Fortune 400* investment company (Lopes *et al.*, 2006b), employees scoring high on the Managing Emotions subscale of the MSCEIT were rated by their peers as being involved in fewer negative interactions with co-workers than employees scoring low on the subscale. Managing Emotions subscale also was related positively to peer and supervisors' rating of employees' contribution to a positive work environment.

The finding that the ability to manage emotion contributes to positive social interactions is corroborated by studies outside the realm of work groups. Among college students, those scoring high on the Managing Emotion MSCEIT subscale were more popular among their peers (Lopes *et al.*, 2005) and had higher quality interactions with friends according to self- and peer-reports (Lopes *et al.*, 2004). Taken together, these findings suggest that having the ability to manage emotions may create positive interactions and an environment conducive to team success.

Application to sport and exercise groups

The importance of regulating emotion is well recognized in the sport domain. Research demonstrates that individuals with a stronger ability to regulate emotion perform better. A study of cricket players reported that athletes who scored higher on a scale measuring perceived ability to regulate negative moods had better batting averages during a match than athletes who scored lower on the scale (Totterdell and Leach, 2001). This relationship persisted over the course of the entire season, such that athletes with high mood regulation scores also had higher total batting averages at the end of the season. Furthermore, emotion regulation is the cornerstone of individual-centered peak performance interventions (Hanin, 1999). A critical component of a sport psychologist's job involves teaching athletes strategies to achieve an emotional state that will allow for optimal performance. The appropriate use of techniques to reduce arousal (e.g. progressive relaxation, meditation) or to increase arousal (e.g. self-talk, imagery) can affect individual performance substantially (Robazza *et al.*, 2004). An interesting question is whether athletes who are high in EI are either naturals in this area or learn these strategies more quickly than athletes who are low in EI.

Within team settings, having the ability to manage emotions may have notable performance consequences. Specifically, knowing that mood linkage occurs in sport teams (e.g. Totterdell, 2000), an athlete's positive or negative emotions could easily influence the emotional tone of the entire team. This possibility is demonstrated in an empirical study of 305 athletes from the UK who played either team or individual sports (Maxwell, 2004). Athletes involved in team sports reported significantly more aggression than their counterparts who played individual sports, regardless of sex. Anecdotally, the NBA brawl described at the beginning of the chapter is an example of how one player's poorly managed disgust and anger can infiltrate not only an entire team but an entire stadium of players, fans and officials. These findings provide preliminary evidence that players' emotion regulation ability (particularly the ability to handle negative emotions) is vital to a team's success; if left unmanaged, the impact of negative emotions on behavior could be amplified in a group setting and sabotage a team's success.

Once again, in the context of exercise groups, having the ability to manage emotion may be an asset for an instructor. Instructing an exercise class is a very public position. Class participants rely on the instructor for a number of different cues, including emotional cues. For example, an instructor's enthusiasm and energy is often mimicked by his students. Given that positive emotion is highly valued and often expected, instructors must be able to regulate their own emotions to meet participant expectations. Thus, to meet this expectation, when an instructor has a bad day he must regulate his emotions to mask any negative feelings he may be having and rather display the expected positive emotions. According to principles of mood linkage, this emotional display in turn will affect the emotional response of participants. It would be interesting to examine whether the ability to regulate emotion is associated with appropriate displays of emotion among exercise class instructors. Because individuals with greater ability to manage emotion are better at disguising their feelings, instructors with this ability should be able to display appropriate emotions during class (i.e. managing their own emotions) and in turn, create positive reactions among their students (i.e. manage other's emotions).

Practical implications and interventions

Implications

A great deal of research is needed before EI and its component abilities in sport and exercise groups can be understood. However, drawing on the research reviewed in the previous section, we suspect that EI affects group processes in sport and exercise and ultimately affects key outcomes such as performance and program adherence. Once research establishes the effects of EI on success of sport and exercise groups and if the effects are positive as we suspect, practitioners might consider using EI as a selection tool. For example, a gym owner might seek to hire aerobics instructors with high EI or a coach might designate an athlete with high EI as captain. In addition to capitalizing on existing EI as a selection tool, researchers and practitioners may consider implementing interventions to promote EI among athletes, exercisers, coaches, exercise instructors and administrators.

Intervention

We believe the skills that comprise EI can be learned and improved with the acquisition of new knowledge (Grewal et al., 2006). Currently interventions teaching EI-related abilities have been implemented successfully in school settings (e.g. Brackett and Katulak, 2006) and have been suggested for businesses (Lopes et al., 2006a). If indeed EI plays a central role in sport and exercise groups, similar intervention strategies could be developed for these settings as well. For example, the third author of this chapter has co-developed a program aimed at promoting awareness of the importance of EI skills in teachers, *The Emotionally Intelligent Teacher* (Brackett and Caruso, 2005). The goal of the program is to provide teachers with strategies to enhance their ability to use EI skills in their professional and personal relationships. This program could be adapted for coaches and fitness instructors. However, we caution that substantial research is needed before interventions aiming to promote EI as a means of improving group outcomes in sport and exercise are justified.

Alternatively, researchers and practitioners working outside the realm of sport and exercise might consider using sport or exercise groups as milieu for teaching EI-related abilities. This type of intervention would promote EI-skills with the goal of increasing social and emotional functioning in all life domains rather than aiming to enhance group performance per se. The emotional experiences that emerge while participating in sport and exercise activities could serve as 'teachable moments' and thus the basis for building the knowledge that fosters the development of EI-related abilities. To determine whether a sport- and exercise-based EI development intervention is a worthwhile endeavor, researchers might first establish the effects of sport and exercise participation on EI. A longitudinal study comparing the trajectories of EI development among athletes/exercisers and non-athletes/exercisers would provide insight into this question.

Future research directions

As we have noted throughout the chapter, the field of EI and its application in the realm of sport and exercise groups requires a significant amount of additional research. In this section we identify several avenues for future research.

The effect of EI on group outcomes

In order for EI research and interventions to advance in the realm of sport and exercise groups, one critical question must be addressed: *'Does emotional intelligence enhance group outcomes in the context of sport and exercise?'* Evidence supporting EI as a key determinant of group success will indicate whether interventions for developing EI in sport and exercise groups are warranted. Furthermore, the findings will provide a platform for a second generation of research examining mechanisms underlying the effects of EI on group outcomes.

To maximize the likelihood of generating support for the role of EI in sport and exercise groups, careful selection of measures is imperative. First when measuring EI, researchers should keep in mind that self-ratings of one's abilities, particularly in the EI domain, tend to be mostly unrelated to objective measures (Brackett *et al.*, 2006); thus, the use of performance measures is recommended. Second, researchers will need to establish the best method for operationalizing EI in a group context. Possible options include using a group aggregate EI score, the minimum or maximum EI score from the group, the range of EI scores in the group or the individual EI scores nested in a group (i.e. multilevel modeling approach; Elfenbein, 2006). Finally, care must be taken in selecting appropriate outcome variables. Failure to select outcomes sensitive to EI-related abilities may result in premature dismissal of EI as a determinant of team effectiveness. For example, in the study of EI and performance in collegiate baseball players, pitching statistics but not hitting statistics were related to EI (Zizzi *et al.*, 2003). The authors suggested that the difference in outcomes may be due to the variation in the EI-ability requirements for each task. Hitting may require little if any EI-related ability whereas pitching may have a more emotional component and thus is affected by a player's level of EI. Thus, in preliminary research, investigators might choose performance outcomes that strongly reflect emotion-laden aspects of sport and exercise. These might include indicators of aggression (e.g. penalty minutes) and arousal regulation (e.g. team scoring percentage on penalty shots).

How does EI operate?

Undoubtedly, establishing the effects of EI on group outcomes will generate subsequent research questions including *'How does EI operate on group outcomes?'* and will require researchers to uncover the mechanisms underlying the observed effects of EI. While discussing mediators of an effect that has not been fully established is somewhat premature, it merits attention given emerging research findings.

Leadership. In the organizational literature, leadership has been identified as an important determinant of group performance (see Hoption *et al.*, Ch. 3, this volume). As Hoption and colleagues suggest, strong leadership results in better job performance, greater job satisfaction and stronger intentions to stay in a job among subordinates. Interestingly, emerging research suggests that EI and its related abilities are important qualities for strong leadership (George, 2000; Wong and Law, 2002). For example, the leadership behavior of managers with a greater ability to recognize emotions in a series of photographs (i.e. higher ability to perceive emotion) was rated more positively by subordinates than among managers who performed poorly on the recognition task (Rubin *et al.*, 2005). In another study, individuals with higher total EI were evaluated by their supervisors as having more leadership potential than individuals with lower EI (Lopes *et al.*, 2006b). Together, these findings suggest that when examining the effects of EI on group performance, leadership might be considered as a possible mediator of these effects. Within the sport and exercise domain this might include examining leadership among athletes (i.e. EI of team captain) and instructional staff (i.e. EI of coach or instructor).

Cohesion. A second mediator that has been suggested as a potential contributor to the EI and group performance relationship is cohesion. It is well established in a number of domains, including sport and exercise, that cohesion affects group performance. Sport teams with greater cohesion have better records than less cohesive sports teams (Carron *et al.*, 2002). In exercise groups increased cohesion leads to better adherence rates (Spink and Carron, 1992). It has been proposed that this sense of cohesion may be attributed to EI (Rapisarda, 2002). Specifically, the EI of group members may be important for creating positive social interactions within the groups – an important component of group cohesion (Carron and Hausenblaus, 1998). Thus, high group EI may be conducive to creating team cohesion which in turn may lead to enhanced team performance.

The effect of EI on psychological skill interventions

As discussed earlier, the influence of EI on the effectiveness of psychological skill interventions (i.e. EI as a moderator of intervention effectiveness) is another important avenue for future research. As suggested previously, athletes and exercisers with higher EI may be better equipped to implement and use psychological skill interventions than those people with lower EI. Knowing whether EI moderates the effectiveness of these types of interventions would allow coaches, sport psychologists and fitness leaders to adapt their approaches to accommodate athletes and exercisers with varying levels of EI. For example, a sport psychologist may encourage an athlete with lower EI to practice his arousal regulation techniques more frequently than an athlete with higher EI.

Conclusion

Echoing the call made by several prominent leaders in the field for group-level emotion research in the sport and exercise domain, this chapter offers an organizing model for directing research in the area. We are proponents of the ability model of EI (Mayer and

Salovey, 1997) as a framework for examining interpersonal aspects of emotion and emotion-related abilities in sport and exercise groups. In a review of literature relevant to each of the model's components (i.e. the perception, use, understanding and management of emotion), we have demonstrated how this model may be useful for addressing the applied issues and research questions related to emotion in sport and exercise groups. In addition, because research in this area is in its incipient stage, we pointed out a number of avenues for future research pursuits. We hope that by providing researchers in sport and exercise psychology with an organizing framework and a direction for future investigations, they will undertake the challenge of advancing the study of emotion in sport and exercise groups.

References

Ayoko, O. B., Hartel, C. and Cullen, V. J. (2002). Resolving the puzzle of productive and destructive conflict in culturally heterogeneous work groups: A communication-accommodation theory approach. *International Journal of Conflict Management*, 13, 165–195.

Bar-On, R. (1997). *Bar-On emotional quotient inventory: Technical manual*. Toronto: Multi-Health Systems.

Barsade, S. G. (2002). The ripple effect: Emotional contagion and its influence on group behavior. *Administrative Science Quarterly*, 47, 644–675.

Botterill, C. and Brown, M. (2002). Emotion and perspective in sport. *International Journal of Sport Psychology*, 33, 38–60.

Boyatzis, R. E. (1982). *The competent manager: A model for effective performance*. New York: Wiley.

Brackett, M. A. and Caruso, D. R. (2005). *The emotionally intelligent teacher workshop*. Ann Arbor, MI: Quest Education.

Brackett, M. A. and Geher, G. (2006). Measuring emotional intelligence: Paradigmatic shifts and common ground. In J. Ciarrochi, J. P. Forgas and J. D. Mayer (Eds), *Emotional intelligence in everyday life* (2nd ed., pp. 27–50). New York: Psychology Press.

Brackett, M. A. and Katulak, N. (2006). Emotional intelligence in the classroom: Skill-based training for teachers and students. In J. Ciarrochi and J. D. Mayer (Eds), *Improving emotional intelligence: A practitioner's guide* (pp. 1–27). New York: Psychology Press/Taylor and Francis.

Brackett, M. A. and Mayer, J. D. (2003). Convergent, discriminant and incremental validity of competing measures of emotional intelligence. *Personality and Social Psychology Bulletin*, 29, 1147–1158.

Brackett, M. A., Mayer, J. D. and Warner, R. M. (2004). Emotional intelligence and its relation to everyday behavior. *Personality and Individual Differences*, 36, 1387–1402.

Brackett, M. A., Rivers, S. E., Shiffman, S., Lerner, N. and Salovey, P. (2006). Relating emotional abilities to social functioning: A comparison of self-report and performance measures of emotional intelligence. *Journal of Personality and Social Psychology*, 91, 780–795.

Brackett, M. A. and Salovey, P. (2004). Measuring emotional intelligence with the Mayer–Salovey–Caruso Emotional Intelligence Test (MSCEIT). In G. Geher (Ed.), *Measuring emotional intelligence: Common ground and controversy* (pp. 179–194). Happauge, NY: Nova Science.

Carron, A. V., Colman, M. M., Wheeler, J. and Stevens, D. (2002). Cohesion and performance in sport: A meta-analysis. *Journal of Sport and Exercise Psychology*, 24, 168–188.

Carron, A. V. and Hausenblaus, H. A. (1998). *Group dynamics in sport* (2nd ed.). Morgantown, WV: Fitness Information Technology.

Cote, S. and Miners, C. T. H. (2006). Emotional intelligence, cognitive intelligence and job performance. *Administrative Science Quarterly*, 51, 1–28.

Crocker, P. R. E. and Graham, T. R. (1995). Emotion in sport and physical activity: The importance of perceived individual goals. *International Journal of Sport Psychology*, 26, 117–137.

Damasio, A. (1994). *Descartes Error*. New York: Penguin Putnam.

Daus, C. S. and Ashkanasy, N. M. (2005). The case for the ability-based model of emotional intelligence in organizational behavior. *Journal of Organizational Behavior*, 26, 453–466.

Desivilya, H. S. and Yagil, D. (2005). The role of emotions in conflict management: The case of work teams. *International Journal of Conflict Management*, 16, 55–69.

Eckmann, T. F. (2004). Emotional intelligence makes a difference: Developing emotional competencies can be the 'little bit extra' that makes ordinary fitness professionals extraordinary. *IDEA Fitness Journal*, 1, 30–37.

Elfenbein, H. A. (2006). Team emotional intelligence: What it can mean and how it can affect performance. In V. Urch Druskat, F. Sala and G. Mount (Eds), *Linking emotional intelligence and performance at work* (pp. 165–184). Mahwah, NJ: Lawrence Erlbaum.

Elfenbein, H. A. and Ambady, N. (2002). Predicting workplace outcomes from the ability to eavesdrop on feelings. *Journal of Applied Psychology*, 87, 963–971.

Fredrickson, B. L. (2001). The role of positive emotions in positive psychology: The broaden-and-build theory of positive emotions. *American Psychologist*, 56, 218–226.

Frijda, N. H. and Mesquita, B. (1994). The social roles and functions of emotions. In S. Kitayama and H. Markus (Eds), *Emotion and culture* (pp. 51–87). Washington, DC: American Psychological Association.

George, J. M. (2000). Emotions and leadership: The role of emotional intelligence. *Human Relations*, 53, 1027–1055.

Goleman, D. (1998). *Working with emotional intelligence*. New York: Bantam Books.

Gordon, S. (2001). Facilitating emotional intelligence in elite sport. *New Zealand Journal of Sports Medicine*, 30, 102–105.

Grewal, D., Brackett, M. A. and Salovey, P. (2006). Emotional intelligence and the self-regulation affect. In D. K. Snyder, J. A. Simpson and J. N. Hughes (Eds), *Emotion regulation in families* (pp. 37–55). Washington, DC: American Psychological Association.

Hanin, Y. L. (1999). Individual zones of optimal functioning (IZOF) model. In Y. L. Hanin (Ed.), *Emotions in Sport* (pp. 65–89). Champagne, IL: Human Kinetics.

Hobman, E., Bordia, P. and Gallois, C. (2003). Consequences of feeling dissimilar from others in a work team. *Journal of Business Psychology*, 17, 301–325.

Isen, A. M. (2001). An influence of positive affect on decision-making in complex situations: Theoretical issues with practical implications. *Journal of Consumer Psychology*, 11, 75–85.

Isen, A. M. and Daubman, K. A. (1984). The influence of affect on categorization. *Journal of Personality and Social Psychology*, 47, 1206–1217.

Isen, A. M., Daubman, K. A. and Nowicki, G. P. (1987). Positive affect facilitates creative problem solving. *Journal of Personality and Social Psychology*, 52, 1122–1131.

Jordan, P.J. and Ashkanasy, N. M. (2006). Emotional intelligence, emotional self-awareness and team effectiveness. In V. Urch Druskat, F. Sala and G. Mount (Eds), *Linking emotional intelligence and performance at work* (pp. 145–163). Mahwah, NJ: Lawrence Erlbaum.

Jordan, P. J., Ashkanasy, N. M. and Hartel, C. E. J. (2002a). Emotional intelligence as a moderator of emotional and behavioral reactions to job insecurity. *Academy of Management Review*, 27, 361–372.

Jordan, P. J., Ashkanasy, N. M., Hartel, C. and Hooper, G. S. (2002b). Workgroup emotional intelligence: Scale development and relationship to team process effectiveness and goal focus. *Human Resource Management Review*, 12, 195–214.

Jordan, P. J. and Troth, A. C. (2004). Managing emotions during team problem solving: Emotional intelligence and conflict resolution. *Human Performance*, 17, 195–218.

Kay, L., Shapiro, D. and Weingart, L. (2001). Maximizing cross-functional new product teams' innovativeness and constraint adherence: A conflict communications perspective. *Academy of Management Executive*, 44, 779–793.

Keltner, D. and Haidt, J. (2001). Social functions of emotions. In T. Mayne and G. Bonanno (Eds), *Emotions: Current issues and future directions* (pp. 192–213). New York: Guilford Press.

Landers, D. M. (1981). Arousal, attention and skilled performance: Further considerations. *Quest*, 33, 271–283.

Lopes, P. N., Brackett, M. A., Nezlek, J. B., Schutz, A., Sellin, I. and Salovey, P. (2004). Emotional intelligence and social interaction. *Personality and Social Psychology Bulletin*, 30, 1018–1034.

Lopes, P. N., Cote, S. and Salovey, P. (2006a). An ability model of emotional intelligence: Implications for assessment and training. In V. Urch Druskat, F. Sala and G. Mount (Eds), *Linking emotional intelligence and performance at work* (pp. 53–80). Mahwah, NJ: Lawrence Erlbaum.

Lopes, P. N., Grewal, D., Kadis, J., Gall, M. and Salovey, P. (2006b). Evidence that emotional intelligence is related to job performance and affect and attitudes at work. *Psicothema*, 18, 132–138.

Lopes, P. N., Salovey, P., Cote, S. and Beers, M. (2005). Emotion regulation abilities and the quality of social interaction. *Emotion*, 5, 113–118.

Lopes, P. N., Salovey, P. and Straus, R. (2003). Emotional intelligence, personality and the perceived quality of social relationships. *Personality and Individual Differences*, 35, 641–658.

Lovaglia, M. J. and Houser, J. A. (1996). Emotional reactions and status in groups. *American Sociological Review*, 61, 867–883.

Maxwell, J. P. (2004). Anger rumination: An antecedent of athlete aggression? *Psychology of Sport and Exercise*, 5, 279–289.

Mayer, J. D. (1986). How mood influences cognition. In N. E. Sharkey (Ed.), *Advances in cognitive science* (pp. 290–314). Chichester, UK: Ellis Horwood.

Mayer, J. D., Caruso, D. R. and Salovey, P. (1999). Emotional intelligence meets traditional standards for an intelligence. *Intelligence*, 27, 267–298.

Mayer, J. D., Caruso, D. R. and Salovey, P. (2007). *The Mayer–Salovey–Caruso Emotional Intelligence Test – Youth Version (MSCEIT-YV)*. Toronto: Multi Health Systems.

Mayer, J. D., Gaschke, Y. N., Braverman, D. L. and Evans, T. W. (1992). Mood-congruent judgment is a general effect. *Journal of Personality and Social Psychology*, 63, 119–132.

Mayer, J. D. and Salovey, P. (1997). What is emotional intelligence? In P. Salovey and D. Sluyter (Eds), *Emotional development and emotional intelligence: Educational implications* (pp. 3–31). New York: Perseus Books Group.

Mayer, J. D., Salovey, P. and Caruso, D. R. (2002). *MSCEIT technical manual*. Toronto: Multi Health Systems.

Mayer, J. D., Salovey, P. and Caruso, D. R. (2004). Emotional intelligence: Theory, findings and implications. *Psychological Inquiry*, 15, 197–215.

Mayer, J. D., Salovey, P., Caruso, D. R. and Sitarenios, G. (2003). Measuring emotional intelligence with the MSCEIT V2.0. *Emotion*, 3, 97–105.

McCann, S. (1999). Emotional intelligence: The secret of athletic excellence. *Olympic Coach*, 9, 8–9.

Montieth, M. (2004). Artest out for season. Suspension of 5 Pacers decimates starting lineup. *The Indianapolis Star*. Online. Available: http://www2.indystar.com/articles/6/196691–5326–237.htm (Accessed August 2006).

Parrott, W.G. (2001). *Emotions in social psychology: Essential readings*. New York: Psychology Press.

Petrides, K. V. and Furnham, A. (2001). Trait emotional intelligence: Psychometric investigation with reference to established trait taxonomies. *European Journal of Personality*, 15, 425–448.

Raglin, J. S. and Morris, M. J. (1994). Precompetition anxiety in women volleyball players – A test of ZOF theory in a team sport. *British Journal of Sports Medicine*, 28, 47–51.

Rapisarda, B. A. (2002). The impact of emotional intelligence on work team cohesiveness and performance. *International Journal of Conflict Management*, 10, 363–379.

Rivers, S. E., Brackett, M. A., Salovey, P. and Mayer, J. D. (in press). Measuring emotional intelligence as a set of mental abilities. In G. Matthews, M. Zeider and R. D. Roberts (Eds), *The science of emotional intelligence*. New York: Oxford University Press.

Robazza, C., Pellizzari, M. and Hanin, Y. L. (2004). Emotion self-regulation and athletic performance: An application of the IZOF model. *Psychology of Sport and Exercise*, 5, 379–404.

Rosenthal, R., Hall, J. A., DiMatteo, M. R., Rogers, P. L. and Archer, D. (1979). *Sensitivity to nonverbal communication: The PONS test.* Baltimore: Johns Hopkins University Press.

Rubin, R. S., Munz, D. C. and Bommer, W. H. (2005). Leading from within: The effects of emotion recognition and personality on transformational leadership behavior. *Academy of Management Journal*, 48, 845–858.

Sallis, J. F. and Owen, N. (1998). *Physical Activity and Behavioral Medicine.* Thousand Oaks, CA: Sage Publications.

Salovey, P. and Birnbaum, D. (1989). Influence of mood on health-relevant cognitions. *Journal of Personality and Social Psychology*, 57, 539–551.

Salovey, P. and Mayer, J. D. (1990). Emotional intelligence. *Imagination, Cognition and Personality*, 9, 185–211.

Salovey, P., Mayer, J. D. and Caruso, D. R. (2002). The positive psychology of emotional intelligence. In C. R. Snyder and J. Lopez (Eds), *The handbook of positive psychology* (pp. 159–171). New York: Oxford University Press.

Salovey, P. and Rodin, J. (1985). Cognitions about the self: Connecting feeling states to social behavior. In P. Shaver (Ed.), *Self, situations and social behavior: Review of personality and social psychology* (pp. 143–166). Beverly Hills, CA: Sage Publications.

Schutte, N. S., Malouff, J. M., Hall, L. E., Haggerty, D. J., Cooper, J. T., Golden, C. J. *et al.* (1998). Development and validation of a measure of emotional intelligence. *Personality and Individual Differences*, 25, 167–177.

Solomon, R. L. (1980). The opponent process theory of acquired motivation: The cost of pleasure and the benefits of pain. *American Psychologist*, 35, 691–712.

Spink, K. S. and Carron, A. V. (1992). Group cohesion and adherence in exercise classes. *Journal of Sport and Exercise Psychology*, 14, 78–86.

Thayer, R. E., Newman, J. R. and McCain, T. M. (1994). Self-regulating of mood: Strategies for changing a bad mood, raising energy and reducing tension. *Journal of Personality and Social Psychology*, 67, 910–925.

Totterdell, P. (1999). Mood scores: Mood and performance in professional cricketers. *British Journal of Psychology*, 90, 317–332.

Totterdell, P. (2000). Catching moods and hitting runs: Mood linkage and subjective performance in professional sports teams. *Journal of Applied Psychology*, 85, 848–859.

Totterdell, P., Kellett, S., Teuchmann, K. and Briner, R. B. (1998). Evidence of mood linkage in work groups. *Journal of Personality and Social Psychology*, 74, 1504–1515.

Totterdell, P. and Leach, D. (2001). Negative mood regulation expectancies and sports performance: An investigation involving professional cricketers. *Psychology of Sport and Exercise*, 2, 249–265.

Turner, P. E. and Raglin, J. S. (1996). Variability in precompetition anxiety and performance in college track and field athletes. *Medicine and Science in Sports and Exercise*, 28, 378–385.

Vallerand, R. J. and Blanchard, C. M. (1999). The study of emotion in sport and exercise. In Y. L. Hanin (Ed.), *Emotions in Sport* (pp. 3–37). Champagne, IL: Human Kinetics.

Wolfe, S. B., Urch Druskat, V., Stubbs Koman, E. and Eira Messer, T. (2006). The link between group emotional competence and group effectiveness. In V. Urch Druskat, F. Sala and G. Mount (Eds), *Linking emotional intelligence and performance at work* (pp. 223–242). Mahwah, NJ: Lawrence Erlbaum.

Wong, C. S. and Law, K. S. (2002). The effects of leader and follower emotional intelligence on performance and attitude: An exploratory study. *Leadership Quarterly*, 13, 243–274.

Zizzi, S. J., Deaner, H. R. and Hirschhorn, D. K. (2003). The relationship between emotional intelligence and performance among college baseball players. *Journal of Applied Sport Psychology*, 15, 262–269.

Photograph by Richard Lam/UBC Athletics. Reprinted courtesy of The University of British Columbia.

2 Personality processes and intra-group dynamics in sport teams

Mark R. Beauchamp, Ben Jackson and David Lavallee

Introduction

Sixty years ago, Kurt Lewin (1947), who is generally regarded as the father of group dynamics research, published an article in the first issue of the journal, *Human Relations*, entitled 'Frontiers in group dynamics: Concept, method and reality in social science.' In this article, Lewin was particularly concerned with engaging in social change and emphasized that 'in social research the experimenter has to take into consideration such factors as the personality of individual members' (p. 9). Leaders and sports coaches are often heard commenting that group functioning is facilitated or debilitated by the presence or absence of certain personnel and so it would seem entirely logical to understand how group composition and members' personality characteristics are related to conjoint functioning. Just over three decades after Lewin's seminal paper another prominent group dynamics theorist, Marvin Shaw (1981) similarly asserted that 'personality characteristics of group members play an important role in determining their behavior in groups. The magnitude of the effect of any given characteristic is small but taken together the consequences for group processes are of major significance' (p. 208).

In spite of the historical impetus behind understanding the role of personality in group functioning, the study of personality within group dynamics research in sport and exercise psychology has been considerably limited. Indeed, the personality *construct* has been viewed with a great deal of skepticism regarding its predictive utility in explaining physical activity and achievement behavior (Morgan, 1980; Vealey, 2002). One likely reason for this skepticism can be traced to research in the 1960s and 1970s that sought to determine whether individual athletic performance could be predicted by particular traits and whether a specific personality profile existed for the elite athlete (Ogilvie, 1968; Tutko *et al.*, 1969). In the years that followed Tutko *et al.*'s (1969) publication of the *Athlete Motivation Inventory* (AMI), which was purported to predict athletic success based on a set of global personality traits, over 1,000 studies were conducted on the relationship between personality and sport performance (Fisher, 1984). While several of these studies found personality traits to be associated with athletic success (e.g. Morgan *et al.*, 1987), the specific associations varied so considerably that it made generalizations difficult (Vealey, 2002). This has led the sport and exercise psychology community to conclude that the findings linking personality characteristics with athletic performance are inconclusive (Van den Auweele *et al.*, 2001).

In sport, performance is determined by a number of factors that include (but are not limited to) skill level, physical conditioning and genetics. In addition, some psychological variables such as self-efficacy beliefs (Bandura, 1997) have been found to be directly predictive of sports performance (e.g. Moritz *et al.*, 2000). However, to dismiss the personality construct on the grounds that specific personality character-istics have not been found to be consistently predictive of individual athletic perform-ance is, from a group dynamics perspective, limited on three main grounds. First, although personal athletic prowess may not directly (and linearly) be determined by specific personality traits, personality variables have been found to be associated with other (i.e. non-performance) interdependent outcomes (e.g. empathy provision, leader-ship emergence/effectiveness) that may have implications for interdependent function-ing. Second, when personality is examined at the group-level in the form of *group personality composition* (Barrick *et al.*, 1998), the distribution of different personalities may indeed influence interdependent behaviors related to group functioning and integration. Third, rather than seek to identify which personality characteristics are directly associated with individual athlete performance, a different paradigm of per-sonality assessment and research exists which suggests that if members of inter-dependent teams can better understand themselves and the personalities of their team-mates then this greater awareness can be used to enhance intra-team dynamics.

The overall purpose of this chapter is to review the personality literature with a specific focus on understanding the role that personality can play within team func-tioning in sport contexts. Personality is defined as 'a dynamic and organized set of characteristics possessed by a person that uniquely influences his or her cognitions, motivations and behaviors in various situations' (Ryckman, 2000, p. 5) and it is the combination of these characteristics that gives each individual their uniqueness. In this chapter we will focus on two major conceptualizations of personality that have received considerable research attention in the group dynamics literature, the *trait*-based (Eysenck, 1952, 1991; McCrae and Costa, 1990, 1997) and *type*-based (Jung, 1921/1971; Myers and Myers, 1995) approaches to the personality construct.

In many disciplines of psychology (outside the sport and exercise field) the study of personality has made a strong comeback in the last two decades (McAdams and Pals, 2006), in particular, in areas as varied as interpersonal counseling (Allen and Brock, 2000; Quenk, 2000), leadership (Judge *et al.*, 2002; Hogan and Kaiser, 2005) and team-building (McCaulley, 2000; Tett and Burnett, 2003). In a similar regard, we believe that the study of personality does have an important role to play within sport and exercise psychology and from a group dynamics perspective may provide invaluable insight into how team members both influence and are influenced by those around them. In this chapter, we present a number of personality-based considerations that have yet to be applied to the group dynamics literature in sport and also present an integrated framework to inform team development interventions in sport psychology.

Theory and research

Personality traits, interpersonal processes and group dynamics

Perhaps the most widely employed conceptualization of personality corresponds to the *trait* perspective. Traits are considered to represent relatively consistent and endur-ing internal attributes or dispositions (McCrae and Costa, 1997), with research in this area made popular by scholars such as Hans Eysenck (1952, 1991) and Raymond Cattell (Cattell, 1965; Cattell *et al.*, 1970). The decline of trait-based research in sport and exercise psychology in the 1980s and early 1990s mirrored its decline in other areas of psychology. Indeed, Kanfer and Heggestad (1997) noted that 'until recently, the status of traits in most work motivation theories has been like that of a distant and not well liked relative attending a family reunion' (p. 13). The prevailing criticisms evident in both sport and exercise psychology as well as its parent discipline, psychology, stemmed from conceptually weak and atheoretical frameworks linking the vast array of traits that were being measured in relation to criterion variables (Judge and Illies, 2002; McAdams and Pals, 2006; Van den Auweele *et al.*, 2001; Vealey, 2002).

The strong resurgence of trait-based research, outside of the sport and exercise domain, can be traced to the widespread acceptance of the five-factor model (FFM; Digman, 1990; McCrae and John, 1992) of personality, or more commonly known as the Big Five (Goldberg, 1993). The five traits conceptualized within the FFM include *extraversion, neuroticism, conscientiousness, agreeableness* and *openness to experience* and are referred to as 'big' because each subsume a number of more specific or 'narrow' (Dudley *et al.*, 2006) traits (e.g. neuroticism is divided into anxiety, self-consciousness, depression, vulnerability, impulsiveness and anger hostility). Although a number of measures have been used to assess the Big Five, arguably the most common is the Revised NEO Personality Inventory (Costa and McCrae, 1992). Evidence for the factor structure of Big Five has consistently been found to generalize across non-English speaking as well as English-speaking populations (McCrae and Costa, 1987; 1997) and appears to explain the extent to which people behave in general ways over-time (Nettle, 2006). In addition, trait-based researchers recognize that these five traits certainly do not (and were not conceptualized to) capture *all* variation in individual differences/personality (Paunonen and Jackson, 2000). However, in light of the fact that these five traits do explain tendencies to behave in general, McAdams and Pals (2006) recently suggested that 'the Big Five factors seem to address the big questions that are likely to arise in the kind of socially intensive patterns of group life that human beings have evolved to live' (p. 208). In the following section we describe the Big Five traits and examine their relationships to interdependent behaviors, giving consideration to the extent to which they may influence group functioning in sport.

Extraversion is characterized by being outgoing, sociable, action oriented and talkative (Costa and McCrae, 1992) and is considered to be diametrically opposite to introversion (i.e. higher levels of one correspond to lower levels of the other), which is characterized by being reflective, reserved and quiet. Extraversion has been found to be associated with general patterns of behavior such as the proactivity of social engagement (Wanberg and Kammeyer-Mueller, 2000), the seeking of social attention (Ashton *et al.*, 1999), as well as greater confidence in speaking in front of others (Pulford and Sohal, 2006). *Agreeableness* involves being collegial, cooperative and affable and is considered an important trait for developing interpersonal relationships. Agreeable individuals tend to prefer greater use of accommodating (e.g. negotiation) strategies in conflict resolution than individuals low on this trait, who in turn prefer greater coercive approaches (e.g. power assertion) (Graziano *et al.*, 1996). Agreeableness has also been found to be closely related to demonstrating greater empathy with others (Nettle, 2007). *Conscientiousness* is concerned with being organized, responsible and diligent and has also been described as an achievement orientation (Barrick and Mount, 1991). *Neuroticism* is characterized by being insecure, anxious, or depressed and is considered diametrically opposite to emotional stability. Finally, *openness to experience* is concerned with being open-minded and inquisitive and has been found to facilitate close relationships (McCrae, 1996).

Although some recent research in sport psychology has sought to utilize the FFM of personality, the majority of these studies have been descriptive and largely atheoretical in nature. For instance, researchers have continued to compare athletes to non-athletes (e.g. Egan and Stelmack, 2003; Hughes *et al.*, 2003) and have sought to predict individual athletic performance (Piedmont *et al.*, 1999) despite the absence of sound theoretical/conceptual bases to support such investigations. Trait theorists purport that personality traits influence social interactions (McCrae, 1996; Tett and Burnett, 2003). In this chapter we focus predominantly on the relationships between intra-group personality traits and two group-dynamics constructs that have received considerable research attention within the sport psychology literature, namely leadership (see also Hoption *et al.*, Ch. 3, this volume) and group cohesion (see also Carron *et al.*, Ch. 7, this volume).

It is perhaps unsurprising that leadership has received substantial empirical attention as leaders (sports coaches and team captains) play such an influential role in the on- and off-field behaviors of athletes and teams. While we are certainly not espousing that a singular trait-profile of successful sports coaches exists, a recent meta-analysis provides some insight into the emergence and effectiveness of leaders within interdependent teams. Specifically, Judge *et al.* (2002) found that extraversion and conscientiousness were the strongest predictors of leadership emergence and that extraversion and conscientiousness were predictive of leadership effectiveness within work settings. Interestingly, 53 per cent of the variance in leadership emergence and 39 per cent of the variance in leadership effectiveness were explained by the FFM. This suggests that although a substantial amount of variance is accounted for by other factors (e.g. situational, organizational), personality is an important variable in leadership research. Interestingly, although extraversion was the strongest predictor of leadership outcomes in this meta-analysis, it was found to be more strongly related to leader emergence than leader effectiveness. This is understandable given that dominant and vocal members will be more likely to assert themselves within group situations allowing them to rise to the fore (Judge *et al.*, 2002). In light of this finding it would certainly seem interesting to examine whether FFM personality traits are similarly related to the emergence or effectiveness of leaders within sport teams, such as team captains or even peer-leaders.

In addition to these *direct* effects, it has also been suggested that team effectiveness may be influenced by the *interaction* of leaders' personality traits with the traits of subordinate team members (Neuman and Wright, 1999). Specifically, Neuman and Wright (1999) theorized that it is the extent to which different personality traits among leaders are *compatible* or *incompatible* with those of their team members that determines salient group outcomes. This question has not been addressed within the sport psychology literature and represents a promising direction for future research.

Beyond leadership, a second area of trait-based research centres on the composition and compatibility of traits within teams (Barrick *et al.*, 1998; Tett and Burnett, 2003) and their relationships to group *cohesion*. In their formative study on work *group personality composition*, Barrick *et al.* (1998) noted that group personality composition has typically been operationalized in one of three ways. The first and most common method, involves calculating mean scores for a given group on specific traits, on the basis that the amount of each trait possessed by each member will contribute to the collective pool of personality resources available to the group. This approach has also been termed *team personality elevation* (Neuman *et al.*, 1999). The second method involves calculating the variability (or variance) of each trait within the group and has also been referred to as *team personality diversity* (Neuman *et al.*, 1999). Such a measure provides an indication of whether the distribution of a particular trait within a group suggests that members are either alike (homogeneous) or unalike (heterogeneous) on specific personality characteristics. The final method outlined by Barrick *et al.* involves identifying extreme (minimum and maximum) scores within the group. Such a measure can be useful when trying to understand the influence of an 'outlier member' (one who is dissimilar to other group members) on either pro-social or disruptive outcomes (e.g. destabilization of group cohesion).

Recent studies have sought to examine how group personality composition (through mean, variance and minimum/maximum methods) is related to group cohesion. Group cohesion refers to 'a dynamic process which is reflected in the tendency for a group to stick together and remain united in the pursuit of its instrumental objectives and/or for the satisfaction of member affective needs' (Carron *et al.*, 1998, p. 213) and includes task as well as social dimensions (see Carron *et al.*, Ch. 7, this volume). Task cohesion represents a general orientation towards achieving the groups' instrumental objectives and social cohesion represents a general orientation toward developing and maintaining social relationships within the group.

Research by Barrick *et al.* (1998) and Van Vianen and De Dreu (2001) found that higher social cohesion was predicted by higher mean levels of extraversion and emotional stability within groups. In light of the fact that extraversion and emotional stability have been described as socially-oriented traits (Mohammed and Angell, 2003) it is understandable that teams characterized by more outgoing and emotionally stable team members will be more likely to interact on a social basis. Barrick *et al.* did not assess task cohesion, however the study by Van Vianen and De Dreu did. Specifically, Van Vianen and De Dreu found that higher mean levels of agreeableness and conscientiousness were related to greater task cohesion and suggested that the more members cooperate towards the team's goals (agreeableness) and strive towards achieving the team goals (conscientious) the more integrated they will be around task-related activities. Collectively, these findings point to the importance of moving beyond individual-level designs and the need to consider the combination of members' individual differences within team environments.

Although the 'mean' method (Barrick *et al.*, 1998) provides some indication of the general level of a trait that may be found within a group, it does not provide any insight into the destructive influence of specific group members. For example, in describing the years preceding the 2003 Rugby World Cup, Sir Clive Woodward (2004), the winning England coach, referred to the destructive influence of 'energy sappers' (i.e. individual members who deplete or weaken the team) who, if they can not be directed to become 'energizers', needed to be cut from the team. From a personality perspective, an 'energy sapper' might represent an individual with markedly different personality characteristics than his or her team-mates, who destabilizes the group's interpersonal processes. Using the 'minimum' scores method Barrick *et al.* and Van Vianen and De Dreu (2001) found that higher minimum levels of extraversion and emotional stability were related to the extent to which groups were united around non-task activities. These studies suggest that it only takes one insular or emotionally unstable member of the group to restrict the extent to which the group as a whole is socially cohesive.

Again, using the minimum scores method, Van Vianen and De Dreu (2001) found that higher minimum levels of conscientiousness and agreeableness within groups were positively related to task cohesion. This suggests that while it is not necessarily important to ensure that all members have the highest possible levels of these traits (i.e. intra-group 'maximum' scores were not significant predictors) it is important to ensure that team members exhibit 'at least' moderate scores on these traits. Indeed, this finding reflects the well-known saying 'one bad apple may spoil the barrel' and if a single member of the group is *very* low on conscientiousness or agreeableness this can disrupt, destabilize and debilitate a team's task-directed processes.

A fundamental question that has concerned group dynamics theorists is whether group composition should ideally be *homogeneous* (i.e. alike) or *heterogeneous* (i.e. dissimilar) in nature (Carron *et al.*, 2005). That is, are teams more likely to succeed if members are alike or if they are different in their personality characteristics? Although homogeneity (i.e. within group similarity) in intra-group conscientiousness has been found to be related to task cohesion, neither homogeneity nor heterogeneity among the other Big Five traits has been found to be associated with elevated team functioning (i.e. cohesion) around task-related activities (Van Vianen and De Dreu, 2001). This suggests that while it is important for all members to strive towards completing group tasks, either diversity or similarity of the other traits should not be viewed as impediments to achieve group tasks.

The choice of whether to use the mean, variance, or maximum/minimum method of assessing group personality composition clearly depends on the nature of the research question being asked. Furthermore, although the nature of tasks carried out in team sport settings are notably different to group tasks carried out in generic work-related environments, we believe that the study of group personality composition has considerable potential for research applications within sport and exercise settings. For example, it would be particularly interesting to observe whether the personality traits of specific individuals (e.g. the 'outlier' or 'energy sapper') have the ability to disrupt team cohesion. Indeed, it seems plausible to suggest that if one member (identified by the 'minimum score' method) of a highly interdependent team does not generally pull his or her weight (i.e. demonstrates very low conscientiousness) then team effectiveness will suffer. Similarly, if generally low levels of emotional stability (i.e. high neuroticism as assessed by the mean method) are in existence within a team then it would seem reasonable to hypothesize that members would demonstrate diminished capabilities to contribute to the team's social climate within highly interactive teams. Research on group composition within sport and exercise psychology has tended to focus on factors such as age, gender, athletic ability and ethnic status (Carron *et al.*, 2005) and, in future, it would seem worthwhile to test the recent hypothesis by Carron *et al.* that 'the "special chemistry" that is thought to exist on successful teams may be nothing more than the effective meshing of a set of personalities' (p. 106). Future research is clearly needed in this area.

Personality types, preferences and intra-group dynamics

An alternative to the trait-based approach relates to the study of personality *types* and *preferences* and stems primarily from the work of C.G. Jung (1921/1971). Research involving this approach has received considerable attention within the fields of counseling psychology (Myers and Myers, 1995), management (Barry and Stewart, 1997;

Gardner and Martinko, 1996) and leadership development (Atwater and Yammarino, 1993). Recent studies from the sport domain have also begun to use this framework to guide both personal development and team building interventions (e.g. Beauchamp *et al.*, in press; Lavallee, 2005).

Jung (1921/1971) recognized, as others do today (e.g. McAdams and Pals, 2006), that the study of personality is concerned with both uniqueness as well as characteristics that are evident across many different people. Indeed, Jung emphasized that 'one can never give a description of a type, no matter how complete, that would apply to more than one individual, despite the fact that in some ways it aptly characterizes thousands of others. Conformity is one side of man, uniqueness is the other' (Jung, 1923/1971, p. 516). Nevertheless, he also underscored that a typology can act as an invaluable 'compass of orientation' and can illustrate *how* different people generally prefer to think and behave. Although sport and exercise psychology textbooks rarely refer to Jung's (1921/1971) writing, it is important to appreciate that trait theorists such as Eysenck (1952; 1991; Eysenck and Eysenck, 1967) were heavily influenced by Jung's model in conceptualizing the dimensions of extraversion and introversion. Although these two psychological 'constructs' have come to be viewed as dimensions within the FFM (McCrae and Costa, 1997), the conceptualization of these 'traits' (cf. Eysenck and Eysenck, 1967) differs subtly from the way in which extraversion and introversion were conceptualized within Jung's (1921/1971) typology. Trait theorists (e.g. Eysenck, 1952; McCrae and Costa, 1990) suggest that general behaviors (i.e. over time and across situations) are causally predicted by traits and that traits are largely independent of one another (e.g. extraversion is conceptually distinct from agreeableness, openness is distinct from neuroticism and so forth). Jung, on the other hand, considered cognitions and behaviors to emerge as a result of the *interaction* of extraversion and introversion (which he described as types of *attitudes*) with four mental processes (which he labeled *functions*) involving *thinking, feeling, sensing and intuition*.

Thinking and feeling were collectively described by Jung (1921/1971) as *rational* functions because they are concerned with decision-making processes. Thinking represents decision-making processes that are based on logic (decisions 'from the head') and feeling involves decisions based on personal values (decisions 'from the heart'). Sensing and intuition, on the other hand, reflect the way people perceive the world and were described by Jung as *irrational*, not because these functions are unfounded or unreasonable, but because they are unconnected with decision-making processes. Sensing reflects preferences for practical experiences that are reflected in the present, whereas intuition is concerned with deeper meanings behind particular situations or future possibilities. According to Jung, when these four functions combine with introversion or extraversion, the result is the manifestation of eight possible *attitudinal-functions* (e.g. introverted feeling, extraverted sensing), which give rise to a range of cognitive and behavioral *preferences* (Table 2.1).

Jung (1921/1971) described the attitudinal-function that we tend to employ most as our *primary* or *dominant* attitudinal-function and the attitudinal-function that we employ least as our *inferior* attitudinal-function. According to his conceptual model, it is possible for auxiliary (i.e. supporting) preferences to support one's dominant attitudinal-function. So, for example, if a person exhibits a strong preference for extraverted feeling (e.g. sociable and selfless), it is possible for a sensing preference (e.g. reflects on fine details) to act in a supportive manner. Similarly, if a person exhibits a primary preference for developing ideas with analytical precision (introverted

Table 2.1 Eight attitudinal-functions

Attitudinal-functions	Preferences
Extraverted thinking	'Seeking order and taking action' Pursuit of order, structure, and objective criteria before making decisions. Likes to be organized and clear about objectives before taking swift actions. May be perceived as bold, decisive, and assertive.
Introverted thinking	'Developing ideas and strategies with analytical precision' Motivated to develop new concepts and logical solutions. Concerned with investigation, observation, and thinking things through carefully before interacting. May be viewed as distant, removed, but with a strong capacity for critical analysis.
Extraverted feeling	'Sociable and selfless' Expressive, talkative, and strong desire to interact with others. Sociable and considerate of the needs of others. May sometimes feel uncomfortable when working independently, and would rather be with others.
Introverted feeling	'Personal reflections and one-on-one connections' Interactions often governed by personally-held values. Supportive and considerate or others needs. May feel uncomfortable in the limelight, but at ease when surrounded by close friends or team-mates.
Extraverted sensing	'Down to earth and practical' Concerned with experiences grounded in the 'here and now'. Seeks out practical experiences that stimulate the senses. Little concern for abstract ideas or future possibilities, and motivated by hands-on activities.
Introverted sensing	'Reflects on fine details' Seeks to take in and study every aspect of the environment. Reflects on and carefully notices expressions, language, and people's behaviors. Although carefully attuned to the present, may be less concerned with how things might be different in the future.
Extraverted intuition	'Creating vision and strategy development' Interested in what might be going on behind the scenes or under the surface. Constantly on the look-out for new possibilities, however, may become oblivious to what might be immediately in front of one's self (in the 'here and now'). Interested in unexplored possibilities, and developing enterprising new strategies.
Introverted intuition	'Introspection and innovation' Considers issues with insight, originality and depth. May have a preference for working independently and seek to understand the real meaning behind concepts. May be viewed by others as a day-dreamer who shows little interest in the real world, only 'what might be'.

Adapted from Lothian (1997).

thinking), it is possible for intuitive preferences to act in a supporting role (e.g. strategy development).

The most extensively used personality instrument with non-clinical populations is an operational definition of Jung's (1921/1971) conceptual model, known as the Myers-Briggs Type Indicator (MBTI: Myers, 1962; Myers *et al.*, 1998). An estimated two million people complete the MBTI annually for employee and/or leadership training as well as personal development (Quenk, 2000). Once completed, the MBTI identifies 16 personality types that represent different combinations of primary and auxiliary attitudinal-functions (e.g. introverted feeling as primary with intuition as auxiliary, extraverted thinking as primary with sensing as auxiliary). Evidence for the convergent and discriminant validity of this instrument has been established by examining the MBTI in relation to trait personality measures such as the Eysenck Personality Inventory (e.g. Saggino and Kline, 1996), as well as the five scales of the FFM (e.g. McCrae and Costa, 1989). Furthermore, psychometric evaluation of the factor structure of the MBTI has provided evidence of construct validity (Johnson and Saunders, 1990) and internal consistencies have been reported for the separate subscales (Myers *et al.*, 1998).

Another operationalization of Jung's conceptual model, but one that has been considerably less used, relates to the *Insights Discovery Evaluator* (IDE; Lothian, 1996). The IDE assesses the extent to which each of the *rational* attitudinal-functions are employed, through the metaphor of 'color'. Specifically, extraverted thinking is represented by 'fiery red' preferences (e.g. strong-willed, purposeful, assertive), extraverted feeling is represented by 'sunshine yellow' preferences (e.g. sociable, enthusiastic, demonstrative), introverted thinking is represented by 'cool blue' preferences (e.g. deliberate, precise, questioning) and introverted feeling is represented by 'earth green' preferences (e.g. caring, patient, encouraging). The IDE does not provide color-based representations of Jung's (1921/1971) *irrational* attitudinal-functions (i.e. sensing and intuitive preferences). However, the visual nature of the 'colorful output', whereby participants can observe the extent to which particular preferences are expressed in both themselves and others, can be effective at facilitating an understanding of self and others among athletes (Beauchamp *et al.*, in press). Recently, Benton *et al.* (2005) provided evidence for the construct validity of the IDE through (a) confirmatory factor analysis supporting the conceptual uniqueness of the four color 'factors', (b) acceptable internal consistencies among the four color subscales and (c) evidence of test-retest reliability. As with the MBTI, the IDE is not a clinical instrument designed to diagnose mental disorders and instead is designed to foster personal awareness and development.

At the heart of Jung's (1921/1971) conceptual model is the philosophy that there are no good or bad types or preferences and that each attitudinal-function possesses *both* strengths and weaknesses. Indeed, one of the major uses of this conceptual model within counseling situations is to foster self-understanding and personal awareness (Myers and Myers, 1995; Quenk, 2000). In a recent study from the sport domain, Lavallee (2005) made use of the MBTI as part of a life development and career transition intervention with 32 recently retired professional soccer players. In this study, the MBTI was used to promote personal awareness and development and within the intervention the participants were encouraged to express their personal reactions associated with career termination. The intervention centred on helping participants to identify how their personal resources (i.e. preferences) could be transferred to the next stages of their lives. Results of the study revealed that in comparison to a control group, significant post-intervention group differences were evident in terms of positive career transition adjustments.

In a recent team building intervention study with an international-level co-acting sports team, Beauchamp *et al.* (in press) made use of the IDE to help athletes better understand themselves and their team-mates. On the basis that cohesion has been found to predict performance within coactive team environments (Carron *et al.*, 2002), this six-month team building intervention was designed to improve the quality of interpersonal communication, reduce intra-team conflict and increase team cohesion. Specifically, the intervention was based on the premise that in order to become more task and socially cohesive (see Carron *et al.*, Ch. 7, this volume), athletes first need to develop an acute understanding of themselves as well as the preferences of their team-mates.

The intervention began with assessment of the athletes' preferences (through the IDE) and was followed up by four experiential workshops over the course of 6 months. These workshops were designed to raise athletes' awareness of their own preferences for interaction as well as those of their team-mates. Athletes were encouraged to highlight potential strengths that they may bring to the team as well as reflect on possible blind-spots (i.e. preferences that are untrained and reluctantly used) through a series of role-playing activities. The intervention included personal and electronic-mail support from the consultant psychologist, as well as a series of on-line learning modules designed to consolidate information presented within the workshops. Athletes were also encouraged through in-depth discussions and traditional experiential activities (e.g. team rowing task, ropes course activities) to consider how their personality preferences may influence their own and team-mates' communication behaviors. Finally, the intervention involved a peer-mentoring system whereby athletes were required to work closely with a partner to share and discuss potentially conflicting preferences. Specifically, athletes were invited to recognize the types of people they may have difficulty communicating with and were encouraged to consider untried strategies that may be particularly well-received by those people with preferences that are different to one's own.

The intervention presented in the Beauchamp *et al.* (in press) study was evaluated through a qualitative methodology (i.e. in-depth interviews with athletes) and themes were allowed to emerge with regard to the strengths and limitations of the six-month program. In comparison to pre-intervention reports of intra-squad conflict and interpersonal stress, athletes reported that the intervention served to facilitate greater self-awareness and greater understanding of others. In terms of perceived outcomes, the athletes reported higher levels of intra-squad trust and greater group cohesion. Furthermore, the athletes also reported that the intervention helped them to more effectively train and compete, by eliminating the existence of interpersonal stressors.

Practical implications

When managers or coaches are faced with the challenge of team building, they have two fundamental options. The first is to *select* (or deselect) the appropriate personnel to fit the team's needs and the second is to *train existing members* to more effectively contribute to the team's objectives. Some within the organizational psychology literature have espoused the potential of personality assessment in the selection of teams.

For example, both Barrick *et al.* (1998) and Neuman and Wright (1999) suggested that because traits such as conscientiousness, agreeableness and emotional stability have been found to predict team performance within work environments, selection might involve ensuring that members have generally high levels of these traits and that no single individual is selected with low levels of these characteristics. Similarly, others such as Tett and Burnett (2003) have suggested that teams could be formed on the basis that members' personality characteristics are compatible. However, it is important to emphasize that the very nature of individual and team performance in sport is conceptually and operationally very different to performance in work settings not least because, in sport, physical and physiological characteristics also need to be considered (and are of major consequence). Furthermore, on the basis that personality characteristics have not been found to predict *individual* athletic performance in sport settings, some sport psychologists have suggested that it is questionable, even unethical, to base team selection in sport on personality assessment (e.g. Sachs, 1993).

Other than selection, the alternative option for team building is to train members. Given that by definition personality is generally consistent and enduring (Ryckman, 2000), it would be a fairly futile effort to seek to bolster or suppress various personality characteristics among members of sports teams. However, team members can be trained to develop a greater understanding of the differences in personalities that may exist among members of sports teams. A number of applied sport psychologists have emphasized the need to better understand one's team-mates as a means to enhance team dynamics (e.g. Crace and Hardy, 1997; Dunn and Holt, 2004). Armed with a greater awareness of what makes others (e.g. coach or team-mate) 'tick', this understanding can be used as a framework to help individuals to communicate and interact more effectively within team situations (Beauchamp *et al.*, 2005; Beauchamp *et al.*, in press). Beauchamp *et al.* (2005) proposed such a framework that included three conceptual phases involving *understanding self* (Phase 1), *understanding others* (Phase 2) and *adapting and connecting* (Phase 3). The fundamental principles of this framework involve:

Phase 1 – understanding self

1   Initially, athletes might employ personality-based measures to reflect on their general preferences or behavioral tendencies. Athletes are encouraged to be 'active' agents in the reflection/review process related to their personality assessment. That is, any personality 'profile' to emerge from the assessment of personality preferences or traits should be used by the athletes as *handrails* to consider typical communication styles, rather than as *handcuffs* to stereotype them into restrictive categories.

2   Athletes are encouraged to identify interpersonal behaviors that they typically employ within group situations (i.e. primary and auxiliary preferences, or behaviors manifested by individual traits) and reflect on personal strengths and potential weaknesses. In particular, it may be particularly challenging for athletes to identify potential weaknesses as it is difficult to 'know what you don't know'. Weaknesses (or blind spots) might correspond to preferences or behavioral tendencies, of which an athlete may be unaware, that impede team functioning. To identify such blind sports, this might involve (under the guidance of an appropriately qualified psychologist) a process of 360 degree appraisal involving one's team-mates, coaches, family members, or friends.

Phase 2 – understanding others

3   Foster an awareness of how those both similar and dissimilar to one's self (i.e. preferences or traits) like to (a) communicate and (b) be communicated with. Role play activities can be encouraged to provide insight into some of the behavioral preferences or tendencies of others.

4   Peer-mentoring schemes can be used to foster empathy among athletes with regard to understanding each others' distinctly different behavioral preferences or communication tendencies.

5   Identify collective strengths and weaknesses. If teams display high mean levels of certain traits or preferences, seek to identify where the shared strengths of the team may be found, but also which resources (as reflected by an absence of certain preferences or traits) are lacking. As one example, consider the case of the homogenous team, whereby all members share similar preferences, attitudes and behavioral tendencies. Although such a team may be quick to agree on key decision-making tasks they may not be quick to consider alternative strategies. Alternatively, the heterogenous team may potentially have more resources available (as reflected by the greater range of personalities within the team) but it may be challenging to have members come to a consensus on decisions. As research by Van Vianen and De Dreu (2001) demonstrates, neither heterogeneity nor homogeneity (in group personality composition) has been found to be superior with regard to team functioning. Clearly, both types of team bring different sets of challenges to the coach or consulting psychologist.

Phase 3 – adapting and connecting

6   Encourage athletes to communicate with team-mates using behaviors and methods that are compatible with the communication preferences of the focal person. This suggests a minor amendment to the well known saying 'treat others as *you* would like to be treated'. Instead, athletes could be encouraged to 'treat others in the way that *they* wish to be treated'.

7   Identify potential barriers for communication that may involve potentially conflicting personality characteristics. Athletes could be encouraged to play devil's advocate with their own opinions and try to see things from the perspective of their team-mates.

8   If members exhibit tendencies that might be in conflict with those of others, develop rules for effective communication. One example corresponds to the 'Four-Sight' model of communication outlined by Lothian (1997), which involves: (step 1 – intuition) using the imagination of all group members to come up with new ideas; (step 2 – sensing) gather the relevant data; (step 3 – thinking) analyze the processes required to implement different objectives; and (step 4 – feeling) give consideration to how the chosen strategy will affect different people.

Future research directions and conclusions

Perhaps the most appropriate way of seeking to propose directions for future group/ personality research is to look to the past and in particular to the comments of Lewin (1951) when he asserted that 'there's nothing so practical as a good theory' (p. 169).

That is, to develop effective and practical solutions to pressing social issues, theory driven-research is required. Unfortunately the study of personality within sport and exercise psychology has, to date, been largely atheoretical. It is our assertion that if researchers are to effectively understand what role personality plays within interdependent settings (and intervene accordingly) then sound conceptual frameworks are needed that drive theoretically considered research hypotheses. The study of groups represents a particularly fascinating context in which to examine interpersonal behaviors. It is possible that the value of personality research in sport and exercise settings lies not in its direct predictive power (or lack thereof) in relation to individual *independent* athletic functioning but, as Carron *et al.* (2005) suggested, in the extent to which personalities 'mesh' within *interdependent* group settings that is of real importance.

Over the course of this chapter a number of possible future research avenues have been highlighted. These include the use of group personality composition models to examine the extent to which maximum/minimum, mean and variance in personality traits are related to salient team dynamics outcomes such as group cohesion. We have also highlighted the importance of identifying personality characteristics that might be associated with the emergence of leaders within sports teams. Another particularly fruitful area of research within sport and exercise psychology relates to the use of type-based personality models that assess athlete preferences. Although a considerable amount of research and professional practice in areas such as counseling and management consulting involves such models, the extent to which they have been employed within sport and exercise has been markedly limited (Beauchamp *et al.*, in press; Lavallee, 2005). Nevertheless, the few intervention studies that have employed personality preference-based frameworks suggest that such approaches can be used to facilitate both salient individual- (e.g. personal growth) and team-level (e.g. cohesion, intra-group trust) outcomes in sport.

Summary

A number of prominent reviews have addressed the role of personality within sport and exercise psychology research, many of which have painted a fairly pessimistic picture regarding the utility of personality assessment. In this chapter, we have outlined conceptual and methodological advances involving sport-based research as well as approaches taken outside of the sport and exercise psychology literature that have potential to inform our understanding of conjoint functioning in groups. A vast amount of behavior in sport exists within group settings and we believe researchers should (re)engage in personality-based research and begin to understand how personalities blend (cf. Carron *et al.*, 2005) to result in highly effective as well as dysfunctional teams.

References

Allen, J. and Brock, S. A. (2000). *Healthcare communication using personality type: Patients are different*. London: Routledge.

Ashton, M. C., Lee, K. and Paunonen, S. V. (1999). What is the central feature of extraversion? Social attention versus reward sensitivity. *Journal of Personality and Social Psychology*, 83, 245–251.

Atwater, L. and Yammarino, F. J. (1993). Personal attributes as predictors of superiors' and subordinates perceptions of military academy leadership. *Human Relations*, 46, 645–668.

Bandura, A. (1997). *Self-efficacy: The exercise of control*. New York: Freeman and Company.

Barrick, M. R. and Mount, M. K. (1991). The big five personality dimensions and job performance: A meta-analysis. *Personnel Psychology*, 44, 1–26.

Barrick, M. R., Stewart, G. L., Neubert, M. J. and Mount, M. K. (1998). Relating member ability and personality to work team processes and team effectiveness. *Journal of Applied Psychology*, 83, 377–391.

Barry, B. and Stewart, G. L. (1997). Composition, process and performance in self-managed groups. The role of personality. *Journal of Applied Psychology*, 82, 62–78.

Beauchamp, M. R., Lothian, J. L. and Timson, S. E. (in press). Understanding self and others: A personality preference-based intervention with an elite co-acting sport team. *Sport and Exercise Psychology Review*.

Beauchamp, M. R., Maclachlan, A. and Lothian, A. M. (2005). Communication within sport teams: Jungian preferences and group dynamics. *The Sport Psychologist*, 19, 203–220.

Benton, S., Schurink, C. van E. and Desson, S. (2005). *Overview of the development, validity and reliability of the English version 3.0 of the Insights Discovery Evaluator (IDE)*. Dundee, UK: Insights Learning and Development.

Carron, A. V., Brawley, L. R. and Widmeyer, W. N. (1998). The measurement of cohesiveness in sport groups. In. J. L. Duda (Ed.), *Advances in sport and exercise psychology measurement* (pp. 213–229). Morgantown, WV: Fitness Information Technology.

Carron, A. V., Colman, M. M, Wheeler, J. and Stevens, D. (2002). Cohesion and performance in sport: A meta analysis. *Journal of Sport and Exercise Psychology*, 24, 168–188.

Carron, A. V., Hausenblas, H. A. and Eys, M. A. (2005). *Group dynamics in sport* (3rd ed.). Morgantown, WV: Fitness Information Technology.

Cattell, R. B. (1965). *The scientific analysis of personality*. Baltimore: Penguin

Cattell, R. B., Ebber, H. W. and Tatsuoka, M. M. (1970). *The 16-Factor Personality Questionnaire*. Champaign, IL: IPAT.

Costa, P. T. Jr. and McCrae, R. R. (1992). *Revised NeEO Personality Inventory (NEO-PI-R) and NEO Five Factor Inventory (NEO-FFI) professional manual*. Odessa, FL: Psychological Assessment Resources.

Crace, R. K. and Hardy, C. J. (1997). Individual values and the team building process. *Journal of Applied Sport Psychology*, 9, 41–60.

Digman, J. M. (1990). Personality structure: Emergence of the five factor model. In M. R. Rosenweig and L. W. Porter (Eds), *Annual Review of Psychology*, 41, 417–440. Palo Alto, CA: Annual Reviews.

Dudley, N. M., Orvis, K. A., Lebiecki, J. E. and Cortina, J. M. (2006). A meta-analytic investigation of conscientiousness in the prediction of job performance: Examining the intercorrelations and the incremental validity of narrow traits. *Journal of Applied Psychology*, 91, 40–57.

Dunn, J. G. H. and Holt, N. L. (2004). A qualitative investigation of a personal-disclosure mutual-sharing team building activity. *The Sport Psychologist*, 18, 363–380.

Egan, S. and Stelmack, R. M. (2003). A personality profile of Mount Everest climbers. *Personality and Individual Differences*, 34, 1491–1494.

Eysenck, H. (1952). *The scientific study of personality*. London: Routledge.

Eysenck, H. (1991). Dimensions of personality: 16, 5, or 3? Criteria for a taxonomic paradigm. *Personality and Individual Differences*, 12, 773–790.

Eysenck, H. J. and Eysenck, S. G. B. (1967). On the unitary nature of extraversion. *Acta Psychologica*, 26, 383–390.

Fisher, A. C. (1984). New directions in sport personality research. In J. M. Silva and R. S Weinberg (Eds), *Psychological foundations of sport* (pp. 70–80). Champaign, IL: Human Kinetics.

Gardner, W. L. and Martinko, M. J. (1996). Using the Myers-Briggs Type Indicator to study managers: A literature review and research agenda. *Journal of Management*, 22, 45–83.

Goldberg, L. R. (1993). The structure of phenotypic personality traits. *American Psychologist*, 48, 26–34.

Graziano, W. G., Jensen-Campbell, L. A. and Hair, E. C. (1996). Perceiving interpersonal conflict and reacting to it: The case for agreeableness. *Journal of Personality and Social Psychology*, 70, 820–835.

Hogan, R. and Kaiser, R. B. (2005). What we know about leadership. *Review of General Psychology*, 9, 169–180.

Hughes, S. L., Case, H. S., Stuempfle, K. J. and Evans, D. S. (2003). Personality profiles of iditasport ultra-marathon participants. *Journal of Applied Sport Psychology*, 15, 256–261.

Johnson, D. A. and Saunders. D. R. (1990). Confirmatory factor analysis of the Myers-Briggs Type Indicator: Expanded analysis report. *Educational and Psychological Measurement*, 50, 561–571.

Judge, T. A., Bono, J. E., Illies, R. and Gerhardt, M. W. (2002). Personality and performance: A qualitative and quantitative review. *Journal of Applied Psychology*, 87, 765–780.

Judge, T. A. and Illies, R. (2002). Relationship of personality to performance motivation: A meta-analytic review. *Journal of Applied Psychology*, 87, 797–807.

Jung, C. G. (1921/1971). Psychological types (Translated by H. G. Baynes, revised by R. F. C. Hull). In *The Collected Works of C. G. Jung* (Vol. 6, pp. 1–495). Princeton, NJ: Princeton University Press. (Original work published 1921).

Jung, C. G. (1923/1971). Psychological types (Translated by H. G. Baynes, revised by R. F. C. Hull). In *The Collected Works of C. G. Jung* (Vol. 6, pp. 510–523). Princeton, NJ: Princeton University Press. (Original work published 1923).

Kanfer, R. and Heggestad, E. D. (1997). Motivation, traits and skills: A person-centred approach to work motivation. *Research in Organizational Behavior*, 19, 1–56.

Lavallee, D. (2005). The effect of a life development intervention on sports career transition adjustment. *The Sport Psychologist*, 19, 193–202.

Lewin, K. (1947). Frontiers in group dynamics: Concept, method and reality in social science; Social equilibria and social change. *Human Relations*, 1, 5–41.

Lewin, K. (1951). *Field theory in social science: Selected theoretical papers* New York: Harper and Row.

Lothian, A. M. (1996). *Insights Discovery Preference Evaluator*. Dundee, Scotland: Insights Learning and Development.

Lothian, A. M. (1997). *Insights into personal effectiveness: Workbook*. Dundee, Scotland: Insights Learning and Development.

McAdams, D. P. and Pals, J. L. (2006). A new Big Five: Fundamental principles for an integrative science of personality. *American Psychologist*, 61, 204–217.

McCrae, R. R. (1996). Social consequences of experiential openness. *Psychological Bulletin*, 120, 323–337.

McCrae, R. R. and Costa, P. T., Jr. (1987). Validation of the five-factor model of personality across instruments and observers. *Journal of Personality and Social Psychology*, 52, 81–90.

McCrae, R. R. and Costa, P. T., Jr. (1989). Reinterpreting the Myers-Briggs Type Indicator from the perspective of the five-factor model of personality. *Journal of Personality*, 57, 17–40.

McCrae, R. R. and Costa, P. T., Jr. (1990). *Personality in adulthood*. New York: Guilford Press.

McCrae, R. R. and Costa, P. T., Jr. (1997). Personality trait structure as a human universal. *American Psychologist*, 52, 509–516.

McCrae, R. R. and John, O. P. (1992). An introduction to the five-factor model and its applications. *Journal of Personality*, 2, 175–215.

McCaulley, M. H. (2000). Myers-Briggs Type Indicator: A bridge between counseling and consulting. *Consulting Psychology Journal: Practice and Research*, 52, 117–132.

Mohammed, S. and Angell, L. C. (2003). Personality heterogeneity in teams: Which differences make a difference for team performance? *Small Group Research*, 34, 651–677.

Moritz, S. E., Feltz, D. L., Fahrbach, K. and Mack, D. (2000). The relation of self-efficacy measures to sport performance: A meta-analytic review. *Research Quarterly for Exercise and Sport*, 71, 280–294.

Morgan, W. P. (1980). Sport personology: The credulous-skeptical argument in perspective. In W. F. Straub (Ed.), *Sport psychology: An analysis of athlete behavior* (2nd ed., pp. 330–339). Ithaca, NY: Mouvement Publications.

Morgan, W. P., Brown, D. R., Raglin, J. S., O'Connor, P. J. and Ellickson, K. A. (1987). Psychological monitoring of overtraining and staleness. *British Journal of Sports Medicine*, 21, 107–114.

Myers. I. B. (1962). *Manual: The Myers-Briggs Type Indicator*. Princeton, NJ: Educational Testing Service.

Myers, I. B., McCaulley, M. H., Quenk, N. L. and Hammer, A. L. (1998). *MBTI manual: A guide to the development and use of the Myers-Briggs Type Indicator*. Palo Alto, CA: Consulting Psychologists Press.

Myers, I. B. and Myers, P. B. (1995). *Gifts differing: Understanding personality type*. Palo Alto, CA: Davis-Black.

Nettle, D. (2006). The evolution of personality variation in humans and other animals. *American Psychologist*, 61, 622–631.

Nettle, D. (2007). Empathising and systemising: What are they and what do they tell us about psychological sex differences? *British Journal of Psychology*, 98, 237–255.

Neuman, G. A., Wagner, S. H. and Christiansen, N. D. (1999). The relationship between work-team personality composition and the job performance of teams. *Group and Organization Management*, 24, 28–45.

Neuman, G. A. and Wright, J. (1999). Team effectiveness: Beyond skills and cognitive ability. *Journal of Applied Psychology*, 84, 376–389.

Ogilvie, B. C. (1968). Psychological consistencies within the personality of high level competitors. *Journal of the American Medical Association*, 205, 156–162.

Paunonen, S. V. and Jackson, D. N. (2000). What is beyond the Big Five? Plenty! *Journal of Personality*, 68, 821–835.

Piedmont, R. L., Hill, D. C. and Blanco, S. (1999). Predicting athletic performance using the five-factor model of personality. *Personality and Individual Differences*, 27, 769–777.

Pulford, B. D. and Sohal, H. (2006). The influence of personality on HE students' confidence in their academic abilities. *Personality and Individual Differences*, 41, 1409–1419.

Quenk, N. L. (2000). *Essentials of Myers-Briggs Type Indicator assessment*. New York: Wiley.

Ryckman, R. M. (2000). *Theories of personality* (7th ed.). Stamford, CT: Wadsworth/Thompson Learning.

Sachs, M. L. (1993). Professional ethics in sport psychology. In R. N. Singer, M. Murphey and L. K. Tennant (Eds), *Handbook of research on sport psychology* (pp. 921–932). New York: Macmillan.

Saggino, A. and Kline, P. (1996). The location of the Myers-Briggs Type Indicator in personality factor space. *Personality and Individual Differences*, 21, 591–597.

Shaw, M. E. (1981). *Group dynamics: The psychology of small group behavior* (3rd ed.). New York: McGraw-Hill.

Tett, R. P. and Burnett, D. D. (2003). A personality trait-based interactionist model of job performance. *Journal of Applied Psychology*, 88, 500–517.

Tutko, T. A., Lyon, L. P. and Ogilvie, B. C. (1969). *Athletic Motivation Inventory*. San Jose, CA: Institute for the Study of Athletic Motivation.

Van den Auweele, Y., Nys, K., Rzewnicki, R. and Van Mele, V. (2001). Personality and the athlete. In R. N. Singer, H. A. Hausenblas and C. M. Janelle (Eds), *Handbook of research on sport psychology* (2nd ed., pp. 239–268). New York: Wiley.

Van Vianen, A. E. M. and De Dreu, C. K. W. (2001). Personality in teams: Its relationship to social cohesion, task cohesion and team performance. *European Journal of Work and Organizational Psychology*, 10, 97–120.

Vealey, R. S. (2002). Personality and sport behavior. In T. Horn (Ed.), *Advances in sport psychology* (2nd ed., pp. 43–82). Champaign, IL: Human Kinetics.

Wanberg, C. and Kammeyer-Mueller, J. D. (2000). Predictors and outcomes of proactivity in the socialization process. *Journal of Applied Psychology*, 85, 373–385.

Woodward, C. (2004). *Winning! The story and rise to rugby world cup glory.* London: Hodder and Stoughton.

Part II
Leadership in groups

Photograph by Action Event Photography. Reprinted courtesy of Laurentian University.

3 Transformational leadership in sport

Colette Hoption, John Phelan and Julian Barling

Introduction

The primary purpose of this chapter is to apply knowledge gained from empirical research on transformational leadership (primarily though not limited exclusively in organizational settings) to assess the extent to which transformational leadership can enable a better understanding of psychological factors within sports. In doing so, a second and equally valuable purpose can be readily achieved, namely facilitating a greater understanding of transformational leadership (Wolfe *et al.*, 2005) by broadening its focus of inquiry. This latter purpose may be especially useful, as an examination of the content of even the most recently published texts on transformational leadership (e.g. Bass and Riggio, 2006) revealed that the application of transformational leadership to sports has received scant attention – despite the fact that today, sports is undoubtedly 'big business'.

We derive the ideas generated in this chapter from two different sources. First, we will extract relevant findings from the extant research on transformational leadership. However, to accentuate the applicability and connection between sports and transformational leadership, we conducted several interviews with 'expert participants'. Specifically, these include top tier (ice) hockey players, coaches and managers such as Wayne Fleming, Assistant Coach of the Calgary Flames and Tom Renney, Head Coach for the New York Rangers. The majority of the interviews conducted focused on the leadership behaviors and characteristics of Wayne Gretzky, an athlete widely known in North American professional sport as 'The Great One'. Observations by people who were close to Gretzky make for a vivid discussion, given his iconic status in professional hockey; as presented in this chapter, Gretzky's colleagues reminisced about how he led them to victory and why they appreciated him as a leader.

To date, the primary approach to leadership in sport psychology has embraced Chelladurai's Multidimensional Model of Leadership (e.g. Chelladurai, 1980; Martin *et al.*, 1999; Price and Weiss, 2000), which identifies three antecedents of leader behavior: situation characteristics, leader characteristics and follower characteristics. Despite the fact that this model has yet to be considered in totality and individuals, rather than teams, have received most attention, its potential appropriateness for athletic contexts made a significant contribution to sport psychology. At the same time, however, developments in understanding leadership in general and transformational leadership in particular – outside of sport psychology – have proceeded, with a sustained focus on the nature and effects of transformational leadership in organizations. Hunt (1999), in fact, has gone as far as to argue that the focus on transformational leadership revived interest in leadership studies which were becoming mundane, detached from reality and unchanging.

The purpose of this chapter is to outline the transformational leadership framework and give consideration to its potential utility within sport psychology. This would not be the first attempt to merge leadership in sports to leadership in organizations. Kellett (1999) explains the complexity of likening sport leadership with corporate leadership and concludes with the following:

> [I]f coaching is a legitimate analog of leadership, then our fundamental conceptions of leadership may need substantial revision . . . Firstly, [an appropriate leadership framework] would include behavioural observations of what it is that coaches actually do when they coach. Secondly, it would compare effective coaches to effective managers (particularly managers who begin from the premise that their role is to empower and facilitate . . .). Thirdly, it would work experimentally to determine whether training managers to use some of the techniques actually used by our best coaches really does make a difference in management outcomes'.
>
> (Kellett, 1999, p. 167)

Kellett's (1999) comments are valid, but transformational leadership addresses many of Kellett's concerns. As will be noted throughout this chapter, transformational leadership focuses on the very behaviors that have been observed in sports teams and among the empirical research supporting the effectiveness of transformational leadership, coaches have been studied and their responses are consistent with findings about other leaders in organizational contexts.

There are five additional reasons to study transformational leadership in sport psychology. First, transformational leadership has been widely studied in organizational behavior; and a plethora of research findings now exist from which sport psychology can borrow, learn and advance. Second, the research on transformational leadership is empirically and rigorously tested, even across culture (e.g. Walumbwa et al., 2005), making it a wide-reaching and extensive framework. Third, evidence exists from quasi-experimental studies showing that transformational leadership can be taught (Barling et al., 1996; Dvir et al., 2002) and such training has been applied in various contexts such as hospitals (e.g. Kelloway et al., 2000), the military (e.g. Dvir et al., 2002) and corporations (e.g. Barling et al., 1996). The ability to hone transformational leadership skills could be a critical competitive advantage for sports teams. Furthermore, a core premise of transformational leadership is to develop followers (Bass, 1998); training athletes to embody transformational leadership behaviors has foreseeable benefits for performance and team dynamics (e.g. cohesion and potency). Thus, coaches, peer leaders and managers can learn the behaviors of transformational leadership and benefit from its positive effects on follower attitudes and behaviors. Fourth, athletics and sports management *are* businesses that require managerial attention (Whisenant and Pedersen, 2004); borrowing from leadership literature in organizational behavior addresses the necessary shift towards incorporating a business mindset to sports.

Fifth and finally, the leader's role in teams and groups has been actively researched and so, it would be intriguing to replicate and augment these findings to a sports context. Examples of such research include the sharing of information among group members (e.g. Hollingshead, 1996), the process of defining one's group members (e.g. Tajfel and Turner, 1979) and protecting one's membership to a group (e.g. Deutsch and

Gerard, 1955). Leaders are also group members and they enact a significant role in group dynamics. For example, a leader functions as a representative of the group and must, therefore, embody the values and characteristics of the collective (e.g. Van Knippenberg and Hogg, 2003). Without leadership, a group can endure hardship because group members lack role clarity (e.g. Weick, 1993). A leader's influence in a group is particularly affected by that leader's demonstration of transformational leadership behaviors: transformational leaders have been found to exert influence that goes beyond their direct subordinates and that ultimately reaches a greater number of organizational members (Bono and Anderson, 2005). Thus, a focus on work teams and groups has now been established and methodologies that contrast individual and team-level effects and look at the interactions, are now common-place in organizations (e.g. Chen *et al.*, 2002; LePine, 2003; Stewart *et al.*, 2005). This brief overview highlights the importance of understanding leadership in groups. In particular, this chapter will review notable effects of transformational leadership on group outcomes that are meaningful in a sports context: group performance, group potency and group cohesion.

Our discussion begins with a description of the major transformational leadership behaviors. Following that, we will review findings from transformational leadership research that attest to its effectiveness in areas relevant to sports psychology, namely follower well-being, attitudes and performance. Thereafter, we will describe the interplay between sport psychology and transformational leadership. Ideas for future research that might benefit both sports psychology and transformational leadership are discussed throughout this chapter.

What is transformational leadership?

Transformational leadership describes four leader behaviors that have been shown to influence followers' values, needs, awareness and performance (Bass and Riggio, 2006). These four behaviors are idealized influence, inspirational motivation, intellectual stimulation and individualized consideration.

Idealized influence. Idealized influence instills pride in followers, setting a good example for followers and earning followers' respect by behaving in ways that maximize values (Bass and Riggio, 2006). A leader's morals and values are especially important; leaders who possess self-interested motivations and enact unethical behavior have been posited as pseudo-transformational (Bass and Steidlmeier, 1999). Pseudo-transformational leaders crave and bask in the spotlight whereas authentic transformational leaders are humble and modest about their personal triumphs.

Several examples from the sports context highlight idealized influence. Wayne Fleming, former Assistant Coach of the Philadelphia Flyers in the National Hockey League, described the Flyers' team captain, Peter Forsberg, in these terms: 'Forsberg goes out of his way to deflect attention to others'. Further illustrative of idealized influence is the following quote from Jim Ramsay, an athletic trainer for the New York Rangers. Ramsay described Gretzky in the following way:

> The best way to describe him is: a good human being, a good person. He has great values and morals . . . He's always had the ability to say the right thing, do the right thing and lead by example by his performance on the ice and off the ice. If you know the man, not just the athlete, you know that he is a quality individual.

What can be deduced from Ramsay's quote is that Gretzky exhibited idealized influence because he earned the respect of those around him and clearly behaved in ways that were consistent with his values. Subsequently, even in the context of a sport that is sometimes brutally physical – indeed, perhaps especially in such a context, values play a substantial role in earning the ability to lead others.

Inspirational motivation. Leaders who reflect inspirational motivation convey optimism and enthusiasm; in so doing they enhance followers' self-efficacy (Bass and Riggio, 2006). Self-efficacy refers to the beliefs that an individual has about his/her capability to manage a situation (Bandura, 1995). Inspirational motivation also includes articulation of a collective purpose so that followers adopt a shared vision for the future which contributes to a team spirit. Part of developing a shared vision for the collective good is bringing individuals together so that they can actively feel part of a group.

In an interview, Jerry Dineen, Video Coach for the New York Rangers, remarked as follows about Gretzky's inspirational motivation:

> He always made you feel part of a team . . . no matter what level you were working, at what capacity you dealt with the team at all . . . he always made everybody feel like they were included . . . and felt like they were part of the big scheme of things.

Even more compelling, Dineen characterized Gretzky as 'doing the common good for the team'.

Intellectual stimulation. Leaders' use of intellectual stimulation encourages followers to be creative, solve problems in innovative ways and question assumptions (Bass and Riggio, 2006). All of this enables followers to experiment with new ideas free from criticism and to develop their strengths. Intellectual stimulation conveys trust and optimism as leaders allow followers to consider and express potentially controversial solutions to problems (Bass, 1985).

Moving away from hockey, the importance of intellectual stimulation was underscored in Corbin's (2005) analysis of cricket players. In particular, Corbin shares insights about the leadership of two players widely regarded as all-time 'greats': Viv Richards and Clive Lloyd. Richards' leadership style recognized that 'even the most talented player would not fulfill his potential if his mental skills are not developed' (p. 41) and Lloyd underscored 'the importance of his "thinking" when he acknowledged that his own success had been the result of a thoughtful, professional approach' (p. 41).

Individualized consideration. Last, individualized consideration addresses the unique needs and capabilities of each follower through coaching, advising, listening, compassion and empathy, thereby promoting followers' development (Bass and Riggio, 2006). The importance of individualized consideration to the leader–follower relationship is underscored in Ramsay's fond memory of Gretzky's compassion:

> He listened to what was going on in our lives . . . and had the ability not just to listen but to take it in and be something meaningful to that person. He wasn't just an athlete . . . he made an impact in my life.

Ramsay's quote explains how Gretzky went above and beyond expectations and symbolized a leader who cared about the individual, not just about the organization. In another example of individualized consideration, Fleming's experience in hockey leads him to the following conclusion: 'To be a leader there must be compassion to team-mates.'

When considering the nature of leadership, reading and witnessing examples of individualized consideration towards one's team-mate(s) might be expected. However, despite the physical nature of a sport such as hockey, there are also examples of individualized consideration directed at one's opponent(s):

> When Brett Hull scored for Dallas in Game 1 of the St. Louis series, Davidson immediately observed that Hull makes a point of not celebrating goals. No reason to embarrass the goalie or incite the opposition.
>
> (Houston, 1999, p. S5)

Although described separately, the four components of transformational leadership are highly correlated (Bycio *et al.*, 1995), meaning that it is likely that leaders who demonstrate one component also exhibit the others.

In addition, the transformational leadership framework is part of Bass and Avolio's (1994) 'Full Range Leadership' model, which also includes *transactional* as well as *laissez-faire* leadership styles. Transactional leadership styles more accurately reflect managerial approaches: contingent reward and management-by-exception leadership (Bass, 1998). Leaders who reward followers for good performance exhibit contingent reward behaviors. Contingent reward requires leaders to recognize followers' successes; in contrast, management-by-exception entails recognizing followers' mistakes. Further, management-by-exception can either be passive or active; the passive form waits for mistakes to occur before pursuing corrective action whereas the active form monitors mistakes and takes corrective action accordingly. Lastly, laissez-faire leadership can also be considered non-leadership behavior; leaders who adopt the laissez-faire style delay actions, do not make decisions and ignore their responsibilities.

Leaders can be both transformational and transactional. However, transformational leadership's components are associated significantly more strongly with leader effectiveness than transactional leadership (Lowe *et al.*, 1996). For example, Rowold (2006) studied leadership behaviors in martial arts sport coaches. Rowold reported that transactional leadership was related to followers' ratings of leadership effectiveness, satisfaction with the leader and the leader's extra effort. In addition, Rowold found that the effects of transformational leadership on these same outcomes (i.e. effectiveness, satisfaction and extra effort) explained *more variance* beyond transactional leadership, hence supporting the augmentation effect of transformational leadership and justifying our focus on transformational leadership in this chapter. Indeed, transformational leadership has been related to many important outcomes to which we now turn our attention.

Transformational leadership behaviors and outcomes

As previously mentioned, one of the reasons for applying the transformational leadership framework to sports is the amount and rigor of research that has been invested into testing this framework in organizational settings (Bass and Riggio, 2006). The field of sport psychology could benefit from this research because it readily applies to the coach–athlete relationship, as well as the coach–team relationship which will be discussed later in this chapter. To begin, we will examine the effects of transformational leadership on individual-level outcomes: follower *well-being, self-efficacy, attitudes and performance*. Each of these are particularly relevant for understanding how transformational leadership can benefit athletes. Later in this chapter we will discuss the coach-team relationship by shedding light on the effect of transformational leadership on group-level outcomes: group performance, potency and cohesion.

Follower well-being. Well-being is an important criterion not only because of its obvious benefits to the individual, but also because it contributes to the team through motivation, absenteeism, turnover and health (Shirom, 1989). Well-being would be incomplete if it did not include both psychological and physical components. Psychological well-being is often operationalized in terms of how negative (e.g. anxious, gloomy, worried) and positive (e.g. calm, relaxed, optimistic) an individual feels (e.g. Martin and Epitropaki, 2001). Physical well-being is frequently operationalized in terms of physiological responses, such as presence of headaches and stomach pains (e.g. Reinboth and Duda, 2006) and injuries (e.g. Barling *et al.*, 2003).

Although they are frequently bifurcated in research, psychological and physical well-being co-occur and influence each other (e.g. Densten, 2005). Transformational leadership is one aspect of organizational life which has been effective in promoting *both* psychological and physical well-being. To illustrate, Densten (2005) found that inspirational motivation mitigated follower burnout; optimistic visions of the future provided burnout victims with a sense of hope. In another example, Barling *et al.* (2002) showed in two separate samples that transformational leaders are able to emphasize the importance of and promote occupational safety, which encompassed cognitions and beliefs about safety in the environment, as well as behaving safely in the environment.

Specific to the sports context, occupational injuries are a concern for athletes: The National Council of Athletic Training (1999) reported that within a year, 30 per cent of interscholastic athletes miss at least 1 day of practice or competition because of injury. Transformational leadership has been effective in promoting occupational safety and thus, is associated with fewer occupational injuries (Barling *et al.*, 2002). The reviewed research suggests that transformational leadership may be useful in promoting physical and mental health in athletes and coaches.

Follower self-efficacy. As argued previously, well-being is an important organizational concern. Subsequently, researchers are devoted to understanding what contributes to individual well-being. An indicator of well-being is self-efficacy: beliefs an individual has about his/her ability to meet a goal or cope effectively in stressful situations (Bandura, 1997). Joekes *et al.* (2007) sampled patients suffering from either congestive heart failure or myocardial infarction; the researchers found that in both of these samples, self-efficacy was strongly associated with psychological well-being. Conversely, researchers have found that individuals low on self-efficacy tend to experience more anxiety and depressive symptoms (e.g. Shnek *et al.*, 2001). The positive effects of self-efficacy also include likelihood of enacting proactive behavior (Parker, 2000) and performance (e.g. Judge *et al.*, 2007; Katz-Navon and Erez, 2005; Richard *et al.*, 2006).

Given these findings, it is beneficial for followers to feel efficacious. Furthermore, transformational leaders have the potential to raise follower self-efficacy through empowerment. Empowerment is the act of raising individuals' perceptions of their individual capabilities, as well as their team or organization's capabilities (Conger and Kanungo, 1988). The positive influence of transformational leadership on followers' beliefs about their competence, confidence and capabilities has been well established in the literature (e.g. Bass, 1998; Kark *et al.*, 2003; Shamir *et al.*, 1993).

Despite the organizational settings in which many of these studies were conducted, belief in oneself, along with general physical and psychological health is also integral to athletic performance and orientations. Slanger and Rudestam (1997) reported that athletes who had confidence in their abilities were less intimidated by the risks involved in extreme sports (i.e. kayaking, rock climbing, stunt flying and skiing) than athletes who were less confident in their abilities. The same authors also note that athletes are characteristically more physically healthy than non-athletes and Raedeke (2004) concluded that coaches themselves need to be in good physical condition so as to project the spirit and drive necessary to lead a team. Due to the amount of studies examining self-efficacy in sports, Moritz *et al.* (2000) conducted a meta-analysis and found a moderate relationship between self-efficacy and sport performance: 0.38. This provides further support for the importance of athletes' efficacious beliefs and under-scores the important role transformational leaders can play in supporting athletes' self-efficacy.

Follower attitudes. We now turn our attention towards followers' beliefs about their work, including perceptions of their colleagues and leaders. An attitude can be defined as 'a general and enduring positive or negative feeling about some person, object, or issue' (Petty and Cacioppo, 1981, p. 7). Two types of attitudes that are frequently studied in organizations are satisfaction and commitment. Satisfaction and commit-ment are important in the current context because they contribute to followers' will-ingness to remain in the leader–follower relationship (e.g. Epitropaki and Martin, 2005) and also influence follower performance (e.g. Barling *et al.*, 1996).

The value of these attitudes in the area of sports psychology has also been acknow-ledged. Wilson *et al.* (2004) concluded that commitment and satisfaction contributed to exercise behavior (e.g. frequency of exercising). Additionally, commitment and sat-isfaction also determine performance in sports (e.g. Theodorakis, 1996), such that higher levels of commitment and satisfaction led to superior performance. It follows that strategies to strengthen athletes' commitment and satisfaction are valuable.

Transformational leadership has been shown consistently to influence follower com-mitment and satisfaction (e.g. Avolio *et al.*, 2004; Butler *et al.*, 1999; Fuller *et al.*, 1999; Rai and Sinha, 2000; Walumbwa *et al.*, 2005) and this is not surprising given the nature of transformational leadership. For example, individualized consideration should fos-ter commitment (e.g. loyalty to the leader, team or organization) because leaders signal that they are not only interested in the collective but also in each individual's personal growth. Moreover, attention to developing followers' strengths and weaknesses is also likely to increase satisfaction as followers master skills and improve upon their performance. Inspirational motivation can also contribute to follower commitment. Specifically, leaders who are optimistic can assuage follower concerns that could limit the amount of effort they invest into a (challenging) project. Treating followers fairly and building their respect are also determinants of follower satisfaction.

This latter rationale could be even more specific; follower *relationship* satisfaction is worthy of discussion especially concerning the focus on leader–follower (or coach–athlete) interactions. To our knowledge, no coach–athlete studies have been conducted to assess relationship satisfaction (as opposed to satisfaction with the sport, or self-satisfaction) and given findings from organizations, this is a promising area for future research. Indeed, satisfaction with the coach–athlete relationship (from both parties) may help explain variance in performance.

Follower performance. Within the organizational behavior literature, two separate forms of performance have been identified and subjected to study, namely task performance (e.g. fulfilling the requirements of the job description) and contextual performance (e.g. behaviors that are not in a formal job description but help the functioning of the organization; see LePine *et al.*, 2002). Research has shown that transformational leadership has been successful in both task and contextual performance, in diverse contexts, such as high school sports teams (e.g. Zacharatos *et al.*, 2000), project teams (e.g. Keller, 2006) and the military (Lim and Ployhart, 2004).

One way in which transformational leadership behaviors translate into exceptional performance is by affecting followers' perceptions of their jobs, such as the meaningfulness of their work (Purvanova *et al.*, 2006). For example, Purvanova *et al.* (2006) argued that transformational leaders' expression of an organization's mission and vision (i.e. inspirational motivation) increases task significance. To reiterate, Ramsay made the following observation of Gretzky's leadership style:

> He's always had the capacity to take a group of individuals and really bring them together . . . and make them have a common goal towards what they were trying to achieve . . . you were part of something bigger.

Particular to a sports context, Charbonneau *et al.* (2001) suggested that transformational leadership enhances sports performance by accentuating the enjoyment of sports regardless of extrinsic rewards (e.g. winning a championship). If Charbonneau *et al.* (2001) are correct, transformational leadership may also help explain athletes' willingness to continue practicing and honing their talents in the face of personal and team failures.

In addition, transformational leadership behaviors can also be exhibited by the athletes themselves. Zacharatos *et al.* (2000) studied high school athletes' transformational leadership behaviors. Team captains in Zacharatos' study were rated as more effective (e.g. satisfying and motivating) when they demonstrated more transformational leadership behaviors and moreover those behaviors were significantly associated with performance variables such as effort. These results emphasize that peer-leadership development merits attention; Fleming of the Calgary Flames, acknowledged that a peer leader may 'help soften the blow of the coach'. Subsequently, transformational leadership is not only pertinent to coaches, but also peer leaders who serve as role models for their contemporaries (Gould *et al.*, 1987).

Group outcomes. Thus far, individual-level outcomes (e.g. coach–athlete relationships) have been the focus of our discussion, but group-level effects are also studied in transformational leadership research. Importantly from a sports context, however, where much performance occurs in teams, transformational leadership has also been addressed within coach–team relationships. In this section we provide an overview of the relationships between transformational leadership and group performance, potency and cohesion.

Performance indicators are varied, for example in organizational research return-on-investments could be an indicator of performance, as could reported satisfaction with one's job and turnaround time on a project. Despite these diverse indicators of performance, researchers consistently find that groups led by a leader with high levels of transformational leadership outperform groups that are led by a leader with lower levels of transformational leadership (e.g. Dvir *et al.*, 2002). The relationship between transformational leadership and performance becomes stronger under the condition of high group potency (e.g. Bass *et al.*, 2003; Sosik *et al.*, 1997). Group potency refers to group members' perceptions of their group's effectiveness, capability, productivity and performance (Guzzo *et al.*, 1993). Similar to group potency is collective efficacy which is sometimes called team efficacy. Collective-efficacy is 'a group's shared belief in its conjoint capabilities to organization and execute courses of actions required to produce given levels of attainment' (Bandura, 1997, p. 477). Group potency and collective efficacy are related concepts and the exact nature of their relationship has been discussed in the literature (e.g. Bandura, 1997; Guzzo *et al.*, 1993). Altogether, evidence for the positive effect of transformational leadership on perceptions of group performance have been well documented in organization behavior literature (e.g. Arnold *et al.*, 2001; Pillai and Williams, 2004; Sosik *et al.*, 1997).

Specific to sports teams, Dirks' (2000) empirical study of basketball teams found that trust in one's leader led to better team performance and, furthermore, trust in one's leader had a more powerful effect on team performance than trust in one's team-mates. In this study, trust in leadership was defined as 'an expectation or belief that the team can rely on the leader's actions or words and that the leader has good intentions toward the team' (Dirks, 2000, p. 1,004). Moreover, Dirks argues that transformational leadership behaviors may be particularly effective in raising team members' expectations in a leader's intentions and abilities.

Group cohesion is another important construct that affects team dynamics and performance. Group cohesion encompasses commitment and attraction to the group (Pillai and Williams, 2004). Not surprisingly, many studies show cohesive groups function better together than groups that are less cohesive; for example, cohesive groups perceive less 'social loafing' among group members, meaning that each group member is seen as a contributor to the collective's goals (Hoigaard *et al.*, 2006).

Transformational leadership affects group cohesion. Pillai and Williams (2004) found that a group of rescue employees at a fire department reported more group cohesion when led by a leader with higher levels of transformational leadership behavior than when led by a leader with lower levels of transformational leadership behavior. Similar to the aforementioned group-potency effects, more cohesion led to a stronger relationship between transformational leadership and performance (Dionne *et al.*, 2004). It is important to note that group effects (e.g. cohesion, potency) can occur regardless of leadership. Nonetheless, transformational leadership has been found to increase perceptions of trust, commitment and collective efficacy *over and above* levels of these variables reached through group norms and values (Arnold *et al.*, 2001).

One caveat to interpreting research at the group level is that group-level constructs are often construed as an average or sum of individual-level scores/observations. This assumes that the sum is always equal to its parts, whereas some groups are purposefully composed so that the sum is *greater* than the parts combined. In many cases this would be true of sports teams. Therefore, it may be particularly interesting to study the antecedents and consequences of transformational leadership in sports teams because in many sports (e.g. hockey, football, basketball, soccer) one team member is not a substitute for another and in fact each team member is chosen to complement the others. Therefore, averaging scores for these team members (to obtain a group-level construct) would discard their unique perspectives and specialties.

Transformational leadership and sport psychology

There is every reason to believe that the effects (i.e. well-being, attitudes, performance and group outcomes) of transformational leaders in organizations should also occur in sports teams. Understanding the intersection of transformational leadership and sports behaviors will bring benefits to both leadership research *and* sport psychology. However, research uniting these topics is scarce. This section discusses four studies that have related transformational leadership to sports. Collectively, they shed a preliminary light on the intersection of transformational leadership and sport performance and dynamics.

Sport performance and transformational leadership. Corbin (2005) conducted a content analysis of biographies, journals and any other relevant information of two West Indies Cricket leaders: Clive Lloyd and Viv Richards. These two athletes were chosen for the content analysis based on their impressive winning records; they helped the West Indies team dominate world cricket for many years throughout the 1970s. Corbin's analysis allows us to conclude that all four aspects of transformational leadership were inherent in Lloyd's and Richards' leadership styles. For example, Richards was known as a 'respected captain', reflecting idealized influence. And in another example, it was written that Lloyd motivated his team-mates to be 'part of a greater whole'. Note that these examples are similar to the qualities mentioned about Gretzky's leadership style; it follows that there is strong qualitative evidence that transformational leadership relates to performance in sports.

Transformational leadership and sportsmanship. Although performance is important to competitive sports, sportsmanship conduct is also critical. According to Tom Renney, coach of the New York Rangers, player conduct is more of a determinant of peer leadership than performance: 'Your best player may not be captain' because being a leader concerns '[helping] others be better'. One way to demonstrate sportsmanship is through modesty and humility. These qualities relate to an athlete's respect for others (including opponents) and an athlete's avoidance of negative behavior in sports (Vallerand et al., 1996). Tucker et al. (2006) investigated the role of humility in sports. They found a positive relationship between apologies and ratings of transformational leadership. This finding provides the groundwork for future research on the intersection of transformational leadership and sportsmanship and it suggests that transformational leadership training may be particularly useful in a sports context because it could inform sportsmanship behavior.

Motivation, performance and leadership. University athletes participated in Charbonneau et al.'s (2001) study. These researchers found that intrinsic motivation (see Standage and Vallerand, Ch. 10, this volume) mediated the relationship between transformational leadership and performance. In their study, intrinsic motivation was defined as individuals' desire to engage in sports activities because of the pleasure they get out of it. The researchers measured three factors of intrinsic motivation: (1) knowledge (e.g. 'For the pleasure of discovering new training techniques'), (2) stimulation (e.g. 'For the intense emotions I feel doing a sport that I like') and (3) accomplishment (e.g. 'For the satisfaction I experience while I am perfecting my abilities'). The results revealed that coaches' intellectual stimulation and individualized consideration significantly correlated with all three aspects of athletes' intrinsic motivation. These results reinforce the importance of mental challenges and receiving personalized attention. Furthermore, a leader's intellectual stimulation and individualized consideration should complement an athlete's physical abilities to produce superior performance. Overall, Charbonneau *et al.*'s research contends that transformational leadership has the capability to motivate athletes by arousing their love and appreciation for the sport.

Antecedents of transformational leadership

Perhaps the most enduring questions across contexts about leadership in general and transformational leadership in particular, focus on how it is developed. Two of the specific questions asked most frequently concern the role of parental socialization and whether it is possible to train or teach leaders (as opposed to whether leaders are 'born'). There are studies addressing both of these possibilities, the findings of which will have implications for transformational leadership in the sporting context.

Zacharatos *et al.* (2000) sought to understand the antecedents or development of transformational leadership and chose to examine parental leadership style and its influence on children's leadership style in high school sports teams. They assumed that parenting behaviors could be conceptualized within a transformational framework and operationalized parenting in terms of idealized influence, inspirational motivation and so forth. The major finding from their study merits attention. Zacharatos *et al.* (2000) found that adolescents modeled their parents' leadership skills (specifically those of their fathers), inasmuch as there was a significant relationship between the adolescents' transformational leadership behaviors (as rated by themselves and their peers) and the extent to which they believed their parents manifested transformational behaviors in their parenting. This allows us to infer that transformational leadership can be socialized and modeled; and that coaches who are transformational would likely serve as a model to the team captain (and other team members) to also exhibit transformational behaviors. Anecdotal evidence of this modeling effect is also evident in Ken Gernander's reflection of his 14 years of experience in the American Hockey League. When asked where leaders learn to be leaders, Gernander replied: '[from watching] others, [learning] from coaches and old players'.

A second question related to the development of leadership that is asked frequently is whether it is possible to teach transformational leadership. Two studies by Barling *et al.* (1996) and Dvir *et al.* (2002) allow for a positive response to this question. In the Barling *et al.* (1996) study, bank managers were either placed into a control or experiment group. Those in the experiment group underwent a one-day group training session, which included reminiscing about effective leaders, learning about the research findings on transformational leadership and role playing exercises. After the group training session, managers underwent individual booster sessions that consisted of evaluating feedback from that manager's subordinates' about his/her leadership style and the manager's own self-rated leadership style. The booster session also established an action plan for each manager: specific goals about behavior changes were set. Three subsequent booster sessions took place and focused on the manager's progress with regards to the action plan. Managers in the control group did not undergo any leadership training. After the training intervention, it was found that the managers in the experimental group were perceived as more intellectually stimulating, charismatic and individually considerate than managers in the control group. Furthermore, subordinates of managers in the experimental group reported significantly more organizational commitment than subordinates of managers in the control group. Barling *et al.*'s results support the contention that transformational leadership can be taught and bring forth organizational benefits.

In another field experiment, Dvir *et al.* (2002) randomly assigned platoon leaders of the Israel Defense Forces to a transformational leadership training condition or a control group condition. Participants in the experimental condition attended a 3-day workshop on transformational leadership. Participants in the control condition also attended a 3-day workshop but the content of this workshop focused on more general psychological processes that occur between and within individuals and groups. Both workshops included similar activities such as role-playing, group discussions and presentations. After the training intervention, many positive effects of transformational leadership emerged. Specifically, subordinates of leaders who underwent transformational leadership training reported higher self-efficacy and extra effort than subordinates of leaders in the control group and also outperformed the control group on tasks that were specific to their training (i.e. obstacle course, a written test of their knowledge on weapons, physical fitness). Dvir *et al.*'s results demonstrate that it is possible to train transformational leadership behaviors and improve follower performance.

These two studies allow us to infer that it might also be possible to teach sports leadership; and future research should address this issue specifically. Focus on either the socialization or the training of sports leaders speaks to the question that has long been asked: Are leaders born or made? Given the research presented, we see the potential to develop transformational leaders and in this same endeavor, advance our knowledge of transformational leadership in research and practice.

Practical implications

In consideration of the research presented in this chapter, we have provided a list of five recommendations for applying transformational leadership to sports:

- A transformational leader does not only direct the team but also considers him/herself *part of* the team.
- Star performers are not necessarily leaders; effectiveness at helping *others* perform their best constitutes transformational leadership.
- Remember that leaders' values and attitudes on and off the field contribute to followers' perceptions of leadership and gamesmanship.
- Transformational leadership training for *all* team members (i.e. athletes, coaches, peer leaders) can be a competitive advantage for teams.
- Transformational leaders recognize each individual on a team.
- To detect the effectiveness of transformational leadership, measures beyond performance should be included, such as attitudes towards the sport, physical and mental health, satisfaction with the team and efficacious beliefs at the individual and collective level.

Summary

Unlike other leadership frameworks in organizational research, transformational leadership is not intended to give rise to the depiction of 'what is a great leader', but rather to understand how to develop better followers. The concern for followers in the transformational framework is particularly salient in the individualized consideration and intellectual stimulation components; nevertheless, inspirational motivation and idealized influence work to establish that a transformational leader is not focused on his/her own achievements, but on the achievements of the team. These fundamental emphases communicate the uniqueness of the transformational leadership framework.

This exploration of sports leadership through a transformational-leadership lens can uncover rich opportunities, in practice and research, to consolidate two areas that have largely been evolving independently of each other. The research linking transformational leadership to sport psychology is at a fledgling state, but the insights from sports experts inserted throughout this chapter demonstrate that the core tenets of transformational leadership are aptly recognized and appreciated in practice. We urge leadership researchers to embrace the opportunities offered by the sports context for observing theory in practice and likewise we urge sport psychologists to apply the transformational leadership framework for fostering better coaches, peer leaders *and* athletes.

References

Arnold, K. A., Barling, J. and Kelloway, E. K. (2001). Transformational leadership or the iron cage: Which predicts trust, commitment and team efficacy? *Leadership and Organization Development Journal*, 22, 315–320.

Avolio, B. J., Zhu, W., Koh, W. and Bhatia, P. (2004). Transformational leadership and organizational commitment: Mediating role of psychological empowerment and moderating role of structural distance. *Journal of Organizational Behavior*, 25, 951–968.

Bandura, A. (1995). *Self-efficacy in changing societies*. New York: Cambridge University Press.

Bandura, A. (1997). *Self-efficacy: The exercise of control*. New York: Freeman.

Barling, J., Kelloway, E. K. and Iverson, R. D. (2003). Accidental outcomes: Attitudinal consequences of workplace injuries. *Journal of Occupational Health Psychology*, 8, 74–85.

Barling J., Loughlin, C. and Kelloway, E. K. (2002). Development and test of a model linking safety-specific transformational leadership and occupational safety. *Journal of Applied Psychology*, 87, 488–496.

Barling, J., Weber, T. and Kelloway, E. K. (1996). Effects of transformational leadership training on attitudinal and financial outcomes: A field experiment. *Journal of Applied Psychology*, 81, 827–832.

Bass, B. M. (1985). *Leadership and performance beyond expectations*. New York: The Free Press.

Bass, B. M. (1998). *Transformational leadership: Industrial, military and educational impact*. Mahwah, NJ: Lawrence Erlbaum.

Bass, B. M. and Avolio, B. J. (1994). *Improving organizational effectiveness through transformational leadership*. Thousand Oaks, CA: Sage Publications.

Bass, B. M., Avolio, B. J., Jung, D. I. and Berson, Y. (2003). Predicting unit performance by assessing transformational and transactional leadership. *Journal of Applied Psychology*, 88, 207–218.

Bass, B. M. and Riggio, R. E. (2006). *Transformational leadership* (2nd ed.). Mahwah, NJ: Lawrence Erlbaum.

Bass, B. M. and Steidlmeier, P. (1999). Ethics, character and authentic transformational leadership behavior. *Leadership Quarterly. Special Issue: Charismatic and Transformational Leadership: Taking Stock of the Present and Future* (Part 1), 10, 181–217.

Bono, J. E. and Anderson, M. H. (2005). The advice and influence networks of transformational leaders. *Journal of Applied Psychology*, 90, 1306–1314.

Butler, J. K., Jr., Cantrell, R. S. and Flick, R. J. (1999). Transformational leadership behaviors, upward trust and satisfaction in self-managed work teams. *Organization Development Journal*, 17, 13–28.

Bycio, P., Hackett, R. D. and Allen, J. S. (1995). Further assessments of Bass's (1985) conceptualization of transactional and transformational leadership. *Journal of Applied Psychology*, 80, 468–478.

Charbonneau, D., Barling, J. and Kelloway, E. K. (2001). Transformational leadership and sports performance: The mediating role of intrinsic motivation. *Journal of Applied Social Psychology*, 31, 1521–1534.

Chelladurai, P. (1980). Leadership in sports organizations. *Canadian Journal of Applied Sport Sciences*, 5, 226–231.

Chen, G., Webber, S. S., Bliese, P. D., Mathieu, J., Payne, S. C., Born, D. H. and Zaccaro, S. J. (2002). Simultaneous examination of the antecedents and consequences of efficacy beliefs at multiple levels of analysis. *Human Performance*, 15, 381–410.

Conger, J. A. and Kanungo, R. N. (1988). The empowerment process: Integrating theory and practice. *Academy of Management Review*, 13, 471–482.

Corbin, E. (2005). Leadership issues in West Indies cricket: A theoretical analysis of the leadership styles of a purposive group of captains. *Journal of Eastern Caribbean Studies*, 30, 31–53.

Densten, I. L. (2005). The relationship between visioning behaviours of leader and follower burnout. *British Journal of Management*, 16, 105–118.

Deutsch, M. and Gerard, H. (1955). A study of normative and informational social influence upon individual judgment. *Journal of Abnormal and Social Psychology*, 51, 629–636.

Dionne, S. D., Yammarino, F. J., Atwater, L. E. and Spangler, W. D. (2004). Transformational leadership and team performance. *Journal of Organizational Change Management*, 17, 177–193.

Dirks, K. T. (2000). Trust in leadership and team performance: Evidence from NCAA basketball. *Journal of Applied Psychology*, 85, 1004–1012.

Dvir, T., Eden, D., Avolio, B. J. and Shamir, B. (2002). Impact of transformational leadership on follower development and performance: A field experiment. *Academy of Management Journal*, 45, 735–744.

Epitropaki, O. and Martin, R. (2005). From ideal to real: A longitudinal study of the role of implicit leadership theories on leader-member exchanges and employee outcomes. *Journal of Applied Psychology*, 90, 659–676.

Fuller, J. B., Morrison, R., Jones, L., Bridger, D. and Brown, V. (1999). The effects of psychological empowerment on transformational leadership and job satisfaction. *Journal of Social Psychology*, 139, 389–391.

Gould, D., Hodge, K., Peterson, K. and Petlichkoff, L. (1987). Psychological foundations of coaching: Similarities and differences among intercollegiate wrestling coaches. *The Sport Psychologist*, 1, 293–308.

Guzzo, R. A., Yost, P. R., Campbell, R. J. and Shea, G. P. (1993). Potency in groups: Articulating a construct. *British Journal of Social Psychology*, 32, 87–106.

Hoigaard, R., Safvenbom, R. and Tonnessen, F. E. (2006). The relationship between group cohesion, group norms and perceived social loafing in soccer teams. *Small Group Research*, 37, 217–232.

Hollingshead, A. B. (1996). The rank-order effect in group decision-making. *Organizational Behavior and Human Decision Processes*, 68(3), 181–193.

Houston, W. (1999, May 11). Truth and Rumours: William Houston's world of sports. *The Globe and Mail*, p. S5.

Hunt, J. G. (1999). Transformational/charismatic leadership's transformation of the field: An historical essay. *Leadership Quarterly*, 10, 129–144.

Joekes, K., Van Elderen, T. and Schreurs, K. (2007). Self-efficacy and overprotection are related to quality of life, psychological well-being and self-management in cardiac patients. *Journal of Health Psychology*, 12, 4–16.

Judge, T. A., Jackson, C. L., Shaw, J. C., Scott, B. A. and Rich, B. L. (2007). Self-efficacy and work-related performance: The integral role of individual differences. *Journal of Applied Psychology*, 92, 107–127.

Kark, R., Shamir, B. and Chen, G. (2003). The two faces of transformational leadership: Empowerment and dependency. *Journal of Applied Psychology*, 88, 246–255.

Katz-Navon, T. Y. and Erez, M. (2005). When collective- and self-efficacy affect team performance: The role of task interdependence. *Small Group Research*, 36, 437–465.

Keller, R. T. (2006). Transformational leadership, initiating structure and substitutes for leadership: A longitudinal study of research and development project team performance. *Journal of Applied Psychology*, 91, 202–210.

Kellett, P. (1999). Organisational leadership: lessons from professional coaches. *Sport Management Review*, 2, 150–171.

Kelloway, E. K., Barling, J. and Helleur, J. (2000). Enhancing transformational leadership: The role of training and feedback. *Leadership and Organization Development Journal*, 21, 145–149.

LePine, J. A. (2003). Team adaptation and postchange performance: Effects of team composition in terms of members' cognitive ability and personality. *Journal of Applied Psychology*, 88, 27–39.

LePine, J. A., Erez, A. and Johnson, D. E. (2002). The nature and dimensionality of organizational citizenship behavior: A critical review and meta-analysis. *Journal of Applied Psychology*, 87, 52–65.

Lim, B. and Ployhart, R. E. (2004). Transformational leadership: Relations to the five-factor model and team performance in typical and maximum contexts. *Journal of Applied Psychology*, 89, 610–621.

Lowe, K. B., Kroeck, K. G. and Sivasubramaniam, N. (1996). Effectiveness correlates of transformational and transactional leadership: A meta-analytic review of the MLQ literature. *Leadership Quarterly*, 7, 385–425.

Martin, R. and Epitropaki, O. (2001). Role of organizational identification on implicit leadership theories (ILTs), transformational leadership and work attitudes. *Group Processes and Intergroup Relations*, 4, 247–262.

Martin, S. B., Jackson, A. W., Richardson, P. A. and Weiller, K. H. (1999). Coaching preferences of adolescent youths and their parents. *Journal of Applied Sport Psychology*, 11, 247–262.

Moritz, S. E., Feltz, D. L., Fahrbach, K. R. and Mack, D. E. (2000). The relation of self-efficacy measures to sport performance: A meta-analytic review. *Research Quarterly for Exercise and Sport*, 71, 280–294.

National Council of Athletic Training. (1999). *Certified athletic trainers in U.S. high schools.* Online. Available: http://www.aahperd.org/naspe/pdf_files/pos_papers/resource-trainer.pdf (Accessed April, 2007).

Parker, S. K. (2000). From passive to proactive motivation: The importance of flexible role orientations and role breadth self-efficacy. *Applied Psychology: An International Review*, 49, 447–469.

Petty, R. E. and Cacioppo, J. T. (1981). *Attitudes and persuasion: Classic and contemporary approaches.* Boulder, CO: Westview Press.

Pillai, R. and Williams, E. A. (2004). Transformational leadership, self-efficacy, group cohesiveness, commitment and performance. *Journal of Organizational Change Management*, 17, 144–159.

Price, M. S. and Weiss, M. R. (2000). Relationships among coach burnout, coach behaviors and athletes' psychological responses. *Sport Psychologist*, 14, 391–409.

Purvanova, R. K., Bono, J. E. and Dzieweczynski, J. (2006). Transformational leadership, job characteristics and organizational citizenship performance. *Human Performance*, 19, 1–22.

Raedeke, T. D. (2004). Coach commitment and burnout: A one-year follow-up. *Journal of Applied Sport Psychology*, 16, 333–349.

Rai, S. and Sinha, A. K. (2000). Transformational leadership, organizational commitment and facilitating climate. *Psychological Studies*, 45, 33–42.

Reinboth, M. and Duda, J. L. (2006). Perceived motivational climate, need satisfaction and indices of well-being in team sports: A longitudinal perspective. *Psychology of Sport and Exercise*, 7, 269–286.

Richard, E. M., Diefendorff, J. M. and Martin, J. H. (2006). Revisiting the within-person self-efficacy and performance relation. *Human Performance*, 19, 67–87.

Rowold, J. (2006). Transformational and transactional leadership in martial arts. *Journal of Applied Sport Psychology*, 18, 312–325.

Shamir, B., House, R. J. and Arthur, M. B. (1993). The motivational effects of charismatic leadership: A self-concept based theory. *Organization Science*, 4, 577–594.

Shirom, A. (1989). Burnout in work organizations. In C. L. Cooper and I. T. Robertson (Eds), *International Review of Industrial and Organizational Psychology* (pp. 25–48). New York: Wiley.

Shnek, Z. M., Irvine, J., Stewart, D. and Abbey, S. (2001). Psychological factors and depressive symptoms in ischemic heart disease. *Health Psychology*, 20, 141–145.

Slanger, E. and Rudestam, K. E. (1997). Motivation and disinhibition in high risk sports: Sensation seeking and self-efficacy. *Journal of Research in Personality*, 31, 355–374.

Sosik, J. J., Avolio, B. J. and Kahai, S. S. (1997). Effects of leadership style and anonymity on group potency and effectiveness in a group decision support system environment. *Journal of Applied Psychology*, 82, 89–103.

Stewart, G. L., Fulmer, I. S. and Barrick, M. R. (2005). An exploration of member roles as a multilevel linking mechanism for individual traits and team outcomes. *Personnel Psychology*, 58, 343–365.

Tajfel, H. and Turner, J. C. (1979). An integrative theory of intergroup conflict. In W. Austin and S. Worchel (Eds), *The social psychology of intergroup relations* (p. 33–47). Monterey, CA: Brooks/Cole.

Theodorakis, Y. (1996). The influence of goals, commitment, self-efficacy and self-satisfaction on motor performance. *Journal of Applied Sport Psychology*, 8, 171–182.

Tucker, S., Turner, N., Barling, J., Reid, E. M. and Elving, C. (2006). Apologies and transformational leadership. *Journal of Business Ethics*, 63, 195–207.

Vallerand, R. J., Deshaies, P., Cuerrier, J., Brière, N. M. and Pelletier, L. G. (1996). Toward a multidimensional definition of sportsmanship. *Journal of Applied Sport Psychology*, 8, 89–101.

Van Knippenberg, D. and Hogg, M. A. (2003). A social identity model of leadership effectiveness in organizations. *Research in Organizational Behavior*, 25, 245–297.

Walumbwa, F. O., Orwa, B., Wang, P. and Lawler, J. J. (2005). Transformational leadership, organizational commitment and job satisfaction: A comparative study of Kenyan and U.S. financial firms. *Human Resource Development Quarterly*, 16, 235–256.

Weick, K. E. (1993). The collapse of sensemaking in organizations: The Mann Gulch disaster. *Administrative Science Quarterly*, 38, 628–652.

Whisenant, W. A. and Pedersen, P. M. (2004). The influence of managerial activities on the success of intercollegiate athletic directors. *American Business Review*, 22, 21–26.

Wilson, P. M., Rodgers, W. M., Carpenter, P. J., Hall, C., Hardy, J. and Fraser, S. N. (2004). The relationship between commitment and exercise behavior. *Psychology of Sport and Exercise*, 5, 405–421.

Wolfe, R. A., Weick, K. E., Usher, J. M., Terborg, J. R., Poppo, L., Murrell, A. J., Dukerich, J. M., Core, D. C., Dickson, K. E. and Jourdan, J. S. (2005). Sport and organizational studies: Exploring synergy. *Journal of Management Inquiry*, 14, 182–190.

Zacharatos, A., Barling J. and Kelloway, E. K. (2000). Development and effects of transformational leadership in adolescents. *Leadership Quarterly*, 11, 22–226.

Photograph by Action Event Photography. Reprinted courtesy of Laurentian University.

4 Coach–athlete relationships ignite sense of groupness

Sophia Jowett

The coach–athlete relationship within the coaching context

Much of human interaction consists of attempts to influence the behavior of other people. Within the context of sport, coaches are key people who attempt to influence athletes in many important ways. For example, coaches aim to produce an environment where athletes can acquire the technical, tactical and strategic skills needed to succeed both individually and as members of a team. A productive working environment is usually the result of a social environment in which coaches relate, interact and communicate effectively with everyone in the team. Hence, the resourcefulness of a coach to develop effective dyadic relationships (dyadic refers to the unit relationship the coach and the athlete establish) with his/her athletes can be instrumental in influencing them to experience sport situations positively.

The main objective of the chapter is to highlight the processes by which coaches' dyadic relationships with their athletes become the glue that holds sport teams together. The chapter aims to fulfill this objective by (a) covering areas related to the role and significance of the coach–athlete relationship in team and individual sports, (b) discussing the psychological constructs of the coach–athlete relationship within a conceptual model, (c) reviewing relevant research, (d) exploring the facilitative qualities of the coach–athlete relationship and (e) highlighting future research directions in this area.

The coach–athlete relationship within team and individual sports

Contextually team and individual sports are different. For example, although athletes in individual sports (e.g. athletics, swimming) do not *necessarily* have to be interdependent with the other athletes in the squad to achieve personal performance goals, athletes in team sports (e.g. hockey, soccer) need to form a well coordinated and collective unit in order to perform effectively. Athletes in team sports not only need to have the support and guidance of their coaches to succeed but also the attention, support, assistance and trust of their team-mates. In effect, the final performance outcome is the result of the effort exerted by all participating athletes in a single team. Thus, athletes in team sports need to be personally (e.g. to like and trust each other) and instrumentally (e.g. to have a common identity and fate) interdependent.

In this chapter it is reasoned that a coach who has the capacity and the resources can ignite a sense of groupness. Groupness is formed when members of a team (i.e. coach/es and their athletes) feel, think and act like one. A coach is viewed as central in turning a collection of individuals into a group (i.e. a team unit) by building and managing the various dyadic coach–athlete relationships. It is through these dyadic relationships and the interactions contained within them that enable the coach and each athlete in the team to get to know one another while making the most of each other's abilities and resources. Ultimately, the coach–athlete relationship can act as a vehicle through which each member in the team understands their personal and team goals and objectives, performance roles and start to consciously (or unconsciously) form a sense of groupness and an interdependent team.

The 3 + 1 Cs conceptual model of the coach–athlete relationship

The 3 + 1 Cs conceptual model has been developed in an attempt to describe the content and quality of the dyadic coach–athlete relationship (see Jowett, 2007a). The development of this model aims to identify and define the nature of the coach–athlete relationship, as well as prescribe a means for evaluating it. Its development was based on a definition of dyadic relationships that stated that a relationship is defined as the situation in which *two persons' feelings, cognitions and behaviors are mutually and causally interconnected* (Kelley et al., 1983). Using this definition as a guide, Jowett (2001) conducted a relationship-specific literature review in order to identify how researchers have investigated relationship members' interpersonal feelings, thoughts and behaviors and their interconnections.

The results of this review highlighted that a range of distinct interpersonal psychological constructs have been offered to assess feelings, thoughts and behaviors of relationship members. For example, some scholars have focused on interpersonal behaviors of two-person relationships employing such constructs as complementarity (Kiesler, 1997) while others have used behavioral closeness (e.g. Berscheid et al., 1989) to represent the type of interaction as well as the activities relationship members are engaged in and the degree to which they are influential to one another. Some scholars have emphasized emotional closeness, which includes interpersonal feelings of love and trust (e.g. Rubin, 1973) to describe the emotional attachment of relationship members. Others have focused on interpersonal thoughts employing such constructs as commitment (e.g. Rosenblatt, 1977; Rusbult and Buunk, 1993) and co-orientation (e.g. Newcomb, 1953). The literature review highlighted that these psychological constructs were conceptualized independently from each other despite the definition of dyadic relationships proposed by Kelley et al. (1983), which emphasized that the affective, cognitive and behavioral components of relationships are causally and mutually interdependent.

The apparent disparity within relationship literature signaled the need to think about dyadic relationships in a more integrative and encompassing way. Subsequently, the mutually exclusive psychological constructs of closeness, co-orientation and complementarity (known as the original 3 Cs) were selected and incorporated into a conceptual model to represent the dyadic relationship that coaches and their athletes form in the course of their athletic partnership. In effect, the original 3 Cs represented coaches' and athletes' interdependent and interpersonal feelings, thoughts and behaviors respectively. Jowett and colleagues (e.g. Jowett, 2001; Jowett and Meek, 2000) defined the 3 Cs in ways that reflected both the original definitions of the constructs and the sport context in which they were applied. Closeness refers to the emotional connection or affective ties that coaches and their athletes experience in their daily interactions and include trust, care, support and concern. Co-orientation reflects coaches' and athletes' common ground or shared knowledge and understanding about each other's roles, aspirations, beliefs and values. It was postulated that co-orientation is established as a result of open channels of communication; thus communication was thought of as an integral part of co-orientation. Complementarity describes coaches' and athletes' cooperative (e.g. 'give and take' attitude) and affiliative (e.g. friendly attitude) interactions as these occur largely in training and practice.

Following this initial conceptual work, a series of qualitative case studies were conducted, to explore whether these constructs represented the reality of coaches' and athletes' perceptions and experiences of the coach–athlete relationship. Jowett and Meek (2000) conducted the first research study employing the constructs of closeness, co-orientation and complementarity in which the coach–athlete relationship in marital couples was explored. Four married couples all of whom participated at high performance levels in track and field athletics were selected. Interviews were conducted with each coach and athlete separately and the data were content analyzed. The findings revealed that the marital coach–athlete relationship involved strong affective bonds such as love and liking, care, value, trust and faith. It was also reported that there was a continuous exchange of information through verbal and non-verbal communication that contributed to the dyads' level of shared knowledge and understanding. It was further evident that the dyads' roles were complementary in that the coach led and the athlete executed in a friendly sporting environment.

In another study, Jowett and Cockerill (2003) investigated the perceptions of 12 Olympic medalists regarding the role and significance of the coach–athlete relationship to performance success. Qualitative data described the content of the coach–athlete relationship in terms of closeness, co-orientation and complementarity and their impact on performance success. Although the nature of the coach–athlete relationship was viewed as instrumental to performance success, it was vulnerable to antagonistic tendencies, for example, power struggles ('who is the boss') resulting in the relationship members' disagreements and misunderstandings.

In an attempt to further understand the content and functions of coach–athlete relationships that experience interpersonal conflict, Jowett (2003) investigated a coach–athlete relationship in crisis. An Olympic silver medal winner and her coach of four years experienced conflictual issues following their major success. The analysis of the qualitative data revealed that although the athlete described the coach–athlete relationship in terms of affective closeness and complementary transactions, the level at which these were experienced at the time of the interviews were nowhere near the levels experienced prior to and during the Olympic Games. The coach's ostensible resistance to adopt his coaching practices to accommodate the athlete's additional needs (e.g. desire to renew their common goal, to feel in charge) led to the experience of tension on a daily basis. It was noticeable that the dyad lacked co-orientation caused by the dyad's unwillingness to communicate effectively. It was concluded that their level of interdependence was weak and ineffective leading to performance disappointments and eventually relationship dissolution (Jowett, 2003).

Further qualitative studies (e.g. Jowett, in press; Jowett and Timson-Katchis, 2005; Jowett *et al.*, 2007) have been conducted to investigate the parental coach–athlete relationship in which the parent is also the coach of the athlete. The findings reveal the complex interpersonal dynamics involved in such dual-role relationships and highlight that the quality of the parent–child relationship is an important determinant for the effectiveness of the coach–athlete relationship. Moreover, these findings highlight the 'paradoxical mix' of roles which typically occur during periods of transitions (e.g. child's adolescent years, sport specialization years). The paradoxical mix refers to the child/athlete desire to experience a sense of dependence within the coach–athlete relationship yet increased independence within the parent–child relationship (see Jowett, in press; Jowett *et al.*, 2007).

This series of qualitative case studies describe and explain the coach–athlete relationship phenomenon including coaches' and athletes' interactions, experiences, roles and perspectives. They provide support for the original conceptual 3 Cs model suggesting that the coach–athlete relationship can be defined by the constructs of affective closeness, co-oriented thoughts and behavioral complementarity. In addition, the results of these studies highlight the interconnections of these relationship constructs and their functions for performance accomplishments and subjective well being (e.g. satisfaction, fulfillment, frustration, anxiety).

In a quest to accelerate the knowledge gained about coach–athlete relationships, Jowett and Ntoumanis (2004) developed a brief instrument to measure coaches' and athletes' *self*-perceptions of their interpersonal feelings, thoughts and behaviors. Utilizing the results generated from several qualitative case studies an initial 23-item self-report measure was developed and administered to 120 British athletes and coaches. Results from a principal component analysis indicated that while closeness and complementarity were supported, co-orientation was no longer a viable component. In its place another component emerged, termed 'commitment' and this was defined as coaches' and athletes' desire to maintain the relationship in the present and in the future (Jowett and Ntoumanis, 2004). In terms of co-orientation, Jowett and Ntoumanis (2004) suggested that both the operationalization and the method used to measure coaches' and athletes' co-oriented views were less precise and hence erroneous.

Jowett and Ntoumanis (2004) continued the validation of a coach–athlete relationship questionnaire with the constructs of closeness, complementarity and the newly emerged construct of commitment. A confirmatory factor analysis was conducted employing data from 214 coaches and athletes. The analysis confirmed the multidimensional structure and existence of the three constructs. Moreover, it was shown that closeness, commitment and complementarity were associated with the variable of interpersonal satisfaction, lending support to the predictive validity of the developed measure. Subsequent psychometric assessments of the self-perceptions version of the Coach–Athlete Relationship Questionnaire (CART-Q) have revealed its sound psychometric properties including reliability and factorial validity (e.g. Jowett, 2007c; Jowett and Chaundy, 2004; Jowett and Clark-Carter, 2006).

The extended coach–athlete relationship model: the 3+1 Cs

The construct of co-orientation has been strongly supported by a series of qualitative case studies (e.g. Antonini Phillippe and Seiler, 2006; Jowett, 2003; Jowett and Meek, 2000) indicating the importance of co-orientation in describing and defining the content and quality of the coach–athlete relationship. Considering its importance, Jowett and colleagues (see Jowett, 2001, 2007a,b; Jowett and Cockerill, 2002; Jowett *et al.*, 2005) attempted to re-define the content and re-establish the position of co-orientation within the Closeness, Commitment and Complementarity conceptual model of the coach–athlete relationship, as well as identify an accurate method of measurement.

In this attempt, Laing *et al.*'s (1966) interperception method was employed. According to Laing *et al.* (1966) there are at least two sets of perceptions that people use in assessing their dyadic relationships: the direct perspective (self-perceptions) and the meta-perspective (meta-perceptions). The direct perspective reflects a relationship member's personal thoughts and feelings for the other member. In the case of the coach–athlete relationship, an athlete's direct perspective would be 'I am committed to my coach' and a coach's direct perspective would be 'I am committed to my athlete'. The meta perspective reflects a relationship member's effort to perceive the relationship from the other member's perspective. In the case of the coach–athlete relationship, an athlete's meta-perspective would be 'My coach is committed (to me)' and a coach's meta perspective would be 'My athlete is committed (to me)'. Laing *et al.* explained that combinations of relationship members' perspectives can yield three distinct co-orientation dimensions: (a) actual similarity; (b) assumed similarity; and (c) empathic understanding. The following section explains how these dimensions can be determined.

Coaches and athletes' actual similarity can be ascertained by comparing the self-perceptions of both coaches and athletes from such statements as 'I am committed to my coach' and 'I am committed to my athlete'. Athletes' assumed similarity with their coaches can be determined by comparing an athlete's self-perceptions (e.g. 'I am committed to my coach') with his/her meta-perceptions ('My coach is committed to me'). Whereas coaches' assumed similarity with their athletes can be determined by comparing a coach's self- and meta-perceptions (e.g. 'I am committed to my athlete' and 'My athlete is committed to me'). Finally, athletes' empathic understanding of their coaches can be discerned by comparing an athlete's meta-perception (e.g. 'My coach is committed to me') with his/her coach's self-perceptions (e.g. 'I am committed to my athlete'). Correspondingly, coaches' empathic understanding of their athletes can be discerned by comparing a coach's meta-perception with his/her athlete's self-perceptions (e.g. 'My athlete is committed to me' and 'I am committed to my coach').

The adoption of Laing *et al.*'s (1966) interperception method was valuable in defining and operationalizing the construct of co-orientation in the coach–athlete relationship. In the coach–athlete relationship, co-orientation refers to the broader notion of coaches' and athletes' common ground or perceptual congruence as this pertains to the status of their dyadic relationship and includes actual and assumed similarity as well as empathic understanding (see Jowett, 2005, 2007b). The integration of the three dimensions of co-orientation into the revisited 3 Cs model (Figure 4.1) opens up conceptual, empirical and practical avenues for research studies that aim to address problems that revolve around the coach–athlete relationship and sport coaching more generally.

As mentioned earlier, the self-perceptions version of the CART-Questionnaire measures coaches' and athletes' self-perceptions of closeness (e.g. 'I like my athlete'), commitment (e.g. 'I am committed to my athlete') and complementarity (e.g. 'When I coach my athlete, I am at ease'). A simple modification of the self-perception items allows the measurement of coaches' and athletes' (meta) perceptions of meta-closeness (e.g. 'My athlete likes me'), meta-commitment (e.g. 'My athlete is committed') and meta-complementarity (e.g. 'When I coach my athlete, my athlete is at ease'). The psychometric properties, namely internal consistency and factorial validity, of the meta-perception version of the CART-Q have been shown to be satisfactory (see Jowett, 2007b).

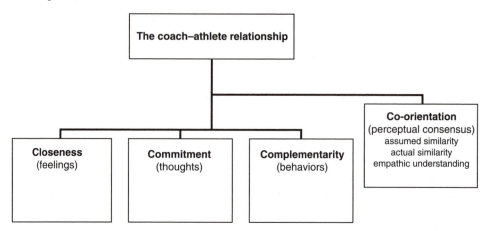

Figure 4.1 The 3 + 1 Cs conceptual model of coach–athlete relationship.

Research employing the 3+1 Cs model and the CART-Questionnaires

The extended conceptual model and its accompanied measures allow researchers to explore and discover a more complete landscape of the interpersonal dynamics of the coach–athlete relationship. One piece of this landscape that this section focuses on is the position adopted in the beginning of the chapter that the coach–athlete relationship forms the 'glue' that holds the team together. The research presented next highlights the associations of the dyadic coach–athlete relationship with group processes in sport.

Jowett and Chaundy (2004) investigated the premise that athletes' sense of groupness (defined and measured as team cohesion) is influenced by a leadership that is shared between the coach and the athlete. A total of 111 athletes participating in university team sports (American football, basketball, field hockey, lacrosse, rugby, soccer, water polo) completed a questionnaire that measured athletes perceptions of coach leadership behaviors, relationship variables (both self and meta-perceptions of closeness, commitment and complementarity) and team cohesion. Team cohesion was defined and measured in terms of task cohesion, whereby team members work together towards common goals and social cohesion, whereby team members like and care for each other (see Carron *et al.*, Ch. 7, this volume). Results showed that coach leadership variables predicted more variance in task cohesion than in social cohesion when coach–athlete relationship variables were included suggesting that coaches who want to develop cooperative teams may need to spend their time building better dyadic relationships with their athletes. It was also found that in the prediction of social cohesion, but not task cohesion, an interaction occurred between athletes' self- and meta-perceptions. The presence of the interaction suggested that athletes' assumed similarity with their coach may help establish affiliation with the other athletes in the team.

In a series of studies, Olympiou and colleagues explored the associations of the coach–athlete relationship with a number of team variables including role ambiguity and motivational climate, as well as outcome variables such as satisfaction and performance. One of their studies explored the impact of athletes' perceptions of the coach–athlete relationship on their role ambiguity in a team context (Olympiou *et al.*, 2005a). A total of 779 university athletes who participated in a variety of team sports (e.g. basketball, cricket, field hockey, handball, soccer) were recruited for this study.

Findings indicated that athletes' self- and meta-perceptions of the coach–athlete relationship as defined by closeness, commitment and complementarity predicted significant variance in athletes' role ambiguity perceptions related to their scope of role responsibilities, role behaviors, role evaluation and role consequences (see Eys *et al.*, Ch. 6, this volume). These findings highlight that effective coach–athlete relationships can help increase athletes' role clarity in the team and support previous studies that have found that social-situational factors contribute to perceptions of role ambiguity (e.g. Beauchamp *et al.*, 2005).

In another study, Olympiou *et al.* (2007) explored the associations between the coach–athlete relationship and the team's motivational climate as created by the athletes' coach. The coach-created motivational climate is focused on how the athlete perceives the social-psychological environment of the team in terms of two features: task-involving (e.g. coach creates an environment where the athlete works hard to achieve personal skill improvement) and ego-involving (e.g. coach creates an environment where the athlete works hard to outperform others; see Duda and Balaguer, 2007). A total of 591 athletes who participated in a range of team sports (e.g. basketball, hockey, volleyball) provided data. Findings revealed that the perceived coaching climate of task-involvement in which role importance, fairness and improvement in the team were emphasized, was associated with athletes' experiencing high levels of closeness, commitment and complementarity with the coach. The perceived coaching climate of ego-involvement emphasized unfairness and punishment in the team and was associated with low levels of perceived closeness, commitment and complementarity with the coach. The authors concluded that these results support the notion that the coach–athlete relationship has implications for the motivation of teams.

Finally, Olympiou *et al.* (2005b) guided by Ryan and Deci's (2000) Basic Needs Sub-Theory examined the extent to which athletes' satisfaction and performance depend on the degree to which the coach–athlete relationship provides the necessary conditions for satisfaction of athletes' basic psychological needs of autonomy, competence and relatedness. The data from 936 university team athletes revealed that self- and meta-perceptions of close, committed and complementary coach–athlete relationships were almost evenly predictive of the three basic psychological needs. Fulfillment of autonomy, competence and relatedness in turn were shown to be predictive of athletes' satisfaction with team performance, individual performance and personal treatment from the coach as well as performance accomplishments (defined as execution of plan, tactics and experience of flow).

These studies suggest that a harmonious coach–athlete relationship, a relationship that is characterized by high levels of closeness, commitment and complementarity, is associated with a sense of cohesion in the team, greater role clarity among team-members, a coaching climate that emphasizes skill learning, improvement and fairness, as well as performance accomplishments and satisfaction. Overall, the generated information supplies tentative support regarding the impact of coach–athlete relationships on group dynamics.

Practical applications: building effective and successful relationships in teams

Clive Woodward is one of the most successful contemporary team coaches in the UK. Woodward was a former English rugby union international and a coach of the England rugby union team from 1997 to 2004, who coached the England side to victory at the 2003 Rugby World Cup. He once described his role as a facilitator, as someone who makes sure that nothing is put in the athletes' way to stop them from becoming the best team; he explained that loyalty and team unity were primary concerns in creating the best team in the world (Leyland, 2004). Woodward's coaching focus implies that a coach needs to pay attention to his/her individual athletes in the team – in doing so the coach instills confidence in the athletes that they are worthy of the coach's attention and while a two-person bond (e.g. trust and commitment, shared perceptions) develops, coaches foster a vision and close ties shared by all in the team. The building of effective and successful dyadic coach–athlete relationships in teams is not easy; it is a deliberate activity and it certainly requires coaches' resourcefulness and interpersonal skills.

Enhancing positive perceptions of the 3+1 Cs

An important function of the sport psychology researcher is to use scientific methods to answer practical issues that concern coaches and athletes. The practical guidelines presented in the next section are informed by the findings of a number of studies conducted in the last decade within the area of coach–athlete relationships (e.g. Jowett, 2003; Jowett and Carpenter, 2004; Jowett and Meek, 2000).

Closeness

During the course of the sporting partnership, coaches and athletes experience a magnitude of emotions. Taking part in sports can be painful and fearful as well as exciting and pleasing. Coaches through the relationships they establish with their athletes can create positive environments in which powerful negative feelings such as fear and pain are contained. One aspect of such a positive environment is making athletes feel valued members of the team; coaches could achieve this by treating them with respect, trust and appreciation (see Jowett and Cockerill, 2003). Evidence suggests that lack of respect, trust and appreciation has negative consequences on the athlete, the dyadic coach–athlete relationship, as well as salient outcomes such as athletic performance. For example, Jowett (2003) has shown that lack of affective interpersonal properties such as respect and trust produced competitiveness, envy, distress, reduced relational rewards all of which led a coach–athlete dyad to break down. Gaining respect, trust and appreciation is a slow and laborious process. Coaches can create a positive affective relationship environment by being consistent, fair, empathic and supportive to their athletes' needs.

Commitment

Performance accomplishments require time and effort as well as the ability to overcome unpleasant transitional events (e.g. burnout, injury, failure, de-selection). Therefore, interpersonal commitment between the coach and the athlete can serve as an accommodating component of the relationship. Research has found that highly committed coach–athlete dyads are closely attached and are more likely to accommodate rather than retaliate (see Jowett and Carpenter, 2004; Jowett and Meek, 2000). Jowett and Carpenter (2004) interviewed 15 elite-level athletes and found that commitment is manifested from such interactions as fulfilling one's role (e.g. come prepared for training, provide assistance, be patient) and exerting effort (e.g. turning up for training on time, work hard, be focused). It is thus proposed that one way to avoid relationship disruption is to ensure that the coach and each athlete in the team understand their specific team roles and rules (i.e. codes of interpersonal conduct) by organizing regular meetings.

Complementarity

Complementarity is important because a coach and an athlete are connected by the nature of their relationship in a cycle of reciprocal acts. Research shows that a coach's action in relation to an athlete are meaningless without a response, hence, cooperation is at the heart of complementary transactions in coach–athlete relationships (e.g. Jowett and Cockerill, 2003; Jowett and Frost, in press; Jowett and Ntoumanis, 2004). If the need and desire to learn and improve in sport motivates coaches and athletes, then coaches' attempts to create a motivational climate that emphasizes learning are likely to foster complementary transactions (see Olympiou *et al.*, 2007). Contemporary interpersonal theory and research (Kiesler, 1997) have demonstrated that control and affiliation are two major dimensions of complementary transactions. Our qualitative studies (e.g. Jowett, 2003; Jowett and Cockerill, 2003; Jowett and Timson-Katchis, 2005) have consistently illustrated that the coach–athlete relationship contains transactions or behaviors that display an element of control, dominance and decisiveness on the part of the coach and affiliation, friendliness and responsiveness on the part of both the coach and the athlete. Consequently, coaches and athletes who implement such transactional patterns are likely to form harmonious coach–athlete relationships.

Co-orientation

As mentioned earlier, a dimension of co-orientation is empathic understanding. Coaches' empathic understanding is reflected in their capacity to understand or accurately infer their athlete's actions, thoughts and feelings. The numerous interviews conducted with coaches and athletes (see Jowett and Carpenter, 2004; Jowett and Cockerill, 2003; Jowett and Frost, in press) attest that athletes and coaches are more appreciative of each other when they feel understood. Mutual understanding in the coach–athlete relationship involves knowing the other person either by closely observing their actions and interactions, or exchanging thoughts, ideas, beliefs and information on a regular basis (e.g. Jowett and Cockerill, 2003; Jowett and Meek, 2000). Communication has been considered as the fuel of relationships and is the process that makes the relationship flourish or perish (Duck and Pond, 1989). Open channels of communication (verbal and non-verbal) appear to be an obvious mechanism that would allow coaches and athletes to know and understand each other (see LaVoi, 2007).

Future research directions

The manner by which the coach–athlete relationship can be responsible for differences in group dynamics is discussed next. The aim is to propose new lines of inquiry by examining the coach–athlete relationship alongside the concept of collective efficacy. According to Bandura (1997), collective efficacy refers to a team's shared perception of its capability to successfully perform a specific task. Collective-efficacy is central to group dynamics because it is thought to 'influence the type of future [people] seek to achieve, how they manage their resources, the plans and strategies they construct, how much effort they put into their group endeavor, their staying power when collective efforts fail to produce quick results or encounter forcible opposition and their vulnerability to discouragement' (Bandura, 1997, p. 418). Bandura (1997) has stated that antecedents of efficacy beliefs 'operate in much the same way at the collective level as they do at the individual level' (p. 478). Correspondingly, collective efficacy is determined by enactive mastery experiences, vicarious experiences, verbal persuasion and affective states (Bandura, 1997).

Recently, Beauchamp (2007), in reviewing the concept of collective efficacy beliefs within sport teams, stated that while 'mastery enactments, verbal persuasion and vicarious experiences may prove to be important sources of collective efficacy, a growing body of research suggests that other factors may also be important' (p. 187). Research has shown that the motivational climate within the team (Magyar *et al.*, 2004) and group cohesion (Paskevich *et al.*, 1999) are associated with collective efficacy beliefs. Moreover, Feltz and Chase (1998) postulated that coaches' interpersonal behaviors affect a team's perceived sense of collective competence. Research evidence has supported the link between coaches' confidence in their own abilities to coach effectively (i.e. facilitate the learning and development of their athletes) and athletes' satisfaction and performance success (Feltz *et al.*, 1999). Moreover, in the wider field of psychology there is a growing body of evidence to suggest that leaders influence team members' perceptions of collective efficacy (Hoyt *et al.*, 2003; Pescosolido, 2001). Crucially, collective efficacy has been associated conceptually and empirically to important outcomes such as performance (Bray, 2004; Chase *et al.*, 1997; Gibson, 1999; Hodges and Carron, 1992; Pescosolido, 2001, 2003) and satisfaction (Feltz and Chase, 1998)

Here it is proposed that the coach–athlete relationship is yet another important element that contributes to collective efficacy for the following reasons. First, the coach–athlete relationship exists as the place where the four major sources of self-efficacy information are transmitted. In terms of mastery experiences, if the dyadic coach–athlete relationship is close, committed and complementary then the coach (and athlete) will likely invest a great deal of effort, energy and time to ensure that athletes learn and master the skills necessary to achieve. In terms of vicarious experiences, Bandura (1997) also theorized that efficacy beliefs can be enhanced when a desirable behavior is demonstrated by a similar and valued person. In a similar regard, if an athlete is able to identify with a coach as a trusted *model* (in the demonstration of specific skills), then it is plausible to suggest that close cooperative coach–athlete relationships may serve to enhance personal efficacy beliefs. With regard to the third source, verbal persuasion, if the dyadic relationship is a harmonious one the coach would be more likely to provide ample encouragement or specific performance feedback, while the athlete would be more willing to be receptive and accepting. Finally, the athlete's level of negative affective states such as anxiety, stress, uncertainty and fear would be exacerbated by a conflicting dyadic coach–athlete relationship.

In summary, the quality of the relationship acts as a vehicle from which the major sources of efficacy influence, positively or negatively, an athlete's level of self-efficacy. However, there is *reciprocal causality* between self- and collective efficacy (Bandura, 1997). Hence, the quality of the coach–athlete relationship provides the ground from which the four sources of efficacy information shape essentially self-efficacy and, in turn, collective efficacy beliefs.

Second, Feltz and Chase (1998) conceptualized that coach leadership will affect collective efficacy. Correspondingly, it is suggested that just like coach leadership, the coach–athlete relationship will impact on athletes' perceptions of collective efficacy. For example, individual athletes' perceptions of their relationship with the coach will impact on how these athletes share beliefs about their collective capabilities to perform well and execute the various tasks competently. Finally, the coach–athlete relationship has been associated with the same key variables as collective efficacy, namely, group cohesion, motivational climate, satisfaction and performance. Acknowledging that there is surprisingly limited research that investigates the antecedents of collective efficacy (Tasa *et al.*, 2007), Figure 4.2 presents a research model that illustrates the potential links between the coach–athlete relationship, efficacy beliefs and salient outcomes in sport settings.

The research model (Figure 4.2) is designed to provide an impetus for research in this area. The model illustrates that self- and collective beliefs of efficacy are associated with the coach–athlete relationship and that these associations impact on important outcomes such as performance and satisfaction. The model further proposes that the coach–athlete relationship and both self- and collective efficacy are reciprocally related (just as mastery experiences and efficacy perceptions are related, see Bandura, 1997). For example, the model illustrates that athletes' shared perceptions of the team's capability to perform successfully may strengthen the dyadic relationship as the coach is likely to be viewed as instrumental to the success of individual athletes and the team as a whole. Moreover, the model suggests that the coach and his/her athletes get feedback when a team wins or loses a game; this feedback is likely to affect collective efficacy (and self-efficacy) because it speaks to whether the team as a unit, the individual athlete and the coach–athlete dyad are successful. Finally, athletes' perceptions of collective efficacy may impact on both the coach's self-efficacy and his/her perceptions of the team's efficacy.

Guided by the research model put forward, future research could explore a number of research questions including the degree to which more harmonious coach–athlete relationships (relationships that exhibit high levels of closeness, commitment, complementarity and co-orientation) have a greater influence in determining collective efficacy than less harmonious coach–athlete relationships (relationships that exhibit low levels of closeness, commitment, complementarity and co-orientation). Moreover, because the quality of the relationship and beliefs of collective efficacy are likely to change over time, future research could investigate what events trigger change. Transitional events

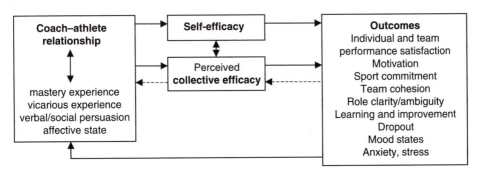

Figure 4.2 A research model of the coach–athlete relationship, collective efficacy and their outcomes.

(e.g. in and out of season, injury, burnout, new coach or team, success versus failure) may be responsible for creating uncertainty in coach–athlete interactions and efficacy beliefs. Longitudinal research designs are capable of determining the temporal patterning of the coach–athlete relationship and collective efficacy when teams are undergoing transitional events and examining the consequences of change on outcome variables such as performance.

Researchers who wish to pursue research in this area would need to pay close attention to two important and interrelated methodological issues: (a) the specific measurements used to assess the coach–athlete relationship and collective efficacy and (b) the levels of analysis. From a theoretical or conceptual point of view, the coach–athlete relationship is a dyadic phenomenon whereas collective efficacy is a group phenomenon. The concept of the coach–athlete relationship has been defined at the dyadic level and has been operationalized and measured via the CART-Questionnaires at the individual level and dyadic level. Consequently, researchers can employ the measure that best fits the purpose of their study and specific focus of their research question. One measure of collective efficacy that has been recently developed and validated, following Bandura's (1997) theorizing, is the Collective-efficacy Questionnaire for Sport (CEQS) (Short et al., 2005). The CEQS measures individual athletes' assessment of five collective efficacy factors that operate in the team: ability, effort, preparation, persistence and unity. According to this questionnaire, individual athletes report the degree to which the team ('we') is capable to confront the opposition. Thus, collective efficacy is measured at the group level.

The level of analysis is an issue that has been addressed somewhat arbitrarily by sport psychology researchers. In general terms, the levels of analysis refer to categories of entities at which a theoretical construct is expected to operate. Essentially, a study that revolves around coach–athlete relationships and collective efficacy is likely to have the following levels of analysis: an individual level (athlete or coach), a dyadic level (coach and athlete) and a team level (several athletes and coaches as members of a team). Paying attention to coach–athlete relationships and collective efficacy from *a levels-of-analysis perspective* would help explain whether individual (coach *or* athlete) and/or dyadic (coach *and* athlete) perceptions of relationship quality are stronger predictors of collective efficacy in sport. Multilevel or hierarchical linear modelling is a statistical method that can analyze simultaneously all three levels, while empirically estimating the degree of non-independence (Kenny et al., 2006). Non-independence is referred to the data supplied by two members of a dyad and/or members of a team that are not independent because they clearly share something in common. It is essential to pay attention to both measurement and levels of analysis issues regardless of whether one pursues basic (focus on theory development) or applied research (focus on practice).

Summary

The coach–athlete relationship as a building block for developing a sense of groupness was at the center of this chapter. The chapter started by highlighting the contextual differences of team and individual sports and the specific role of the coach–athlete relationship in igniting groupness in team sports. A historic overview of the conceptual and operational development of the 3+1 Cs coach–athlete relationship followed to illustrate its content and functions. Empirical evidence was supplied to highlight the associations between the coach–athlete relationship and group processes (e.g. team cohesion) as well as outcomes (e.g. satisfaction). Practical guidelines were offered based on the existing evidence. Finally, future research directions that aim to test the postulate that the ingredients of closeness, commitment, complementarity and co-orientation that connect the coach and the athlete provide the basis for collective efficacy (i.e. the individual athletes' assessment that the team is capable to perform succeed) were put forward. The chapter concluded by emphasizing the importance of methodological considerations in expanding our understanding of the theoretical basis of both the concept of the coach–athlete relationship and collective efficacy.

Acknowledgment

The author would like to thank Sandra Short for the comments supplied on an earlier draft of this chapter.

References

Antonini Phillippe, R. and Seiler, R. (2006). Closeness, co-orientation and complementarity in coach–athlete relationships: What male swimmers say about their male coaches. *Psychology of Sport and Exercise*, 7, 159–172.

Bandura, A. (1997). *Self-efficacy: The exercise of control*. New York: W. H. Freeman.

Beauchamp, M. R. (2007). Efficacy beliefs within relational and group contexts in sport. In S. Jowett and D. Lavallee (Eds), *Social psychology in sport* (pp. 181–194). Champaign, IL: Human Kinetics.

Beauchamp, M. R., Bray, S. R., Eys, M. A. and Carron, A. V. (2005). Leadership behaviors and multidimensional role ambiguity in team sports. *Small Group Research*, 36, 5–20.

Berscheid, E., Snyder, M. and Omoto, A. M. (1989). The relationship closeness inventory: Assessing the closeness of interpersonal relationships. *Journal of Personality and Social Psychology*, 57(5), 792–807.

Bray, S. R. (2004). Collective-efficacy, group goals and group performance of a muscular endurance task. *Small Group Research*, 35, 230–238.

Chase, M. A., Lirgg, C. D. and Feltz, D. L. (1997). Do coaches' efficacy expectations for their team predict team performance? *The Sport Psychologist*, 11, 8–23.

Duck, S. W. and Pond, K. (1989). Friends, Romans, countrymen, lend me your retrospective data: Rhetoric and reality in personal relationships. In C. Hendrick (Ed.), *Review of social psychology and personality*, Vol. 10: *Close relationships* (pp. 3–27). Newbury Park, CA: Sage.

Duda, J. L. and Balaguer, I. (2007). Coach-created motivational climate. In S. Jowett and D. Lavallee (Eds), *Social psychology in sport* (pp. 117–130). Champaign, IL: Human Kinetics.

Feltz, D. L. and Chase, M. A. (1998). The measurement of self-efficacy and confidence in sport. In J. L. Duda (Ed.), *Advances in sport and exercise psychology measurement* (pp. 65–80). Morgantown, WV: Fitness Information Technology.

Feltz, D. L., Chase, M. A., Moritz, S. E. and Sullivan, P. J. (1999). A conceptual model of coaching efficacy: Preliminary investigation and instrument development. *Journal of Educational Psychology*, 91, 765–776.

Gibson, C. B. (1999). Do they do what they believe they can? Group efficacy and group effectiveness across tasks and cultures. *Academy of Management Journal*, 42, 138–152.

Hodges, L. and Carron, A. V. (1992). Collective-efficacy and team performance. *International Journal of Sport Psychology*, 23, 48–59.

Hoyt, C. L., Murphy, S. E., Halverson, S. K. and Watson, C. B. (2003). Group leadership: Efficacy and effectiveness. *Group Dynamics: Theory, Research and Practice*, 7, 259–274.

Jowett, S. (2001). The psychology of interpersonal relationships in sport: The coach–athlete relationship. Unpublished doctoral thesis. The University of Exeter, UK.

Jowett, S. (2003). When the honeymoon is over: A case study of a coach–athlete relationship in crisis. *The Sport Psychologist*, 17, 444–460.

Jowett., S. (2005). On repairing and enhancing the coach–athlete relationship. In S. Jowett and M. Jones (Eds), *The Psychology of Coaching* (pp. 14–26). Sport and Exercise Psychology Division. Leicester: The British Psychological Society.

Jowett, S. (2007a). Interdependence analysis and the 3 + 1 Cs in the coach–athlete relationship. In S. Jowett and D. Lavallee (Eds), *Social psychology in sport* (pp. 15–27). Champaign, IL: Human Kinetics.

Jowett, S. (2007b). Factor structure and criterion validity of the meta-perspective version of the Coach–Athlete Relationship Questionnaire (CART-Q). (Manuscript under review.)

Jowett, S. (2007c). Moderators and mediators of the association between the coach–athlete relationship and physical self-concept. (Manuscript under review.)

Jowett, S. (in press). Outgrowing the 'familial' coach–athlete relationship. *International Journal of Sport Psychology*.

Jowett, S. and Carpenter, P. (2004). Coaches' and athletes' perceptions of rules in the coach–athlete relationship. Poster presented at the annual conference of the Association of the Advancement of Applied Sport Psychology, Minnesota, USA, October.

Jowett, S. and Chaundy, V. (2004). An investigation into the impact of coach leadership and coach–athlete relationship on group cohesion. *Group Dynamics: Theory, Research and Practice*, 8, 302–311.

Jowett, S. and Clark-Carter, D. (2006). Perceptions of empathic accuracy and assumed similarity in the coach–athlete relationship. *British Journal of Social Psychology*, 45, 617–637.

Jowett, S. and Cockerill, I. M. (2002). Incompatibility in the coach–athlete relationship. In I. M. Cockerill (Ed.). *Solutions in Sport Psychology* (pp. 16–31). London: Thomson Learning.

Jowett, S. and Cockerill, I. M. (2003). Olympic Medallists' perspective of the athlete–coach relationship. *Psychology of Sport and Exercise*, 4, 313–331.

Jowett, S. and Frost, T. C. (in press). Race/ethnicity in the all male coach–athlete relationship: Black footballers' narratives. *International Journal of Sport and Exercise Psychology*.

Jowett, S. and Meek, G. A (2000). The coach–athlete relationship in married couples: An exploratory content analysis. *The Sport Psychologist*, 14, 157–175.

Jowett, S. and Ntoumanis, N. (2004). The Coach–Athlete Relationship Questionnaire (CART – Q): Development and initial validation. *Scandinavian Journal of Medicine and Science in Sports*, 14, 245–257.

Jowett, S., Paull, G. and Pensgaard, A. M. (2005). Coach–athlete relationship. In J. Taylor and G. S. Wilson, *Applying Sport Psychology: Four Perspectives* (pp. 153–170). Champaign, IL: Human Kinetics.

Jowett, S. and Timson-Katchis, M. (2005). Social networks in sport: The influence of parents on the coach–athlete relationship. *The Sport Psychologist*, 19, 267–287.

Jowett, S., Timson-Katchis, M. and Adams, R. (2007). Too close for comfort? Dependence in the dual role of parent/coach–child/athlete relationship. *International Journal of Coaching Science*, 1, 59–78.

Kelley, H. H., Berscheid, E., Christensen, A., Harvey, H. H., Huston, T. L., Levinger, G., McClintock, E., Peplau, L. A. and Peterson, D. R. (Eds). (1983). *Close Relationships*. New York: Freeman.

Kenny, D. A., Kashy, D. A. and Cook, W. L. (2006). *Dyadic data analysis*. New York: Guilford.

Kiesler, D. J. (1997). *Contemporary interpersonal theory research and personality, psychopathology and psychotherapy*. New York: Wiley.

Laing, R. D., Phillipson, H. and Lee, A. R. (1966). *Interpersonal perception: A theory and a method of research*. New York: Harper and Row.

LaVoi, N. M. (2007). Interpersonal communication and conflict in the coach–athlete relationship. In S. Jowett and D. Lavallee (Eds), *Social psychology in sport* (pp. 29–40). Champaign, IL: Human Kinetics.

Leyland, A. (2004). A champion of business. *Real Business*, April, 32–35.

Magyar, T. M., Feltz, D. L. and Simpson, I. P. (2004). Individual and crew level determinants of collective efficacy in rowing. *Journal of Sport and Exercise Psychology*, 26, 136–153.

Newcomb, T. M. (1953). An approach to the study of communicative acts. *Psychological Review*, 60, 393–404.

Olympiou, A., Jowett, S. and Duda, J. L. (2005a). *Psychological needs as mediators of social contexts and role ambiguity*. Symposium on interpersonal relationships in sport and exercise. Annual Conference of the British Psychological Society, March, Abstracts (p. 27), Manchester, UK.

Olympiou, A., Jowett, S. and Duda, J. L. (2005b). *Contextual Factors and Optimal Functioning in the Team Sport Context: The Mediating Role of Needs Satisfaction*. 11th World Congress of Sport Psychology, Sydney, Australia, August.

Olympiou, A., Jowett, S., Duda, J.L. (2007). The interface of the coach-created motivational climate and the coach–athlete relationship. Manuscript under review.

Paskevich, D. M., Brawley, L. R., Dorsch, K. D. and Widmeyer, W. N. (1999). Relationship between collective efficacy and team cohesion: Conceptual and measurement issues. *Group Dynamics: Theory, Research and Practice*, 3, 210–222.

Pescosolido, A.Y. (2001). Informal leaders and the development of group efficacy. *Small Group Research*, 32, 74–93.

Pescosolido, A.Y. (2003). Group efficacy and group effectiveness: The effects of group efficacy over time on group performance and development. *Small Group Research*, 34, 20–42.

Rubin, Z. (1973). *Liking and loving: An invitation to social psychology*. New York: Holt, Rinehart and Winston.

Rosenblatt, P. C. (1977). Needed research on commitment in marriage. In G. Levinger and H. L. Rausch (Eds), *Close relationships: Perspectives on the meaning of intimacy*. Amhurst, MA: University of Massachusetts Press.

Rusbult, C. E. and Buunk, B. P. (1993). Commitment processes in close relationships: An interdependence analysis. *Journal of Personality and Social Psychology*, 50, 744–753.

Ryan, R. M. and Deci, E. L. (2000). The 'what' and 'why' of goal pursuits: Human needs and the self-determination of behavior. *Psychological Inquiry*, 11, 227–268.

Short, S. E., Sullivan, P. and Feltz, D. L. (2005). Development and preliminary validation of the collective efficacy questionnaire for sports. *Measurement in Physical Education and Exercise Science*, 9, 181–202.

Tasa, K., Taggar, S. and Seijts, G. H. (2007). The development of collective efficacy in teams: A multilevel and longitudinal perspective. *Journal of Applied Psychology*, 92, 17–27.

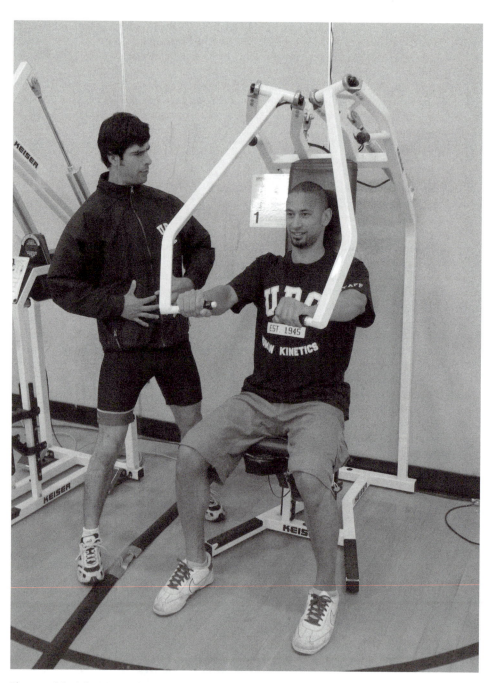

Photograph by John MacLeod. Reprinted courtesy of The University of British Columbia.

5 Proxy agency in physical activity

Steven R. Bray and Christopher A. Shields

Give a man a fish and you feed him for a day. Teach a man to fish and you feed him for a lifetime.

Chinese Proverb

What is proxy agency?

The well-known proverb quoted above illustrates an interesting paradox that applies to interpersonal relationships in many areas of modern life. On the one hand, providing assistance to those who need it helps them to achieve their desired outcomes. However, satisfaction of those needs is likely to be short-lived and through its provision, a dependence on assistance (being given a fish) may develop. On the other hand, helping individuals in an experiential manner and empowering them, while often more difficult, allows them to achieve their desired outcomes independently. In the long-run the person being helped towards independence may have greater opportunities for growth and personal fulfillment.

For most people, there is a balance somewhere between dependence and independence that fluctuates across different areas of life and through time. Certainly, there is little doubt that at every stage of development – from birth and infancy through to old age and death – humans draw on the resources of others to help them pursue their objectives and achieve desired outcomes. Indeed, the interactions people have with benevolent others are powerful forces that shape motivation and behavior. Both in the process of achieving their goals and once they have been achieved, it is not unusual to hear politicians, career scientists, high school valedictorians, Olympic champions and Nobel prize laureates acknowledge the contributions of those who have helped them along the way.

While people can seek out and receive assistance from others in many aspects of life, there are a number of situations involving physical activity in which people look to others to help them manage their participation and performance, achieve their goals or satisfy situational demands. Within the realm of sport and exercise, individuals seeking help may turn to coaches, personal trainers, exercise class instructors, rehabilitation specialists, or physicians to help them achieve outcomes such as weight loss, improvements in performance, or simply regular exercise participation. Throughout this chapter, we will refer to these 'others' as *proxy agents*. According to the Oxford Dictionary (Thompson, 1999), a proxy is 'a person authorized to act as a substitute . . .' (p. 1,103).

Some examples of proxy agents and the assistance they provide to individuals in a variety of physical activity contexts are illustrated in Table 5.1.

The present chapter provides a theoretical overview of proxy agent interactions in physical activity settings. We highlight key conceptual and measurement issues and provide a review of recent empirical work examining proxy agency constructs in exercise settings. Finally, practical implications including suggestions for practitioners in a variety of health-promotion fields and future research are presented.

The social cognitive perspective on agency

The term *proxy agent* is taken from Bandura's social cognitive perspective on thought and action (Bandura, 1986; 1997; 2001; 2004). A fundamental premise of social cognitive theory is that people play an active role in their self-development, adaptation and self-renewal through mechanisms of agency (Bandura, 2001). In Bandura's (2001) words, 'agency refers to acts done intentionally' (p. 6), recognizing that action (or inaction) can also occur unintentionally (e.g. by accident, due to external influences). He differentiates between three modes of agency: personal agency where the self acts as the agent, collective agency in which a group collective is the agent and proxy agency where a third party acts as an agent on one's behalf. In terms of theory, *proxy agency* is defined as a socially-mediated form of control that involves individuals obtaining help from others who act either with them or on their behalf as agents, providing tangible support in order to bring about the individuals' desired outcomes (Bandura, 1997).

While it is often desirable to have direct or self-as-agent control over one's pursuits, Bandura (2001) notes that people simply do not have the resources or skills necessary to master every area of their lives. Evidence to this effect is clearly represented in emerging internet industries such as concierge services where business people and ordinary folks can have someone else orchestrate and deliver everything from mundane shopping and cleaning tasks to extravagant holidays and parties. It is therefore no surprise that our daily lives, at least for most of us, usually involve a combination of personal agency and proxy agency.

Table 5.1 Examples of proxy agents and agency

Proxy agent	Examples of proxy agency
Ice hockey coach	Designs and runs players through drills to encourage skating speed, agility, and other skills development.
Physical therapist	Creates treatment plans and assists in stretching and strengthening movements to facilitate recovery from ACL knee injury.
Physical education teacher	Creates a fun and enthusiastic environment for children to develop motor coordination in the form of structured play.
Exercise class leader	Provides modeling and verbal direction of choreographed exercise-to-music.
Personal trainer	Sets up and supervises a comprehensive resistance training exercise program at the gym.
Sport parent	Persuades coach to give all players equal playing time.
Sport agent	Negotiates lucrative contracts with teams and sponsors.

Three purposes of proxy agents

Bandura (1997, 2001) outlines three main reasons why individuals may turn to a proxy agent for assistance. First, some individuals do not possess (i.e. have not developed or have lost) the means to reach their desired outcome(s). For example, individuals who have never exercised may turn to an exercise instructor or rehabilitation specialist for help in motivating and enabling themselves to become more active. Second, people who do have the necessary skills for goal attainment often turn to a proxy agent because they believe this person can more effectively carry out or facilitate the achievement of desired outcomes. For instance, regular exercisers often experience a plateau in the results they achieve through their self-managed exercise routine and seek assistance from a personal trainer for help with technique and program design. Finally, people who are capable of exerting direct control over their behavior or outcomes may elect to have someone else take control simply because they do not want to shoulder the responsibility of direct control. For example, people who have sufficient knowledge and resources to design and implement their own exercise program often work with a personal trainer or partake in structured (e.g. follow-the-leader) exercise classes designed to result in health or appearance benefits. Doing so removes the individuals' responsibilities of having to monitor intensity or to properly sequence appropriate exercises themselves.

The prevalence and importance of proxy agency may be considerable in sport and exercise situations. Proxy agents can help individuals manage multiple environment and task demands as well as assist with the self-regulatory behaviors necessary for their continued exercise adherence by helping them with lifestyle management and skill development (Rejeski *et al.*, 2003). To help understand how proxy agency may be important, it is useful to have an understanding of how the proxy agent has been studied in the exercise literature.

A key concept in proxy agency research: defining proxy efficacy

As noted above, Bandura (2001) differentiates between three modes of agency: personal, collective and proxy. According to Bandura (1997), efficacy beliefs represent the underlying cognitions of human agency and are defined as: *'capabilities to organize and execute the courses of action required to produce given attainments'* (p. 3). Efficacy beliefs that correspond to personal, collective and proxy agency are self-efficacy, collective - efficacy and proxy efficacy, respectively. A considerable body of research illustrates the important impact of efficacy beliefs on thoughts, affect and behavior and as a major factor in behavior change across a variety of domains including physical activity (see reviews by Bandura, 1997; Beachamp, 2007; Feltz *et al.*, 2008; McAuley and Blissmer, 2000; McAuley and Mihalko, 1998; McAuley *et al.*, 2001; Moritz *et al.*, 2000). What is clearly evident in the reviews listed above is that research has focused largely on self-efficacy and to a much lesser extent on the other forms of efficacy.

Proxy efficacy was first studied by Bray *et al.* (2001) who defined proxy efficacy as: *'one's confidence in the skills and abilities of a third party or parties to function effectively on one's behalf'* (p. 426). This definition strives to capture the concept of a proxy as an empowered agent. Shields and Brawley (2006) have offered a slightly different definition of proxy efficacy as *'an individual's confidence in a proxy agent's abilities to provide assistance to help the individual perform task and/or self-regulatory behaviours required to meet the situational demands'* (p. 911). What this definition draws out is that a proxy can also act as a helper or facilitator who works *with* the individual rather than *for* the individual. As will be discussed in later sections of the chapter, both forms of proxy efficacy have been examined in some initial studies and offer complementary empirical evidence showing that proxy efficacy is associated with numerous cognitive, affective and behavioral variables.

While efficacy beliefs can take multiple forms, Bandura (1997) has suggested various efficacies are determined by similar mechanisms and function in similar ways (Bandura, 1997). Efficacy determinants include: mastery experiences, vicarious experiences or modeling, verbal persuasion and physiological/emotional states; while consequences of efficacy are reflected in motivational manifestations of behavior (e.g. choice, intensity effort and persistence), cognitions (e.g. setting goals) and affect (e.g. anxiety). From a social cognitive standpoint, proxy efficacy might be stronger when people have (a) had experience with a proxy agent working effectively on their behalf, (b) been witness to proxies effectively helping others, (c) heard stories of proxies bringing about successful outcomes for or with others, or (d) felt comfortable or excited to have a proxy carrying out a task for them. Higher proxy efficacy, in turn, should lead to attempting more challenging tasks with a proxy's help than when attempted alone. People with strong proxy efficacy beliefs should also set more challenging goals when assisted by their proxy and feel comfortable when their proxy is empowered to work on their behalf. Given the obvious social interplay surrounding the proxy situation, proxy efficacy may also be affected by intrapersonal factors such as the personalities of both the individual and the proxy, environmental factors (e.g. physical settings in which the proxy-agency occurs), as well as the quality and quantity of proxy interaction.

Measuring proxy efficacy

The discussion above illustrates that there is currently some conceptual ambiguity surrounding proxy efficacy. This ambiguity is also reflected in the attempts thus far to measure proxy efficacy. In the seminal study of proxy efficacy in exercise, Bray *et al.* (2001) operationalized proxy efficacy through a measure of fitness instructor efficacy. Fitness instructor efficacy referred to participants' confidence in the ability of their fitness class instructor to teach, communicate and motivate during the subsequent four weeks. These general capabilities have been identified by researchers (e.g. Oldridge, 1977) and national fitness organizations as necessary skills for a fitness class leader to possess (e.g. National Fitness Leadership Advisory Committee, 1989). The class teaching components that were identified included the warm-up, the cardiovascular component and the cool-down. The communication components included safely cueing the exercises and proper verbal cueing of steps. Finally, the motivational component included the use of appropriate music, providing positive verbal comments, modeling the exercises and visually demonstrating enjoyment. Consistent with Bandura's (2005) recommendations for efficacy measurement participants indicated their confidence (on a 0–100 per cent scale) in their instructor's ability to (a) teach a warm-up that had them breathing moderately hard, (b) communicate effectively and (c) motivate participants within classes.

In a second study of healthy young (i.e. college-aged) exercisers, Bray *et al.* (2004) provided an empirical basis for both the concept of proxy efficacy in exercise settings and an operational definition. That study progressed through a series of stages aimed to clarify the concept of proxy efficacy and its measurement in group exercise class settings. In the first stage, novice exercisers identified behaviors they looked to their group fitness class instructors to perform during classes. This broad list of behaviors was then validated, consolidated and trimmed using input from an independent group of fitness class participants and through expert review to yield a questionnaire measure: the proxy efficacy exercise questionnaire (PEEQ). The authors then gathered data from a large sample ($n = 248$) of novice exercisers using the PEEQ and factor analyzed their results. That analysis showed that this context-specific measure of proxy efficacy could be divided into two distinct beliefs – beliefs about the proxy's abilities to effectively instruct (i.e. instruction and motivation) and beliefs about the proxy's abilities to effectively choreograph the exercises during the class.

Through a controlled experimental study, Bray *et al.* (2004) then manipulated instructor behaviors to illustrate the experiential basis for novice exercise class participants' proxy efficacy perceptions. Specifically, novice exercise participants in the experiment were randomly placed into one of four groups in a 2 (enriched versus bland instruction) × 2 (enriched versus bland choreography) experimental design. In other words, one-quarter of the people were exposed to enriched leadership behaviors as well as enriched choreography, another quarter exercised to an enriched leader but bland choreography, another quarter exercised to enriched choreography but a bland leader and the last quarter experienced a bland leader together with bland choreography. The enriched leadership manipulation was interactive, encouraging and energetic and included general as well as individualized positive feedback and encouragement to participants. The bland leadership manipulation included only vague, general, follow-the-leader style instruction and feedback without any encouraging verbal content from the leader. The enriched exercise choreography consisted of alternating sets of 32-count exercise combinations for use with a step-aerobics platform. The bland exercise choreography consisted of four exercises carried out in repeating sequence. For all four conditions in the experiment, the manipulations were delivered by the same trained exercise leader and carefully scripted to be consistent in their delivery and the exercise sessions lasted 40 minutes.

When the participants completed the PEEQ following their 40-min exercise session, their responses clearly indicated that exercisers who were exposed to the enriched leadership and choreography had greater confidence in their instructor's capabilities – higher proxy efficacy (Figure 5.1a, b). These findings provide initial evidence that novice exercisers' proxy efficacy beliefs are variable and can be shaped through their experiences with a fitness leader.

In the studies by Shields and his colleagues (Shields and Brawley, 2006; Shields *et al.*, 2006), proxy efficacy was measured in a slightly different manner. Consistent with his conceptual definition of proxy efficacy, Shields asked participants to rate their confidence in their instructors' abilities to *provide assistance* with such things as scheduling exercise sessions, using effective exercise technique and monitoring exercise progress. Rather than having participants rate their proxy efficacy for all the items on the list, they first indicated those aspects of their exercise for which they required assistance from their instructor. Proxy efficacy was represented by the composite score derived from only those behaviors for which the participants indicated having received assistance from the proxy. Shields' results also showed substantial variability in participants' responses. Moreover, as one might expect, he found that different exercisers looked to their exercise leaders for assistance with different things.

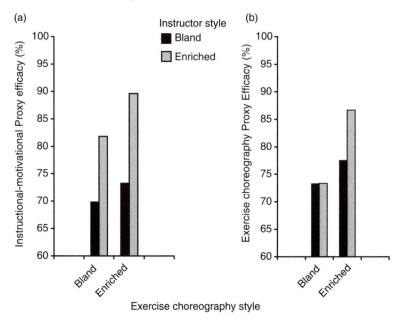

Figure 5.1 Effects of (a) leadership style and (b) exercise choreography style manipulations on proxy efficacy. (From Bray *et al.*, 2004, p. 451. Reprinted with permission from Human Kinetics.)

Although the two approaches to measuring proxy efficacy described above vary somewhat, they each follow considerate principles in establishing close correspondence between the conceptual and operational definitions of proxy efficacy. Importantly, each of these forms of proxy efficacy show further links towards those theoretically-meaningful variables they were aimed to predict. In the case of Bray's research, proxy efficacy predicted intentions, adherence and beliefs about participation in structured group exercise classes. In Shields' research, proxy efficacy was related to self-regulation, exercise preferences and reliance. We should note at this point in time that observed relationships between proxy efficacy and different correlates in the aforementioned research are reflective of the unique research questions examined in the various studies. However, there may be specific correlates or situations in which one form of proxy efficacy may be more influential than another.

Two sides of proxy agency

The term 'proxy agency' and its description thus far may have conjured up images of people relinquishing all personal control, responsibility and accountability when they lack the skills or motivation to attempt control of situations or outcomes independently. This is certainly the case for some people when it comes to their exercise and sport participation. In these situations, because individuals allow the attainment of desired outcomes or behavioral success to rest on the competence and commitment of other people (Bandura, 1997) success may come at the expense of their own skill development. For such individuals, this process can be problematic if the development of independent skills becomes important later on down the road. Consider, for example, many individuals who take part in therapeutic exercise as part of their rehabilitation from cardiac surgery or a heart attack. Outpatient cardiac rehabilitation programs (CRPs) are delivered by well-trained, knowledgeable interventionists (nurses, exercise physiologists) and are designed to help participants initiate a pattern of regular exercise. While adherence to this type of rehabilitation is variable, many programs show high levels of adherence while people are in the program (Oldridge, 1995). Unfortunately, research has consistently shown exercise adherence rates drop to less than 50 per cent within 6 months of completion of a CRP (Bock *et al.*, 2003; Moore *et al.*, 2006). These data are consistent with an all too common scenario for people who graduate from a cardiac rehabilitation program having been behaviorally micromanaged by well-meaning interventionists to the point where they often have little knowledge and few skills that will allow them to carry on exercising on their own.

While proxy agency may have a potential dark side, it can also be employed in situations when people transfer complete or partial control to an intermediary who, through both actions and advice, facilitates the attainment of desired outcomes. On the bright side then, the assistance provided by proxy agents helps individuals to manage aspects of behavioral performance, which in turn, may make it easier to continue the pattern of behavior. Baltes (1996) notes that proxy agency is often a necessary approach to successfully achieving many of one's desired outcomes in life and can be an effective process for self-development and adaptation throughout the life cycle. In an illustrative example, Baltes (1996) tells the story of an elderly gentleman residing in an assisted care facility who one day ceased to perform his own personal grooming. While the staff at the facility capably took up those tasks, they inquired as to why the change in behavior had occurred. The individual then revealed that he was at the point of physical frailty where the energy taken up by personal grooming was interfering with his ability to engage in his favorite daily activity – watching visitors come and go in the lobby. Thus, depending on the situation, utilization of proxy agents may be adaptive, allow greater control over what one feels is important in the face of overwhelming demands or diminishing capacities.

The preceding examples have attempted to illustrate the point that proxy agency may be adaptive or maladaptive, depending on the situation. In the following sections, we will review recent research that provides some empirical evidence pertaining to proxy agency and proxy efficacy in exercise.

Proxy interaction and adaptive cognitions, affect and behaviors

Bandura (1997) has suggested that one way in which people use proxy agency is to allow them to divert control over some tasks while focusing their efforts on developing or preserving personal efficacy or agency capabilities in other areas that are more meaningful to them. In studies of healthy novice exercisers, Bray and his colleagues (Bray *et al.*, 2001) and Shields (2005) have shown that proxy efficacy is positively related to self-efficacy. In those studies, which were carried out in instructor-led aerobics classes, the researchers surveyed exercise class participants' beliefs about their confidence in their instructor's abilities to perform or assist with various behaviors. Both studies showed that, consistent with Bandura's (1997) theorizing, proxy efficacy was positively related to exercisers' self-efficacy beliefs.

In Bray *et al.*'s (2001) study, proxy efficacy was moderately correlated with self-efficacy for scheduling weekly exercise sessions (i.e. *scheduling self-efficacy*) and self-efficacy to complete behaviors that occur during fitness classes (i.e. *in-class self-efficacy*) such as warm-up and stretching, aerobic or step tasks, strength and toning and cool-down and flexibility components ($r = 0.19$ and 0.25, respectively). In other words, people who had greater confidence in their instructors' abilities to do what they were supposed to do (i.e. as exercise instructors) in turn had greater confidence in their own abilities to do what they were supposed to do as exercise class participants. One inter-pretation of these findings is that by utilizing a proxy agent in whom they had high confidence for looking after the content of their exercise session, exercisers allowed themselves to focus on and develop greater mastery and self-efficacy in other areas such as organizing their time to effectively integrate regular exercise sessions into their busy schedules. The study also showed that exercisers who had higher proxy efficacy had stronger intentions to attend their regularly scheduled exercise classes and, in fact, attended more classes during the four-week follow-up period.

One qualifying point for the findings presented above is the pattern of results described was seen only for novice exercisers who had enrolled in an instructor-led class for the first time. Results from experienced exercisers who had been exercising regularly and participated in one or more instructor-led classes in the previous six months showed no significant relationships between proxy efficacy and the other vari-ables. What these findings stand to illustrate is that proxy efficacy may serve different purposes for novice exercisers who may need to develop certain skills for exercising, while proxy efficacy may play a different role or be less important in for experienced exercisers.

Shields *et al.*'s (2006) series of studies examined proxy efficacy in relation to exercise management self-efficacy. This form of self-efficacy reflects exercisers' confidence in their abilities to manage various aspects of their weekly exercise participation such as using safe, effective technique and setting realistic exercise goals. Shields used his measure of proxy efficacy (described above) as well as Bray *et al.*'s (2004) measure. In line with the findings of Bray *et al.* (2001), results indicated exercise management self-efficacy was positively related to Shields' ($r = 0.24$) as well as Bray *et al.*'s ($r = 0.47$) measure of proxy efficacy.

Taken together, the evidence provided by the measurement development studies and prospective empirical investigations of proxy efficacy and self-efficacy in exercise sup-ports the social cognitive perspective on proxy efficacy in terms of both its determin-ants and consequences. While this area of research awaits controlled intervention studies, at this point it seems reasonable to propose that attempts to promote exercise adherence among novice exercisers should look to encourage strong proxy efficacy beliefs by encouraging fitness class instructors to provide assistance with goal setting and self-instruction as well as socially and choreographically enriched environments in their exercise classes.

Proxy interaction and maladaptive cognitions, affect and behaviors

In the previous section, the potential influence of proxy agency in exercise was dis-cussed from the perspective of the positive outcomes that may occur for the person employing proxy-agency. Indeed, Bandura (1997) suggests that in situations of proxy-agency, the interaction of personal capabilities and the capabilities of the proxy agent often facilitate successful behavioral adaptation and promote self-regulatory skill development of proxy users. However, Bandura (1997) also outlines a dilemma that becomes probable the more that proxy-agency is utilized. This dilemma concerns the notion of developing dependence on the proxy. Specifically, he cautions that over-reliance on a proxy may 'impede the cultivation of personal competencies' (Bandura, 2001, p. 13) and 'reduces the opportunities to build skills needed for efficacious action' (Bandura, 1997, p. 17). Thus, individuals may enter into a state of proxy-dependency when it is easier to obtain their desired outcomes by using the proxy rather than developing and using their own skills.

The problematic consequences of dependence become particularly evident when individuals are confronted with a behavioral challenge. In relation to exercise, an example of this challenge may be when individuals no longer have access to their proxy agent and must attempt to self-manage their behavior; such as in the case of cardiac rehabilitation programs discussed above. If individuals are always looking to a proxy agent for assistance with successful behavioral performance an important question is: will they be able to successfully deal with this self-management challenge?

Lent and Lopez (2002) note that understanding the interpersonal context of efficacy beliefs will have valuable implications for individuals attempting to promote the well-being or development of other persons – a point that will be expanded upon later in the chapter. This is especially true in many exercise settings, as individuals often require assistance from a proxy during the adoption phase of exercise when exercise skills, training methods and adherence skills are unknown or erratically used. If those individuals attempting to adopt exercise in a proxy-led context are not taught, or do not otherwise learn, self-regulatory skills because they rely on the proxy, long-term self-managed exercise adherence may suffer. Recent studies, conducted by Shields and Brawley (2006, 2007) and Bray and colleagues (Bray *et al.*, 2006) provide evidence that the dilemma of proxy-agency, as theorized by Bandura (1997) exists in structured exercise contexts.

In two studies of healthy adults participating in structured, exercise classes, Shields and Brawley (2006, 2007) found that when confronted with hypothetical scenarios describing situations in which they would have to continue their exercise outside of their proxy-led class, individuals who preferred a high level of assistance from proxy-agents reported being less confident in performing (i.e. task-efficacy) and managing (i.e. self-regulatory efficacy) exercise independently than did those participants preferring low levels of assistance from a proxy-agent. The interactive effect of preference level and exercise context (in-class versus outside of class) on self-regulatory efficacy is illustrated in Figure 5.2. Also, as can be seen in Figure 5.3, those exercisers who preferred high levels of assistance also perceived independent exercise to be more difficult than did their low assistance counterparts (Shields and Brawley, 2007). Further, when confronted with the cancellation of their exercise classes, participants preferring high-assistance (a) were less likely to choose self-managed activity as an exercise option, (b) were less confident in their ability to pursue their chosen alternative activity, (c) felt it would be more difficult than with a proxy, and (d) expected to be less satisfied with the exercise experience than individuals preferring low-assistance (Shields and Brawley, 2007). These findings seem to suggest that individuals who prefer to use proxy-agency most of the time may be inadequately prepared or unwilling to effectively self-manage their exercise participation.

While these results provide evidence that those individuals preferring a high level of assistance from a proxy-agent may be less well equipped to deal with self-managing physical activity, they do not speak directly to the issue of proxy-reliance outlined by Bandura (1997). However, recent work in both healthy (Shields and Brawley, 2006) and

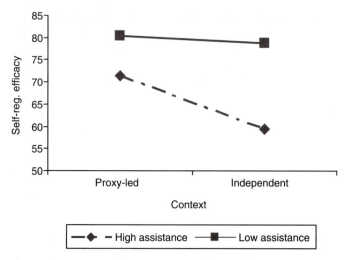

Figure 5.2 Preferences for assistance by exercise context interaction for self-regulatory efficacy. (From Shields and Brawley, 2006, p. 910. Reprinted with permission from Sage Publications.)

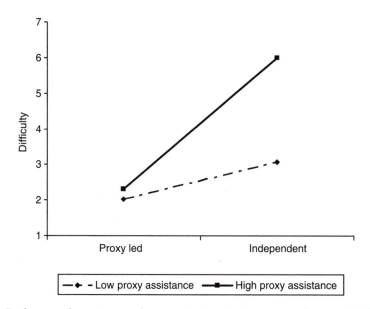

Figure 5.3 Preferences for assistance by exercise context interaction for perceived difficulty. (From Shields and Brawley, 2006, p. 668. Reprinted with permission from Sage Publications.)

symptomatic (Bray *et al.*, 2006) exercise populations sheds some light on the relationships between proxy-efficacy, self-efficacy, reliance on a proxy and behavior in exercise contexts.

In their study of healthy exercise class participants, Shields and Brawley (2006) examined whether self-regulatory efficacy and proxy-efficacy were predictors of reliance on a proxy (exercise class instructor). In this study, it was found that higher proxy-efficacy and lower self-regulatory efficacy were related to higher levels of reliance on the exercise class instructor. Further, both self-regulatory and proxy-efficacy contributed separately and uniquely to the statistical regression model suggesting that both participants' beliefs about their own capabilities and their beliefs about the assistance from their class instructor are independently related to their reliance on the proxy.

Research by Bray *et al.* (2006) examining the impact of proxy-agency on exercise-related cognitions and behavior during the transition from a structured cardiac rehabilitation program (CRP) to home-based exercise also provided insight into the relationships between self-efficacy, proxy-efficacy, reliance as well as exercise behavior. Specifically, greater reliance on the CRP exercise leader was associated with weaker self-regulatory efficacy regarding home-based exercise. It was also found that proxy-efficacy and proxy-reliance were important predictors of how much exercise participants engaged in following completion of the structured CRP program. Higher proxy efficacy and higher reliance were both predictors of less frequent exercise participation. Taken together, the results of both the Shields and Brawley (2006) and the Bray *et al.* (2006) studies suggest that proxy-agents may need to balance the assistance they provide with the provision for self-managed mastery experiences in order to minimize reliance on the part of their clients.

Practical implications and considerations

Given the potential widespread use of proxy-agency in physical activity (e.g. exercise classes: Bray *et al.*, 2001, 2004; Shields and Brawley, 2006) and healthcare settings (e.g. cardiac rehabilitation: Bray *et al.*, 2006; Bray and Cowan, 2004), as well as nursing homes (e.g. Baltes and Baltes, 1990), we believe there are a number of practical and research implications stemming from the current evidence for both exercise professionals and research interventionists. First, it is important to point out that proxy agents often help to promote self-regulatory development and successful behavioral performance of proxy users. It would appear that these developments are facilitated through both the direct actions of the proxy agent in assisting with skill development and indirectly by allowing the proxy user to focus on other pursuits (e.g. developing self-regulatory skills and efficacy) independently. Therefore, professionals working in the health and exercise field must recognize the important role they play in helping people adapt to lifestyle behavior change.

The second implication is that practitioners should be aware of the potential dilemma that may arise when individuals utilize their services as a form of proxy agency (Bandura, 1997). Indeed, persons preferring a high level of proxy-assistance or those who have greater reliance on their proxy may be at risk for nonadherence outside a proxy-led situation, especially if they have lower self-regulatory efficacy for skills that are necessary for the independent management of exercise participation. The key qualification is that although proxy agency my be an effective approach to exercise participation within a proxy-led context, long-term exercise adherence often requires individuals to deal with behavioral challenges that require independent use of self-regulatory skills (Brawley *et al.*, 2003; Marcus *et al.*, 2000). Exercise professionals should therefore attempt to encourage the development of independent (e.g. self-regulatory) skills among clients or patients so they can self-manage their continued exercise behavior. However, it is recognized that such encouragement may be challenging to provide, considering many professionals are highly trained in the delivery of services in the therapeutic environment (e.g. during exercise classes or rehabilitation sessions) and may lack training and skills relating to behavior change, maintenance and relapse prevention.

As a follow-up to the last point, we suggest that one way in which people who are engaged in situations in which there is a great deal of proxy control or assistance would benefit is in the form of planned mastery opportunities. That is, practitioners should plan and promote activities for their clients to independently self-regulate their exercise, that way better insuring the development of essential self-regulatory skills (Bandura, 1997). Brawley *et al.* (2003) have suggested that for the development of the self-regulatory skills required for long-term exercise adherence, proxy agents may need to actively collaborate with participants to encourage planned development of independent skills through practice of those skills while still in the proxy context. For example, the proxy may devise various 'homework' tasks that allow the proxy user to attempt, practice and master the sorts of activities that are normally carried out with proxy assistance. Through experiential tasks such as these, the proxy's role as a facilitator rather than a provider could be expanded in many ways including efforts to develop client skills in self-monitoring, goal setting and contingent reinforcement (e.g. provision of self-rewards when desired behaviors are performed).

The above recommendations are in alignment with those of Meichenbaum and Turk (1987), who have suggested that a collaborative relationship between the practitioner and participant is necessary to develop commitment and learn self-regulatory skills, which should translate into better treatment adherence. In other words, the effective nurturing of and eventual weaning from the proxy relationship necessitates a collaborative atmosphere in which proxy users assume increasing amounts of responsibility for their behavior (e.g. adherence) rather than simply following a practitioner's (i.e. proxy) instructions.

Based on the evidence as it stands at this early point in the research on proxy agency, we believe that in order to promote long-term exercise adherence, proxy agents must maintain a balance between providing assistance to participants and encouraging the development of self-regulatory capabilities. Assistance from proxy-agents can be an effective way to promote adherence (Brawley *et al.*, 2003; Meichenbaum and Turk, 1987) with positive relationships being demonstrated between proxy-efficacy and a number of social-cognitions and actual exercise behavior (Bray *et al.*, 2006; Bray and Cowan, 2002, 2004; Bray *et al.*, 2001, 2004). However, the current findings suggest the use of proxy-agency may be associated with lower perceived capabilities in managing exercise *away from a proxy-led context* (Shields and Brawley, 2006, 2007). As long-term exercise adherence often requires the capacity to deal with multiple behavioral challenges (e.g. cancelled classes), encouraging the development of the self-regulatory skills needed to *independently* manage exercise is essential for the long term participation required to accrue health benefits.

Future research directions

Research carried out thus far examining proxy agent beliefs such as efficacy and reliance point to numerous ways in which proxy agents may affect self-efficacy and behavior for exercisers who take part in group exercise classes. However, this research barely scratches the surface of the complex inter-relationships that are likely to emerge among cognitive, affective and behavioral variables within proxy agent – proxy user relationships. Three broad avenues for future research are presented. The first avenue includes the continued and more elaborate examination of the effects of proxy agency and proxy relationships on proxy users. Not only should this research focus on a larger assortment of cognitive, affective and behavioral variables, it should broaden to examine proxy agency in areas of physical activity other than group exercise; such as coach – athlete and teacher – student relationships. Another area in need of further examination is one that considers the characteristics and behaviors that might make an effective proxy. A third avenue leads towards gaining a better understanding of situations necessitating the weaning from a proxy and processes linked to effective nurturing of independence.

As is evident from the content of the chapter thus far, research has attempted to understand ways in which proxy agency can affect the thoughts and behaviors of proxy users. For example, Shields and Brawley's (2006) initial work illustrated a relationship between the use of proxy-agency and efficacy beliefs; however, self-efficacy theory (Bandura, 1997) suggests that proxy-agency may be related to more than efficacy beliefs. Specifically, the use of proxy-agency is theorized to be related to the perceived difficulty of tasks when they are enacted, or activities that are selected, satisfaction with those tasks and behavioral choices. When individuals are assisted by a proxy agent, perceived difficulty may be lessened, satisfaction with the experience higher and choices about continuance of exercise behavior more straightforward. As discussed earlier in the chapter, these issues have been explored using hypothetical scenarios (Shields and Brawley, 2006, 2007). However, in situations where proxy users find themselves without a proxy, a number of potentially interesting questions arise. How, if at all, does their perception of the exercise context change . . . and in what ways? How do they perceive their ability to pursue self-managed exercise? To what extent might they view the absence of a proxy as a challenge or a threat? What exercise choices do they make? Future research should aim to explore and provide further answers to such questions.

The work to date examining proxy agency and related constructs offers new perspectives and avenues for examining and studying exercise-related cognitions, affect and behavior. However, research from the social-psychological literature suggests that there may be additional efficacy-related constructs relevant to proxy-agency that are worthy of attention. For example, Lent and Lopez (2002) present a 'tripartite' model outlining several forms of efficacy that may occur in interpersonal relationships. In their model, *self-efficacy* perceptions (person A's beliefs in his/her own capabilities) co-exist with perceptions of *other efficacy* (person A's beliefs in person B's capabilities) and *relationship-inferred self-efficacy* or *RISE* which represents person A's beliefs about person B's beliefs about person A's capabilities. Preliminary evidence in sporting dyads and group exercise settings (Jackson *et al.*, 2007; Shields *et al.*, 2006) provides initial support that other efficacy and RISE are related, yet independent constructs and that these relational efficacies appear to be significant predictors of exercise-related social-cognitions (e.g. self-efficacy beliefs, reliance, satisfaction, commitment).

Specifically, Jackson *et al.* (2007) examined the inter-relationships between self-, other- and relation inferred efficacy beliefs within doubles tennis pairs. Further, they examined how these efficacy perceptions related to athletes' commitment and satisfaction with their playing partner. Using actor-partner interdependence models (e.g. Kashy and Kenny, 2000) Jackson *et al.* found that all three efficacy cognitions were interrelated and that an increase in one form of efficacy was associated with an increase in the other efficacy perceptions. For instance, as an individual's RISE beliefs increased so did their self-efficacy. Further, it was found that self-efficacy and other-efficacy were predictive of athletes' commitment to and satisfaction with their partners, respectively. These findings highlight the potential impact these efficacy perceptions may have in situations of interdependence.

Research by Shields *et al.* (2006) also examined relational efficacies, however, this work focused on the perceptions of participants in proxy-led, structured, exercise classes. Findings indicated that RISE beliefs were predictive of self-regulatory efficacy. It was also demonstrated that participants reporting higher RISE beliefs attributed their exercise success to more internal, personally controllable and stable factors. While additional research is needed, these initial findings suggest that social-cognitions in situations involving proxy-agency are associated with what people see in themselves, how they perceive the proxy and how they believe the proxy perceives them in return.

Another area for future research is to examine what makes an effective proxy agent. Research by Bray *et al.* (2004) indicates that efficacy in a proxy agent (e.g. exercise leader) is determined by the proxy's abilities to motivate, communicate and model behavior effectively. These are key areas of good exercise leadership that have been identified by other researchers (e.g. Oldridge, 1977; see also Hoption *et al.*, Ch. 3, this volume). However, there are many other ways in which a proxy could gain the confidence of his or her users. For example, in a novel study in which the exercise leader proxy took the form of a video instructor, Martin Ginis *et al.* (2006) showed that higher proxy efficacy in the video instructor was predicted by participants' enjoyment of the video and perceived similarities in age between the participants and the instructor. These findings are consistent with social cognitive theory. First, affective experiences are theorized to be one of the primary determinants of self-efficacy (Bandura, 1997). Concerning Martin *et al.*'s second finding, Bandura (1997) has suggested that vicarious experiences are most effective at increasing self-efficacy beliefs when the behavior of interest is modelled by a similar other. This rationale is often used in promoting exercise for older adults by having an older instructor lead the exercise class. Other ways in which characteristics of the proxy could be influential include such things as his or her reputation, qualifications or certifications and experience. This is particularly important in studying proxy-agency within a social cognitive framework as it has been suggested that social persuasion is most effective when done by a knowledgeable or significant other. Research is currently lacking in each of these areas, but should be undertaken to help understand how proxies can be made more effective.

Balanced against the notion that it might be valuable to know what makes an effective proxy is the qualification that prolonged dependence on a proxy may be maladaptive – especially if the proxy user needs to develop independent capabilities in order to sustain a behavior or to grow as an individual. Often people fail to realize, or avoid altogether, the possibility of taking greater personal control over important aspects of their lives such as preventive health care maintenance (e.g. exercising regularly, healthy eating, managing stress). Indeed, the dilemma of proxy agency is one that fuels many service industries and a good many people make a living by convincing others that they may not achieve what they want to, or have potential for, without their help. These situations may be all well and good when the proxy user knowingly and willingly empowers the proxy agent, can withdraw that power voluntarily and face the consequences whatever they may be. However, the proxy dilemma may often arise unintentionally in many instances where well-meaning proxies focus on expert provision and dependence arises as an unplanned and unwanted fallout. Anecdotal and empirical evidence to this effect can be seen in instances where athletes have difficulties performing and self-managing without their coaches in attendance and patients fail to adhere to treatment when separated from their therapist (cf. Meichenbaum and Turk, 1987). As noted throughout this chapter, our collective research programs are looking at factors that lead to the proxy dilemma (e.g. preference for high proxy contact). The challenge for future researchers and practitioners intent on understanding proxy dependence is how the various personalities and social interactions within the proxy relationship may be effectively managed to minimize the development of dependencies and promote effective methods of weaning proxy users from their proxy agents.

Summary

Proxy agency is a common form of social interaction that occurs in many important aspects of life including physical activity involvement. Proxy relationships are often adaptive, allowing opportunities to develop personal efficacy and skills in areas that are of fundamental importance in people's lives. However, proxy relationships may also cause difficulties when dependency on a proxy results in a failure to nurture one's own capabilities to function independently. This proxy dilemma is one in which exercisers may find themselves and could be a key contributor of high levels of nonadherence to exercise in both asymptomatic (Shields and Brawley, 2006, 2007) and therapeutic (Bray *et al.*, 2006) populations. As with the other areas covered in this volume, ample opportunities exist to further investigate this fledgling area of research in exercise, sport and rehabilitation settings.

References

Baltes, M. M. (1996). *The many faces of dependency in old age*. Cambridge: Cambridge University Press.

Baltes, P. B. and Baltes, M. M. (1990). Psychological perspectives on successful aging: The model of selective optimization with compensation. In P. B. Baltes and M. M. Baltes (Eds), *Successful Aging* (pp. 1–34). Cambridge: Cambridge University Press.

Bandura, A. (1986). *Social foundations of thought and action: A social cognitive theory*. Englewood Cliffs, NJ: Prentice-Hall.

Bandura, A. (1997). *Self-efficacy: The exercise of control*. New York: W. H. Freeman.

Bandura, A. (2001). Social cognitive theory: An agentic perspective. *Annual Review of Psychology*, 52, 1–26.

Bandura, A. (2004). Health promotion by social cognitive means. *Health Education and Behavior*, 31, 143–164.

Bandura, A. (2005). Guide for creating self-efficacy scales. In F. Pajares and T. Urdan (Eds), *Self-efficacy beliefs of adolescents* (pp. 307–337). Greenwich, CT: Information Age.

Beachamp, M. R. (2007). Efficacy beliefs within relational and group contexts in sport. In S. Jowett and D. Lavallee (Eds), *Social psychology in sport* (pp. 181–193). Champaign, IL: Human Kinetics.

Bock, B. C., Carmona-Barros, R. E., Esler, J. L. and Tilkemeier, P. L. (2003). Program participation and physical activity maintenance after cardiac rehabilitation. *Behavior Modification*, 27, 37–53.

Brawley, L. R., Rejeski, W. J. and King, A. C. (2003). Promoting physical activity for older adults: The challenges of changing behavior. *American Journal of Preventive Medicine*, 25, 172–183.

Bray, S. R., Brawley, L. R. and Millen, J. A. (2006). Proxy efficacy and proxy reliance predict self-efficacy and independent home-based exercise following supervised cardiac rehabilitation. *Rehabilitation Psychology, 51*, 224–232.

Bray, S. R. and Cowan, H. (2002). Personal and proxy efficacy in exercise-based cardiac rehabilitation. *Journal of Sport and Exercise Psychology, 24*, S37–S38.

Bray, S. R. and Cowan, H. (2004). Proxy efficacy: Implications for self-efficacy and exercise intentions in cardiac rehabilitation. *Rehabilitation Psychology, 49*, 71–75.

Bray, S. R., Gyurcsik, N. C., Culos-Reed, S. N., Dawson, K. A. and Martin, K. A. (2001). An exploratory investigation of the relationship between proxy efficacy, self-efficacy and exercise attendance. *Journal of Health Psychology, 6*, 425–434.

Bray, S. R., Gyurcsik, N. C., Martin Ginis, K. A. and Culos-Reed, S. N. (2004). The Proxy Efficacy Exercise Questionnaire: Development of an instrument to assess female exercisers' proxy efficacy beliefs in structured group exercise classes. *Journal of Sport and Exercise Psychology, 26*, 442–456.

Feltz, D. L., Short, S. E. and Sullivan, P. (2008). *Self-efficacy in sport*. Champaign, IL: Human Kinetics.

Jackson, B., Beauchamp, M. R. and Knapp, P. R. (2007). Relational efficacy beliefs in athlete dyads: An investigation using actor-partner interdependence models. *Journal of Sport and Exercise Psychology, 29*, 170–189

Kashy, D. A. and Kenny, D. A. (2000). The analysis of data from dyads and groups. In H. T. Reis and C. M. Judd (Eds), *Handbook of research methods in social and personality psychology* (pp. 451–477). New York: Cambridge University Press.

Lent, R. and Lopez, F. (2002). Cognitive ties that bind: A tripartite view of efficacy beliefs in growth-promoting relationships. *Journal of Social and Clinical Psychology, 21*, 256–287.

Marcus, B. H., Forsyth, L. H., Stone, E. J., Dubbert, P. M., McKenzie, T. L., Dunn, A. L. and Blair, S. N. (2000). Physical activity behaviour change: Issues in adoption and maintenance. *Health Psychology, 19*(Suppl.), 32–41.

Martin Ginis, K. A., Bray, S. R. and Prapavessis, H. (2006). 'Great Teachers Inspire': Exercise video instructor characteristics that inspire motivation and confidence in beginner exercisers. *Medicine and Science in Sport and Exercise, 38*, S570.

McAuley, E. and Blissmer, B. (2000). Self-efficacy determinants and consequences of physical activity. *Exercise and Sports Sciences Reviews, 28*, 85–88.

McAuley, E. and Mihalko, S. L. (1998). Measuring exercise-related self-efficacy. In J. L. Duda (Ed.), *Advances in sport and exercise psychology measurement* (pp. 371–390). Morgantown, WV: Fitness Information Technology.

McAuley, E., Pña, M. M. and Jerome, G. J. (2001). Self-efficacy as a determinant and outcome of exercise. In G. C. Roberts (Ed.), *Advances in motivation in sport and exercise* (pp. 235–262). Champaign, IL: Human Kinetics.

Meichenbaum, D. and Turk, D. C. (1987). *Facilitating treatment adherence: A practitioner's guidebook*. New York: Plenum.

Moore, S. M., Charvat, J. M., Gordon, N. H., Pashkow, F., Ribisl, P., Roberts, B. L., Rocco, M. (2006). Effects of a CHANGE intervention to increase exercise maintenance following cardiac events. *Annals of Behavioral Medicine, 31*, 53–62.

Moritz, S. E., Feltz, D. L., Fahrbach, K. R. and Mack, D. E. (2000). The relation of self-efficacy measures to sport performance: A meta-analytic review. *Research Quarterly for Exercise and Sport, 71*, 280–294.

National Fitness Leadership Advisory Committee. (1989). *Performance standards for the basic fitness leader*. Ottawa: Government of Canada.

Oldridge, N. B. (1977). What to look for in an exercise class leader. *The Physician and Sport Medicine, 5*, 85–88.

Oldridge, N. B. (1995). Patient compliance. In M. L. Pollock and D. H. Schmidt (Eds), *Heart Disease and Rehabilitation* (3rd ed., pp. 209–228). Champaign, IL: Human Kinetics.

Rejeski, W. J., Brawley, L. R., Ambrosius, W. T., Brubaker, P. H., Focht, B. C., Foy, C. G. and Fox,

L. D. (2003). Older adults with chronic disease: Benefits of group-mediated counseling in the promotion of physically active lifestyles. *Health Psychology, 22*, 414–423.

Shields, C. A. (2005). The dilemma of proxy-agency in exercise: A social-cognitive examination of the balance between reliance and self-regulatory ability. Unpublished doctoral dissertation, University of Waterloo, Ontario, Canada.

Shields, C. A. and Brawley, L. R. (2006). Preferring proxy agency: Impact on self-efficacy for exercise. *Journal of Health Psychology, 11*, 906–917.

Shields, C. A. and Brawley, L. R. (2007). Limiting exercise options: Depending on a proxy may inhibit exercise self-management. *Journal of Health Psychology, 12*(4), 663–671.

Shields, C. A., Brawley, L. R. and Jung, M. E. (2006). Is my exercise leader confident in my abilities to self-manage exercise? Relational efficacy beliefs as predictors of self-regulatory efficacy. *Journal of Sport and Exercise Psychology, 28*, S166.

Thompson, D. (1999). *The concise Oxford dictionary of current English.* Oxford: Clarendon Press.

Part III
Group environment

Photograph by Action Event Photography. Reprinted courtesy of Laurentian University.

6 Role perceptions in sport groups

Mark A. Eys, Robert J. Schinke and
Sarah M. Jeffery

Introduction

> Call them the Disrupters: Their unsung handiwork can change the flow of a game
> and the outcome of a series. 'The pretty stuff makes the highlights,' says [National
> Basketball Association's] Dallas Mavericks coach Avery Johnson, 'but it's the guys
> who do the down-and-dirty work who can make or break a team.'
>
> (McCallum, 2005, p. 32)

As the above quotation highlights, there are a number of different role responsibilities
present within a group that are essential to the group's overall success. Among other
concepts such as group norms, status and leadership, roles represent one of the structural aspects of groups (Carron *et al.*, 2005). Specifically, a role has been defined as a set
of behaviors expected from a person occupying a position in a specific social context
(e.g. Biddle and Thomas, 1966; Katz and Kahn, 1978).

Historically, the study of roles within a group's structure originated outside the
fields of sport and exercise. The emergence of terminology and concepts related to
roles can be found in sociological and psychological literature dating as far back as the
early twentieth century (e.g. Cottrell, 1933). However, research on roles within social
psychology was really brought to the fore by two prominent groups of researchers in
the middle of the last century. The first involved Bales and his colleagues (e.g. Bales and
Slater, 1955; Parsons and Bales, 1955) and the second corresponded to the work by
Kahn *et al.* (1964). This literature, related to the types of roles that could exist in groups
as well as the processes involved in how role information and responsibilities are
conveyed among group members, is discussed in the subsequent section.

Types of roles

Two different, yet compatible, general categorizations of role *types* have been advanced
(Bales and Slater, 1955; Mabry and Barnes, 1980). Bales and colleagues (e.g. Bales and
Slater, 1955) suggested that roles within a group could be differentiated on the basis of
the functions they serve. The first function outlined by Bales was task related – role
responsibilities that are directly oriented toward the instrumental objectives of the
group. A sport example of a task related role could be the team's captain. The second
general function of roles outlined by Bales was social in nature – role responsibilities
that are related to the maintenance and harmony of the group. A team clown or social
organizer would be examples of this type of social role in a team sport environment. It

should be noted that this task versus social differentiation follows along the lines of propositions advanced by Lewin (1935) who suggested that the two primary concerns of any group are locomotion (i.e. reaching the group's goals) and maintenance (i.e. ensuring the group continues to exist by satisfying members' affiliation needs).

Although Bales' conceptualization of roles focused on function, Mabry and Barnes' (1980) conceptualization focused on the level of *formality* that may exist within roles. Specifically, Mabry and Barnes (1980) proposed that roles could be formal or informal in nature. Formal roles are those that are prescribed by the organization for the individual while informal roles are those that arise over time through the interactions among group members. To use the previous examples, it is likely that any prescribed leadership roles in sport would be formal in nature (e.g. the coach or team as a whole would designate players to leadership roles). However, it is also likely that a team's social coordinator could be a role that arises naturally through the interactions of the team. Different levels of formality of the role will likely have implications for how responsibilities are communicated and performed. For example, informal role expectations might be transmitted through more subtle cues (e.g. reinforcement, praise) rather than direct communication and prescription necessary for formal roles.

While the scope of the above two categorizations are general, other researchers have sought to identify specific roles in their social contexts from a task and social perspective, including both formal and informal responsibilities. For example, in the business domain, Belbin (1981) identified nine key roles that are present for effective management. These include team worker, chairperson, completer/finisher and monitor evaluator (Fisher *et al.*, 1998). From a team sport perspective, Eys (2000) identified eight types of responsibilities in an interactive environment including positional, formal and informal team leadership, social, communication, motivational, organizational and peer leadership (e.g. guiding specific others).

Transfer of role information

As can be inferred from the previous discussion, there is the potential for many roles and responsibilities to be present in a group environment. In some cases, individuals must carry out more than one responsibility simultaneously (Fisher *et al.*, 1998), progress through multiple responsibilities over the course of a season or career, or share responsibilities with others. These situations have the potential to be confusing for group members. Thus, proper role communication is necessary to ensure effective team functioning. Kahn *et al.* (1964), in their work on role ambiguity and conflict in organizations, provided a *role episode model* that has since been adapted for a sport environment by Eys *et al.* (2005a; Figure 6.1). This model highlights a number of events that occur between two individuals, in which a *role sender* communicates a set of role responsibilities to a *focal person*. In the sport context, the individuals who typically occupy these positions are *the coach* (i.e. the role sender) and *the athlete* (i.e. the focal person). However, it is likely that in a group environment, the majority of individuals can fulfill the roles of both role sender and focal person at one point in time or another. For example, in a collegiate or professional setting, the coach consistently provides role information to his or her athletes but also receives (i.e. is the focal person) coaching role information from an athletic director or owner. Likewise, an athlete will receive information from a head or assistant coach but might also transmit information to other players on the team.

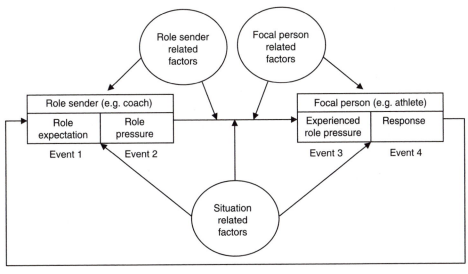

Figure 6.1 A theoretical framework of factors influencing the transmission and reception of role responsibilities. (Adapted from Kahn *et al.*, 1964, p. 30, by Eys *et al.*, 2005, p. 385. Reprinted with permission from Sage Publications.)

Regardless of who specifically sends or receives role information, the role episode model highlights five events in this transfer. The first event highlights that the role sender will develop certain expectations for the focal person. In a sport context, a coach will likely spend a fair amount of time determining which player should fill each position on the team. Once expectations for the focal person (or people) are determined, the role sender will then exert role pressure (Event 2) on the focal person to accept and comply with these expectations. In most cases, the third event in the process occurs when the focal person perceives that the role sender has developed certain expectations for him or her and subsequently responds (Event 4). It would be hoped that the focal person perceives the expectations to be clear, fair and consequently complies by engaging in the behavior required by the role sender. However, as we will explain, there are many role elements (or perceptions) that can lead to negative responses (e.g. not performing the behavior correctly or simply not performing the behavior).

In the subsequent sections of this chapter these role elements are defined and research that has examined specific questions related to each is introduced. In addition, practical implications are discussed regarding the development of positive role perceptions and the implementation of role interventions with sport teams. Finally, future research directions are suggested to build on a growing body of role-related literature, taking into account both the sport and exercise contexts.

Theory and research

In earlier research about roles in industrial and organizational psychology, the label of 'role theory' was given to describe the body of knowledge related to this topic (Biddle and Thomas, 1966). However, a theory represents 'a set of interrelated facts that presents a systematic view of some phenomenon in order to describe, explain and predict its future occurrences' (Weinberg and Gould, 2003, p. 13). As a consequence, research-ers (e.g. Shaw and Costanzo, 1982) have suggested that the present body of knowledge reflects a system of concepts that revolve around the topic of roles as opposed to an all encompassing theory. From a sport perspective, a number of these concepts have been discussed and examined including cognitive elements such as *role ambiguity/ clarity, role efficacy, role conflict, role overload* and *role acceptance*. In addition, the affec-tive element of *role satisfaction* has been discussed, but investigated to a much lesser degree. Finally, the behavioral element of *role performance* has been integrated and examined in relation to some of the aforementioned cognitive and affective elements.

Role ambiguity/clarity

Role ambiguity has been defined as a lack of clear information regarding the expect-ations associated with one's position (Kahn *et al.*, 1964). The term 'role clarity' is another accepted term to describe this element but it refers to the other extreme of the role understanding continuum (i.e. possessing clear information about role responsi-bilities). To date, role ambiguity is the most extensively researched aspect of role involvement in sport.

Recently, Beauchamp *et al.* (2002) proposed a four dimension conceptual model of role ambiguity for sport based on their earlier research (e.g. Beauchamp and Bray, 2001; Eys and Carron, 2001) as well as Kahn *et al.*'s (1964) influential work. Their conceptual model indicates that it is necessary for athletes to be clear regarding (a) the scope of their responsibilities (i.e. a person's range of responsibilities on the team), (b) the behaviors necessary to fulfill their responsibilities, (c) how they will be evaluated with regard to their performance of assigned roles and (d) what the consequences will be in the case that responsibilities go unfulfilled. In addition to these four dimensions, Beauchamp and colleagues proposed that in the interactive team environment, athletes could differ in their perceptions of these four dimensions in the separate contexts of offensive and defensive play.

Role efficacy

Efficacy related research in sport has typically addressed the concepts of self-efficacy (i.e. 'beliefs in one's capabilities to organize and execute the course of action required to produce given attainments'; Bandura, 1997, p. 3) or collective efficacy (i.e. beliefs in the capabilities of the group; Bandura 1986, 1997). Bandura noted that these efficacy beliefs can have a strong influence over an individual's choice, effort and persistence in performing an activity. However, in addition to beliefs related to the individual (i.e. self-efficacy) and the group as a whole (i.e. collective efficacy), Bray *et al.* (2002) suggested that in a group setting where members' roles overlap and require a high level of inter-dependence, it is likely that individuals will develop efficacy beliefs about their ability to carry out their roles in combination with others' responsibilities and competencies. These are referred to as role efficacy beliefs, which are specifically defined as team members' beliefs about their capabilities to successfully carry out interdependent for-mal role functions.

Role conflict

A cognitive element that has been closely linked with role ambiguity is role conflict (e.g. Kahn *et al.*, 1964). Role conflict is the presence of incongruent expectations for a focal person. For example, in a sport environment, an individual who has a desire to coach may not be able to devote time to this activity because of family role responsibilities. Thus, the family role (e.g. mother or father) conflicts with the sport role.

Kahn *et al.* (1964) highlighted a number of different types of role conflict that can exist. The above example represents one of these types; namely, *inter-role conflict*. Inter-role conflict occurs when expectations from two or more contexts interfere with one another (e.g. family versus physical activity). However, *intra-role conflict* (i.e. conflict occurring within the same role context) can also exist in three different forms. First, intra-sender conflict occurs when a single role sender develops multiple expectations (i.e. two or more) for the focal person that are inconsistent with one another. One example that describes this particular type of conflict is an ice-hockey coach who emphasizes aggression and physicality for his or her players but also expects the players to stay out of the penalty box.

A second type of intra-role conflict is termed inter-sender conflict. Likely a very common form of conflict, this occurs when two role senders apply incongruent expectations to a focal person regarding the same role. This might occur in a sport setting when multiple coaches (e.g. a head coach and an assistant coach) advise an athlete on how to perform his or her responsibilities. Finally, a third type of intra-role conflict is termed person-role conflict and occurs when the expected role responsibilities conflict with the values or motivation of the focal person. This last type of interpersonal conflict is exemplified when an athlete is asked to perform a lower status role (e.g. a bench player or non-starter) that is at odds with his or her expectations.

A related term that is often associated with role conflict is *role overload*. In general, there has been a lack of conceptual clarity regarding this construct. In some cases it has been likened to role conflict itself (e.g. a high number of incompatible expectations that are impossible to complete in a required length of time; Kahn *et al.*, 1964). In a discussion on this topic, Eys *et al.* (2006) noted that role overload might manifest itself in different ways in an athletic environment. First, an athlete might feel that a single role responsibility is beyond his or her personal capabilities. This was referred to as a qualitative overload. Conversely, an athlete may be expected to perform an excessive number of responsibilities and in such instances could be said to experience quantitative role overload (Eys *et al.*, 2006). Overall, while role conflict and role overload are conceptually somewhat similar, the former relates to *incompatibility* of responsibilities while the latter refers to an excessive *amount* of responsibilities.

Role acceptance

A final cognitive role element is role acceptance. At present, role acceptance is the least examined of the cognitive elements due in part to a lack of conceptual clarity. Recently, Eys *et al.* (2006) suggested that role acceptance represents 'a dynamic, covert process that reflects the degree to which an athlete perceives his or her own expectations for role responsibilities as similar to and agreeable with, the expectations for role responsibilities determined by his or her role senders' (p. 246). In the past some researchers have used the terms role acceptance and role satisfaction interchangeably

(Carron and Hausenblas, 1998), despite the fact that the two constructs appear to be conceptually different. Not only does the above definition highlight how these two role perceptions differ, but also by emphasizing that acceptance involves a similarity of expectations shared among the role sender and focal person, this definition deviates from the term 'compliance', which would only involve the overt behavioral response from the focal person.

Role satisfaction

Generally, role satisfaction represents the degree of fulfillment the role gives the individual (e.g. how happy people are with their responsibilities). In an attempt to define role satisfaction, Eys *et al.* (2006) adapted a definition of job satisfaction (Locke, 1976) from the industrial-organizational literature to the role domain in sport. Specifically, they defined role satisfaction as 'a pleasurable emotional state resulting from the perception of one's [role] as fulfilling or allowing the fulfillment of one's important [role] values' (p. 246).

   Rail (1987) suggested that there are four major perceptions that lead individuals to feel that their roles are satisfying. The first is the perceived degree to which their abilities and strengths are being utilized. A second perception is how important members view their role in relation to and within the group's context. Receiving feedback and recognition for role efforts was identified as being a third perception relevant to role satisfaction. Finally, the degree to which individuals are given autonomy in performing their role responsibilities is also important for role satisfaction. Therefore, it would be predicted that role satisfaction would be elevated if an individual's abilities are being utilized correctly, the role is considered important within the group, feedback and recognition regarding the role performance is relatively consistent and constructive and the individual is given some control over how responsibilities are fulfilled.

Role performance

The final role element that has been discussed is behavioral in nature and is termed role performance. This particular element would seem to be an outcome related to the individual's general ability to complete the role responsibilities as well as his/her understanding of and motivation to perform them. Therefore, all the previous role elements discussed will likely influence role performance and consequently, role performance has been examined in many of the recent studies conducted in sport. These and other research findings are discussed in the subsequent section.

Review of sport-related role research

Prior to 2001, there was a limited amount of sport research that focused specifically on the topic of roles. As examples of this early research both Dawe (1990) and Grand and Carron (1982) examined the concepts of role clarity and role acceptance/satisfaction in sport teams. However, in both cases the role elements examined were not necessarily the prime focus. In the case of the former study, role clarity and role acceptance were studied in relation to another major variable of concern; cohesion. For the latter study, role elements were considered as part of a larger group evaluation measure termed the Team Climate Questionnaire. In both cases, the conceptualization of the role elements was unidimensional in nature. A final example of earlier sport research was conducted in two studies by Capel (1986 and Capel et al., 1987). The results of these investigations suggested that increased role conflict and role ambiguity were associated with an increased possibility of burnout in athletic trainers and high school coaches.

More recently, conceptual advances in the above role elements have resulted in an enhanced understanding of (a) the inter-relationships between the role elements, (b) the importance of optimizing perceptions of role responsibilities, (c) the influence of potential antecedents of poor role perceptions and (d) possible moderators of role relationships. Each of these recent additions to the literature is discussed in turn.

Inter-relationships of role elements

It would be logical to suggest that some role elements are related to one another and, in some cases there may be a great deal of overlap (e.g. role overload and role conflict). Recently, researchers have sought to examine the inter-relationships and pathways that link the role variables. For example, Beauchamp and Bray (2001) found that role ambiguity mediated the relationship between intra-role conflict and role efficacy. More specifically, a higher degree of role conflict was associated with greater role ambiguity, which in turn was related to lower perceptions of competence with regard to role responsibilities (i.e. role efficacy). In a similar example that was primarily focused on assessing the validity of their operationalization of role ambiguity, Beauchamp et al. (2002) found that role efficacy mediated the role ambiguity–role performance relationship in such a way that clarity of role responsibilities was positively related to beliefs in performing successfully, which in turn were positively associated with actual role performance. Finally, Beauchamp et al. (2005a) found a negative association between role ambiguity and role satisfaction.

In a series of studies examining role efficacy as the focal point, Bray and colleagues (Beauchamp et al., 2005c; Bray et al., 2004; Bray and Brawley, 2002) identified similar relationships between role efficacy, role performance and role ambiguity. First, in a study with Spanish youth soccer players, Bray et al. (2004) again found support for the role efficacy-role performance link. Using a slightly different approach, Bray and Brawley (2002) examined whether perceptions of role ambiguity *moderated* this relationship. Specifically, they discovered that the role efficacy-role performance relationship was more salient under conditions where athletes were clear about their roles. This result is perhaps unsurprising given that if an athlete does not understand his/her role to begin with, it would be very difficult to have accurate perceptions of efficacy to perform the role. As a final example, Beauchamp et al. (2005c) examined relationships between role efficacy and role ambiguity from a multilevel perspective and uncovered that role ambiguity accounted for approximately one-fifth of the variance related to role efficacy and that this variance was explained mostly at the individual level.

Relationships of role elements with other variables

In addition to the work outlined above that demonstrates an interplay between the role elements, some of these variables have also been examined in relation to other group and individual level constructs. For example, Settles et al. (2002) found that the degree to which individuals could psychologically separate the dual roles of 'athlete' and 'student' (i.e. reduce inter-role conflict) was positively related to general perceptions of well-being. Also, Bray (1998) linked the role elements of efficacy (positive relationship) and ambiguity (negative relationship) to task cohesion. In general, the vast majority of these studies have focused on role ambiguity as the main variable of interest and demonstrated the potential consequences of dysfunctional role perceptions.

As a brief summary, role ambiguity has been found to be negatively linked to task self-efficacy and task cohesion (Eys and Carron, 2001), general athlete satisfaction (Eys et al., 2003b) and intention to return to the same competitive team (Eys et al., 2005b). Also, a positive relationship has been found between role ambiguity and competitive state anxiety (Beauchamp et al., 2003). It should be noted that many of the above studies were correlational and as such, causation cannot be inferred. However, from a conceptual standpoint, it is reasonable to suggest that these associated variables (e.g. decreased satisfaction) might be consequences of not having a full understanding of one's role.

Potential antecedents of role elements

Another avenue of research has been to try to determine the *antecedents* of role elements. Overall, these investigations have typically focused on the antecedents of role ambiguity. However, there are some exceptions. For example, Mellalieu and Juniper (2006) examined the perceptions of 11 male soccer players in relation to the role episode previously discussed (Kahn et al., 1964). Their in-depth qualitative analysis revealed a number of potential antecedents of the degree to which an individual will *accept* their role including (a) the individual's perception of the effectiveness of the role, (b) its overall importance, (c) how others view the individual's role responsibilities, (d) the perceived competency level of coach and (e) the congruency between the actual and preferred leadership styles of the coach.

As mentioned previously, a somewhat larger amount of information is available with regard to sources of role ambiguity. Eys et al. (2005a) asked athletes to identify reasons why they might not fully understand their roles. As Figure 6.1 depicts, these reasons were classified as being related to or under the direct control of the role sender, focal person, or the situation. Specific role sender factors included perceptions that the role sender (e.g. the coach) did not communicate enough, did not communicate clearly and/or provided conflicting information to the focal person (e.g. the athlete). While the athletes typically identified the coach as being the primary role sender, they also indicated that ambiguity could arise through the communication practices among their team-mates. Examples that were included under the factors related to the focal person were issues such as the athlete not having the capacity to understand the instructions or not paying attention to instruction in practice. Examples of situation-related factors influencing role understanding included having to switch to a more elite and complex level of competition (e.g. high school to university) or changing positions within the team. In general, these findings were also supported by Mellalieu and Juniper (2006) who, in their qualitative study of the role episode, found that the development of role clarity was facilitated by the explicit instruction of role senders and through each individual's learning experiences within the sport.

Beyond the Mellalieu and Juniper (2006) and Eys et al. (2005a) studies, two other investigations are worthy of note, having highlighted the importance of role sender factors. First, Cunningham and Eys (in press) examined the association between intra-team communication practices and role ambiguity. For male sport teams, they found that the more athletes perceived their teams to engage in communications that built and conveyed trust among the group, the more likely they were to have a better understanding of their role responsibilities. This relationship was not replicated with females. A second study conducted by Beauchamp *et al.* (2005b) found that the perceived quantity of training and instruction received from the coach was related to perceptions of role ambiguity. However, this relationship was only found among non-starting players. As an aside, it is worth pointing out that both the quantity *and* quality of instruction should be taken into account. For example, previous research has found that qualities of instruction associated with transformational leadership behaviors (see Hoption *et al.*, Ch. 3, this volume) have been found to bring about greater role clarity (Shoemaker, 1999).

Moderators of role relationships

The above two studies highlight another important consideration for the examination of role elements in a sport context. Essentially, researchers need to be aware and control potential moderators of relationships involving role perceptions. In the above examples, gender and team starting status were variables that were influential in how salient the relationships were between constructs. However, these are not singular examples. Eys and Carron (2001) found that males and females differed in terms of the association between multidimensional role ambiguity and task cohesion. Also, Bray *et al.* (2002) discovered that starting players had a significantly greater degree of role efficacy than non-starters and suggested this was due to the ability and opportunity to execute their role responsibilities more often in real competitive situations. Other potential moderators related to roles include the athletes' tenure on the team and the time of season when perceptions of roles are assessed. Eys *et al.* (2003a) found that senior university athletes (in their second to fifth seasons with their sport teams) had greater clarity about their role responsibilities than first year players but that this difference dissipated by the end of the season.

A final moderator of interest related to role ambiguity that was examined by Bray *et al.* (2005) corresponds to the *need for clarity*. Bray and his colleagues hypothesized that individuals differ in terms of how critical it is to have role responsibilities fully delineated to them. Therefore, the consequences for those who have a high need for clarity but are ambiguous about their role should be greater than for those who are ambivalent about receiving role information. Bray and colleagues' study demonstrated this effect quite clearly as the relationship between role ambiguity and athlete satisfaction was evident for individuals with a high need for clarity but did not exist for those with a low need. In general, taking into consideration moderating influences is extremely important because it will 'help validate theory and identify conditions under which antecedent-consequence relationships may be most evident and should also help guide effective interventions to alleviate the potential negative effects of stress on athletes' (Bray *et al.*, 2005, p. 317).

Practical implications and interventions

The research findings regarding the consequences of poor role perceptions highlight the need to consider role differentiation and communication within sport groups. Individuals who do not have positive role perceptions are also likely to have associated group (e.g. cohesion) and individual (e.g. satisfaction, efficacy) perceptions that are less positive. Consequently, a major applied implication is the need to develop practices within a team that will facilitate positive role perceptions. However, there are a number of issues that should be kept in mind. As some of the previous research has suggested (e.g. Eys *et al.*, 2003a), for example, an intervention would likely have the most effect toward the earlier part of group development and with individuals who are lower in the status hierarchy (e.g. non-starters and/or new players). The present section will address the limitations of the role perception literature and suggestions for applied practice will subsequently be proposed.

Limitations and practical implications

Perhaps the largest overarching limitation that can be made, under which several smaller concerns are housed, is that the role literature has typically targeted amateur (e.g. school, university and club-level) athletes. As such, relating to the present theme, the generalizability of relationships among role variables beyond these competitive levels is somewhat speculative. Consider the aforementioned negative relationship between role ambiguity and role satisfaction, which might become less salient within national amateur and professional sport teams. Among professional sport teams, for example, athletes shift positions regularly, change in formal appointments to and from roles of leadership and even alter their playing role within a specific game, perhaps due to unforeseen momentary circumstances. Over the course of these experiences, they may be able to amass considerable competitive experiences, sometimes sustaining their satisfaction while fulfilling unanticipated and previously undefined roles. Consequently, it also becomes plausible that the acceptance of the continued presence of role ambiguity, a probable athlete adaptation strategy at the elite level, becomes an inherent part of performance within team sports such as ice-hockey, basketball and soccer.

The nature and direction of communication among role actors would also likely change at a more elite or professional level with the direction of communication being revised from a top-down (during instances when coaches are viewed as above the athlete in position, stature and decision-making capabilities) to bi-directional approach. Within elite amateur teams, Bloom *et al.* (1998) found that university level coaches commonly use a top-down approach exemplified by the coach most often depicted as the role sender and the athlete commonly regarded as the focal person. Interestingly, Bloom *et al.* found that as coaches transition to the national level they adapt their communication strategies to include more frequent bottom-up feedback from veterans and team leaders. The integration of frequent two-way communication is partly explained by the athletes within elite teams being regarded as becoming more equal partners leading up to and within international tournaments. At the professional level, the direction of communication refines once more, with athletes often considered on par with coaches (in terms of knowledge and experience). When the second author worked with professional boxers who were world champions, it became clear that coaches were employed (and sometimes unemployed) by the athletes they trained. Hence, role assignment and the processes of communicating role responsibilities are not always consistent across levels of sport.

The limitations of current role literature also extend to cultural variability. To the present, this literature has not necessarily reflected multicultural values across nationalities. Within North American mainstream sport, for instance, it is reasonable to believe that athletes who do not receive playing time would be unhappy (or unsatisfied). When data are gathered from North American athletes in contexts such as university settings, a major focal point from the athletes' point of view is the self. However, among Canadian Aboriginals, as reflected within two recent reports by Schinke and colleagues (see Schinke *et al.*, 2006a,b), team and group objectives were reported to be more valued over personal aspirations. Consequently, if an athlete from a collective-minded culture is assigned a role that entails less playing time and more social support (e.g. from the bench), it becomes possible that the reasons for satisfaction or dissatisfaction might deviate from what is currently being regarded as the norm. Within collective cultures, group affiliation and group acceptance might supersede personal aspirations.

Reflecting on the current limitations within the sport role literature, it becomes clear that what is known can only be regarded as a starting point. It is hoped that role researchers explore the topics falling within the boundary of the role domain with athletes spanning all levels, age groupings and cultures. In addition, it is suggested that role researchers employ a wider number of research methods (e.g. qualitative methodologies) whenever appropriate to glean a clearer (and more in-depth) understanding of the area. As just one example integrating the above points, qualitative approaches (e.g. interviews, focus groups, or talking circles) would be a positive first step to understanding role communication strategies within Aboriginal sport and physical activity groups.

Interventions

Building on what has been presented, it is worth considering intervention strategies for applied practitioners, including coaching staff, administrators and sport psychology consultants. It would seem that effective communication is a pivotal aspect of effective intervention strategies. For developmental and varsity level athletes, such communication may be based on a coach's pre-established seasonal plan and style of play, which in turn are founded upon athletes' strengths and weaknesses. At the beginning of each season, effective coaching communication practices would include the utilization of team and individual goal setting as well as delineating clearly defined roles for each player. As such, the effective pre-elite level team would be exemplified by a clear understanding of the coach's expectations, the athletes' competencies and beliefs of those competencies and ongoing clear directives regarding how to progress in terms of ability, playing time and performance.

Among effectively managed elite amateur contexts, the importance of clear communication remains constant. However, as the level of competition increases the contribution of athletes in relation to the team's vision and collective maintenance becomes more influential. National team athletes are often recognized for their athletic prowess and as such, are regarded by coaching staff as a creditable and valuable source of ongoing information. When elite athletes are consulted throughout the development of their team, Schinke *et al.* (1997) noted that their emotional investment and commitment is retained. That said, elite athletes typically expect to play and these expectations are confounded by the inevitable; athletes within interactive teams do not receive equal playing time, or equal game opportunities. Consequently, it becomes critical for elite coaches to sell the team's vision to their athletes and make each member's respective part important within the unit. Creative thinking among coaching staff and team captains is necessary to retain group harmony given the number of designated roles and varying responsibilities. Further, as roles become increasingly ambiguous within critical games, the task of the coaching staff ought to include information that clarifies roles and encourages and reinforces self-exploration on the part of each athlete.

Finally, as mentioned previously for the professional level, the direction of communication *among* athletes and coaching staff is often bi-directional. Given the sometimes unclear role of stakeholders (athletes, coaching staff, administration) in terms of the decision-making of the team (or sport organization) and the close tie within professional sport between performance success and financial viability, it may become increasingly important to clarify and/or simplify the scope of each member's duties. The process of designating roles and subsequently holding one accountable for them, increases in challenge as athletes and coaches both struggle to retain (and enhance) contracts. Consequently, a third-party (e.g. a sport psychology consultant) is often sought in such instances to liaise among members and encourage and maintain effective bi-directional communication throughout the season. It is proposed that effective communication, which would include the ongoing buy-in among all stakeholders of their designated roles, could include a standard communication protocol that can be followed as pressures and expectations mount. An example of this protocol would be for professional athletes to only challenge the coach in private, away from the scrutiny of team-mates, media and the public. Clearly, the importance of role clarity, role acceptance and effective communication strategies by all involved, are essential aspects within professional sport.

Future research directions

Conceptualizing role elements

With the relative paucity of research conducted with certain role elements, four general suggestions for future research are offered based on their various stages of development. The first general suggestion is for future research to further our understanding of the conceptual basis of role constructs. In general, recent literature on role ambiguity and role efficacy has provided definitional and conceptual clarity to these topics. Consequently, this has also provided an opportunity to measure athlete perceptions and properly test propositions in relation to other variables. However, research into other role elements such as role conflict, role satisfaction and role acceptance has likely been stunted by a lack of conceptual clarity. It is only recently (Eys *et al.*, 2006) that initial definitions related to sport have been advanced and further research into the nature of these role elements (e.g. are they unidimensional versus multidimensional constructs) is warranted.

Another point related to underdeveloped areas is that virtually all research into the topic of roles has been focused on formal, prescribed responsibilities. The relative ease with which to assess these types of roles (versus informal roles that are not quite so visible) is a likely reason for this focus. However, anecdotal evidence can be found consistently through media accounts of athletes and teams highlighting the prevalence and importance of informal roles in groups. As mentioned previously, some positive informal roles might include the team's comedian/clown or the individual who manages to arrange for the group to get together (i.e. social coordinator). However, negative informal roles can also exist to the detriment of teams. A quote by NCAA basketball player Emeka Okafor highlights one of these negative roles in response to being denied playing time because of foul problems:

> My first time in the Final Four, I didn't want to miss a minute and I was going to miss 16 . . . It was eating me up inside. I blew off steam for like two or three minutes. But I knew I couldn't stay sour-faced for the whole half. I didn't want to be a cancer on the team.'
>
> (quoted in Wolff, 2004, p. 51)

In the sporting context, a person who is disruptive to the group and without whom the group would likely perform better is often referred to as a team cancer. Overall, an in-depth examination of positive and negative informal roles in addition to their effect on team performance and harmony would be a vital addition to our understanding in group dynamics.

Examining complex role relationships

A second general area for future research is a focus on more complex research questions. Earlier information presented in this chapter highlighted a number of different issues that could modify or explain relationships that are present for role elements. Moderators that have found research support in the sport role literature include gender, starting status, tenure on the team, need for clarity (in the case of role ambiguity), time of season and suggestions have been made in this chapter that it is necessary to also account for differences due to competitive level and culture. In addition, similar to work conducted by Beauchamp *et al.* (2002), it is necessary to move beyond descriptive relationships to more explanatory (i.e. mediational) investigations. As Salzinger (2001) noted, determining 'an underlying mechanism . . . is the main function of research' (p. B14). For example, previous research has suggested a link between perceptions of role clarity and task cohesion but it is possible that there are intermediary variables (e.g. enhanced quality/quantity of communication) that play a part in this link. Understanding these mediational pathways would be vital for the determination of effective interventions in group dynamics.

A final suggestion with regard to designing more complex research questions is to take into account both individual and group level effects. Multilevel analyses are becoming increasingly common in group oriented research. Essentially, this type of analysis (i.e. multilevel modeling) allows for data contained in hierarchical structures (e.g. athletes nested within teams nested within competitive level) to be examined simultaneously. A typical approach to study group data has been to examine either individual perceptions or a group aggregate of this information. However, examining only a single level (either at the athlete-level or team-level) has drawbacks (Rousseau and House, 1994). First, it may lead to the assumption that relationships obtained at one level are relevant to another level when, in fact, this may not be true. For example, in a study with ice-hockey teams by Feltz and Lirgg (1998), perceptions of efficacy held for the group (i.e. collective efficacy) were found to be related to team success whereas individual perceptions of efficacy (i.e. self-efficacy) were not. Second, cross-level effects (i.e. effect of the group on the individual and vice versa) may be underestimated. With regard to this second point and the communication of role responsibilities, it is reasonable to suggest that a team environment provides ample opportunity to see effects at both levels. More specifically, personality differences and background experiences could likely lead to individual variation of role perceptions among athletes. However, common stimuli within the team (e.g. exposure to the same coach) could also provide for commonalities among in-group members but differences between groups. To date, only one study has examined a sport role issue (Beauchamp *et al.*, 2005a; perceptions of role ambiguity and role efficacy) from a multilevel perspective and found that the majority of variance was accounted for at the individual level.

Antecedents of role perceptions

The third general suggestion for future research relates to previous points made about both practical implications and gaining an understanding about the antecedents of role perceptions. With an eye towards providing theoretically driven and tested intervention strategies in the future, it is necessary to first understand which of the proposed antecedents are salient in the sport environment. To date, through either sport or industrial/organizational literature, antecedents have been identified that could be tested with regard to their impact on three role elements. Eys *et al.* (2005a) highlighted factors related to the *role sender, focal person* and *context* that could influence perceptions of role ambiguity. The quantity of coach leadership behaviors (e.g. the amount of training and instruction behaviors perceived by athletes) and intra-team communication practices are the only variables that have been examined at present.

Role efficacy is another element where potential antecedents have been identified. Bandura (1986) hypothesized four determinants of efficacy beliefs. These included the provision of mastery experiences, vicarious experiences/modeling, verbal persuasion and physiological states. Examining the effect of these four potential determinants (individually and in combination) would aid in successful intervention development. A similar process could occur for the examination of antecedents and interventions related to role satisfaction as the suggestions by Rail (1987) would provide a solid basis from which to proceed. As highlighted in the role satisfaction section, these potential determinants include the degree to which relevant and existing abilities are utilized, the importance of the role within the group, the amount and quality of feedback, recognition of the role and the degree of autonomy that one may have in performing various responsibilities. It is likely that the salience of this last determinant within the interdependent sport environment would differ among various competitive levels (e.g. high school sports versus the professional level). However, this suggestion could only be validated through examination of these research questions.

Roles in an exercise context

The fourth general future research suggestion relates to the context in which roles are investigated. Examination of interdependent role functions has to date focused on the sport environment. However, the potential applications and benefits of exploring group dynamics principles in an exercise setting have been communicated in previous research. Typically, these studies have focused on the formal exercise environment (i.e. exercise classes). Carron and Spink (1993) highlighted a team building process that took advantage of the group's environment (e.g. developing a group identity), structure (e.g. developing group norms) and process (e.g. enhancing interaction and communication) to maintain physical activity adherence. More recently, Brawley *et al.* (2000) developed an approach to exercise program delivery that utilized properties of the group to promote adherence to a 12-week program of exercise (termed a group-mediated cognitive-behavioral intervention) and facilitate the participants' commitment to physical activity after the structured program had ended. In both cases, a group structure was created and consequently formal (e.g. mentors for new members, attendance monitor) and informal roles (e.g. class clown, social coordinator) and expectations for interdependent behaviors were likely developed within this environment.

A concept that would likely have some overlap with role responsibilities would be social support. General social support functions in an exercise group might consist of the provision of emotional support and verbal encouragement as well as tangible support functions (e.g. providing a drive to the exercise facility). Within these groups, who provides these functions, how often they are performed, whether they are formally prescribed responsibilities (e.g. fitness instructor versus classmate) and the effect of role perceptions on adherence may be an important avenue of research.

Summary

Roles represent an important structural component to all groups including interactive sport teams. Thus, athletes hold a number of perceptions related to their role and these perceptions are associated with many important group and individual level variables. Overall, sport teams comprised of talented athletes and technically competent coaching staff, provide a foundation for their viability and success. The multifaceted role literature provides coaching staff, athletes and sport science practitioners with clear indications regarding how best to develop and refine sport teams, with several markers (variables and classification schemes) worth considering throughout the process. Underpinning all of these, from developmental to professional teams, is the basic tenet of effective communication.

References

Bales, R. F. and Slater, P. E. (1955). Role differentiation in small decision-making groups. In T. Parsons and R. F. Bales (Eds), *Family socialization and interaction process* (pp. 259–306). Glencoe, IL: The Free Press.

Bandura, A. (1986). *Social foundations of thought and action: A social cognitive theory.* Englewood Cliffs, NJ: Prentice-Hall.

Bandura, A. (1997). *Self-efficacy: The exercise of control.* New York: W. H. Freeman.

Beauchamp, M. R. and Bray, S. R. (2001). Role ambiguity and role conflict within interdependent teams. *Small Group Research*, 32, 133–157.

Beauchamp, M. R., Bray, S. R., Eys, M. A. and Carron, A. V. (2002). Role ambiguity, role efficacy and role performance: Multidimensional and mediational relationships within interdependent sport teams. *Group Dynamics: Theory, Research and Practice*, 6, 229–242.

Beauchamp, M. R., Bray, S. R., Eys, M. A. and Carron, A. V. (2003). The effect of role ambiguity on competitive state anxiety. *Journal of Sport and Exercise Psychology*, 25, 77–92.

Beauchamp, M. R., Bray, S. R., Eys, M. A. and Carron, A. V. (2005a). Multidimensional role ambiguity and role satisfaction: A prospective examination using interdependent sport teams. *Journal of Applied Social Psychology*, 35, 2560–2576.

Beauchamp, M. R., Bray, S. R., Eys, M. A. and Carron, A. V. (2005b). Leadership behaviors and multidimensional role ambiguity perceptions in team sports. *Small Group Research*, 36, 5–20.

Beauchamp, M. R., Bray, S. R., Fielding, A. and Eys, M. A. (2005c). A multilevel investigation of the relationship between role ambiguity and role efficacy in sport. *Psychology of Sport and Exercise*, 6, 289–302.

Belbin, M. R. (1981). *Management teams: Why they succeed and why they fail*. Oxford: Butterworth-Heinemann.

Biddle, B. J. and Thomas, E. J. (1966). *Role theory: Concepts and research*. New York: John Wiley and Sons.

Bloom, G. A., Schinke, R. J. and Salmela, J. H. (1998). Assessing the development of perceived communication skills by elite basketball coaches. *Coaching and Sport Science Journal*, 6, 3–10.

Brawley, L. R., Rejeski, W. J. and Lutes, L. (2000). A group-mediated cognitive-behavioral intervention for increasing adherence to physical activity in older adults. *Journal of Applied Biobehavioral Research*, 5, 47–65.

Bray, S. R. (1998). Role efficacy within interdependent teams: Measurement development and tests of theory. Unpublished doctoral thesis. University of Waterloo, Ontario, Canada.

Bray, S. R., Balaguer, I. and Duda, J. L. (2004). The relationship of task self-efficacy and role efficacy beliefs to role performance in Spanish youth soccer. *Journal of Sports Sciences*, 22, 429–437.

Bray, S. R., Beauchamp, M. R., Eys, M. A. and Carron, A. V. (2005). Need for clarity as a moderator of the role ambiguity – satisfaction relationship. *Journal of Applied Sport Psychology*, 17, 306–318.

Bray, S. R. and Brawley, L. R. (2002). Role efficacy, role clarity and role performance effectiveness. *Small Group Research*, 33, 233–253.

Bray, S. R., Brawley, L. R. and Carron, A. V. (2002). Efficacy for interdependent role functions: Evidence from the sport domain. *Small Group Research*, 33, 644–666.

Capel, S. A. (1986). Psychological and organizational factors related to burnout in athletic trainers. *Athletic Training*, 21, 322–327.

Capel, S. A., Sisley, B. L. and Desertrain, G. S. (1987). The relationship between role conflict and role ambiguity to burnout in high school coaches. *Journal of Sport Psychology*, 9, 106–117.

Carron, A. V. and Hausenblas, H. A., (1998). *Group dynamics in sport* (2nd ed.). Morgantown, WV: Fitness Information Technology.

Carron, A. V., Hausenblas, H. and Eys, M. A. (2005). *Group dynamics in sport* (3rd ed.). Morgantown, WV: Fitness Information Technology.

Carron, A. V. and Spink, K. S. (1993). Team building in an exercise setting. *The Sport Psychologist*, 7, 8–18.

Cottrell, L. S. (1933). Roles and marital adjustment. *Publications of the American Sociological Society*, 27, 107–115.

Cunningham, I. and Eys, M. A. (in press). Role ambiguity and intra-team communication in interdependent sport teams. *Journal of Applied Social Psychology*.

Dawe, S. L. (1990). Cohesion, performance, role clarity and role acceptance. Unpublished master's thesis, University of Western Ontario, London, Ontario, Canada.

Eys, M. A. (2000). Development of a measure of role ambiguity in sport. Unpublished master's thesis, The University of Western Ontario, London, Ontario, Canada.

Eys, M. A., Beauchamp, M. R. and Bray, S. R. (2006). A review of team roles in sport. In S. Hanton and S. D. Mellalieu (Eds), *Literature reviews in sport psychology* (pp. 227–255). Hauppauge, NY: Nova Science.

Eys, M. A. and Carron, A. V. (2001). Role ambiguity, task cohesion and task self-efficacy. *Small Group Research*, 32, 356–373.

Eys, M. A., Carron, A. V., Beauchamp, M. R. and Bray, S. R. (2003a). Role ambiguity in sport teams. *Journal of Sport and Exercise Psychology*, 25, 534–550.

Eys, M. A., Carron, A. V., Beauchamp, M. R. and Bray, S. R. (2005a). Athletes' perceptions of the sources of role ambiguity. *Small Group Research*, 36, 383–403.

Eys, M. A., Carron, A. V., Bray, S. R. and Beauchamp, M. R. (2003b). Role ambiguity and athlete satisfaction. *Journal of Sports Sciences*, 21, 391–401.

Eys, M. A., Carron, A. V., Bray, S. R. and Beauchamp, M. R. (2005b). The relationship between role ambiguity and intention to return. *Journal of Applied Sport Psychology*, 17, 255–261.

Feltz, D. L. and Lirgg, C. D. (1998). Perceived team and player efficacy in hockey. *Journal of Applied Psychology*, 83, 557–564.

Fisher, S. G., Hunter, T. A. and Macrosson, W. D. K. (1998). The structure of Belbin's team roles. *Journal of Occupational and Organizational Psychology*, 71, 283–288.

Grand, R. R. and Carron, A. V. (1982). Development of a team climate questionnaire. In *Proceedings of the Annual Conference of the Canadian Society for Psychomotor Learning and Sport Psychology, Edmonton, Alberta* (pp. 217–229).

Kahn, R. L., Wolfe, D. M., Quinn, R. P., Snoek, J. D. and Rosenthal, R. A. (1964). *Organizational stress: Studies in role conflict and ambiguity*. New York: Wiley.

Katz, D. and Kahn, R. L. (1978). *The social psychology of organizations* (2nd ed.). New York: Wiley.

Lewin, K. (1935). *A dynamic theory of personality*. New York: McGraw-Hill.

Locke, E. A. (1976). The nature and causes of job satisfaction. In M. D. Dunnette (Ed.), *Handbook of industrial and organizational psychology*. Chicago: Rand McNally.

Mabry, E. A. and Barnes, R. E. (1980). *The dynamics of small group communication*. Englewood Cliffs, NJ: Prentice-Hall.

McCallum, J. (2005). Let's get physical: To advance in the postseason, a team's stars must shine, but the critical difference is often made by the players who wreak the most havoc. *Sports Illustrated*, 102, 30–39.

Mellalieu, S. D. and Juniper, S. W. (2006). A qualitative investigation into experiences of the role episode in soccer. *The Sport Psychologist*, 20, 399–416.

Parsons, T. and Bales, R. F. (1955). *Family, socialization and interaction process*. Glencoe, IL: The Free Press.

Rail, G. (1987). Perceived role characteristics and executive satisfaction in voluntary sport associations. *Journal of Sport Psychology*, 9, 376–384.

Rousseau, D. M. and House, R. J. (1994). Meso organizational behavior: Avoiding three fundamental biases. In C. L. Cooper and D. M. Rousseau (Eds), *Trends in Organizational Behavior* (Vol. 1, pp. 13–30). London: Wiley.

Salzinger, K. (2001). Scientists should look for basic causes, not just effects. *Chronicle of Higher Education*, 157, B14.

Schinke, R. J., Draper, S. P. and Salmela, J. H. (1997). A conceptual model of team building in high-performance sport as a season-long process. *Avante*, 3, 47–62.

Schinke, R. J., Eys, M. A., Danielson, R., Michel, G., Peltier, D., Pheasant, C., *et al.* (2006a). Cultural social support for Canadian Aboriginal elite athletes during their sport development. *International Journal of Sport Psychology*, 37, 1–19.

Schinke, R. J., Hanrahan, S., Michel, G., Danielson, R., Peltier, D., Pheasant, C., *et al.* (2006b). The pre-competition and competition practices of Canadian Aboriginal elite athletes: A purposive sample. (Manuscript submitted for publication.)

Settles, I. H., Sellers, R. M. and Damas, A., Jr. (2002). One role or two? The function of psychological separation in role conflict. *Journal of Applied Psychology*, 87, 574–582.

Shaw, M. E. and Costanzo, P. R. (1982). *Theories of social psychology* (2nd ed.). New York: McGraw-Hill.

Shoemaker, M. E. (1999). Leadership practices in sales managers associated with self-efficacy, role clarity and job satisfaction of individual industrial salespeople. *Journal of Personal Selling and Sales Management*, 14, 1–19.

Weinberg, R. S. and Gould, D. (2003). *Foundations of sport and exercise psychology* (3rd ed.). Champaign, IL: Human Kinetics.

Wolff, A. (2004). The Conn game. *Sports Illustrated*, 100, 46–53.

Photograph by Richard Lam/UBC Athletics. Reprinted courtesy of The University of British Columbia.

7 Group cohesion in sport and exercise

Past, present and future

Albert V. Carron, Kim M. Shapcott and Shauna M. Burke

Introduction

For centuries, cohesion has been considered a crucial factor in the success of groups. The earliest records of cohesion are written descriptions of military battles in ancient Greece (Siebold, 1999). Specifically, the battle in 480 BC between the Spartan warriors and the Persian army has been used to depict the powerfulness of group cohesion. The outnumbered Spartans managed to hold their ground for several days against the powerful Persians. They did so not only with their physical strength but their unity; they stood 'shoulder to shoulder, shield to shield, in the narrow pass to prevent the Persians from invading' (Siebold, 1999, p. 8). This courageous stand by the Spartans was viewed as 'a symbol of unity and cohesion' (Siebold, 1999, p. 8).

Likewise, cohesion has played a major role in sport for decades. Numerous sport dynasties from the past, such as the New York Yankees, Montreal Canadians, Manchester United and Chicago Bulls, have credited their success to team chemistry. Lack of cohesion has also been a factor for losing teams. Recent performances in both the winter and summer Olympics highlight the fact that effective teams are more than just a collection of talented members. To be successful, a team has to be able to combine the efforts and abilities of all members in a united fashion. An example where, apparently, talent was abundant but team chemistry was relatively lacking was Canada's 2006 Olympic Men's hockey team. Despite Team Canada's all-star line-up, the team was barely capable of scoring a goal and was not in contention for a gold medal. Head coach Pat Quinn attributed the poor performance to lack of chemistry and cohesion (CBC Sports, 2006). Another so called Dream Team – the heavily favored 2004 US Olympic Men's basketball team – was reported to have experienced a similar shortcoming in cohesiveness and was defeated by Puerto Rico in the opening round.

These recent failures by talented teams suggest that developing a cohesive sport team in the twenty-first century represents an immense challenge. This sentiment is shared by some professional coaches, such as National Basketball Association coach Phil Jackson who noted:

> In the 1960s and '70s, players asked: 'Where do I fit in? How can I help this team win?' Now they ask: 'How do I get what *I* want?' Given this selfish mind-set, it is remarkable actually that teams play with any cohesiveness . . . Good teams become great ones when the members trust each other enough to surrender the 'me' for the

'we'. Individuals are required to surrender their self-interest for the greater good so that the whole adds up to more than the sum of its parts.

(Jackson 2004, p. 25)

In addition to a focus on the increasing challenge of developing cohesion in sport teams, there has also been an increase in interest in recent years on the role cohesion might play in the exercise setting. With the rise of obesity (Centers for Disease Control and Prevention, 2006), greater emphasis is being placed on getting people fit and healthy. Perhaps one of the most well known group fitness initiatives of the past decade is American talk-show host Rosie O'Donnell's Chub Club. Overweight viewers were encouraged to form local groups of several people who wanted to eat less, exercise more and become fitter. There were monthly group weigh-ins to monitor the group's progress and groups losing the most weight were rewarded. The monthly updates revealed the powerful role the group's unity played in losing weight and becoming healthy.

The above examples clearly emphasize the importance and the challenge of creating a cohesive group. Cohesion is one of those often talked about yet difficult to define intangibles of a group. This chapter provides an overview of the past, present and possible future of cohesion research in the domain of sport and exercise. In the first two sections, the definition, conceptual framework and measurement of cohesion in both sport and exercise are presented. The third and fourth sections contain a literature review of cohesion in sport and exercise settings. In the fifth section, practical implications of these findings are discussed. Future directions and recommendations are provided in the final section.

Definition of cohesion

Cohesion is considered a distinguishing attribute of successful groups, whether it be in the domain of work, military, sport, or exercise. It plays such an important role in group dynamics that some social scientists have called cohesion the most important small group variable (Golembiewski, 1962; Lott and Lott, 1965). As a result, researchers in several domains such as sport psychology, social psychology, military psychology, organizational psychology and educational psychology have studied the construct.

Across domains, cohesion has proven to be a difficult concept to define given that it is a theoretical construct – an abstract, general scientific term that is not housed in any specific domain or school of thought. In an early classic definition, group cohesion was defined as 'the total field of forces which act on members to remain in a group' (Festinger *et al.*, 1950, p. 164). Groups that contain members strongly attracted to the collective stay intact; those that do not dissolve. Other researchers have defined cohesion in terms of the commitment of members to a group task (Goodman *et al.*, 1987).

Over the years, the definition of cohesion evolved to incorporate both the factors that attracted members to a group and also the group's goals and objectives. Thus, a relatively recent accepted definition in group dynamics is that cohesion is 'a dynamic process which is reflected in the tendency for a group to stick together and remain united in the pursuit of its instrumental objectives and/or for the satisfaction of member affective needs' (Carron *et al.*, 1998, p. 213). This definition highlights four main characteristics of cohesion:

- *Multidimensional*: There are numerous factors that cause a group to remain united and these factors can vary from group to group.
- *Dynamic*: Cohesion can vary across time; it is not a stable personality-like group trait.
- *Instrumental*: Cohesion reflects the reason(s) a group forms and remains together.
- *Affective*: Cohesion is associated with positive affect.

This definition and nature of cohesion form the basis for a conceptualization of the construct and, ultimately, its measurement.

Conceptual framework and measurement of cohesion

Considering the difficulty in obtaining consensus for a definition of cohesion, it is not surprising that its measurement has posed similar problems. To overcome these problems, Carron *et al.* (1985) developed a conceptual model to represent cohesion in sport teams. As illustrated in Figure 7.1, Carron *et al.* proposed that each team member develops and holds perceptions about his/her team that are related to the group as a totality and to the manner in which the group satisfies personal needs and objectives. In turn, the strength of these perceptions, singly or in combination, account for why groups stick together. These perceptions are labeled:

- *Individual Attractions to the Group*, which reflects the individual's perceptions about personal motivations acting to attract and to retain him/her in the group, as well as his/her personal feelings about the group.
- *Group Integration*, which reflects the individual's perceptions about the closeness, similarity and bonding within the group as a whole, as well as the degree of unification of the group.

As Figure 7.1 also illustrates, Carron *et al.* suggested that there are two fundamental foci to a group member's perceptions:

- A *Task* orientation representing a general orientation or motivation towards achieving the group's instrumental objectives.

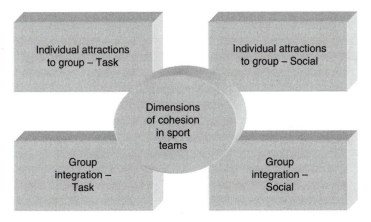

Figure 7.1 A conceptual model of group cohesion. (From Carron *et al.*, 1985, p. 248. Reprinted with permission from Human Kinetics.)

- A *Social* orientation representing a general orientation or motivation toward developing and maintaining social relationships and activities within the group.

The result is four manifestations of cohesiveness: Group Integration-Task (GI-T), Group Integration-Social (GI-S), Individual Attractions to the Group-Task (ATG-T) and Individual Attractions to the Group-Social (ATG-S). This conceptual model resulted in the development of the Group Environment Questionnaire (GEQ: Carron *et al.*, 1985).

The GEQ was developed to measure cohesion in sport teams. Because exercise classes differ from sport teams in task, social, individual and group level characteristics, the original GEQ was modified for use in the exercise domain. In later years the Physical Activity Group Environment Questionnaire (PAGEQ: Estabrooks and Carron, 2000) was developed specifically to assess cohesiveness in older adult exercise samples. Both the GEQ and PAGEQ have been found to be internally consistent and to have sound predictive, concurrent, content and factorial validity (Carron *et al.*, 1998; Estabrooks and Carron, 2000).

Research on cohesion in sport teams

The development of the GEQ resulted in a substantial amount of research investigating the correlates of cohesion in sport settings. For convenience sake, these correlates typically have been categorized into four categories: (1) environmental factors, (2) personal factors, (3) leadership factors and (4) group (team) factors. Consistent with the notion of correlation, no conclusions about causation are possible. However, it is important to note that the relationships between cohesion and these correlates may be (are likely) reciprocal. For example, as is discussed below, cohesion is correlated with role acceptance. It is probable that cohesion increases role acceptance and role acceptance increases cohesiveness. A brief overview of some of the research within each of the four categories is provided here.

Environmental factors

Two environmental factors that are related to cohesion are the size of the team and the level of competition. As a general rule, cohesion decreases as group size increases (Carron *et al.*, 2005). One explanation for this finding is that as group size increases it becomes more difficult to communicate effectively and coordinate team activities (Steiner, 1972).

Widmeyer *et al.* (1990) carried out two studies that demonstrated cohesion-size relationship. In the first study, 3-on-3 recreational basketball league teams were formed consisting of 3, 6, or 9 members. Results indicated that task cohesion decreased as the roster size increased and that social cohesion was the highest in the 6-member team. In the second study, Widmeyer and colleagues investigated the relationship between group size and cohesion in a recreational volleyball league. Teams competed in 3 versus 3, 6 versus 6 and 12 versus 12 competitions. The level of group cohesion was greatest in the 3-member teams and as team size increased there was a progressive decrease in cohesiveness.

The level of competition has been found to be related to the amount of group cohesion present (Granito and Rainey, 1988; Gruber and Gray, 1982). Specifically, cohesion decreases as level of competition increases. Granito and Rainey (1988) assessed the cohesion of high school and college football teams and found that task cohesion was greater in high school teams. Similarly, Gruber and Gray found that social cohesion was higher in elementary school and junior high school basketball teams than in senior high school teams. Carron *et al.* (2005) suggested that perhaps cohesion is higher in lower level teams because consensus regarding task and social unity are achieved more easily with less experienced athletes.

Personal factors

Personal factors influencing cohesion revolve around individual characteristics such as demographic attributes, cognitions, affect and behavior. Two important correlates in this category are individual satisfaction and adherence behavior. Individual athlete satisfaction has been identified as a significant personal factor related to cohesion (Carron and Chelladurai, 1981; Martens and Peterson, 1971; Williams and Hacker, 1982). For example, Martens and Peterson (1971) found that individuals on highly cohesive basketball teams reported more individual satisfaction than individuals on less cohesive teams. Consequently, the authors proposed that cohesion, satisfaction and performance are related to each other in a circular fashion. That is, the presence of cohesiveness contributes to athlete satisfaction and, ultimately, to team success. In turn, team success produces higher satisfaction in the individual athlete and this leads to the development of a greater sense of cohesiveness. Williams and Hacker (1982) tested the cause–effect relationship among performance, cohesion and satisfaction in women's intercollegiate field hockey and found support for Martens and Peterson's proposal.

Given that cohesion is the construct representing the tendency for individuals to remain together, it is not surprising that cohesion is related to adherence in sport teams (Brawley *et al.*, 1988, Study 1; Prapavessis and Carron, 1997; Widmeyer *et al.*, 1988, Study 2). Research has shown that athletes who hold the perception that their team is more cohesive are more likely to be on time for practice, to be present at practices and games (Carron *et al.*, 1988, Study 1) and to feel that their team is able to withstand the negative impact of disruptive events (Brawley *et al.*, 1988, Study 1).

Leadership factors

Two elements of leadership that are related to the development of group cohesion are the leader's behavior and decision style. Concerning a coach's behavior, Gardner *et al.* (1996) and Westre and Weiss (1991) found that coaches could promote higher levels of task cohesion for their players by using more training and instruction, democratic behavior, social support, positive feedback styles and decreasing the use of autocratic coaching strategies. More recently, Turman (2003) investigated the impact of coaching techniques on the team cohesion of university athletes. Results identified numerous techniques that deter (i.e. inequity, embarrassment and ridicule) and promote (i.e. bragging, sarcasm and teasing, motivational speeches, quality of opponent, athlete directed techniques, team prayer and dedication) team cohesion levels. These results indicate the instrumental role a coach's behavior has in the development of team cohesion.

Concerning decision style, stronger perceptions of cohesiveness are present when a more participative (democratic) approach is used to arrive at a decision. For example,

Brawley *et al.* (1993) found that athletes who had greater participation in team goal setting also possessed a stronger sense of task and social cohesion. Other researchers, such as Kozub (1993) and Westre and Weiss (1991) reported that athletes who perceived their coach to use a democratic style also perceived the group to be more task cohesive.

Team factors

Team factors are associated with the group as a totality. The team factors discussed here include roles, norms, collective efficacy and performance. In both team and individual sports, various aspects of role involvement and cohesion are strongly related (Brawley *et al.*, 1987). For example, Brawley *et al.* reported correlations of 0.56, 0.63 and 0.57 between task cohesion (i.e. Group-Integration-Task) and role clarity, role acceptance and role performance respectively for individual sport athletes. For team sport athletes, the comparable correlational values were 0.38, 0.49 and 0.43. Furthermore, recent research conducted by Eys and Carron (2001) found a negative relationship between role ambiguity and cohesion; that is, as role ambiguity increased task cohesion decreased.

In contrast, research on cohesion and conformity to group norms has yielded a positive relationship. Conformity to group norms is greater in teams high in cohesion. A classic study by Schacter *et al.* (1951) examined the norm of productivity in high- and low-cohesive groups in a laboratory experiment that involved cutting cardboard squares. The results revealed that high-cohesive groups conformed to the norm more than the low-cohesive group, independent of whether the norm was for high or low productivity. Similar findings have been found with sport teams (e.g. Gammage *et al.*, 2001; Kim, 1995). For example, Gammage and her colleagues found performance norms to be positively related to cohesion.

Collective-efficacy is the 'sense of collective competence shared among individuals when allocating, coordinating and integrating their resources in a successful concerted response to specific situational demands' (Zaccaro *et al.*, 1995, p. 309). Recent research has found collective efficacy to be positively related to group cohesion. For example, Spink (1990) found that perceptions of cohesion were higher for elite athletes and recreational volleyball players who perceived high collective efficacy in their respective teams. Subsequent research (e.g. Kozub and McDonnell, 2001; Paskevich, 1995), produced similar findings and also found that task measures of cohesion were stronger predictors of collective efficacy than social measures of cohesion. Furthermore, a recent study by Heuze *et al.* (2006) investigated the mediating effects in the relationships between collective efficacy, cohesion and performance in professional basketball players. The results showed collective efficacy as a mediator for the performance – group integration-task relationship. That is, athletes' individual performances contributed to their perceptions of collective efficacy, which in turn contributed to their perceptions of task cohesion. Likewise, task cohesion was found to be a mediator of the performance – collective efficacy relationship. Thus, athlete's individual performances influenced their perceptions of group integration-task, which in turn influenced perceived collective efficacy.

As the introduction to the present chapter highlighted, one of the most important correlates of cohesion is team performance. Also, from the perspective of causation, does cohesion breed success? Or does success breed cohesion? The relationship between group cohesion and team success has been a heavily debated topic in the sport sciences for years. Conclusions from early research seemed equivocal. To overcome these inconsistencies, Carron *et al.* (2002) carried out a meta-analysis of 46 studies that examined the association between team cohesiveness and team success in sport. An overall moderate to large positive relationship was found. Furthermore, both task and social cohesion were positively related to team success and team success was positively related to both task and social cohesion. The results suggest that highly successful teams are more likely to develop a sense of togetherness. On the other hand, unsuccessful teams that begin to develop greater cohesiveness should increase their chances of becoming successful.

Research on cohesion in exercise groups

In addition to the interest in cohesion in sport, in recent years there has been an increased interest in the role that cohesion plays in the exercise domain. The literature examining the impact of group cohesion on exercise participation has also been based on the conceptual model of group cohesion developed by Carron *et al.* (1985). Similar to sport, the factors related to group cohesion in exercise groups can be considered in relation to four categories: (1) environmental factors, (2) personal factors, (3) leadership factors and (4) group (class) factors.

Environmental factors

One environmental factor influencing cohesion in exercise groups is the size of the physical activity class. As mentioned earlier, in sport teams an increase in size generally results in a decrease in cohesion. Does the same hold true for physical activity classes? In a series of studies, Carron and Spink (1995) examined the relationship between class size and perceptions of cohesion. Group cohesion was assessed at different times in small and large physical activity classes. When cohesion was assessed at the beginning of the program, only individual attractions to the group components of cohesion could effectively distinguish members of small and large groups. However, when cohesion was assessed later in the program (i.e. the 8th week of a 13-week program), the researchers determined that the group integration components of cohesion could discriminate members. In both cases participants in large groups held lower perceptions of cohesion. Therefore, similar to sport teams, members of small exercise groups held stronger perceptions of cohesion than do members of large groups.

Personal factors

Personal factors related to cohesion in the exercise setting consist of individual characteristics such as demographic attributes, behavior, affect and cognitions. A considerable amount of research in organizational psychology has investigated the role that diversity in such characteristics plays in the dynamics of task-oriented groups (Jackson *et al.*, 1995; Webber and Donahue, 2001). Recently Shapcott *et al.* (2006) examined the relationship of group member diversity in task-related attributes (i.e. diversity in self-efficacy, in level of previous physical activity and in personal goals) and task-unrelated attributes (i.e. diversity in ethnicity and in gender) to task cohesiveness and task performance in walking groups. Insofar as the task-related attributes were concerned, only diversity in level of previous physical activity was significantly related to task cohesion – as diversity increased, task cohesion decreased. Insofar as the task-unrelated attributes were concerned, only diversity in gender was related to task cohesion – as gender diversity in the composition of the group increased, task cohesion decreased.

The most frequently examined personal variable in cohesion research in the exercise setting has been adherence behavior. In their meta-analysis, Carron *et al.* (1996), reported that being in a highly task cohesive class setting (i.e. versus classes lower in task cohesiveness) had a moderate to large effect on adherence (effect size = 0.62).

The research included in the Carron *et al.* meta-analysis had been conducted with university-aged students to young adults. Thus, Estabrooks and Carron (1999a,b), carried out research with older adults. Not surprisingly, Estabrooks and Carron found in both studies that a positive relationship also exists between task and social cohesion and attendance and dropout behavior in older adults.

Furthermore, a recent meta-analysis by Burke *et al.* (2006) examined the effectiveness of group versus individual interventions utilized in the physical activity literature in relation to a wide variety of outcomes. Four physical activity contexts were examined. These included (a) home-based programs not involving contact from researchers or health professionals, (b) home-based programs that involved some contact, (c) standard ('typical') exercise classes and (d) exercise classes where group-dynamics principles were used to increase cohesiveness ('true groups'). With regard to adherence behavior, exercising in a true group was superior to exercising in a standard exercise class, which in turn, did not differ from exercising at home with contact. In addition, exercising at home with contact was superior to exercising at home without contact in terms of adherence to the exercise program.

In sum, these findings provide evidence for the conclusion that individuals are more likely to adhere to an exercise program if they exercise in a group. Furthermore, the greater task and social bonds that exist between exercisers the increased likelihood for adherence.

Leadership factors

Researchers have also been interested in the role that exercise leaders play in developing class cohesion. For example, in the Carron *et al.* (1996) meta-analysis discussed above, exercise leaders were found to have a small to moderate effect on adherence behavior (effect size = 0.31). Loughead *et al.* (2001) extended these findings by examining whether older adults' perceptions of class cohesion served as a mediator between exercise class leader behavior and adherence in exercise programs. They reported that the leader behaviors of enthusiasm, motivation and availability were positively related to task cohesion. The authors further suggested that for older adults, these three leader behaviors may 'foster an environment that promotes adherence by making the task more attractive (i.e. ATG-T) and increasing the perception of class unity around common objectives (i.e. GI-T)' (Loughead *et al.*, 2001. p.571). Therefore, similar to coaches, exercise leaders play an important role in developing group cohesion.

Group factors

Similar to sport, group factors in the exercise setting refer to group structure and group processes, such as group goals. The role of group goals on group performance has been well documented in work and sport groups. For example, the results of a meta-analysis conducted by O'Leary-Kelly *et al.* (1994) showed that the mean performance level of work groups that set goals was almost one standard deviation higher than that of groups that did not set goals. Furthermore, sport researchers have found that group goals not only increase athlete commitment but can also increase cohesion and performance (Weingart, 1992; Widmeyer and DuCharme, 1997).

A study conducted by Heath *et al.* (1991) provides some evidence of the positive effects of group goal setting in an exercise environment. Participants with diabetes took part in a 10-week weight-loss competition. Individuals were placed on teams and group goals were established. Each week, the teams' total weight loss was calculated. The results showed that group exercise programs were effective in aiding individuals in weight loss. Heath *et al.* suggested that group exercise competitions are successful in terms of long-term behavior change because they provide increased social support which leads to enhanced interest and commitment (e.g. Brownell and Felix, 1987).

More recently, Burke *et al.* (2007) also examined the relationship between group goal setting and team performance in an exercise setting. Specifically, close to 6,500 participants were recruited and registered in teams of 6 for a community-based, 8-week walking program. The teams were instructed to develop group goals for the number of miles to be walked over the course of the program. The results revealed a positive moderate relationship between group goal setting and team performance ($r = 0.44$), indicating that group goals are indeed effective in physical activity contexts.

Practical implications and intervention strategies

What can be taken from the above discussion? Babe Ruth, the famous New York Yankees baseball player observed:

> The way a team plays as a whole determines its success. You may have the greatest bunch of individual stars in the world, but if they don't play together, the club won't be worth a dime.
>
> (Quote Garden, 2007)

Ruth's comment highlights the fact that it is not merely the talent of each individual on a team that leads to success; rather it is how effectively those individuals are able to work together. In other words, success is not necessarily inevitable, even when a team consists of several 'all-star' players.

As was discussed earlier in this chapter, enhanced group cohesiveness – in the task and/or social aspects of the group – is positively related to team performance in sport settings (Carron *et al.*, 2002). Similarly, in the physical activity domain, perceptions of group cohesion have been shown to be related to increased adherence behaviors (e.g. greater attendance, fewer dropouts) in a number of settings including universities (Carron and Spink, 1993; Carron *et al.*, 1988; Spink and Carron, 1992, 1993, 1994, Study 1), private fitness facilities (Annesi, 1999; Spink and Carron, 1994, Study 2) and community centers (Estabrooks and Carron, 1999a). Thus, it is clear that in both sport and exercise settings enhancing group unity is important for successful sport performance and increased adherence to exercise programs.

Perhaps the most widely used method for increasing the level of cohesiveness present in any type of group, whether in the military, business, healthcare, sport, or exercise domain, is *team building*. Within the organizational psychology literature, it has been suggested that most team building interventions have focused primarily:

> on improving team operations or processes. Group processes can be improved by removing barriers, clarifying roles, improving interpersonal relations, establishing agreed upon goals, or through other targeted intervention strategies.
>
> (Tannenbaum *et al.*, 1992, p. 119)

This statement further supports the notion that team building influences team performance via enhanced team synergy or team cohesion. Likewise, in the sport and exercise psychology domain, it has been suggested that the fundamental objective of team building interventions is to enhance group effectiveness by increasing perceptions of group cohesion (Carron *et al.*, 1997). Thus, the basis of any team building intervention is the expectation that the group will become more unified (Carron *et al.*, 1997).

Approaches to team building

Team building interventions are generally implemented using either an indirect or a direct approach. In workplace settings, team building interventions are typically *direct* in nature such that a team building specialist is hired to work directly with employees in an attempt to increase group unity. Conversely, in sport and exercise settings, an *indirect* approach to team building is more often adopted (Carron *et al.*, 1997). An indirect approach is one in which the team building specialist works with the coach or instructor in the development of relevant team building strategies and the coach or instructor then delivers the intervention to his or her team or exercise class. This is considered an indirect approach because the intervention must filter through the coach or instructor before reaching participants (Carron *et al.*, 2005).

In their research in both sport and exercise settings, Carron and his colleagues (e.g. Carron and Spink, 1993; Carron and Widmeyer, 1987; Estabrooks and Carron, 1999a, Study 2; Prapavessis *et al.*, 1996; Spink and Carron, 1993) have successfully utilized a four-stage model of team building based on the indirect approach discussed above. The first three stages – the *introductory stage*, the *conceptual stage* and the *practical stage* – are typically carried out in a workshop setting with the sport psychology specialist and the coaches/instructors. The fourth and final stage – the *intervention stage* – involves the delivery of the intervention by the coach or fitness instructor to the members of the team or class.

Essentially, the purpose of the introductory stage is to provide the coach/instructor with a general understanding of the benefits of group cohesion (e.g. increased team performance/class attendance). In the second stage – the conceptual stage – a theoretical model for the implementation of a team building intervention is introduced to the coach/instructor. This model generally consists of three categories that are important to consider when attempting to increase the level of cohesiveness in a group. These categories are the *group's environment*, the *group's structure* and the *group's processes*. Within each of these categories, specific factors that can lead to effective group functioning have also been identified. For instance, the group environment category contains a factor entitled 'distinctiveness.' This relates to the idea that group members are likely to feel more united if their team or class is distinctive or clearly identifiable in some unique way. The group structure category contains two factors that are important for group functioning and cohesiveness – 'group norms' and 'group positions'. Finally, the group processes category contains two factors entitled 'interaction and communication' and 'sacrifice'. These factors were developed based on group dynamics theory which suggests that cohesion is intensified when standards of behavior and group roles are clearly outlined, when group interaction and communication are facilitated and when group members are encouraged to make personal sacrifices for other group members.

Using the model described above as a framework, the team building specialist and the coach/exercise leader then work together to generate specific strategies that could be used to enhance the cohesiveness of the team or exercise class. This is the practical stage. Finally, in the intervention stage, the coach or instructor implements, maintains and consistently re-evaluates the team building strategies identified in the practical stage on an ongoing basis for the duration of the season/program.

Team building strategies in sport and exercise

When attempting to implement team building interventions, coaches and exercise instructors face a number of challenges. Coaches of any sport (and at any competitive level) must use their expertise to lead a group of individual athletes with different and sometimes conflicting temperaments, abilities, goals and attitudes into a single cohesive and unified team (Schmidt *et al.*, 2005). Exercise leaders, on the other hand, face a unique situation in that often, the group of individuals attending an exercise class may differ from one session to the next. Also, people exercise for individual, not group outcomes. Thus, although the benefits of cohesion have been reliably demonstrated, creating a sense of 'team' in a sport or exercise group is not always an easy task.

Despite some of the challenges associated with enhancing group cohesion, there are a number of team building strategies that have been successfully used in both sport and exercise settings. A number of these strategies are presented in Table 7.1. Additionally, specific team building techniques that have been used to: (a) facilitate group goal setting, (b) enhance group interaction and communication and (c) promote a sense of group identity are discussed in greater detail below.

Group goal setting

Sport

The process of enhancing cohesiveness is best initiated by the development of clear goals for the team (Schmidt *et al.*, 2005). To provide a foundation and focus for the team goal setting process, Bull *et al.* (1996) have suggested that coaches initiate a process called *team profiling*. The specific steps associated with team profiling are as follows:

1   Have all athletes collectively identify a team they consider to be 'ideal'.
2   Ask athletes to brainstorm to come up with a list of qualities (e.g. mental, physical, technical) they feel best describe this ideal team.
3   Have the athletes rate the ideal team (on a scale from 1 to 10) on each of the qualities listed, producing a target or 'ideal score'.
4   Ask the team to collectively arrive at a 'current score' (i.e. a score from 1 to 10) that reflects their *own* team's level for each of the qualities listed.

Table 7.1 Examples of team building strategies for coaches and exercise class instructors

Factor		Intervention strategies
Distinctiveness	Sport	Provide the team with unique identifiers (e.g. sweatsuits, shirts, logos, etc.). Emphasize unique traditions and/or history associated with the team.[a,c]
	Exercise	Have a group name. Make up a group T-shirt. Hand out neon headbands and/or shoelaces. Make up posters or slogans for the class.[a]
Individual positions	Sport	Create a team structure in which there is a clear differentiation in team positions/roles. Clarify and discuss role expectations for all athletes.[c] [f]Ensure that players accept their roles.[f]
	Exercise	Use three areas of the pool depending on fitness level. Have signs to label parts of the group. Use specific positions for low-, medium-, and high-impact exercisers. Let them pick their own spot and encourage them to remain in it for the duration of the program.[a]
Group norms	Sport	Establish positive group standards. [b]Show all team members how the group's standards contribute to effective team performance and a greater sense of team unity. Point out to team members how their individual contributions contribute to team success. Reward team members who adhere to the group's standards.[f]
	Exercise	Establish positive group standards. Encourage exercise leaders in the class to set high standards of achievement.[a] Have members introduce each other to increase social aspects. Establish a goal to lose weight together. Promote a smart work ethic.[f]
Individual sacrifices	Sport	Encourage important team members to make sacrifices for the team (e.g. ask a veteran athlete to sit out to give a novice athlete more playing time).[c]
	Exercise	Use music in aqua fitness (some may not want music). Ask two or three people for a goal for the day. Ask regulars to help new people and encourage becoming fitness friends. Ask people who are not concerned with weight loss to make a sacrifice for the group on some days (more aerobics) and people who are concerned with weight loss to make a sacrifice on other days (more mat work).[a]
Interaction and communication	Sport	Provide opportunities for athlete input. Reduce uncertainty by being supportive. Understand that there are individual differences in the way athletes respond to you. Be a good role model.[e] Have all players identify (on paper) why they want their fellow players on the team, then create a summary sheet for each player.[d]
	Exercise	Use partner work and have them introduce themselves. Introduce the person on the right and left. Work in groups of five and take turns showing a move. Use partner activities.[a]

Adapted from [a]Carron and Spink, 1993 and Spink and Carron, 1993; [b]Zander, 1982; [c]Bull *et al.*, 1996; [d]Munroe et al., 2002; [e]Yukelson, 2006; [f]Weinberg and Gould, 2003.

Note: From Eys *et al.* (2005, p. 169). Reprinted with permission from McGraw-Hill.

5   Calculate a discrepancy or 'difference score' by subtracting the current score from the ideal score for each quality.
6   Highlight the qualities with the largest discrepancy scores. These qualities will then be the focus for team goal setting.

Once two or three specific target areas have been identified using the team profiling technique, the process of team goal setting can begin. In addition to the acknowledgement that all group goals should be challenging, specific and realistic, Widmeyer and Ducharme (1997) have outlined six additional principles for coaches interested in establishing a goal setting program with their team. These include the following:

1   Set long-term goals (e.g. for the season) first and then set short-term goals.
2   Develop strategies and establish clear paths to reach the long-term goals (this will involve setting several short-term goals).
3   Involve all athletes in the team goal setting process.
4   Monitor progress and provide regular feedback concerning team goals. It is also useful to display goals and team statistics in a highly visible location such as a locker room.
5   Provide public praise for team progress (rather than or in combination with individual athlete incentives).
6   Foster a sense of team confidence/collective efficacy (see Chow and Feltz, Ch. 12, this volume) toward team goals (e.g. schedule exhibition games against lesser-skilled opponents, adequately prepare the team and develop realistic expectations for team outcomes).

Exercise

As mentioned above, setting group goals in exercise settings presents a unique challenge. In many cases, the group or 'team' of individuals in a class differs from one day to the next. Further, class members typically have little concern for the success of the collective. However, as the research evidence discussed above shows, the use of group goal setting in exercise classes is also likely to be effective.

So what does this mean for the 'typical' exercise class setting? A group goal setting strategy that was used successfully to enhance task cohesion in exercise classes (Estabrooks and Carron, 1999a, Study 2) involved equating 10 min of class participation to 1 km of walking (e.g. across the state/province). Participants then set a collective goal for the total number of kilometers the class would 'walk' over a 4-week period. Thus, high participation rates were necessary for all class members in order to achieve the target distance set for the class.

Alternatively, in a situation where weight loss is a group goal, the exercise leader could focus on the total number of pounds lost within the group as a collective. Then class members could (confidentially) record and submit their weekly weight loss/gain and the instructor could create a chart displaying the results for the class as a whole. This type of approach was recently used in the American reality television series 'The Biggest Loser', a weight-loss competition involving 12–14 participants who competed against one another to lose the most weight and to win US$250,000. During the 'team-based phase' of the series (i.e. before there are too few competitors to make up two groups), competitors were divided into two teams and each was assigned a personal trainer. A weekly weigh-in was used to determine which team lost the greatest percentage of total team weight and the team with the lowest overall weight loss had to vote one group member off the show (Wikipedia, 2007).

Weinberg and Gould (2003) have also suggested the use of a goal-setting staircase that includes a series of short-term goals (one on each step) leading to an 'ultimate' long-term goal. Thus, for example, short-term group goals could be set for the amount of weight lifted per week, distance walked per week, or weight lost per week. Similarly, a goal-setting mountain could be used whereby exercisers would be encouraged to 'climb the mountain of lifestyle change' together, in order to achieve a final group goal (Weinberg and Gould, 2003).

Creating opportunities for group interaction and communication

Sport

Effective communication and interaction are essential for team success (Yukelson, 2006). Therefore, athletes and the coaching staff must maintain open communication channels so that problems, suggestions and feedback can be discussed in a democratic environment (Bull *et al.*, 1996). However, creating opportunities for regular team interaction and communication presents a challenge for many coaches. According to Yukelson (1997), coaches should schedule regular team meetings to openly and honestly discuss team-related issues. Such discussions are extremely valuable. It has been recommended that these discussions take place prior to or following practice sessions rather than immediately before a competition (Bull *et al.*, 1996). In his widely-cited work on communication in sport, Yukelson (2006) has presented several recommendations for enhancing coach–athlete communications. The following list includes a number of these suggestions:

1   Coaches should aim to consistently use effective communication techniques which include being sincere, honest, genuine, fair and consistent.
2   Coaches should strive to be empathetic by showing genuine concern for and actively listening to athletes' feelings and concerns.
3   Coaches should encourage and create a supportive atmosphere in which praise, encouragement and positive reinforcement are plentiful.
4   Coaches must be aware of their nonverbal communication skills and consequently, the messages they may be sending to athletes.
5   Coaches should attempt to provide clear rationales for why athletes should or should not engage in specific behaviors.

Finally, when carried out in a comfortable and supportive environment, team communication and interaction may also be facilitated through the use of the goal setting strategies discussed above.

Exercise

As was pointed out earlier, the Carron and Spink (1993) conceptual framework for team building interventions acknowledges that group interaction and communication also contribute directly to perceptions of cohesion in exercise contexts. Although communication and interaction occur naturally in most settings including exercise classes, the instructor can employ strategies to facilitate this process (Carron *et al.*, 2003). Specifically, participants can be encouraged to introduce themselves to other exercisers and partner or group work can be worked into the exercise routine on a regular basis.

Additionally, many of Yukelson's (2006) recommendations for enhancing coach–athlete communications in sport can also be applied in an exercise setting. For instance, the exercise leader should strive to be sincere, honest, genuine and consistent and he or she should show concern for class participants. Instructors should also be aware of their non-verbal communication skills and strive to create a supportive atmosphere that is rich in praise, encouragement and positive reinforcement.

Creating a sense of group identity

Sport

It has been suggested that the presence of team distinctiveness or group identity contributes to perceptions of cohesion in sport teams (e.g. Prapavessis *et al.*, 1996). Feelings of distinctiveness are somewhat inherent in sport, whereby team uniforms, initiation rites, team rituals and the amount of time spent together as a team all contribute to a sense of 'groupness' (Weinberg and Gould, 2003). In their recommendations for team building in sport, Bull *et al.* (1996) have suggested that coaches can create or enhance team identity by:

1   Gathering all athletes together prior to competition.
2   Setting up residential training camps.
3   Providing the team with unique identifiers such as shirts, logos, mottos and/or identical sweat suits.
4   Emphasizing unique history and/or traditions within the team.
5   Recognizing the importance of pride in the team and striving to develop its sources.

Exercise

Exercise classes also can be made distinctive from other classes or groups (Carron *et al.*, 2003). For example, instructors can work with participants to develop a group name and the class can be encouraged to wear distinctive and matching apparel such as group T-shirts, shoelaces and headbands (Carron and Spink, 1993). Personal trainers can also create unique T-shirts for exercisers training at the same fitness center or with the same trainer (Weinberg and Gould, 2003). Additionally, Carron and Spink (1993) have suggested that class instructors create unique slogans and/or posters for their class. Finally, utilizing some of the group goal setting ideas discussed above (e.g. creating and displaying posters/charts showing group successes) may also be effective in terms of creating a sense of distinctiveness and class pride.

Future directions and recommendations

Coming to an understanding in a domain of inquiry – group dynamics in general or cohesion in sport and exercise specifically – involves inquiry through research. In regard to the foundation for research, the famous British scientist, Sir William Thomson (Lord Kelvin), emphasized that 'when you can measure what you are speaking about and express it in numbers, you know something about it; but when you cannot measure it, when you cannot express it in numbers, your knowledge is of a meagre and unsatisfactory kind' (Thompson, 1891, p. 80).

It should be noted that Lord Kelvin was not denigrating the qualitative approach to research – he was a physical scientist and measurement was essential to the paradigms he used. Further, the qualitative approach has been used effectively to provide valuable insights into the dynamics of sport teams (e.g. Birrell and Richter, 1994; Eys *et al.*, 2005; Hardy *et al.*, 2005) and to answer some meaningful questions. Nonetheless, however, it is informative to consider another observation by Thompson (1891) that if you cannot measure it, you cannot improve it. In short, it is difficult (at best) to know the state of a group and/or whether an intervention such as team building is necessary or even essential if we have no assessment tools.

In the introduction to this chapter, we pointed out that cohesion plays such an important role in group dynamics that some social scientists have called it the most important small group variable (Golembiewski, 1962; Lott and Lott, 1965). It influences and is influenced by a myriad of small group variables. With only few exceptions, few of the small group variables influencing cohesion can be assessed reliably and validly. Thus, one fundamental need corresponds to the development of psychometrically robust protocols/inventories to measure theorized *sources* of group cohesion in sport and exercise.

Sport

One construct, important in the dynamics of sport teams, for which an inventory or measurement protocol should be developed is *group norms*. Norms represent the standards for behavior expected of members of a team. They are informal; that is, they are not rules or policies although they could evolve (a) around the importance attached to team rules or policies, or (b) into team rules once they have been decided upon or formalized. For example, the team may have a policy that members must be in bed prior to midnight on the eve of competition. However, the athletes may come to expect that team-mates need not adhere to the rule. This latter expectation would be a group norm.

Carron and his colleagues spent a considerable amount of time attempting to identify important norms in sport teams (Munroe *et al.*, 1999) and then to develop an inventory to assess those norms (Carron *et al.*, 1999). That inventory was subsequently used in research projects (e.g. Colman and Carron, 2001). However, because of psychometric concerns, development of the inventory has halted. Thus, we have no means of assessing group norms for productivity or civility or punctuality or attendance and so on.

Recently, however, Eys *et al.* (2006b) examined group norms in an exercise setting using an adapted version of Carron *et al.*'s survey. Interestingly, the findings provided preliminary evidence for the presence of normative expectations for communication, support, effort and attendance in an exercise environment. A positive relationship between exercise norms and task cohesion was also found. Nonetheless, it is evident that further research is necessary in both sport and exercise settings.

A second construct, important in the dynamics of sport teams, for which an inventory or measurement protocol should be developed is *role acceptance*. Role acceptance has been defined as 'the degree to which an athlete perceives his or her own expectations for role responsibilities as similar to and agreeable with, the expectations for role responsibilities determined by his or her role senders' (Eys *et al.*, 2006a, p. 245). Carron *et al.* (2005) have suggested that:

> overall, the degree to which all athletes on a team accept and attempt to perform their role responsibilities (regardless of the prestige associated with the role) is absolutely vital to the proper functioning of the group as a whole. It is likely that this element of role involvement is the most critical in terms of how well the group performs together.
>
> (Carron *et al.*, 2005, p. 166)

Most competitive sport involves an autocracy where, largely, what the coach wants is what happens. So if an athlete is assigned to a role, he or she has little choice but to carry out the responsibility. However, an athlete who begrudgingly carries out a role without full enthusiasm represents a cancer in the team. Without some way of assessing athlete role acceptance, that cancer can go undetected.

A third construct, important in the dynamics of sport teams, for which an inventory or measurement protocol should be developed is *status congruency*. Status differences in any group are inevitable. Individuals differ in a variety of characteristics to which, depending upon the group, others attach importance. Some of these characteristics, for example, are age, experience, ability and group role. The inevitability of status differences is not necessarily a problem on every sport team. What could be a problem, as Carron *et al.* (2005) pointed out,

> is a discrepancy in group members' perceptions about where they lie in the status hierarchy relative to where they perceive they belong. Research has shown that a lack of consensus on status ranking within a group contributes to conflicting expectations, feelings of injustice and discomfort . . .
>
> (Carron *et al.*, 2005, p. 142)

To paraphrase Lord Kelvin, if we are unable to assess the degree to which status congruency is absent (that is, is a problem) on a team, we are unable to take steps to improve the situation.

A fourth important need is an inventory to assess cohesiveness in youth sport teams. The Group Environment Questionnaire was developed for teams populated by athletes 18 years of age and older. Many of the items are nonsensical for athletes considerably younger. Yet if we are to gain a better understanding of the dynamics of youth sport teams – and such negative outcomes as drop out behavior (the ultimate reflection of low cohesiveness) – we must be able to assess athlete perceptions of cohesiveness.

Exercise

Historically, the exercise leader has been identified as the single most important agent insofar as adherence in structured programs is concerned (Franklin, 1984; Oldridge, 1977). In fact, Oldridge (1977) proposed that leaders are 'the pivot on which the success or failure of a program will depend' (p. 86). Nonetheless, as Remers *et al.* (1995) noted, although 'researchers cite leadership as a factor that influences exercise, rarely do they study or even control for it' (p. 40). One major reason there may be a paucity of research on exercise leadership is that published inventories used to assess leader behavior in an exercise setting are not available.

In their research on leadership in exercise settings, Loughead and Carron (2004) used the Chang (1998) Scale of Quality in Fitness Services (SQFS) inventory. This 45-item inventory assesses nine dimensions of fitness services. Three of those dimensions pertain to fitness leader behavior; commitment to service quality, interpersonal interaction and task interaction. Although the SQFS appears promising, the scale has not yet been published.

In addition to the need for inventories for the above-mentioned constructs, future research examining group cohesion and its correlates should employ multilevel statistical methodologies that account for individual level, group level and cross-level effects (Kenny *et al.*, 2002). Multilevel modeling analyzes hierarchal data which consists of lower level observations (i.e. individuals) nested within higher level units, such as a sport team or exercise group (Kreft and de Leeuw, 2002). Hierarchal linear modeling is a methodology that has been used extensively in educational and organizational domains as a procedure for conducting multilevel analysis (Hox, 1995). However, despite its applicability to group dynamics in sport and exercise settings, the majority of research in this area has focused on a single level of analysis. Kashy and Kenny (2000, p. 451) noted that 'examining groups at the individual level may not be suitable given that when studying individuals in group situations observations do not refer to a person but, rather, refer to many individuals nested within a social context'.

In any group, be it a sport team or an exercise class, individuals interact with one another. Individuals are influenced by group members and in turn the properties of that group are influenced by the individuals who make up the group (Hox, 1995). As mentioned earlier, the relationships between cohesion and factors such as norms, role acceptance and collective efficacy are likely reciprocal in nature. Specifically, a team's cohesion can influence an athlete's cognitions, emotions and behaviors which in turn will influence other group member's cognitions, emotions and behaviors. For example, a hockey team high in cohesion would likely cause a team member to exhibit positive group behavior such as role acceptance and compliance to team norms. In turn, the athlete's actions would contribute to subsequent team behaviors by increasing the level of cohesion among team-mates. This example highlights how simultaneously exploring cohesion at multiple levels may help develop a better understanding of the construct and its influence on performance in sport teams and exercise groups.

Summary

Throughout history, group cohesion has been identified as an important factor in the success of a wide variety of groups. Today, cohesion remains an essential group variable that researchers in a wide variety of disciplines have concluded deserves considerable thought and attention. As this chapter has shown, research in the area of cohesion continues to thrive, with exciting new developments in the domains of sport and exercise. Specifically, research conducted in these areas has provided the foundation for several practical steps that coaches and exercise leaders can now effectively employ to enhance the level of cohesiveness present in – and consequently, the success of – sport teams and exercise classes. Finally, it is inevitable that cohesion will also be recognized as an essential element in the formula for group success in the future and the development of new and innovative inventories and methodologies will help to shed additional light on the value of this dynamic and instrumental construct.

References

Annesi, J. J. (1999). Effects of minimal group promotion on cohesion and exercise adherence. *Small Group Research*, 30, 542–557.

Bacharach, S. B., Bamberger, P. and Mundell, B. (1993). Status inconsistency in organizations: From social hierarchy to stress. *Journal of Organizational Behavior*, 14, 21–36.

Birrell, S. and Richter, D. M. (1994). Is a diamond forever? Feminist transformations of sport. In S. Birrell and C. L. Cole (Eds), *Women, sport and culture* (pp. 221–244). Champaign, IL: Human Kinetics.

Brawley, L. R., Carron, A. V. and Widmeyer, W. N. (1987). Assessing the cohesion of teams: Validity of the Group Environment Questionnaire. *Journal of Sport Psychology*, 9, 275–294.

Brawley, L. R., Carron, A. V. and Widmeyer, W. N. (1988). Exploring the relationship between cohesion and group resistance to disruption. *Journal of Sport and Exercise Psychology*, 10, 199–213.

Brawley, L. R., Carron, A. V. and Widmeyer, W. N. (1993). The influence of the group and its cohesiveness on perceptions of group-related variables. *Journal of Sport and Exercise Psychology*, 15, 245–260.

Brownell, K. D. and Felix, M. R. J. (1987). Competitions to facilitate health promotion: Review and conceptual analysis. *American Journal of Health Promotion*, 2, 28–36.

Bull, S. J., Albinson, J. G. and Shambrook, C. J. (1996). *The mental game plan: Getting psyched for sport*. Cheltenham, UK: Sports Dynamics.

Burke, S. M., Carron, A. V., Eys, M. A., Ntoumanis, N. and Estabrooks, P. A. (2006). Group versus individual approach? A meta-analysis of the effectiveness of interventions to promote physical activity. *Sport and Exercise Psychology Review*, 2, 13–29.

Burke, S. M., Shapcott, K. M., Carron, A. V., Bradshaw, M. H. and Estabrooks, P. A. (2007). Group goal setting and team performance in a physical activity context. (Manuscript submitted for publication.)

Carron, A. V., Brawley, L. R. and Widmeyer, W. N. (1998). The measurement of cohesiveness in sport groups. In J. L. Duda (Ed.), *Advances in sport and exercise psychology measurement* (pp. 213–226). Morgantown, WV: Fitness Information Technology.

Carron, A. V. and Chelladurai, P. (1981). The dynamics of group cohesion in sport. *Journal of Sport Psychology*, 3, 123–139.

Carron, A. V., Colman, M. M., Wheeler, J. and Stevens, D. (2002). Cohesion and performance in sport: A meta-analysis. *Journal of Sport and Exercise Psychology*, 24, 168–188.

Carron, A. V., Hausenblas, H. A. and Estabrooks, P. A. (2003). *The psychology of physical activity*. New York: McGraw-Hill.

Carron, A. V., Hausenblas, H. A. and Eys, M. A. (2005). *Group dynamics in sport* (3rd ed.). Morgantown, WV: Fitness Information Technology.

Carron, A. V., Hausenblas, H. A. and Mack, D. (1996). Social influence and exercise: A meta-analysis. *Journal of Sport and Exercise Psychology*, 18, 1–16.

Carron, A. V., Prapavessis, H. and Estabrooks, P. A. (1999). Team norm questionnaire. Unpublished.

Carron, A. V. and Spink, K. S. (1993). Team building in an exercise setting. *The Sport Psychologist*, 7, 8–18.

Carron, A. V. and Spink, K. S. (1995). The group size-cohesion relationship in minimal groups. *Small Group Research*, 26, 86–105.

Carron, A. V., Spink, K. S. and Prapavessis, H. (1997). Team building and cohesiveness in the sport and exercise setting: Use of indirect interventions. *Journal of Applied Sport Psychology*, 9, 61–72.

Carron, A. V. and Widmeyer, W. N. (1987, May 2). *Developing effective groups*. Workshop presented for the Faculty of Part-Time and Continuing Education, University of Western Ontario, London, Ontario, Canada.

Carron, A. V., Widmeyer, W. N. and Brawley, L. R. (1985). The development of an instrument to assess cohesion in sport teams: The Group Environment Questionnaire. *Journal of Sport Psychology*, 7, 244–266.

Carron, A. V., Widmeyer, W. N. and Brawley, L. R. (1988). Group cohesion and individual adherence to physical activity. *Journal of Sport and Exercise Psychology*, 10, 119–126.

CBC Sports (2006). *What happened to Team Canada?* Online. Available: http://www.cbc.ca/olympics/sports/icehockey/stories/index.shtml?/story/olympics/national/2006/02/22/Sports/teamcanada-torino060222.html (Accessed August, 2006).

Chang, K. (1998). A systems view of quality in fitness services: Development of a model and scales. Unpublished doctoral dissertation, Ohio State University, Columbus.

Centers for Disease Control and Prevention. (2006). State-specific prevalence of obesity among adults: United States 2005. *Morbidity and Mortality Weekly Report*, 55, 985–988.

Colman, M. M. and Carron, A. V. (2001). The nature of norms in individual sport teams. *Small Group Research*, 32, 206–222.

Estabrooks, P. A. and Carron, A.V. (1999a). Group cohesion in older adult exercisers: Prediction and intervention effects. *Journal of Behavioral Medicine*, 22, 575–588.

Estabrooks, P. A. and Carron, A. V. (1999b). The influence of the group with elderly exercisers. *Small Group Research*, 30, 438–452.

Estabrooks, P. A. and Carron, A. V. (2000). The Physical Activity Group Environment Questionnaire: An instrument for the assessment of cohesion in exercise classes. *Group Dynamics: Theory, Research and Practice*, 4, 230–243.

Eys, M. A., Beauchamp, M. R. and Bray, S. R. (2006a). A review of team roles in sport. In S. Hanton and S. D. Mellalieu (Eds), *Literature reviews in sport psychology* (pp. 227–256). Hauppauge, NY: Nova Science Publishers.

Eys, M. A., Burke, S. M., Carron, A. V. and Dennis, P. W. (2005). The sport team as an effective group. In J. M. Williams (Ed.), *Applied sport psychology: Personal growth to peak performance* (5th ed., pp. 157–173). New York: McGraw-Hill.

Eys, M. A. and Carron, A. V. (2001). Role ambiguity, task cohesion and task self-efficacy. *Small Group Research*, 32, 356–373.

Eys, M. A., Carron, A.V., Beauchamp, R. and Bray, S. R. (2005). Athletes' perceptions of the sources of role ambiguity. *Small Group Research*, 36, 383–403.

Eys, M. A., Hardy, J. and Patterson, M. M. (2006b). Group norms and their relationship to cohesion in an exercise environment. *International Journal of Sport and Exercise Psychology*, 4, 43–56.

Festinger, L., Schachter, S. and Back, K. (1950). *Social pressures in informal groups*. New York: Harper and Brothers.

Franklin, B. (1984). Exercise program compliance: Improvement strategies. In J. Storlie and H. Jordan (Eds), *Behavioral management of obesity* (pp. 105–135). New York: Spectrum.

Gammage, K. L., Carron, A. V. and Estabrooks, P. A. (2001). Team cohesion and individual productivity: The influence of the norm for productivity and the identifiability of individual effort. *Small Group Research*, 32, 3–18.

Gardner, D. E., Shields, D. L., Bredemeier, B. J. and Bostrom, A. (1996). The relationship between perceived coaching behaviors and team cohesion among baseball and softball players. *Sport Psychologist*, 10, 367–381.

Golembiewski, R. (1962). *The small group*. Chicago: University of Chicago Press.

Goodman, P. S., Ravlin, E. and Schminke, M. (1987). Understanding groups in organizations. In

L. L. Cummings and B. M. Staw (Eds), *Research in organizational behavior* (pp. 121–173). Greenwich, CT: JAI.

Granito, V. J. and Rainey, D. W. (1988). Differences in cohesion between high school and college football teams and starters and nonstarters. *Perceptual and Motor Skills*, 66, 471–477.

Gruber, J. J. and Gray, G. R. (1982). Response to forces influencing cohesion as a function of player status and level of male varsity basketball competition. *Research Quarterly for Sport and Exercise*, 53, 27–36.

Hardy, J., Eys, M. A. and Carron, A. V. (2005). Disadvantages from high task cohesion? A qualitative approach. *Small Group Research*, 36, 166–189.

Heath, G. W., Wilson, R. H., Smith, J. and Leonard, B.E. (1991). Community-based exercise and weight control: Diabetes risk reduction and glycemic control in Zuni Indians. *American Journal of Clinical Nutrition*, 53, 1642S–1646S.

Heuze, J. P., Raimbault, N. and Fontayne, P. (2006). Relationships between cohesion, collective - efficacy and performance in professional basketball teams: An examination of mediating effects. *Journal of Sport Sciences*, 24, 59–68.

Hox, J. J. (1995). *Applied multilevel analysis*. Amsterdam: TT-Publikaties.

Jackson, P. (2004). *The last season: A team in search of its soul*. New York: Hyperion.

Jackson, S. E., May, K. E. and Whitney, K. (1995). Understanding the dynamics of diversity in decision-making teams. In R. A. Guzzo and E. Salas (Eds), *Team effectiveness and decision-making in organizations* (pp. 383–396). San Francisco: Jossey-Bass.

Kashy, D. A. and Kenny, D. A. (2000). The analysis of data from dyads and groups. In H. T. Reis and C. M. Judd (Eds), *Handbook of research methods in social and personality psychology* (pp. 451–477). New York: Cambridge University Press.

Kenny, D. A., Mannetti, L., Pierro, A., Livi, S. and Kashy, D. A. (2002). The statistical analysis of data from small groups. *Journal of Personality and Social Psychology*, 83, 126–137.

Kim, M. (1995). Performance norms and performance by teams in basketball competition. *Perceptual and Motor Skills*, 80, 770.

Kozub, S. A. (1993). Exploring the relationships among coaching behavior, team cohesion and player leadership. Unpublished doctoral dissertation, University of Houston, Texas.

Kozub, S. A. and McDonnell, J. F. (2001). Exploring the relationship between cohesion and collective efficacy in rugby teams. *Journal of Sport Behavior*, 23, 120–129.

Kreft, I. and de Leeuw, J. (2002). *Introducing multilevel modeling*. Thousand Oaks, CA: Sage.

Lott, A. J. and Lott, B. D. (1965). Group cohesiveness as interpersonal attraction: A review of relationships with antecedent and consequent variables. *Psychological Bulletin*, 64, 259–309.

Loughead, T. M. and Carron, A.V. (2004). The mediating role of cohesion in the leader behavior-satisfaction relationship. *Psychology of Sport and Exercise*, 5, 355–371.

Loughead, T. M., Colman, M. M. and Carron, A.V. (2001). Investigating the mediational relationship of leadership, class cohesion and adherence in an exercise setting. *Small Group Research*, 32, 558–575.

Martens, R. and Peterson, J. (1971). Group cohesiveness as a determinant of success and member satisfaction in team performance. *International Review of Sport Sociology*, 6, 49–71.

Munroe, K., Estabrooks, P., Dennis, P. and Carron, A. (1999). A phenomenological analysis of group norms in sport teams. *The Sport Psychologist*, 13, 171–182.

Munroe, K., Terry, P. and Carron, A. (2002). Cohesion and teamwork. In B. Hale and D. Collins (Eds), *Rugby tough* (pp. 137–153). Champaign, IL: Human Kinetics.

Oldridge, N. (1977). What to look for in an exercise class leader. *Physician and Sports Medicine*, 5, 85–88.

O'Leary-Kelly, A. M., Martocchio, J. J. and Frink D. D. (1994). A review of the influence of group goals on group performance. *Academy of Management Journal*, 37, 1285–1301.

Paskevich, D. M. (1995). Conceptual and measurement factors of collective efficacy in its relationship to cohesion and performance outcome. Unpublished doctoral dissertation, University of Waterloo, Ontario, Canada.

Prapavessis, H. and Carron, A. V. (1997). Sacrifice, cohesion and conformity to norms in sport teams. *Group Dynamics*, 1, 231–240.

Prapavessis, H., Carron, A. V. and Spink, K. S. (1996). Team building in sport. *International Journal of Sport Psychology*, 27, 269–285.

Quote Garden. (2007). *Quotations about teamwork*. Online. Available: http://www.quotegarden.com/teamwork.html (Accessed July, 2006).

Remers, L., Widmeyer, W. N., Williams, J. M. and Myers, L. (1995). Possible mediators and moderators of the class size-member adherence relationship in exercise. *Journal of Applied Sport Psychology*, 7, 38–49.

Schacter, S., Ellertson, N., McBride, D. and Gregory, D. (1951). An experimental study of cohesiveness and productivity. *Human Relations*, 4, 229–238.

Schmidt, U., McGuire, R., Humphrey, S., Williams, G. and Grawer, B. (2005). Team cohesion. In J. Taylor and G. S. Wilson (Eds), *Applying sport psychology: Four perspectives* (pp. 171–183). Champaign, IL: Human Kinetics.

Shapcott, K. M., Carron, A. V. Burke, S. M., Bradshaw, M. and Estabrooks P. A. (2006). Member diversity and cohesion and performance in walking groups. (Manuscript submitted for publication.)

Siebold, G. L. (1999). The evolution of the measurement of cohesion. *Military Psychology*, 11, 5–26.

Spink, K. S. (1990). Cohesion and collective efficacy of volleyball teams. *Journal of Sport and Exercise Psychology*, 12, 301–311.

Spink, K. S. and Carron, A. V. (1992). Group cohesion and adherence in exercise classes. *Journal of Sport and Exercise Psychology*, 14, 78–96.

Spink, K. S. and Carron, A. V. (1993). The effects of team building on the adherence patterns of female exercise participants. *Journal of Sport and Exercise Psychology*, 15, 39–49.

Spink, K. S. and Carron, A. V. (1994). Group cohesion effects in exercise classes. *Small Group Research*, 25, 26–42.

Steiner, I .D. (1972). *Group processes and productivity*. New York: Academic.

Tannenbaum, S. I., Beard, R. L. and Salas, E. (1992). Team building and its influence on team effectiveness: An examination of conceptual and empirical developments. In K. Kelley (Ed.), *Issues, theory and research in industrial/organizational psychology* (pp. 117–153). Amsterdam: Elsevier.

Thompson, W. (1891). *Popular lectures and addresses: Constitution and Matter*. London: Macmillan.

Turman, P. D. (2003). Coaches and cohesion: The impact of coaching techniques on team cohesion in the small group sport setting. *Journal of Sport Behavior*, 26, 86–104.

Webber, S. S. and Donahue, L. M. (2001). Impact of highly and less-job-related diversity on work group cohesion and performance: A meta-analysis. *Journal of Management*, 27, 141–162.

Weinberg, R. S. and Gould, D. (2003). *Foundations of sport and exercise psychology*. Champaign, IL: Human Kinetics.

Weingart, L. R. (1992). Impact of group goals, task component complexity, effort and planning on group performance. *Journal of Applied Psychology*, 77, 682–693.

Westre, K. R. and Weiss, M. R. (1991). The relationship between perceived coaching behaviors and group cohesion in high school football teams. *Sport Psychologist*, 5, 41–54.

Widmeyer, W. N., Brawley, L. R. and Carron, A. V. (1988, June). How many should I carry on my team? Consequences of group size. Paper presented at the meeting of the North American Society for the Psychology of Sport and Physical Activity, Knoxville, TN.

Widmeyer, W. N., Brawley, L. R. and Carron, A. V. (1990). The effects of group size in sport. *Journal of Sport and Exercise Psychology*, 12, 177–190.

Widmeyer, W. N. and DuCharme, K. (1997). Team building through team goal setting. *Journal of Applied Sport Psychology*, 9, 97–113.

Wikipedia. (2007). *The Biggest Loser*. Online. Available: http://en.wikipedia.org/wiki/The_Biggest_Loser (Accessed August, 2006).

Williams, J. M. and Hacker, C. M. (1982). Causal relationships among cohesion, satisfaction and performance in women's intercollegiate field hockey teams. *Journal of Sport Psychology, 4,* 324–337.

Yukelson, D. (1997). Principles of effective team building interventions in sport: A direct services approach at Penn State University. *Journal of Applied Sport Psychology, 9,* 73–96.

Yukelson, D. (2006). Communicating effectively. In J. M. Williams (Ed.), *Applied sport psychology: Personal growth to peak performance* (5th ed., pp. 174–191). New York: McGraw Hill.

Zaccaro, S. J., Blair, V., Peterson, C. and Zazanis, M. (1995). Collective-efficacy. In J. E. Maddux (Ed.), *Self-efficacy, adaptation and adjustment: Theory, research and application* (pp. 305–328). New York: Plenum Press.

Zander, A. (1982). *Making groups effective*. San Francisco: Jossey-Bass.

Zimmerman, E., (1985). Almost all you wanted to know about status inconsistency but never dared to measure: Theoretical deficits on status inconsistency. *Social Behavior and Personality, 13,* 195–214.

Photograph by John MacLeod. Reprinted courtesy of The University of British Columbia.

8 Group integration interventions in exercise

Theory, practice and future directions

Paul A. Estabrooks

Introduction

Groups have a long history of influencing individual behavior. For example, Christians believe that the very existence of humankind had its origins in group influenced behavior. Without the existence of the first small group, Adam and Eve, Eve would not have exerted group pressure on Adam to bite the apple. Without Adam eating the apple, this first small group would not have been sent out from the Garden of Eden to populate the earth. This (mostly) frivolous example of the influence of groups on individual behavior highlights some fundamental characteristics that define groups (Marrow, 1969). First, the minimum number of people necessary for a group is two. Second, the influence of groups does not always lead to positive outcomes. Third, group members usually have a common fate (e.g. both Adam and Eve were kicked out of the garden). Fourth, there are important group processes related to interaction and communication that move the group towards a common goal. Fifth, these group processes can exert an exceptional motivational influence on members (Marrow, 1969).

Exercise and physical activity interventions often target small groups as a vehicle to enhance motivation and change behavior. From a practical standpoint promoting physical activity in groups is less expensive than a one-on-one counseling approach, there are resources within the group that can foster member enjoyment (e.g. a good leader; funny classmate) and the general social environment can be attractive to existing and new members (Carron et al., 1988; Estabrooks, 2000; Estabrooks et al., 2004; Fox et al., 2000). As a gestalt, the primary rationale for using small group interventions is that the group, however defined, can exert a positive influence on individual behavior.

Yet, the use of group-based interventions for physical activity promotion is not without controversy. For example, some researchers question the ability of group-based interventions to promote sustained physical activity once the intervention is complete (King et al., 1998). In addition, a series of reviews on the effectiveness of group-based interventions relative to individually targeted strategies provide conflicting results. For example, one quantitative review of 127 physical activity interventions completed in community, school, worksite, home and health care settings found that interventions delivered to groups were more effective than those delivered to individuals (Dishman and Buckworth, 1996). In contrast, a qualitative review of 39 studies, reached the conclusion that, in community samples, home-based exercise was superior to group-based exercise (Atienza, 2001). Finally, van der Bij et al. (2002) completed a narrative review of 38 physical activity intervention studies and they concluded that individual and group-based interventions were equally effective.

Theory and research

So, are group-based or individually targeted interventions superior? To answer this question, it may be helpful to briefly re-visit early group dynamics theory. Although seldom referenced in group-based physical activity intervention work, Kurt Lewin is generally regarded as the father of group dynamics (Marrow, 1969). Group dynamics is the field of study that examines the positive and negative forces that reside within groups. The original theoretical basis of group dynamics is quite resilient and can be summarized as in the following way: (a) by joining a group one is significantly changed, (b) one's interactions with fellow members changes both the individual and the other group members and (c) a highly attractive group can exert much influence on its members whereas a weak group does not have the same ability (Lewin, 1939). In addition, Lewin (1939) described cohesion to be the essential characteristic underlying group dynamics and that without it, it is doubtful that a group could be said to exist at all.

The final point of the preceding paragraph has strong implications for research and practice professionals when they consider the utility of group-based interventions – that is, there is a distinction between an aggregate of people (e.g. no group cohesion) and a group. Until recently, this implication was not addressed in the extant literature on group-based physical activity programs and yet, it may be the key to understanding the seemingly discrepant findings in the literature. More plainly, all physical activity interventions that are delivered to an aggregate of individuals do not necessarily include strategies based on the theoretical underpinnings of group dynamics – just as, for example, all interventions delivered to individuals do not necessarily include strategies that target social cognitions. Therefore it is possible that interventions based on group dynamics may be superior to interventions that target aggregates of people but do not have formal strategies to enhance perceptions of cohesion.

To untangle the issue of the relative effectiveness of group-based physical activity interventions our research group recently completed a meta-analysis to compare individually targeted physical activity interventions (with and without additional social support), standard class-based physical activity interventions and interventions that used group-dynamics principles to increase their cohesiveness (Burke *et al.*, 2006). This final category of interventions (i.e. those that used group dynamics principles) was termed 'true groups' to reflect interventions that used group goal setting, targeted group norms and methods to enhance a collective perception of distinctiveness as well as other group dynamics strategies. The primary outcomes examined within the meta-analysis included adherence, social interactions, quality of life, physiological effectiveness and functional effectiveness.

When looking across the outcome variables the meta-analysis demonstrated a specific hierarchy of effectiveness (Burke *et al.*, 2006). True groups were more effective than standard physical activity class interventions which were more effective than individually targeted interventions with social support which, in turn, were more effective than individual interventions without additional social support. Based on these findings, we concluded that 'clearly, others – in the form of members of cohesive classes, members of collectives, interested family and friends, interested and concerned professionals and researchers – do have an effect on the [peoples'] involvement in and benefits derived from physical activity' (p. 30).

Although there are a number of intervention models that are based on group dynamics principles (Lorig and Holman, 1993; Rejeski *et al.*, 2003), a model developed by Carron and Spink (1993) directly flows from the initial theorizing of Lewin and proposes that group cohesion is a key target in the development of true group interventions for physical activity promotion. Specifically, their conceptual model indicates that a fundamental consideration in physical activity interventions – adherence – is related to participant perceptions of group cohesion (Carron and Spink, 1993). Figure 8.1 presents a pyramid view of interventions based on this model. As is figuratively described, group cohesion is thought to be the pinnacle of a process that is developed on a foundation of a consistent (a) group structure, (b) environment and (c) targeted processes related to group outcomes.

Distinct from the initial theoretical framework of group dynamics, Carron and colleagues (Carron and Brawley, 2000; Carron and Spink, 2000; Carron *et al.*, 1988), propose that cohesion is a multidimensional construct – rather than a unidimensional one – that is made up of four independent, but related dimensions (see Carron *et al.*, Ch. 7, this volume). The dimensions are distinguished by a social versus task basis and by an individual attractions versus group integration basis. Thus, an individual can be attracted to a group's task function (e.g. to get some exercise) and by its social function (e.g. opportunity to interact with other people). Similarly, an individual can become integrated into the task functioning of a group (e.g. provides input on the types of exercises completed during class) and into the social function (e.g. participates in the organization of social functions for the group).

Group structure includes four basic components (Carron *et al.*, 2005). First, participants occupy specific locations relative to the class and other members. Regular participants will typically migrate to a consistent location in the group which provides a sense of comfort and belonging. Second, participants in the group may differ on status within the group. This can be based on characteristics such as longevity in the program

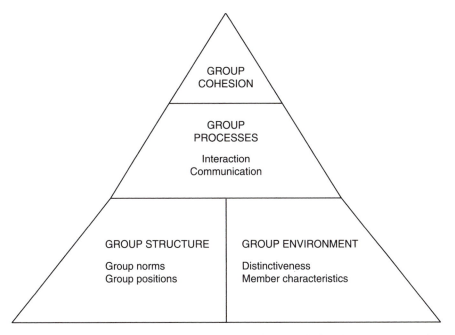

Figure 8.1 Carron and Spink's (1993) conceptual framework for designing group dynamics-based physical activity interventions.

or athletic capabilities. Third, participants in the group may have specified or informal roles. Typical roles could include a resident class clown or attendance tracker. Fourth, group norms reflect an expectation of behavior that is acknowledged as being appropriate for group members. Norms can develop around timeliness and quality of exercise completion. In the physical activity group context, issues related to creating differential status among class members has not been targeted as an intervention component. Roles, norms and encouraging regular position in the groups have all been used across a number of intervention trials (Brawley et al., 2000; Carron and Spink, 1993; Estabrooks et al., 2005b; Estabrooks and Carron, 1999; Spink and Carron, 1994).

In Carron and Spink's model the group environment was operationalized as issues related to creating a sense of distinction within a group and issues related to group size (Carron et al., 2005; Carron and Spink, 1993). As groups form and become more cohesive they naturally develop a sense of 'us' and perceptions of non-group members or other similar groups as 'them' (Tajfel and Turner, 2004). Group size also has an impact on the group environment by influencing the opportunity for members to interact and find commonalities. In the physical activity context, small and large groups are both superior to medium sized groups when considering attendance and retention (Carron, 1990). In contrast to medium-sized groups, small groups are thought to provide greater opportunities for member interaction and familiarity while larger groups are thought to provide greater opportunities to meet interesting and attractive contemporaries (Carron et al., 2005).

Group processes can be characterized by collective goals, cooperation and competition, interaction and communication and collective efficacy. First, in the context of physical activity, group goal-setting has played an integral part of team building interventions and typically involve group participants defining personal goals and a larger plan of group performance (Carron and Spink, 1993; Estabrooks et al., 2005b; Estabrooks and Carron, 1999). Second, cooperation in physical activity groups is primarily associated with supporting one another in partnered exercises during class or providing assistance to help group members achieve personal goals. Third, competition in group interventions typically occurs between small groups rather than between individual group members and is often tied to the group goal (Estabrooks and Glasgow, 2006). For example, teams within the larger group could compete to see who had more people attend classes. Fourth, group interaction and communication can be operationalized through peer sharing and problem solving activities. Finally, collective - efficacy, has not be addressed in physical activity groups, but it reflects the group's confidence to achieve a common outcome (Bandura, 1997). For specific examples of strategies that are based on these processes see Table 8.1.

When considered with the underlying group structure, environment and process, the multidimensional model of group cohesion provides 12 basic targets for intervention development (Table 8.1). These processes and cohesion outcomes are hypothesized to include reciprocal causality (Carron and Hausenblas, 1998). For example, as one perceives the physical activity norms of a group to align with his/her personal beliefs, this process engenders stronger perceptions of task cohesion which in turn reinforces and strengthens the norms within the group. Also, of note, is that a specific strategy that is developed to target one dimension of cohesion may also concurrently enhance another dimension of cohesion. For instance, in Table 8.1 the strategy to use small groups to identify underlying motives and barriers to living a healthy lifestyle allows for conversation and the uncovering of shared experiences with behavior

Table 8.1 Underlying theoretical principles of group-dynamics interventions and potential related intervention strategies

Dimension of cohesion	Group characteristic	Potential strategy
Individual attractions to the group-task	Group environment	Identify a group name that is attractive to a specific population that would participate. *Example:* 'Cardiopump' – Designates specific task-related exercises to help women tone muscles.
	Group structure	Develop strategies that enhance group norms for appropriate exercise during class. *Example:* Reward individual group members for prompt and regular attendance.
	Group processes	Provide opportunities for group interaction around exercises. *Example:* Incorporate partner stretching exercises.
Individual attractions to the group-social	Group environment	Consider the appropriate group size to allow for participant social interactions. *Example:* Small classes (5–17 members) are best for higher attendance and provide the opportunity for social interactions.
	Group structure	Develop strategies that enhance group norms for appropriate social activities during class. *Example:* Celebrate individual group members' birthdays or other special occasions.
	Group processes	Provide opportunities for group social interaction. *Example:* Offer time and space for post-class water and fruit.
Group integration-task	Group environment	Develop sense of group distinctiveness. *Example:* Get participant input on refining group name or developing subgroup names to reflect the group's specific identity (e.g. 'Cardiopump: Pumped Park Hill Parents').
	Group structure	Develop group roles for class participants. *Example:* Develop a telephone tree and identify who will follow-up with who when someone is absent or unable to attend.
	Group processes	Develop strategies that involve the group working together to achieve a common goal. *Example:* Set a group goal for amount of physical activity over the course of 3 or 6 months and set a group reward for when the goal is achieved.
Group integration-social	Group environment	Develop strategies that ensure class participants occasionally come in close proximal distance of each other to heighten the sense of causal relatedness. *Example:* Use games like a modified musical chairs format that allow group members to be in close proximity to one another without feeling uncomfortable.

(Continued overleaf)

Table 8.1 Continued

Dimension of cohesion	Group characteristic	Potential strategy
Group integration-social	Group structure	Encourage structured social interactions with participants both within and outside of the formal class time. *Example*: Monthly potluck lunches or dinners have been used to encourage social belongingness.
	Group processes	Provide opportunities for participants to share challenges and complete problem solving activities to feel a sense of collective similarity and support. *Example*: Use small groups to identify underlying motives and barriers to living a healthy lifestyle.

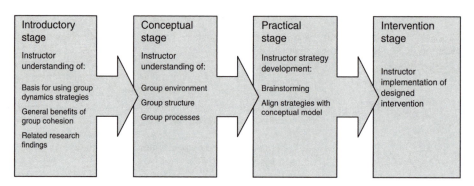

Figure 8.2 Stages of group dynamics-based physical activity intervention development.

change. This enhances the social integration of individuals within the group. At the same time, the strategy can focus group member attention to the common goal of improved lifestyle behaviors and enhance the integration of the group around the task of increasing physical activity.

Practical implications and intervention design

In addition to providing a sound theoretical basis for group dynamics based physical activity interventions, Carron and Spink (1993) also provided a practical framework for developing interventions based on group-dynamics principles. The framework, which targets those who will ultimately implement the intervention, includes four stages. Figure 8.2 highlights each stage and their respective foci. Briefly, the stages provide those who will deliver the program with: (1) an understanding of the basis for using group dynamics interventions; (2) a clear conceptualization of the group environment, structure, processes and cohesion; (3) an opportunity to dynamically develop strategies that target enhanced group properties; and (4) the ability and confidence to deliver a successful intervention.

This section of the chapter will describe three recent projects that used this framework, to varying degrees, in the design of group dynamics interventions to increase physical activity of adults across different contexts – two community-based and one clinical in nature (Estabrooks *et al.*, 2005b; Estabrooks *et al.*, 2006; Estabrooks and Glasgow, 2006). Each intervention reflects a progression in our research team's pursuit of group dynamics enhanced physical activity interventions that can be translated and delivered in regular community or clinical practice. As such, each is unique in the frequency of group sessions (i.e. once per week, once per month, or no formal group sessions), target population (i.e. frail older adults, adult community residents, or adult patients) and type of delivery agent (i.e. graduate students, health educators, or cooperative extension agents). Conversely, all three interventions were based on an identical theoretical framework.

Activity for the Ages

Activity for the Ages was developed in partnership with the local Kansas Area Agencies on Aging and Kansas State University Research and Extension (Estabrooks *et al.*, 2005a,b). During the development stage of this intervention, each of the partner agencies met with the research team to determine, first, the feasibility of offering programs in Area Agency on Aging congregate meal sites for frail older adults and, second, the conceptual underpinnings of group dynamics enhanced physical activity sessions. For this implementation, graduate students were designated as instructors with the explicit target of identifying and training an older adult group member to take over the group after an initial 3-month implementation.

Table 8.2 describes the group dynamics strategies identified and used over the 12 weekly sessions. In addition to identifying sessions that would increase group cohesion through group environmental, structure and processes we also used a basic guiding principle – the sessions should include activities that were fun and could improve the affect of the participants. In many cases, typical children's games such as hot potato were the most successful in developing excitement and humor for the groups. Specific communication and interaction strategies for this age were also used to foster task and social cohesion. The Physical Activity Timeline, for example, allowed not only for identifying physical activities that were enjoyed across the lifespan, but also allowed for members to reminisce about events from a shared past. The fundamental group dynamics strategies of group goal setting, name identification and shared problem solving were also prominent through the program and across sessions.

Activity for the Ages reflected the first of our group dynamics intervention studies that met less than 3 times per week. This was in response to participant surveys on the preferred number of sessions and on the reduced resources needed to deliver a physical activity intervention in this context. As a result, it was also the first project that included a need to promote physical activity while participants were away from the location where the primary intervention content was delivered. In this study we added in a personal goal setting session that was completed in small groups and followed this with our group goal setting activity to ensure that the group goal was more than the sum of the activity that was completed on site (i.e. they had goals to be active in other locations while away from the meal site). When compared with a control group of participants who received standard physical activity and health lectures in an aggregate (i.e. no structured physical activity class or group dynamics strategies), the participants in the Activity for the Ages intervention completed significantly more physical activity at program completion (Estabrooks *et al.*, 2005b). In fact, Activity for the Ages

Table 8.2 Session by session group dynamics strategies used during Activity for the Ages

	Strategies
Session 1	Name tags (used for first few sessions) Participant sharing of motives for joining program Partnered exercises (i.e. need others to complete exercises).
Session 2	Leader welcomes using participant names and handshake Participant input on exercises *Physical Activity Timeline*: Participants share their physical activity histories in the context of childhood, young and early adulthood, prior to joining the group.
Session 3	Self-monitoring tool is provided and described (to be used as basis for group goals) *Personal Action Planning*: Small group discussions around the benefits of regular physical activity and personal motives to stick with it *Hoops*: Integrate strength and skill exercises using tennis balls and small garbage can – small teams compete on who can fill the basket most quickly.
Session 4	Participants brainstorm and select team name Partner exercises.
Session 5	Introduce and define group goal for physical activity Develop individual goals for 4 weeks of activity that will support group goal Display group name (e.g. poster with future schedule/pictures) *Hot Potato*: Participants pass tennis balls between them – rules similar to musical chairs.
Session 6	Group goal map introduced to track group progress Participants identify incentive for completing first half of group goal (e.g. T-shirts with group name) Small group discussion of home physical activity barriers and strategies to overcome barriers.
Session 7	Feedback on group progress towards goal Small group discussion on other resources for physical activity in community (e.g. mall for walking) *On Your Toes*: Participants complete short synchronized physical activity routines.
Session 8	Feedback on progress towards group goal *I Lead*: Participants take turns leading favorite exercises throughout the session Give incentives for half way towards group goal.
Session 9	Feedback on group progress towards goal *Hot Seat*: Participants hear from others about why they are appreciated members of the group Re-set individual goals for the next 6 months in light of team goal and personal goal.
Session 10	Feedback on group goal Group photographs *How Are Things?* Participants provide input for ways to keep program fresh.
Session 11	Feedback on group goal Small group work on benefits that have been gained since the beginning of the program *Relay*: Population appropriate relay races.
Session 12	Celebrate group goal Participant certificates of merit (e.g. best attender) *Kick the Ball*: participants call one another's names as they kick utility balls.

participants increased, on average, by 100 min/week while control participants decreased by about 25 min/week. This reflected a large effect and, suggesting that the shortening of duration did not have a deleterious effect, was similar in magnitude to our earlier work that used 3 times/week sessions (Estabrooks and Carron, 1999).

Move More!

Move More! was developed for integration and delivery within a healthcare organization (Estabrooks and Glasgow, 2006; Estabrooks and Smith-Ray, 2005). Similar to Activity for the Ages, a research partnership was developed that included members of the potential healthcare delivery system. Specifically, the practice partners included the Chief and Director of Preventive Medicine, the Director of Health Education, health educators who would ultimately deliver the physical activity intervention and, finally, the clinical Physician in Charge and Medical Office Administrator. These partners from the Kaiser Permanente Colorado managed care organization provided ongoing guidance to our research team so that a practical pilot physical activity intervention would be developed. The primary purpose of testing Move More! was to determine first, if a group dynamics based intervention for insufficiently active adults could be successfully implemented within a system of limited resources for preventive care and second, if so, could the intervention sustain physical activity beyond the completion of group sessions.

The most challenging aspect of this partnership was the limited resources available to deliver the program once the research project was complete. In short, the intervention was limited to two 2-hour sessions per group and the availability of personnel to complete a single telephone follow-up session for each participant. Nonetheless, our partnership agreed that a focus on developing a sense of group distinctiveness, targeting norms through group goal setting, comprising groups of individuals within geographic proximity of one another, fostering ongoing group interactions and communication to provide feedback, information sharing and collective problem solving were still appropriate principles for strategy development. However, the primary outcome targeted with each of the strategies was designed to support individual self-management and increase physical activity that occurred exclusively away from the group sessions. By fostering strong self-management skills it was hypothesized that participants could continue to improve beyond the duration of the formal intervention (Glasgow et al., 2006; Scholz et al., 2006).

The intervention sessions were spread over a 3-month period. Participants attended the two 2-hour group sessions with a gap of 4 weeks between sessions. During the initial session, participants completed a 'name game' activity as an ice-breaker and were then assigned to small groups. This was followed by specific 15-min education sessions on strength training, flexibility and cardiovascular exercise. In each 15-min block, participants completed small group physical activities within their assigned smaller groups. These activities filled the initial hour of the session and created a sense of comfort and familiarity of participants within their small groups. During the second hour of the initial session, small groups identified team names and participated in friendly competitions on team understanding of simple physical activity concepts. Each team then completed a small group discussion around appropriate goals for physical activity for the following 4 weeks, barriers to participation and strategies to overcome the barriers. Each team also set a group goal for the following 4 weeks. Class instructors described a friendly competition based on attendance at the next session for each team – the team that had the highest attendance would receive a prize.

The second 2-hour group session took place 1 month following the first. The primary purpose of this second session was to check in with participants on their progress during their first month. Instructors once again facilitated group discussion reinforcing progress made toward goals while addressing barriers encountered. In addition, to promote the supportive network among participants, team goals and achievement were celebrated using team prizes and awards. Participants reviewed the concepts of and practiced additional, strengthening, flexibility and cardiovascular exercise. Each participant also completed a new personal action plan in small groups focusing on 8-week goals. Specific attention was given to identifying ways that the participants could continue to increase physical activity – even after the program was over. At 8 weeks after the second session, participants received a telephone call from an instructor that reinforced the group-based activities and content.

Participants in Move More! were compared with participants who were randomly assigned to receive a print-based physical activity intervention that also included a telephone support session. The delivery of materials for the control group coincided with the timing of the Move More! intervention components. The results of the study again supported the use of Carron and Spink's (1993) model of intervention development. After the 3 months of intervention, participants in both groups increased physical activity by an average of 75 min/week (Figure 8.3). Interestingly, 6 months after the programs had both completed, participants from Move More! increased their physical activity, on average, by an additional 30 min/week, while those in the control condition saw a 40 min drop in weekly activity.

Walk Kansas

Rural Americans are at higher risk for obesity and less active than their urban counterparts and this was the basis for the development of Walk Kansas (McMurray *et al.*, 1999; Patterson *et al.*, 2004; Wilcox *et al.*, 2000). In this case, our research team

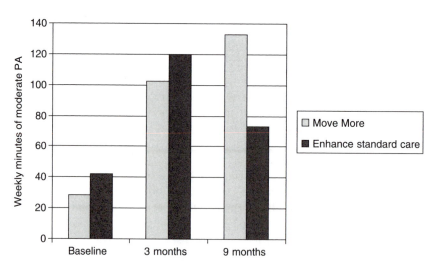

Figure 8.3 The effectiveness of Move More!

partnered with the state Extension Health Specialist, who held the decision-making authority to make health programs available for implementation within the Kansas State University Research and Extension Service. The development team also included marketing personnel, a journalist, a local county extension agent who would ultimately deliver the program and community members.

Again, the conceptual model developed by Carron and Spink (1993) to apply group dynamics' principles to physical activity interventions was used as a template to identify the appropriate properties of Walk Kansas. However, Walk Kansas included three primary innovations that were not components of previous interventions based on Carron and Spink's (1993) model. First, participants were allowed to self-select teams. Second, completing physical activity with the team was not required (i.e. participants could do physical activity on their own without other team members). These innovations were adopted in response to criticisms of group-based physical activity programs (King *et al.*, 1998) and to allow for a broader dissemination potential of the program. For example, one criticism of group-based physical activity is that when the research program is completed, the group dissolves, thereby increasing the likelihood of participant relapse (King *et al.*, 1998). To overcome this barrier and increase the likelihood that participants' support structures for physical activity would be sustained beyond the conclusion of the 8-week program, participants were allowed to self-select teams from people within their peer group (e.g. family, friends, co-workers). A second criticism of group-based physical activity is that attendance at group sessions is more difficult to adhere to than allowing participants to complete physical activity on their own schedule at multiple locations (Hillsdon *et al.*, 1995). Allowing participants to be physically active on their own, while retaining their feelings of responsibility to the group through team goal setting, was included to overcome this barrier. Third, because the intervention was not designed to bring team members together for group exercise, the conceptualization of participant position in the group (e.g. where one stands during each exercise session) was redefined to reflect geographic proximity of team members to ensure that contact and interaction would still likely occur (e.g. same house; workplace; faith-based organization).

Table 8.3 provides an overview of the group dynamics principles and strategies used in Walk Kansas. The program targeted teams of six individuals who would collectively walk the 423-mile distance across Kansas over an 8-week period. Individual miles were accumulated by participating in any moderate intensity physical activity. To operationalize this, besides walking and jogging, which were documented as miles covered, 15 min of moderate intensity physical activity was defined and reported as 1 mile. Teams of six were used to correspond to the recommended guidelines for regular physical activity (US Department of Health and Human Services, 1996). That is, if six people walked for 30 min at a moderate intensity (based on the compendium of physical activities; Ainsworth *et al.*, 2000), 5 days a week, for 8 weeks, they would meet the team goal of 423 miles (which is the distance across Kansas).

A captain was designated for each team and was responsible to collect weekly reports of miles from each team member. Captains then provided an update of team miles to their county extension agent who subsequently mailed a weekly update to all Walk Kansas participants and/or posted team progress in a common community location. The updates included the names and progress of all the teams participating within a given county.

Walk Kansas was an exceptionally successful physical activity intervention from

Table 8.3 The principles and strategies of Walk Kansas

Group dynamics principle	Walk Kansas strategy
Develop a sense of group distinctiveness	Unique self-determined team names Capitalize on existing perceptions of distinctiveness through self-selected teams of friends, family, or co-workers Walk Kansas T-shirts.
Group goal setting	Cooperative goal rather than competitive Weekly individual goals to complete 30 min of moderate intensity physical activity on at least 5 days Group goal to figuratively walk 423 miles across Kansas.
Geographic proximity	Self-selection of team members to allow for geographic or emotional proximity Target recruitment locations where people already aggregate to benefit from pre-existing proximity (e.g. worksites, faith-based institutions, community centers).
Ongoing group interactions	Weekly reporting of physical activity to team captain Promote occasional group 'get togethers' Self-selection of team members with pre-existing and consistent interactions.

a number of perspectives. First, in the initial year of delivery, almost 50 per cent of the counties in Kansas offered the program. By the third year of delivery, over 90 per cent of the counties were delivering the program. Second, in the initial year of delivery approximately 6,000 residents participated; this reflected about 1 per cent of the population. By the third year of delivery over 18,000 residents participated, reflecting 3 per cent of the population. Third, the program was effective and significantly increased physical activity by over 150 min/week for participants who were inactive or insufficiently active prior to participation – and it maintained the physical activity levels of those who were active prior to participation in Walk Kansas. In addition, 6 months after the program was complete, inactive and insufficiently active participants were still being physically active at a significantly higher rate that they were prior to participation in Walk Kansas. Fourth, extension agents found the program to be easy to implement (Estabrooks *et al.*, 2006).

Future research directions

There are a number of promising directions for future work examining the utility of group dynamics approaches to physical activity promotion. This section of the chapter will address three areas that may be considered critical. First, there are issues related to testing the underlying group dynamics framework that is used as the basis for physical activity interventions. Group cohesion is proposed to be the primary mediating variable of intervention effectiveness, yet when it is assessed and mediational analyses are applied, group cohesion is only a partial mediator (Estabrooks *et al.*, 2005b). In our meta-analysis comparing true groups (i.e. groups that worked toward becoming more cohesive) to aggregates (i.e. collections of individuals not necessarily viewing group membership as salient) and individually delivered interventions, we found very few true group studies that even assessed group cohesion and no studies that quantified group environment, structure, or processes (Burke *et al.*, 2006). Clearly, focused attention on assessing the proposed causal pathways of group dynamics intervention effectiveness is an understudied and important avenue for future studies. Studies that develop measures for group dynamics principles and test the relative need and interaction of constructs are needed (Gammage *et al.*, 2001). Additionally, clarifying the interplay between individual and group level variables in the behavior change process would be an excellent contribution to the literature (Paskevich *et al.*, 2001). For example, how do perceptions of group cohesion and individual attitudes and social cognitions interact to predict enhanced adherence? Combined, the findings of such research would allow for a more effective and efficient method of group dynamics intervention development.

Second, there is a need to conduct trials that demonstrate the cost-effectiveness of group dynamics based interventions. As demonstrated by Move More! and Walk Kansas there are methods to delivery group dynamics interventions in ways that do not impact organizational resources in the same intensive way as traditional 3-day/week group sessions. This is not to say that all group dynamics based interventions need to be at a low intensity or incorporate a low frequency of contact time. It could be that there are differing levels of group dynamics physical activity interventions that could be applied dependent upon the potential cost savings of the behavior change. For example, Toobert *et al.* (2005) targeted increased physical activity (along with healthy eating and stress management) using a very intensive group dynamics intervention for postmenopausal women with type 2 diabetes. The intervention included a 2-day retreat and as much as 4 hours of group work per week for 6 months. In women with diabetes, changes in behavior can have considerable cost savings in healthcare delivery – hence more resources can be dedicated to encouraging behavior change (Ritzwoller *et al.*, 2006; Toobert *et al.*, 2005).

Third, to ensure an optimal public health benefit of group dynamics physical activity interventions, identifying and integrating with existing geographic locations or organizational structures where high need populations already aggregate may be a productive avenue for future research. By adding group dynamics strategies at locations where people already gather there is a strong likelihood that significant behavior change could be achieved (Burke *et al.*, 2006). In addition, in physical activity group dynamics contexts, homogeneity on gender or other personal characteristics may facilitate improved exercise adherence (Shapcott *et al.*, 2006) suggesting that similarity on social identity could enhance participant preferences for exercise groups (Beauchamp *et al.*, 2007). Lee and colleagues are currently conducting a trial – Health Is Power – that targets low income housing projects populated predominantly by minority populations (Lee, 2007). In this study, a group dynamics physical activity intervention based on Carron and Spink's (1993) model is integrated into community facilities where minority women aggregate. By using the existing the public housing structure the intervention attempts to engender not only group cohesion but also social advocacy of the participants to facilitate physical environment changes. In that study participants are encouraged to complete community needs assessments and provide feedback to local government organizations on strategies to encourage physical activity in their neighborhoods. In a clinical example, Scott and colleagues developed a group visit model for geriatric medical care (Beck *et al.*, 1997; Scott *et al.*, 1998, 2004) that includes monthly meetings of a physician, nurse and approximately 15 patients for a 90-min session. Although there have yet to be studies integrating group goal setting and other group dynamics principles into the visit, this reflects an ideal setting for integration.

Summary

Group dynamics has a rich research history in physical activity. There is strong evidence to support that interventions based on group dynamics are effective across populations and in both community and clinical settings. More recent work has demonstrated that these types of interventions need not be resource intensive from an organizational perspective, nor are regular formal group sessions necessary to see significant increases in physical activity. Nonetheless there is a need for additional research and refining of the current theories of group dynamics that are being applied to physical activity promotion. Further, research is needed to determine what types or intensity of interventions are appropriate for existing aggregates of individuals and the costs related to implementation.

References

Ainsworth, B. E., Haskell, W. L., Whitt, M. C., Irwin, M. L., Swartz, A. M., Strath, S. J., O'Brien, W. A., Bassett, D. R., Schmitz, K. H., Emplaincourt, P. O., Jacobs, D. R. and Leon, A. S. (2000). Compendium of physical activities: An update of activity codes and MET intensities. *Medicine and Science in Sports and Exercise*, 32, S498–S516.

Atienza, A. A. (2001). Home-based physical activity programs for middle-aged and older adults: Summary of empirical research. *Journal of Aging and Physical Activity*, 9(Suppl.), S38–S58.

Bandura, A. (1997). *Self-efficacy: The exercise of control*. New York: W. H. Freeman.

Beauchamp, M. R., Carron, A. V., McCutcheon, S. and Harper, O. (2007). Older adults preferences for exercising alone versus in groups: Considering contextual congruence. *Annals of Behavioral Medicine*, 33, 200–206.

Beck, A., Scott, J., Williams, P., Robertson, B., Jackson, D., Gade, G. and Cowan, P. (1997). Randomized trial of group outpatient visits for chronically ill older HMO members: The Cooperative Health Care Clinic. *Journal of the American Geriatrics Society*, 45, 543–549.

Brawley, L. R., Rejeski, W. J. and Lutes, L. (2000). A group-mediated cognitive-behavioral intervention for increasing adherence to physical activity in older adults. *Journal of Applied Biobehavioral Research*, 5, 47–65.

Burke, S. M., Carron, A. V., Eys, M. A. and Estabrooks, P. A. (2006). Group versus individual approach: A meta-analysis of the effectiveness of interventions to promote physical activity. *Sport and Exercise Psychology Review*, 2, 19–35.

Carron, A. V. (1990). Group size in sport and physical activity: Social psychological and performance consequences. *International Journal of Sport Psychology*, 21, 286–304.

Carron, A. V. and Brawley, L. R. (2000). Cohesion: Conceptual and measurement issues. *Small Group Research*, 31, 89–106.

Carron, A. V. and Hausenblas, H. A. (1998). *Group dynamics in sport* (2nd ed.). Morgantown, WV: Fitness Information Technology.

Carron, A. V., Hausenblas, H. A. and Eys, M. A. (2005). *Group dynamics in sport* (3rd ed.). Morgantown, WV: Fitness Information Technology.

Carron, A. V. and Spink, K. S. (1993). Team building in an exercise setting. *The Sport Psychologist*, 7, 8–18.

Carron, A. V. and Spink, K. S. (2000). Internal consistency of the group environment questionnaire modified for an exercise setting. *Perceptual and Motor Skills*, 74, 304–306.

Carron, A. V., Widmeyer, W. N. and Brawley, L. R. (1988). Group cohesion and individual adherence to physical activity. *Journal of Sport and Exercise Psychology*, 10, 127–138.

Dishman, R. K. and Buckworth, J. (1996). Increasing physical activity: A quantitative synthesis. *Medicine and Science in Sports and Exercise*, 28, 706–719.

Estabrooks, P. A. (2000). Sustaining exercise participation through group cohesion. *Exercise and Sport Sciences Reviews*, 28, 63–67.

Estabrooks, P. A., Bradshaw, M., Dzewaltowski, D. A. and Smith-Ray, R. L. (2006). Determining the impact of Walk Kansas: Applying a team-building approach to community physical activity promotion. Unpublished manuscript.

Estabrooks, P. A., Bradshaw, M., Toner, S. and Fox, E. H. (2005a). *Activity for the Ages: A team-building program to promote fun and physical activity in congregate meal sites for older adults.* Manhattan: Kansas State University Agricultural Experiment Station and Cooperative Extension Service.

Estabrooks, P. A. and Carron, A. V. (1999). Group cohesion in older adult exercisers: Prediction and intervention effects. *Journal of Behavioral Medicine*, 22(6), 575–588.

Estabrooks, P. A., Fox, E. H., Doerksen, S. E., Bradshaw, M. H. and King, A. C. (2005b). Participatory research to promote physical activity at congregate-meal sites. *Journal of Aging and Physical Activity*, 13, 121–144.

Estabrooks, P. A. and Glasgow, R. E. (2006). Translating effective clinic-based physical activity interventions into practice. *American Journal of Preventive Medicine*, 31, 45–56.

Estabrooks, P. A., Munroe, K. J., Fox, E. H., Gyurcsik, N. C., Hill, J. L., Lyon, R., Rosenkranz, S. and Shannon, V. R. (2004). Leadership in physical activity groups for older adults: A qualitative analysis. *Journal of Aging and Physical Activity*, 12, 232–245.

Estabrooks, P. A. and Smith-Ray, R. L. (2005). Clinical social cognitive physical activity interventions. *Annals of Behavioral Medicine*, 29, SO30.

Fox, L. D., Rejeski, W. J. and Gauvin, L. (2000). Effects of leadership style and group dynamics on enjoyment of physical activity. *American Journal of Health Promotion*, 14(5), 277–283.

Gammage, K. L., Carron, A. V. and Estabrooks, P. A. (2001). Team cohesion and individual productivity: The influence of the norm for productivity and the identifiability of individual effort. *Small Group Research*, 32, 3–18.

Glasgow, R. E., Nutting, P. A., Toobert, D. J., King, D. K., Strycker, L. A., Jex, M., O'Neill, C., Whitesides, H. and Merenich, J. (2006). Effects of a brief computer-assisted diabetes self-management intervention on dietary, biological and quality-of-life outcomes. *Chronic Illness*, 2, 27–38.

Hillsdon, M., Thorogood, M., Anstiss, T. and Morris, J. (1995). Randomised controlled trials of physical activity promotion in free living populations: A review. *Journal of Epidemiology and Community Health*, 49, 448–453.

King, A. C., Rejeski, W. J. and Buchner, D. M. (1998). Physical activity interventions targeting older adults: A critical review and recommendations. *American Journal of Preventive Medicine*, 15, 316–333.

Lee, R. E. (2007). *Maintaining physical activity in ethnic minority women.* National Cancer Institute Grant No. R01CA109403–02.

Lewin, K. (1939). Experiments in social space. *Harvard Educational Review*, 9, 32.

Lorig, K. and Holman, H. (1993). Arthritis self-management studies: A twelve-year review. *Health Education Quarterly*, 20, 17–28.

Marrow, A. J. (1969). *The practical theorist: The life and work of Kurt Lewin.* New York: Basic Books.

McMurray, R. G., Harrell, J. S., Bangdiwala, S. I. and Deng, S. (1999). Cardiovascular disease risk factors and obesity of rural and urban elementary school children. *Journal of Rural Health*, 15, 365–374.

Paskevich, D. M., Estabrooks, P. A., Brawley, L. R. and Carron, A. V. (2001). Cohesion in sport and exercise. In R. Singer, H. A. Hausenblas and C. Janelle (Eds), *Handbook of research on sport psychology* (2nd ed.). New York: Macmillan.

Patterson, P. D., Moore, C. G., Probst, J. C. and Shinogle, J. A. (2004). Obesity and physical activity in rural America. *Journal of Rural Health*, 20, 151–159.

Rejeski, W. J., Brawley, L. R., Brubaker, P. H., Ambrosius, W. T., Fox, L. D., Focht, B. P. and Foy,

C. G. (2003). Older adults with chronic disease: Benefits of group-mediated counseling in the promotion of physically active lifestyles. *Health Psychology*, 22, 414–423.

Ritzwoller, D. P., Toobert, D. J., Sukhanova, A. and Glasgow, R. E. (2006). Economic analysis of the Mediterranean Lifestyle Program. *Diabetes Educator*, 32, 761–769.

Scholz, U., Knoll, N., Sniehotta, F. F. and Schwarzer, R. (2006). Physical activity and depressive symptoms in cardiac rehabilitation: Long-term effects of a self-management intervention. *Social Science and Medicine*, 62, 3109–3120.

Scott, J. C., Conner, D. A., Venor, I., Gade, G., McKenzie, M., Kramer, A. M., Bryant, L. and Beck, A. (2004). Effectiveness of a group outpatient visit model for chronically ill older health maintenance organization members: A 2-year randomized trial of the Cooperative Health Care Clinic. *Journal of the American Geriatrics Society*, 52, 1463–1470.

Scott, J. C., Gade, G., McKenzie, M. and Venohr, I. (1998). Cooperative health care clinics: A group approach to individual care. *Geriatrics*, 53, 68–81.

Shapcott, K. M., Carron, A. V., Burke, S. M., Bradshaw, M. H. and Estabrooks, P. A. (2006). Member diversity and cohesion and performance in walking groups. *Small Group Research*, 37, 701–720.

Spink, K. S. and Carron, A. V. (1994). Group cohesion effects in exercise classes. *Small Group Research*, 25, 26–42.

Tajfel, H. and Turner, J. C. (2004). The social identity theory of intergroup behavior. In J. T. Jost and J. Sidanius (Eds), *Political psychology: Key readings* (pp. 276–293). New York: Psychology Press.

Toobert, D. J., Strycker, L. A., Glasgow, R. E., Barrera, M. and Angell, K. (2005). Effects of the Mediterranean lifestyle program on multiple risk behaviors and psychosocial outcomes among women at risk for heart disease. *Annals of Behavioral Medicine*, 29, 128–137.

U.S. Department of Health and Human Services (1996). *Physical activity and health: A report of the Surgeon General, Superintendent of Documents*. Pittsburgh, PA.

van der Bij, A. K., Laurant, M. G. H. and Wensing, M. (2002). Effectiveness of physical activity interventions for older adults. *American Journal of Preventive Medicine*, 22, 120–133.

Wilcox, S., Castro, C., King, A. C., Housemann, R. A. and Brownson, R. C. (2000). Determinants of leisure time physical activity in rural compared with urban older and ethnically diverse women in the United States. *Journal of Epidemiology and Community Health*, 54, 667–672.

Photograph by Richard Lam/UBC Athletics. Reprinted courtesy of The University of British Columbia.

9 Gendered social dynamics in sport

Vikki Krane

Introduction

What is the interplay between gender and group dynamics? Are group interactions gendered? These are precarious questions. Intentioned or not, direct comparisons of males and females often are colored by our cultural milieu in which males and masculinity are privileged over females and femininity. The institution of sport magnifies this effect as male athletes consistently receive greater resources, status and social and economic power than female athletes (e.g. Messner, 2002). Approaching the realm of group dynamics by emphasizing gender differences essentializes *male* and *female* characteristics (i.e. generalizes attributes across all females or all males) and promotes that there are innate characteristics we are born with and that cannot be changed. For example, the stereotype that females are more emotional than males connects the personality characteristic of being emotional to the biology of being female. Conflating personality characteristics, learned behaviors and biology leads to the assumptions that certain groups of people are identical, irrespective of social and cultural influences and that these characteristics will not change (Fuss, 1989).

Still, some coaches strongly believe that the social dynamics among members of male teams are qualitatively different than the dynamics among members of female teams (e.g. DeBoer, 2004). As such, recommendations often are made regarding how males and females should be coached differently. However, to describe all women or all men as identical is fraught with inferences and assumptions. If one believes, for example, that males are inherently more competitive than females and that competitiveness is an essential quality for success in sport, then females will be perceived as less successful in sport as males. No amount of physical training, sport psychology consultation, or even athletic success will change this conclusion. In our society, no matter how it is framed when comparing male and female athletes, very often females are perceived as 'other' or 'less than'. Alternatively, if we consider the socialization factors or motivational climates that may lead to differing behaviors in female and male athletes, then we recognize that advantageous behaviors can be developed. Doing so is a much more meaningful and promising view of group dynamics in sport.

Therefore, this is not a chapter about gender differences in team dynamics. Rather, a social identity perspective (Turner and Reynolds, 2001) is used to explain the interplay of gender and group dynamics in sport. This perspective has been applied in sport psychology primarily to examine sexual identity (e.g. Krane and Barber, 2003) and fan identity (e.g. Laverie and Arnett, 2000). However, as a whole, the social identity perspective has many applications when examining group dynamics in sport. It provides a foundation for understanding the development of team norms and team cohesion as well as potential divisiveness among team members or conflict between groups of athletes.

Theory and research

Overview of social identity perspective

Social identity perspective examines group behavior through the combined processes described in social identity (Tajfel and Turner, 1979) and social categorization theories (Turner *et al.*, 1987). This perspective posits that 'people categorize and define themselves as members of a distinct social category or assign themselves a social identity' (Hogg and McGarty, 1990, p. 14). That is, individuals recognize similarities among group members, notice that they are similar to these group members and then place themselves within that group. This concept is elucidated in the title of Beverly Daniel Tatum's (2003) book, 'Why are All the Black Kids Sitting Together in the Cafeteria?' People sharing important attributes tend to congregate together, forming a social group. Individuals' social identity emerges from their recognition of this group membership (Tajfel and Turner, 1979) and it becomes important to be recognized as a group member.

Moreover, individuals have multiple social identities based on alliances with numerous social groups reflecting race, profession, religion and social class, to name a few. In many cases, group membership is chosen based on factors such as one's profession or becoming a member of a club or team. Membership in these groups, according to social identity perspective, should lead to feelings of positive self-worth and self-esteem. As individuals embrace their social identities, they learn the expected behaviors, attitudes and social values of a group. That is, they adopt the social norms or the accepted customs within a social group. Norms, unlike rules or laws, are implicit standards maintained through seemingly *normal* social practices and 'they usually remain implicit, difficult to read, [and] discernible most clearly and dramatically in the results they produce' (Butler, 2004, p. 41).

Over time, depersonalization occurs in which individuals' behavior becomes more normative and loyalty to the group increases (Turner *et al.*, 1987). Individuals act in manners consistent with group sanctioned accepted and unaccepted behavior (i.e. group social norms). Such changes in behavior assimilate individuals into the group and increase social acceptance by group members. As group membership is sustained, collective esteem (i.e. group pride) develops and, consequently, self-esteem and self-worth increase (Crocker and Luhtanen, 1990). These positive feelings, when coupled with adherence to group norms, also should increase collective efficacy and team cohesion. When group membership does not enhance one's sense of self, social identity perspective conjectures that individuals may attempt to change social affiliations (Abrams and Hogg, 1990). For example, a young man may be a talented figure skater, yet he loathes the stereotype that male skaters are gay. Therefore, he may quit figure skating and join an ice hockey team to distance himself from what he perceives as a negative label and become part of a group perceived as heterosexual and masculine. This change in group membership will lead to an improved sense of self and greater self-worth.

Not all group memberships are consciously self-selected and may not be amenable to change. In general, one cannot simply move among different gender and racial groups, for example. Social groups into which people are born usually include diverse individuals with a vast range of defining characteristics such as religion, sexuality, or social class. Thus, even within the broad group of women, clearly not all women are identical. For these reasons, it may be difficult to identify common social norms across these large, typically immutable, social groups. Consequently, some theorists (e.g. Skevington and Baker, 1989) caution against making the assumption that all women, for example, perceive womanhood similarly. Likewise, a diversity in masculine/male identities also exists (Greenleaf and Krane, 2007). Still many individuals are quite proud of their gender or racial identities. Membership in these social groups does draw people together and bonds among group members are apparent. Consider, for example, the empowering effects of sporting events that cater to specific social groups, such as the Gay Games, Maccabiah Games (for Jewish athletes), or the North American Indigenous Games (Krane, 2004). As Worchel (1999) highlighted:

> Groups need to provide us with a relatively safe and secure sense of being, a shield that both defines and protects us. As such, these groups need to be large and powerful, capable of defending and rewarding. The ideal candidate groups must have ways to heighten their salience by constantly reminding us that we are members. We'd also like these groups to be enduring so that our sense of self is stable and grounded.
>
> (Worchel, 1999, p. 8)

Regardless of how a person obtains a social identity (born into or self-selected), a social identity becomes most salient when it is threatened (Hurtado, 1997). For instance, when an athlete is a member of a racial minority or is faced with racial bigotry, her or his social identity based on race is most likely to be more salient than social identities such as gender or athlete. Under these circumstances, individuals sharing a superordinate identity (i.e. an overarching identity composed of many subgroups) likely will focus on this identity and the need to enhance the group's social position and status (Hornsey and Hogg, 2000; Skevington and Baker, 1989). Consider a Black athlete who hears a racial slur from the crowd during a game. Likely, most athletes (and fans) of color in this competition will be offended, regardless of team membership. In this situation, race is the superordinate identity, including males and females, athletes and non-athletes and the experienced racism reinforces the need to improve race relations.

Focusing on a superordinate identity does not necessarily negate other social identities. Rather, meaningful superordinate identities embrace and involve other component identities (Hornsey and Hogg, 2000). An example recently occurred after a college football game. Spontaneously, at the end of the game, a number of players joined a prayer circle in the center of the field. Members from both teams came together 'as Christians and not just opponents' (Dunavan, 2006, p. 1). Here, the superordinate identity was Christian, while the subordinate identity was based on team membership.

Further, social identity perspective recognizes the constant struggle among social groups for status, power and resources (Hogg and Abrams, 1990). Dominant groups often will do what is necessary to sustain the status quo that supports their social power and access to resources. Low status groups, conversely, may engage strategies to enhance their social status. One such strategy is *social creativity* which occurs when group members emphasize their unique characteristics, creating a new, positive image

(Tajfel and Turner, 1979). For instance, while stereotypes depict lesbians in a negative manner, Bredemeier *et al.* (1999) re-defined physical educators who were openly lesbian as moral exemplars and positive role models who displayed honesty and high ethical character, traits held in high regard by most dominant groups in society.

Social competition is another strategy to enhance the social standing of a social group. It entails a direct challenge to the high status group in an effort to gain increased power and resources (Tajfel and Turner, 1979). A remarkable example of social competition occurred when the Yale women's rowing team, in 1976, marched into the athletic director's office, disrobed and revealed the words 'Title IX' across their breasts and backs (Mazzio *et al.*, 2002). This protest against their second-class treatment by the athletics department led to greater equity between the women's and men's rowing programs, including a new locker room and improved facilities for the women. Ultimately, social groups are vibrant, dynamic entities; power and status are continuously contested and individual group members constantly negotiate their social identities with social expectations and social perceptions (Breakwell, 1979; Kauer and Krane, 2006; Krane and Barber, 2005).

Gender as a social identity

Whether or not gender should be treated as a social identity has been debated. Some theorists believe that *gender* as a social group category is too broad to be self-descriptive (e.g. Skevington and Baker, 1989). That is, the social category of *female* is multifaceted and contains a myriad of different social groups based on other attributes (e.g. social class, religion, physical ability). Further, examination of a *male* social identity has received little attention by researchers. Conceivably, this inattentiveness to a male social identity occurs because group consciousness is most likely to develop when members of a social group recognize that they are treated unfairly by society (Skevington and Baker, 1989) and this is far more likely to occur in females than males. When a social group is threatened in some manner and the concomitant social identity is important, there is greater group identification, commitment and readiness for social action (Ellemers *et al.*, 2002).

Accordingly, it may be theorized that under conditions of no threat, there is minimal group commitment and involvement. In fact, research shows *female* as a social group is more salient for women who identify as non-traditional or feminist (i.e. who recognize gender biases) than for women who identity as traditional (e.g. Cameron and Lalonde, 2001). Additionally, social status explains why some majority group identities, such as male or White, do not seem to become conscious identities. For example, in North America, *White* is viewed as *normal* whereas people of color are viewed as *other*. The privilege of Whiteness in such a society is not noticing Whiteness or its privileges (Mahoney, 1997). That said, it is important to point out that that taken-for-granted identities, such as *White* or *male*, refer to very specific forms of that identity that typically are shaped by heterosexuality and an upper-middle class status.

Conversely, other researchers have considered gender a core aspect of identity. For example, Worchel (1999) described that 'our [gender] group is clear, enduring, large and powerful. It is at the foundation of our social identity' (p. 23). In our society, gender is highly salient, especially for females. The term *gender* evokes recognition of the status differential between males and females apparent in our society. Ridgeway (2001) described,

. . . gender is an institutional system of social practices for constituting males and females as different in socially significant ways and organizing inequality in terms of those differences (Ridgeway and Smith-Lovin, 1999). Widely shared gender stereotypes are in effect the 'genetic code' of the gender system, since they constitute the cultural rules or schemas by which people perceive and enact gender difference and inequality.

(Ridgeway, 2001, p. 637)

Undeniably, one of the first characteristics noticed about an individual is her or his gender categorization; immediately, people are labeled as female or male. When it is difficult to discern an individual's gender, dissonance occurs. As there are unmistakable gendered social norms and expectations, confusion occurs about how to interpret gender ambiguity. Consider common interactions with infants; knowledge of their gender guides how adults interact with them. For example, girls often are given dolls and pink clothes while boys often are dressed in blue and provided with sports paraphernalia.

Western society has clear gendered expectations about appearance, demeanor and behavior (Butler, 2004). Girls and women are expected to be feminine; boys and men are expected to be masculine. Females learn the strong social code that requires being quiet, dependent and maternal. Appropriate female appearance includes being soft, sexy, clean and toned (Krane *et al.*, 2004). Prevailing social codes encourage males to be competitive, assertive, strong and muscular (Connell and Messerschmidt, 2005). In Butler's (1990, 2004) view, gender is a performance and we learn to *do our gender right*. While gender performance may seem voluntary, there are formidable constraints on this performance. Individuals who fail to perform their gender correctly incur social punishments (Butler, 1990, 2004). Feminine males and masculine females often face social ostracism. To avoid social repercussions, males and females correctly perform accepted, gendered behaviors. In athletic contexts, gender is a highly salient social identity.

Group dynamics and gendered social norms in sport

Power relations

In sport, hegemonic gender norms are stridently upheld; there are strong social codes for acceptable behavior of male and female athletes. Ample evidence exists that sport teaches and reinforces allowable female and male behavior, which coincides with narrow definitions of femininity and masculinity, respectively (e.g. Choi, 2000; Messner, 2002). Referred to as hegemonic (i.e. privileged and powerful), these forms of masculinity and femininity are not necessarily the most common; rather, they are the most valued and create an ideal to which males and females are compared. Those who most resemble this idealized form garner social rewards and power. Star male athletes have become the model of hegemonic masculinity; they are strong, competitive, muscular, dominant and powerful (Burgess *et al.* 2003; Light and Kirk, 2000). In their analysis of televised sport, Messner *et al.* (2000) found 'a remarkably stable and concrete view of masculinity as grounded in bravery, risk taking, violence, bodily strength and heterosexuality' (p. 392). Using excessive force or competing while injured, for instance, conjures social accolades, encouraging male athletes to reify such behavior.

Although the term hegemonic typically is used in conjunction with masculinity and male privilege in sport, there also is merit in recognizing that a particular form of femininity evokes a power hierarchy among females and is upheld as the standard for female athletes (Choi, 2000; Krane, 2001). This privileged form of femininity (i.e. White, heterosexual, upper-middle class femininity) creates a paradox for female athletes:

> Sportswomen must balance some traits essential for athletic success with presentation of an acceptable appearance conforming to the heterosexist norms of society. They must be physically and mentally strong, yet also portray an image of vulnerability to be perceived as feminine.
>
> (Krane, 2001, p. 122)

The hegemonic forms of femininity and masculinity emphasize power relations. Hegemonic masculinity positions males as privileged over females and traditionally masculine males are privileged over other males (Anderson, 2005; Connell and Messerschmidt, 2005). Hegemonic femininity positions *appropriately feminine* women as *normal* (Krane *et al.*, 2004), also invoking a social hierarchy among women.

Further, the indicators of both masculinity and femininity in our society have become linked to heterosexuality (Connell and Messerschmidt, 2005; Krane, 2001). In sport, heterosexuality is a revered social norm, *proven* through strict adherence to correct performances of femininity and masculinity. As such, femininity and masculinity have become social scripts for male and female behavior in most sports. For example, females may wear make-up or bows in their hair to emphasize that indeed they are female (Krane *et al.*, 2004) whereas males may strive to accentuate their muscularity and mental toughness (Greenleaf and Krane, 2007).

Peer acceptance

Messner (2002) imparts a poignant model of gendered behavior for males in youth sport. As he explains, the typical male peer group in youth sport is dominated by a small group of boys who model ideal masculine behavior. These athletes typically are the team leaders or most skilled players and they have high social status because of their athletic prowess. These leaders, then, are able to use their social status to act in a manner that may not be wholly acceptable in other contexts, such as being misogynist or heterosexist, or by hazing team-mates. They are able to act in this manner because other boys on the team are complicit in supporting these dysfunctional norms. The 'leaders', in Messner's terms, are supported by a group of 'wanna be' followers, who desperately want to be accepted by the leaders. To this end, they applaud and encourage the raucous behavior of the leaders. Another group, the 'marginals', may not agree with what their team-mates are doing, yet they realize that if they openly disagree they will face repercussions such as being socially rejected or becoming the target of ridicule. The drive for social acceptance and concomitant desire to avoid social rejection, encourages obedience and support for the leaders.

Waldron and Krane (2005) illustrated how this model of social status and need for acceptance also fits girls' and women's sport. As social acceptance of sport for girls and women has increased, they have adopted many social norms from the *more prestigious* male model of sport. For example, members of girls' teams participate in hazing and excessive alcohol consumption, behaviors previously more common in boys' sport settings. For males and females in sport, there seems to be a strong desire to fit into a team structure. Messner's (2002) model and Waldron and Krane's elaboration of it, is consistent with social identity perspective in that individuals' drive for social acceptance can lead to reckless adherence to social norms. For example, in a study of middle and high school aged athletes, Moulton *et al.* (2000) found that the expectation of fitting in socially compelled student-athletes to drink alcohol. However, this expectation also was associated with a variety of negative consequences such as an inability to do homework or getting into fights. Moulton *et al.* concluded that social expectations may be associated with increased alcohol consumption and that 'adolescents' expectation that alcohol will provide social benefits is a very powerful motivator for alcohol use' (p. 20).

Athletes who do not acquiesce to team norms or who deviate from team expectations risk rejection. Further, as explained by the social identity perspective, nonnormative behavior is perceived to reflect badly on the whole group and often is met with hostility (Marques *et al.*, 2001). Ironically, these hostile reactions enhance commitment to the group, especially when the disregarded norm is highly valued. Thus, group response to nonconformity can result in paradoxical outcomes. When a group member deviates from a valued social norm, that person will likely be derogated by other group members (causing disruption to team unity). Yet, through this exclusionary process, the conforming team members tend to unite in their support of the norm and their disdain toward the non-conforming team member (Marques *et al.* 2001). For example, if appearing feminine is highly valued among members of a volleyball team, a team member with very short hair and wearing no make-up will be ostracized. Teammates may taunt her or exclude her from team activities. They also may emphasize their own femininity, reinforcing its importance. Caution regarding team norms is necessary since uncritical adherence to team norms can lead male and female athletes to engage in a number of risky or health-compromising behaviors (e.g. aggressive actions out of sport, bar fights, unhealthy eating and overtraining) (Crosset, 2000; Curry, 2000; Nixon, 1997; Waldron and Krane, 2005).

Gender conflict in sport

Social identity perspective posits that across groups, there is continuous competition for resources, which leads group members to band together, support their group and fight to maintain or gain access to needed resources. Thus, members of a group are motivated to protect group resources and social status (Abrams and Hogg, 1990). When the group is threatened and commitment to the group is high, strong expressions of loyalty are likely and a readiness to take collective action emerges (Ellemers *et al.*, 2002). In sport, women and men often are pitted against one another in the dispersal of resources, which are disproportionately allocated. In the USA, approximately 60 per cent of all school-related (i.e. high school and post-secondary levels) sporting opportunities are designated for males and 2/3 of sport budgets are allocated for male sport teams (NCAA, 2006; Women's Sports Foundation, 2002a). Thus, males may become motivated to protect their assets and privileged status.

While considering gender discord in sport, it also is fitting to contemplate how groups attain positive distinctiveness. That is, groups aim to differentiate themselves from other groups based on positively perceived characteristics. As Hornsey and Hogg

(2000) explained, 'prejudice, discrimination, negative stereotyping and other aggressive intergroup behaviors form a subset of strategies that are capable of maintaining or achieving positive distinctiveness' (p. 144). Although not encouraged, denigrating other groups and concomitant self-aggrandizing, can increase a group's social status as well as group members' self-esteem and self-worth. Michelle Dumaresq experienced this disparagement as she competed at the highest level of Canadian mountain biking. Michelle, a transgender athlete, was accused of having an unfair advantage (counter to medical research and International Olympic Committee policy). When Michelle won the national championship in 2006, another competitor on the award podium donned a T-shirt with the words '100 per cent pure woman' scrawled in marker (Zurowski, 2007). As predicted by social identity perspective, this protest discriminated against Dumaresq while emphasizing that her competitor was a *real woman*, distancing herself from the transgender sportswoman. Altogether, members of privileged social groups, such as male athletes, are most likely to discriminate against lower status groups, such as female athletes, when their privilege is in jeopardy (Hornsey and Hogg, 2000). Perceived threat to one's social status accentuates adherence to group norms, sharpens group boundaries and reinforces a 'hierarchical leadership and power structure' (i.e. the most privileged males will react in this manner) (Hornsey and Hogg, 2000, p. 145).

As long as male sport is privileged over female sport (Messner, 2002), some males will do whatever it takes to sustain their power. As activists have fought for increased resources for sportswomen, some male sport participants and administrators have become concerned that they may lose funding or other resources. Parallel to women gaining prestige in sport, men's resources have become more threatened. Such consternation has led some males to become discriminatory against women's sport. A current example of this reaction in the USA corresponds to the renewed offensive by some politicians against Title IX (the law that forbids gender discrimination in education, which houses US collegiate sport). As Heywood and Dworkin (2003) pointed out, as women's sport has received more social acceptance and society has become enthusiastic about elite female athletes (e.g. US national soccer team, Women's National Basketball Association), Title IX has come under attack. This threatened stance also is evident when highly muscled, successful female athletes are accused of using steroids (Davis and Delano, 1992) or are labeled lesbian (Krane, 2001). By painting successful female athletes as deviant or 'not real women', it is easy to dismiss their deserved status (Blinde and Taub, 1992).

Interestingly, even within men's sport, certain sports have greater prestige, institutional support and resources. For example, US men's basketball and American football tend to garner a disproportionate amount of university athletic department resources relative to all other men's and women's teams (Lopiano, 2007). Still, battle lines have been drawn along gender boundaries. Rather than all *minor sport* athletes (male and female) who receive reduced resources coalescing, males in these sports tend to side with high status football or basketball players. Why? Because male athletes, as a whole, have higher status than female athletes. As Messner (2002) described, some male athletes have lower status than other male athletes. When these *low status athletes* claim the identity of *male athlete* (i.e. the superordinate identity), they enhance their identity and status. This proclivity helps explain why, for example, the National Wrestling Coaches Association has taken such a strong stance against Title IX, including suing the US government to change the law. As the Women's Sports Foundation espoused, 'the Wrestling Coaches Association's lawsuit does nothing more then pit the "have-nots" (wrestlers whose teams have been dropped) against the "have-nots" (women who are still not getting equal participation opportunities and benefits)' (Women's Sports Foundation, 2002b, p. 6). Consistent with social identity perspective, this strategy of being discriminatory against female sport enhances male *minor sport* athletes' social identity by claiming the superordinate identity of *male athlete*. Whereas aligning themselves with female athletes would diminish their social status, especially among other male athletes. Unfortunately, this strategy supports the status quo within the male sport structure in that the high status athletes continue to reap a greater proportion of the resources than low status male athletes.

Homonegativism has become a common tactic in the gender clash in sport. This prejudicial behavior is composed of 'negative stereotypes, prejudice and discrimination' against lesbian, gay male, bisexual and transgender people (Krane, 1997, p. 145). When aimed at females in sport, homonegativism is a vehicle of social control that demands conformity to traditional female gender roles and hegemonic femininity (Veri, 1999). When women *act out* by demanding equity, they are called lesbian and this lesbian label is used to *keep women in their place*. In many current sport climates, women fear being labeled as lesbian because of the stigma and marginalization associated with the label (Krane and Barber, 2003, 2005). Such stereotyping is a form of social comparison; it preserves the status quo (Leyens *et al.*, 1994) by subordinating female athletes while sustaining male status in sport. Stereotyping successful, muscular and/or outspoken sportswomen as lesbian negatively affects all females in sport. As Wright and Clarke (1999) aptly stated, 'this is pervasive discourse that keeps heterosexual women in their place and lesbian women closeted' (p. 239). Wielding the lesbian stereotype also serves to divide sportswomen, creating dissension among them and limiting their ability to work together to challenge women's inferior status in sport (i.e. minimizing the superordinate identity).

Group dynamics and sexual identity

Because heterosexuality is a cherished social norm in sport, deviation from it can be met with ruthless antagonism. Not only are non-conforming gender performances chastised, unconventional gender performance frequently is conflated with sexual orientation. Because female athletes are thought by some people to contradict ideal femininity, they often are stereotyped as lesbian. Their athletic bodies and competitive nature belie the social discourse that females should be passive, weak, graceful and small (Krane, 2001). Alternatively and stereotypically, it often is considered inconceivable that masculine males can be gay; thus, it is assumed that gay males do not exist in sport (a patently inaccurate precept). Although very different stereotypes surround lesbians and gay males in sport, similar outcomes can transpire. As explained by social identity perspective, when comparing social groups, there is a strong tendency for individuals to describe the group to which they belong (i.e. the in-group) favorably while describing the outgroup unfavorably (Hinkle and Brown, 1990). This process of social comparison results in developing and perpetuating stereotypes, which are used to distinguish between groups (e.g. 'we are not like that') and that generalize characteristics across all group members (Hogg and Abrams, 1990). Additionally, these stereotypes maintain and legitimize the higher status of the ingroup (Leyens *et al.*, 1994). Heterosexual team-mates attempting to protect their privileged social status may denigrate lesbian or gay male team-mates and distance themselves from lesbian or gay male social groups (Barber and Krane, 2005a). Such behaviors disintegrate overall team unity as one or more members are metaphorically, if not literally, estranged.

Having team-mates who differ in sexual orientation can lead to divisiveness when intolerance pervades the team environment. Conversely, it can lead to greater team commitment if respect for all team members becomes the predominant social norm. Current research reveals that some sport teams are accepting of gay and lesbian team-mates (Anderson, 2005; Kauer and Krane, 2006; Mennesson and Clément, 2003). Kauer and Krane (2006) found several positive outcomes within open and accepting team climates: heterosexual athletes realized the fallacy of previously held stereotyped beliefs, the lesbian and bisexual athletes were able to discuss their lives openly and all team members challenged stereotypes about female athletes. In respectful team climates, athletes learn from one another and focus on achieving team goals. In such settings, the multiplicity of gender and sexual identities becomes normalized and athletes recognize their collective struggles (Krane and Kauer, 2007). Challenging stereotypes and discrimination creates alliance among all athletes.

Practical applications: developing productive team dynamics

Social identity perspective provides important practical implications relevant to encouraging productive social dynamics among team members and across social groups in sport as well as for enhancing gender relations in sport. A number of issues need to be considered when attempting to ensure positive group interactions: (a) individuals want to associate with a group that will enhance self-worth, (b) fitting in and being accepted are strong motivators for engaging in normative behavior and (c) distinctions in social status need to be minimized. Another important issue in developing team unity is the subjective meaning of group membership. Individuals need to value membership and perceive it in a similar manner as their team-mates.

Often strategies that encourage productive group dynamics will incorporate several of the above considerations. As social identity perspective suggests, group identity is likely to be strong when membership positively distinguishes its members from other groups (Hogg and Abrams, 1990). On sport teams, this positive distinction will enhance team pride and lead to increased feelings of self-worth among team members. Hornsey and Hogg (2000) suggested that having team symbols or totems could provide this distinctiveness and enhance group solidarity. Having team jackets or t-shirts identify individuals as a member of a specific team (e.g. Falcon women's basketball). There also have been examples where all team members shave their heads in solidarity of a team-mate being treated for cancer. Such simple strategies are celebratory and prideful. When emphasizing team distinctiveness, it is important that the characteristics highlighted are productive and healthy (Waldron and Krane, 2005) because as Ellemers *et al.* (2002) explained, 'the quest for clear intergroup differentiation may paradoxically lead highly committed group members to cultivate negative traits and/or behaviors, insofar as they seem to underline the group's distinct identity' (p. 178). Thus, team leaders and team members need to develop and sustain productive social norms.

When attempting to develop or change team norms, coaches should recognize that the drive for social acceptance can lead to unquestioned adherence to team norms, reinforcing the importance of creating appropriate norms. To create a team identity centered on productive achievement behaviors and pro-social behaviors, coaches and team members can identify important and healthy attributes of a successful team (Barber and Krane, 2002). They may decide, for example, that it is important to engage in community service or achieve high grades. Denouncing heterosexist language and behaviors also can become a team norm. On the field, collective improvement and positive communication may be emphasized. Athletes should be encouraged to suggest what reputation they would like have. Then, as a group, they can brainstorm about how to enhance or sustain the identified characteristics.

It is especially important that athlete leaders (e.g. captains, senior players) reinforce appropriate behaviors; within social identity perspective, leadership is viewed as a group process (Hogg, 2001). Influential team leaders will embody prototypical charac-teristics, which are those deemed most valued and central to distinguishing this group from other groups. Team members likely will emulate the characteristics exhibited and validated by their leaders. If being stereotypically masculine is valued within a team, then, as Messner (2002) explained, team leaders often will be prone to model hetero-sexist, aggressive and dominating behaviors. However, if being compassionate and encouraging team-mates are the norms modeled by team leaders, then these behaviors will be imitated by team members. Paradoxically, strategies to reinforce team norms also can be used to fuel segregation of non-conforming team members (Marques *et al.*, 2001). Careful attention to the value placed on various norms may be advantageous. For example, if a team member dresses differently than team-mates, this should not become cause for disavowal. In contrast, if a team-mate engages in sexist or heterosex-ist behavior, counter to team norms, then a negative response may be warranted.

As previously noted, an important avenue to positive team dynamics is to minimize status differences among team members. One strategy to do so, is to create a super-ordinate goal (Barber and Krane, 2005b), one that reinforces productive norms and requires cooperation among all team members to achieve. When faced with a super-ordinate goal, athletes have to ensure that all team members are able to accomplish their part, or the team as a whole will not succeed. If, for example, there seems to be a split among male team members based on traditionally masculine characteristics (i.e. dominant team members are more assertive and stronger than their peers), the super-ordinate goal should necessitate the expertise of everyone to be achieved. For exam-ple, problem solving capabilities should be considered as important as strength and muscularity.

Consider a team engaged in a ropes challenge course. One of the activities may be to move all team members through a particular course (i.e. the superordinate goal). Team-mates will need to develop collective strategies, invoke problem-solving and leadership, as well as encourage each other. If this course includes crossing a narrow bridge high up in the trees, very likely some athletes (regardless of team status) may need much encouragement from team-mates to complete the course. Overall, everyone on the team will have to cooperate to successfully navigate the whole course. As players help each other, team loyalty and cohesion will increase (Barber and Krane, 2005a,b).

A similar strategy can be used to reduce tension *between* teams. In situations where there is conflict between male and female teams over facilities, a superordinate goal can be used to get them to work together. An athletic director may assign the boys' and girls' tennis teams, for example, to spend a day together cleaning the area around the courts. The teams also could be engaged in a joint fundraiser to earn money to improve their facility. One goal of such actions is to reinforce the superordinate identity, whereby athletes unite based on their school affiliation (e.g. *Bobcat tennis players*). As athletes embrace this superordinate identity, between-group friction should dissipate.

If coaches want to reduce unproductive or unhealthy behaviors and encourage constructive training, these new behaviors need to become entrenched in team norms. Appropriate training will occur when coaches reinforce athletes' strong efforts and openly discuss the hazards of unhealthy behaviors associated with sport. For example, hazing and excessive drinking by athletes have been linked to masculinity in boys' and men's sport (e.g. Allan and DeAngelis, 2004; Curry, 2000). Enduring hazing rituals or drinking more than one's peers reinforces idealized masculine behaviors which, in turn, reinforce one's status on the team. These behaviors also have become common in girls' and women's sport as they emulate the accepted practices in the *higher status* male sport (cf. Waldron and Krane, 2005). To reduce the likelihood of hazing or excessive drinking as accepted team norms, coaches and team leaders can stress the importance of respecting team-mates and engaging in healthy training behaviors. As such, athletes can be offered an alternative to the discouraged behaviors. Further, team rules can make hazing and drinking alcohol unacceptable. When creating team rules, athletes should engage in discussion about why hazing is counterproductive to achieving team goals. If athletes are involved in decisions about the team rules, it is more likely that they will accept them. In this discussion, athletes should be empowered to enforce these rules among themselves. When athletes believe that being respectful includes challenging team-mates who break team rules, team members will self-regulate appropriate actions, without coach intervention.

Furthermore, care is needed that valued subsidiary (i.e. minority) social identities are not belittled within team settings. That is, teams typically are not comprised of identical members and athletes will have a range of additional social identities (e.g. race, sexual identity, academic major, year in school) that also are important to them. As Hornsey and Hogg (2000) proposed, 'social harmony is most likely to be achieved by maintaining, not weakening, subgroup identities, provided they are nested within a coherent superordinate identity' (p. 143). These subgroups do not need to detract from the collective esteem of the team. In other words, team-mates respect individual differences. Cory Johnson's experience provides an example: Cory was a high school football player who came out to his team-mates as a gay male (Cassels, 2000). Rather than rebuking him, his team-mates were supportive. They openly talked and joked about Cory's revelation. Importantly, they also perceived harassment from members of other teams as inappropriate and unacceptable. Although Cory was a minority as an openly gay male football player, it did not create tension within the team nor did it detract from team cohesion.

Cory's example is similar to Kauer and Krane's (2006) findings that respecting individual differences will lead to positive outcomes, such as speaking out against discriminatory actions. One strategy to encourage impartiality is to create a team norm based on diversity, thus expecting that everyone brings something different, yet important to the team. While discussing team strengths, coaches can highlight the importance of each individual comprising the group and underscore that each team member provides important contributions to team success (Barber and Krane, 2005a). Pointing out the different contributions or unique abilities of each player also will enhance team functioning. This activity can be quite powerful if the athletes identify each others' talent. As Rink and Ellemers (2007) suggested, the availability of various resources and skills can lead to enhanced innovation and creativity. Team identity, then, becomes based on 'individual actions on behalf of the team' (Rink and Ellemers, 2007, p. S20). These social norms allowing individuality within the team structure can create a safe environment where athletes are not compelled to conceal lesbian, gay, bisexual, or transgender identities, for example. Social norms embracing individuality also will 'allow people to maintain a degree of distinctiveness within the broader group while still maintaining a sense of belonging with that group' (Hornsey and Jetten, 2004, p. 254).

As Hornsey and Hogg (2000) explained, recognizing subgroup identities is important, as is the development of an overall team identity that is 'a source of pride and positive identity that does not conflict with or contradict cherished attributes of subgroup identity' (p. 153). Ideally, administrators and coaches encourage team norms that respect all athletes, regardless of individual differences. As coaches model appropriate behavior, athlete leaders also will be socialized to value these characteristics and will transmit them to their team members.

Directions for future research

Since few sport researchers have employed social identity perspective in their work, there are many avenues for further research in group dynamics. Most of the research that has been conducted has used a social identity perspective to understand the experiences of a specific, marginalized group within sport (e.g. lesbians; Krane and Barber, 2005). Thus, any application of the broader principles related to group interactions, team leadership and social hierarchy in sport will extend our understanding of gendered group dynamics.

An initial entrée into this area of research is to identify productive and unproductive norms within sport teams. This can occur through use of ethnographic methodology (cf. Krane and Baird, 2005). Participant observation combined with interviewing members of a particular team, or even a whole sport league, would be enlightening concerning the group dynamics. Researchers could learn how sexist and heterosexist norms are developed and sustained within teams. This knowledge, then, would provide the first step toward eradicating such behavior.

Social identity perspective predicts that collective esteem will be related to positive attributes (e.g. Crocker and Luhtanen, 1990). In sport, the Collective Self-Esteem Scale (CSES; Luhtanen and Crocker, 1992) rarely has been used. With this scale, researchers can examine how collective esteem is related to mental states such as sport competence, intrinsic motivation, or goal orientation. Similarly, associations among collective esteem and group characteristics such as cohesion should be investigated. Luhtanen and Crocker showed that slight modification of the scale, to correspond to a specific social group, did not compromise the validity and reliability of the scale. Thus, as Dworsky (2004) did, the scale can become sport-specific, or possibly even team-specific. Additionally, there are scales that assess conformity to femininity (Mahalik *et al.*, 2005) and conformity to masculinity (Mahalik *et al.*, 2003). While many measures of masculinity and femininity are fraught with stereotypical connotations, if the focus of a study is on stereotyped or hegemonic masculinity and femininity, such scales may be beneficial. Combining assessment of collective esteem and conformity to femininity or masculinity can shed light on the strength of team norms surrounding femininity and masculinity, which would provide the foundation for investigations about how these norms are related to other behaviors (e.g. aggression, hazing, eating, or drinking alcohol).

Understanding how athletes' commitment to femininity or masculinity may instigate sexist and heterosexist behavior, is another avenue for future research.

An important area for subsequent research is to examine the effectiveness of the strategies or interventions suggested in this chapter. For example, group cohesion and collective esteem could be assessed in conjunction with an intervention aimed at increasing respect for diversity and acceptance of team-mates who differ in sexual orientation. Pre- and post-assessments could identify changes in group dynamics as social norms change. Interviews with athletes about their experiences during the intervention as well as changes in the team climate also would be enlightening.

These examples are only a few directions for future research. As noted, there is much room for advancement of our knowledge concerning gendered group dynamics. Using either qualitative or quantitative methods will be informative. Importantly, studies should be theoretically grounded as well as have practical application. Social identity perspective easily can guide our future efforts to study the role of gender, sexual identity, femininity and masculinity in shaping the behaviors of athletes. Ultimately research in this area will lay the foundation for nurturing diverse, accepting and constructive team environments.

Summary

It is impossible to ignore gender when examining the social institution of sport. Clear cut social norms, based on gender, guide much behavior in sport. As explained, that does not necessitate a focus on gender differences in sport. Rather, consideration of socially enforced gender norms, guided by social identity perspective, provides an entrée into understanding how gender influences sporting behaviors. Hegemonic femininity and masculinity create social norms often adopted in sport. These norms can lead to discriminatory behaviors if alternative norms are not created and reinforced.

Athletes are motivated to have an affirming social identity, based on group membership. Teams that encourage supportive, constructive social norms will have loyal, committed and cohesive members. Further, acceptance of diverse team members will lead to constructive and productive team climates. Conversely, the preponderance of bias against athletes for not fitting the social norms of appropriately feminine females and appropriately masculine males can negatively affect intra-team dynamics as well as gender relationships in sport. Such prejudicial behavior likely will be unproductive, detract attention from achieving group goals and create hostile climates in sport. Coaches and team leaders can employ numerous tactics to increase the likelihood of constructive social norms and rewarding sport climates. Sport teams that adopt social norms of inclusion and respecting team-mates will have relaxed and productive sport climates (Hornsey and Hogg, 2000).

Recognizing the influence of social acceptance, leadership from athletes will have a strong effect on team norms and behaviors. The desire to fit in encourages newer team members to adopt the accepted behaviors of the more senior team members. Social identity perspective helps us understand the important role of social acceptance in the strict adherence to norms, even those that may impede team cohesion or athletic success. This perspective also provides guidance for enhancing team unity and intergroup relationships. As such, social identity perspective is a much needed, yet largely overlooked, foundation for examining group dynamics in sport.

Acknowledgment

The author extends her appreciation to Sandra Short for her valuable feedback and constructive comments on an earlier version of this manuscript.

References

Abrams, D. and Hogg, M. A. (1990). An introduction to the social identity approach. In D. Abrams and M. Hogg (Eds), *Social identity theory: Constructive and critical advances* (pp. 1–9). New York: Springer-Verlag.

Anderson, E. (2005). *In the game: Gay athletes and the cult of masculinity*. Albany, NY: State University of New York Press.

Allan, E. J. and DeAngelis, G. (2004). Hazing, masculinity and collision sports: (Un)becoming heroes. In J. Johnson and M. Holman (Eds), *Making the team: Inside the world of sport initiations and hazing* (pp. 61–80). Toronto: Canadian Scholar's Press.

Barber, H. and Krane, V. (2002, October). A theory-to-practice approach to creating positive team climates: A social identity perspective. Colloquium presented at the meeting of the Association for the Advancement of Applied Sport Psychology, Tucson, Arizona.

Barber, H. and Krane, V. (2005a). The elephant in the lockerroom: Opening the dialogue about sexual orientation on women's sport teams. In M. Andersen (Ed.), *Sport psychology in practice* (pp. 259–279). Champaign, IL: Human Kinetics.

Barber, H. and Krane, V. (2005b, April). The elusive elephant in the lockerroom: Creating positive climates for lesbian and gay youth in physical education and sport. Symposium presented at the American Alliance for Health, Physical Education, Recreation and Dance national conference, Chicago, Illinois.

Blinde, E. and Taub, D. (1992). Women athletes as falsely accused deviants: Managing the lesbian stigma. *The Sociological Quarterly*, 33, 521–533.

Breakwell, G. M. (1979). Women: Group and identity? *Women's Studies International Quarterly*, 2, 9–17.

Bredemeier, B. J. L., Carlton, E. B., Hills, L. A. and Oglesby, C. A. (1999). Changers and the changed: Moral aspects of coming out in physical education. *Quest*, 51, 418–431.

Burgess, I., Edwards, A. and Skinner, J. (2003). Football culture in an Australian school setting: The construction of masculine identity. *Sport, Education and Society*, 8, 199–212.

Butler, J. (1990). *Gender trouble: Feminism and the subversion of identity*. New York: Routledge.

Butler, J. (2004). *Undoing gender*. New York: Routledge.

Cameron, J. E. and Lalonde, R. N. (2001). Social identification and gender-related ideology in women and men. *British Journal of Social Psychology*, 40, 59–77.

Cassels, P. (2000). A brave athlete, supportive school: The Massconomet Regional High football team's co-captain comes out and finds a world of support. *Bay Windows Magazine*. Online. Available: http://www.outsports.com/gaymassplayer.htm (Accessed March, 2007).

Choi, P. Y. L. (2000). *Femininity and the physically active woman*. New York: Routledge.

Connell, R. W. and Messerschmidt, J. W. (2005). Hegemonic masculinity: Rethinking the concept. *Gender and Society*, 19, 829–859.

Crocker, J. and Luhtanen, R. (1990). Collective self-esteem and ingroup bias. *Journal of Personality and Social Psychology*, 58, 60–67.

Crosset, T. (2000). Athletic affiliation and violence against women: Toward a structural prevention project. In J. McKay, M. A. Messner and D. F. Sabo (Eds), *Masculinities, gender relations and sport* (pp. 147–161). Thousand Oaks, CA: Sage.

Curry, T. J. (2000). Booze and bar fights: A journey to the dark side of college athletics. In J. McKay (Ed.), *Masculinities, gender relations and sport* (pp. 162–175). Thousand Oaks, CA: Sage.

Davis, L. R. and Delano, L. C. (1992). Fixing the boundaries of physical gender: Side effects of anti-drug campaigns in athletics. *Sociology of Sport Journal,* 9, 1–19.

DeBoer, K. J. (2004). *Gender and competition: How men and women approach work and play differently.* Monterey, CA: Coaches Choice Books.

Dunavan, N. (2006)). In the spirit: UND gridders take a page from Jesus' playbook. Online. Available: *GrandForksHerald.com.* http://72.14.203.104/search?q=cache:POQ0kbGG1rkJ: www.grandforksherald.com /articles/index.cfm per cent3Fid per cent3D18204 per cent26section per cent3Dcolumnists per cent26columnist per cent3DNaomi per cent2520Dunavan-+sioux+football+prayerandhl=enandgl=usandct=clnkandcd=1andclient=firefox-a (Accessed March, 2007)

Dworsky, D. (2004). The psychosocial development of collegiate student-athletes and student-musicians. Unpublished doctoral dissertation, Bowling Green State University, Ohio.

Ellemers, N., Spears, R. and Doosje, B. (2002). Self and social identity. *Annual Review of Psychology,* 53, 161–186.

Fuss, D. (1989). *Essentially speaking: Nature and difference.* New York: Routledge.

Greenleaf, C. and Krane, V. (2007). 'The more muscles you have, the more masculine you are': How male athletes and exercisers construct and negotiate masculinity. (Manuscript submitted for publication.)

Heywood, L. and Dworkin, S. L. (2003). *Built to win: The female athlete as cultural icon.* Minneapolis: University of Minnesota Press.

Hinkle, S. and Brown, R. (1990). Intergroup comparisons and social identity: Some links and lacunae. In D. Abrams and M. A. Hogg (Eds), *Social identity theory: Constructive and critical advances* (pp. 48–70). New York: Springer-Verlag.

Hogg, M. A. (2001). A social identity theory of leadership. *Personality and Social Psychology Review,* 5, 184–200.

Hogg, J. and Abrams, D. (1990). *Social identifications: A social psychology of intergroup relations and group processes.* New York: Routledge.

Hogg, M. A. and McGarty, C. (1990). Self-categorization and social identity. In D. Abrams and M. Hogg (Eds), *Social identity theory: Constructive and critical advances* (pp. 10–27). New York: Springer-Verlag.

Hornsey, M. J. and Hogg, M. A. (2000). Assimilation and diversity: An integrative model of subgroup relations. *Personality and Social Psychology Review,* 4, 143–156.

Hornsey, M. J. and Jetten, J. (2004). The individual within the group: Balancing the need to belong with the need to be different. *Personality and Social Psychology Review,* 8, 248–264.

Hurtado, A. (1997). Understanding multiple group identities: Inserting women into cultural transformation. *Journal of Social Issues,* 53, 299–328.

Kauer, K. and Krane, V. (2006). 'Scary dykes and feminine queens': Stereotypes and female athletes. *Women in Sport and Physical Activity Journal,* 15, 43–56.

Krane, V. (1997). Homonegativism experienced by lesbian collegiate athletes. *Women in Sport and Physical Activity Journal,* 6, 141–163.

Krane, V. (2001). We can be athletic and feminine, but do we want to? Challenging hegemonic femininity in women's sport. *Quest,* 53, 115–133.

Krane, V. (2004). Fair treatment and discrimination in sport. In C. Spielberger (Ed.), *Encyclopedia of Applied Psychology.* San Diego, CA: Academic Press.

Krane, V. and Baird, S. M. (2005). Using ethnography in applied sport psychology. *Journal of Applied Sport Psychology,* 17, 1–21.

Krane, V. and Barber, H. (2003). Lesbian experiences in sport: A social identity perspective. *Quest,* 55, 328–346.

Krane, V. and Barber, H. (2005). Identity tensions in lesbian college coaches. *Research Quarterly for Exercise and Sport,* 76, 67–81.

Krane, V., Choi, P. Y. L., Baird, S. M., Aimar, C. M. and Kauer, K. J. (2004). Living the paradox: Female athletes negotiate femininity and muscularity. *Sex Roles,* 50, 315–329.

Krane, V. and Kauer, K. J. (2007). Out on the ball fields: Lesbians in sport. In E. Peele and V.

Clark (Eds), *Out in Psychology: Lesbian, gay, bisexual and transgender perspectives* (pp. 273–290). Chichester, West Sussex: John Wiley and Sons.

Laverie, D. A. and Arnett, D. B. (2000). Factors affecting fan attendance: The influence of identity salience and satisfaction. *Journal of Leisure Research, 32*, 225–247.

Leyens, J., Yzerbyt, V. and Schadron, G. (1994). *Stereotypes and social cognitions*. London: Sage.

Light, R. and Kirk, D. (2000). High school rugby, the body and the reproduction of hegemonic masculinity. *Sport, Education and Society, 5*, 163–76.

Lopiano, D. (2007). *The state of women's sports 2006*. Online: Available from the Women's Sport Foundation website: http://www.womenssportsfoundation.org/cgi-bin/iowa/issues/history/article.html?record=1168 (Accessed March, 2007).

Luhtanen, R. and Crocker, J. (1992). A collective self-esteem scale: Self-evaluation of one's social identity. *Personality and Social Psychology Bulletin, 18*, 302–318.

Mahalik, J. R., Locke, B. D., Ludlow, L. H., Diemer, M. A., Scott, R. P. J., Gottfried, M. and Freitas, G. (2003). Development of the conformity to masculine norms inventory. *Psychology of Men and Masculinity, 4*, 3–25.

Mahalik, J. R., Morray, E. B., Coonerty-Femiano, A., Ludlow, L. H., Slattery, S. M. and Smiler, A. (2005). Development of the conformity to feminine norms inventory. *Sex Roles, 52*, 417–435.

Mahoney, M.R. (1997). The social construction of Whiteness. In R. Delgado and J. Stefancic (Eds), *Critical White studies: Looking behind the mirror* (pp. 330–333). Philadelphia: Temple University Press.

Marques, J. M., Abrams, D., Paez, D. and Hogg, M. A. (2001). Social categorization, social identification and rejection of deviant group members. In M. A. Hogg and S. Tinsdale (Eds), *Blackwell handbook of social psychology: Group processes* (pp. 425–460). Malden, MA: Blackwell.

Mazzio, M. (Writer/Director), Mazzio, T. (Producer) and Hamilton, E. (Producer). (2002). *A Hero for Daisy*. [Motion picture]. USA: 50 Eggs Films.

Mennesson, C. and Clément, J. P. (2003). Homosociability and homosexuality: The case of soccer played by women. *International Review for the Sociology of Sport, 38*, 311–330.

Messner, M. A. (2002). *Taking the field: Women, men and sports*. Minneapolis: University of Minnesota Press.

Messner, M. A., Dunbar, M. and Hunt, D. (2000). The televised sports manhood formula. *Journal of Sport and Social Issues, 24*, 380–394.

Moulton, M., Moulton, P., Whittington, A. N. and Cosio, D. (2000). The relationship between negative consequence drinking, gender, athletic participation and social experiences among adolescents. *Journal of Alcohol and Drug Education, 45*, 12–22.

NCAA. (2006). *2003–04 NCAA Gender-Equity Report*. Online. Available from the NCAA website: http://www.ncaa.org/library/research/gender_equity_study/2003–04/2003–04_gender-_equity_report.pdf (Accessed March, 2006).

Nixon, H. L. (1997). Gender, sport and aggressive behavior outside sport. *Journal of Sport and Social Issues, 21*, 379–391.

Ridgeway, C. L. (2001). Gender, status and leadership. *Journal of Social Issues, 57*, 637–655.

Rink, F. and Ellemers, N. (2007). Diversity as a basis for shared organizational identity: The norm congruity principle. *British Journal of Management, 18*, S17–S27.

Skevington, S. and Baker, D. (1989). Introduction. In S. Skevington and D. Baker (Eds), *The social identity of women* (pp. 1–14). Newbury Park, CA: Sage.

Spears, R., Doosje, B. and Ellemers, N. (1999). Commitment and the context of social perception. In N. Ellemers, R. Spears and B. Doosje (Eds), *Social identity: Context, commitment, content* (pp. 59–83). Oxford: Blackwell.

Tajfel, H. and Turner, J. C. (1979). An integrative theory of intergroup conflict. In S. Worshel and W. G. Austin (Eds), *The social psychology of intergroup relations* (pp. 33–47). Monterey, CA: Brooks-Cole.

Tatum, B. D. (2003). *'Why are all the Black kids sitting together in the cafeteria?' and other conversations about race*. New York: Basic Books.

Turner, J. C. and Reynolds, K. J. (2001). The social identity perspective in intergroup relations: Theories, themes and controversies. In R. Brown and S. L. Gaertner (Eds), *Blackwell handbook of social psychology: Intergroup processes* (pp. 133–152). Malden, MA: Blackwell.

Turner, J. C., Hogg, M. A., Oakes, P. J., Reichter, S. D. and Wetherell, M. S. (1987). *Rediscovering the social group: A self-categorization theory.* Oxford: Basil Blackwell.

Veri, M. J. (1999). Homophobic discourse surrounding the female athlete. *Quest,* 51, 355–368.

Waldron, J. J. and Krane, V. (2005). Whatever it takes: Health compromising behaviors in female athletes. *Quest,* 57, 315–329.

Women's Sports Foundation (2002a). *Title IX at 30: Report Card on Gender Equity.* Washington, DC: National Coalition for Women and Girls in Education.

Women's Sports Foundation (2002b). *Title IX and the Wrestling Coaches Association's lawsuit* (May 30th). Online. Available: http://www.womenssportsfoundation.org/cgi-bin/iowa/issues/rights/article.html?record=894 (Accessed October, 2006).

Worchel, S. (1999). *Written in blood: Ethnic identity and the struggle for human harmony.* New York: Worth Publishers.

Wright, J. and Clarke, G. (1999). Sport, the media and the construction of compulsory heterosexuality. *International Review for the Sociology of Sport,* 34, 227–243.

Zurowski, J. (2007, Jan/Feb). It's a girl thing. *Vancouver Magazine.* Online. Available: http://www.thepinkseats.com/archive/2007/01/18 (Accessed March, 2007).

Part IV
Motivation in groups

Photograph by Richard Lam/UBC Athletics. Reprinted courtesy of The University of British Columbia.

10 Self-determined motivation in sport and exercise groups

Martyn Standage and Robert J. Vallerand

Introduction

A considerable amount of sport, exercise and physical activity behavior occurs within group settings. Every day, an untold number of individuals participate in team sports, exercise classes and school physical education (PE) lessons. In our endeavors to understand why disparities exist between individuals' behavior, reported investment and personal experiences of such social settings, the concept of motivation provides valuable insight. Indeed, motivation has been repeatedly advanced as a key factor when attempting to predict outcomes such as sporting success, exercise persistence and athlete/exerciser well-being (see Vallerand, 2007 for a review). Further, since past work has shown individuals to have a need to relate, connect and belong (cf. Baumeister and Leary, 1995; Deci and Ryan, 2000), comprehending motivation in group settings is crucial to our understanding of how others influence our, and we their, experiences and behaviors in group/team physical activity settings.

A fundamental starting point to this chapter is a definition of motivation. At a basic level, individuals are said to be motivated when they are *moved* to do something (Ryan and Deci, 2000). Accordingly, motivation is evident in all human actions, encompassing essential functions (e.g. eating), behaviors that one must do (e.g. attend school) and actions that are selectively engaged (e.g. one's hobbies). Clearly, however, the reasons and foci of *why* individuals partake in activities differ greatly. Addressing the *energizing*, *direction*, *regulation* and *persistence* of human behavior, it is this overarching question of 'why' behavior occurs that guides the study of motivation (Deci and Ryan, 1985; McClelland, 1985). During the past 15 years a burgeoning line of empirical work has employed a Self-Determination Theory (SDT) (Deci and Ryan, 1991, 2000) perspective to explore and explain motivational processes in physical activity settings (see Hagger and Chatzisarantis, 2007 for reviews).

The purpose of this chapter is to review past SDT research with a keen eye towards applying these findings to group physical activity settings. To facilitate this objective, we have adopted an approach akin to the motivational sequence of SDT and one identified by Vallerand (1997) in his Hierarchical Model of Intrinsic and Extrinsic Motivation (HMIEM). This sequence is represented by 'social factors → psychological mediators → types of motivation → consequences' and is shown in Figure 10.1. Following a review of extant work grounded in SDT, we then discuss a number of issues pertaining to measurement of motivational processes at the group level. In the penultimate section we suggest some practical applications grounded in SDT. Finally, we conclude by highlighting a number of research directions that appear promising for future SDT work.

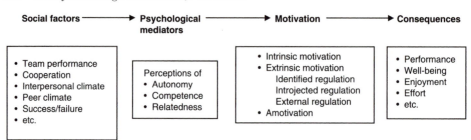

Figure 10.1 Motivational sequence proposed by SDT and the HMIEM. (Adapted from Vallerand and Losier, 1999.)

Theory and research

Self-determination theory (Deci and Ryan, 1991, 2000) embraces a multidimensional perspective of motivation. That is, rather than viewing motivation as a dichotomy (e.g. internal versus external motivation; deCharms, 1968), SDT distinguishes between different reasons that form the impetus for action or inaction. SDT categorizes motivation into three types; namely *intrinsic motivation, extrinsic motivation* and *amotivation*. See Figure 10.2 for a schematic overview of the types of motivation embraced by SDT and their associated regulatory processes.

Intrinsic motivation is the prototype of self-determined regulation. When intrinsically motivated, individuals are fully self-regulated, engage in activities out of interest, experience a sense of volition and function without the aid of external rewards and/or constraints (Deci and Ryan, 1985, 2000). Put more simply, when intrinsically motivated an individual takes part in an activity for its own sake. For example, hockey players who play the sport simply for the pleasure and satisfaction that they gain from learning new skills would be displaying intrinsic motivation.

While intrinsically motivated actions represent behaviors that are performed for the inherent pleasure that emanates directly from an activity, extrinsic motivation embraces a broad variety of behaviors that are characterized by an individual's goal of action being governed by some separable consequence. While traditional approaches to extrinsic motivation considered the construct to be antithetical to intrinsic motivation by reflecting non-autonomous behavior directed at obtaining a tangible a reward (e.g. deCharms, 1968), SDT views this type of extrinsic motivation to capture just one type of extrinsically motivated behavior (Ryan and Deci, 2000). Arguing that such a one-dimensional approach does not capture the vast range of behaviors that are pursued for extrinsic reasons, Deci and Ryan (1985) proposed a typology of extrinsic motivation in which some types are autonomously pursued. The different types of extrinsic motivation outlined by SDT are hypothesized to form a quasi-simplex pattern reflecting a continuum of self-determination and from most to least autonomous these are labeled *identified regulation, introjected regulation* and *external regulation*.[1] Empirical support for the self-determination continuum has been reported in numerous contexts including sport, exercise and PE (Chatzisarantis et al., 2003; Li and Harmer, 1996).[2]

External regulation is the least self-determined form of extrinsic motivation, referring to actions controlled by external contingencies such as rewards and constraints (Deci and Ryan, 1985). For example, tennis players who participate in the sport to

MOTIVATION	AMOTIVATION	EXTRINSIC MOTIVATION				INTRINSIC MOTIVATION
TYPE OF REGULATION	Non-regulation	External	Introjection	Identified	Integration	Intrinsic
PERCEIVED LOCUS OF CAUSALITY	Impersonal	External	Somewhat external	Somewhat internal	Internal	Internal
INTERNALIZATION	No	No	Partial	Almost full	Full	Not required
QUALITY OF BEHAVIOR	Non-self-determined		Self-determined			
RELEVENT REGULATORY PROCESSES	Lack of • competence • contingency • intention • activity value	Presence of external • constraints • rewards • compliance • punishments	Focus on • approval (i.e. self or others) • ego involvement • internal rewards and punishment	• Activity valued • Personally important • Consciously pursued	Synthesis of identified regulations to self • Awareness • Congruence	Inherent • enjoyment • fun • satisfaction • pleasure

Figure 10.2 Schematic overview of the self-determination continuum outlining the types of motivation advanced by SDT and related processes. (Adapted from Ryan and Deci, 2000, 2002.)

receive trophies and awards would be acting out of external regulation. The next type of extrinsic motivation is referred to as introjected regulation which is characterized by an individual partly internalizing external regulation (Ryan and Deci, 2002). Rather than external contingencies directing the behavior, the impetus for introjected action is regulated by self-imposed sanctions (e.g. shame, self-guilt, ego enhancement, pride). It is important to stress that while the contingencies are internal, introjection is still quite a controlling motivation type. An example of introjected regulation would be exercisers who take part in aerobics classes, not because they like the class, but rather because they would feel a sense of personal guilt if they were not to attend. Identified regulation refers to a relatively self-determined form of extrinsic motivation in which an individual freely chooses to perform an activity as they accept the underlying value of the behavior (Deci and Ryan, 2000). Although identified regulation refers to behaviors that have been accepted as ones own, behavior is still instrumental as it is the usefulness of the activity, rather than the activity's inherent interest that guides participation (Deci and Ryan, 2000). An example of identified regulation would be individuals who go running, not because they like the activity, but because they recognize that running regularly has benefits for their health.

Deci and Ryan (1985) have also proposed that amotivation should be included when trying to comprehend human motivation. Amotivation occurs when individuals lack an intention to act or when they passively perform activities (Ryan and Deci, 2000). Amotivation stems from a lack of competence, the belief that an activity is unimportant and/or when an individual does not perceive contingencies between her/his behavior and the desired outcome(s) (Ryan and Deci, 2000; Vallerand, 1997). An example of amotivation would be students in school PE who are just 'going through the motions'.

The arrangement of the motivational types along the self-determination continuum is helpful when one wants to hypothesize their associations with outcome variables (Deci and Ryan, 1991). SDT advances that intrinsic motivation will lead to the most positive consequences followed by integrated regulation and identified regulation. In contrast, external regulation and amotivation are hypothesized to be associated with negative consequences. Introjected regulation is hypothesized to lead to consequences that lie between external regulation and identified regulation. Research in a variety of physical activity contexts has shown autonomous forms of motivation (intrinsic motivation and identified regulation) to be associated with adaptive outcomes such as behavioral persistence (Pelletier *et al.*, 2001), concentration (Ntoumanis, 2005), positive affect (Standage *et al.*, 2005a), reported effort (Ntoumanis, 2001), physical self-esteem (Wilson and Rodgers, 2004), flow (Kowal and Fortier, 1999), positive sportspersonship (Donahue *et al.*, 2006) and quality of life (Gillison *et al.*, 2006). In contrast, controlling types of extrinsic motivation and amotivation have been shown to be linked with maladaptive consequences such as drop-out (Pelletier *et al.*, 2001), unhappiness (Standage *et al.*, 2005a), boredom (Ntoumanis, 2001) and poor sportspersonship (Donahue *et al.*, 2006; Vallerand and Losier, 1994) (see Vallerand, 2007 for a review).

Self-determination theory contains both organismic and dialectic elements to address motivated behavior. The organismic aspect of SDT considers humans to be growth-oriented organisms who actively seek optimal challenges and new experiences to master and integrate (Ryan and Deci, 2002). However, since the engagement in activities does not exist in social isolation, the dialectic component addresses the interaction between the growth-oriented individual and social factors that either facilitate or impede personal growth and development (Deci and Ryan, 1991; Ryan and Deci, 2002). According to SDT, this growth and development is achieved through being exposed to social environments that satisfy three innate psychological needs. The needs outlined by SDT are for autonomy (i.e. the need to endorse and be the origin of one's behavior), competence (i.e. the need to interact effectively within the environment) and relatedness (i.e. the need to feel connected, cared for and close to others and one's community) (Ryan and Deci, 2002). When these psychological needs are met self-determined motivation and well-being are promoted, however if thwarted then self-determined motivation and well-being are undermined (Deci and Ryan, 2000). Empirical support for the veracity of SDT's basic needs approach has been found in physical activity contexts such as team sports, exercise groups and school PE classes (see Hagger and Chatzisarantis, 2007 for reviews). Since the psychological needs advanced by SDT are considered essential nutriments that mediate the 'social context – motivation relationship', an understanding of the various social factors that promote, as opposed to forestall, need satisfaction in group settings is central to the objectives of this chapter. It is to a number of these social factors that our attention now turns.

Autonomy support

Coaches, instructors and teachers in physical activity settings have the potential to promote or thwart the motivational strivings of group members. Indeed, the way in which those in supervisory positions act engenders perceptions of the social environment that can, according to SDT, be perceived as being autonomy-supportive or controlling. SDT hypothesizes that autonomy-supportive environments (i.e. social contexts that support choice, initiation and understanding, while minimizing the need to perform and act in a prescribed manner) as opposed to controlling environments facilitate self-determined motivation and optimal psychological functioning.

Using a sample of competitive swimmers, Pelletier *et al.* (2001) conducted a prospective study to examine the relationships between the coaches' interpersonal behavior (autonomy support versus control), the types of motivational regulation and behavioral persistence (i.e. persistence versus drop-out). Structural equation modeling analyses revealed that perceiving the coach to be autonomy-supportive positively predicted self-determined forms of motivation (i.e. intrinsic motivation and identified regulation) and negatively predicted reported amotivation. To a lesser extent, autonomy-support positively predicted introjected regulation. In contrast, perceiving the coach to be controlling positively predicted amotivation and controlling forms of extrinsic motivation (i.e. external regulation and introjected regulation). Swimmers who reported self-determined types of motivation at the first time point showed greater persistence as assessed 10 and 22 months later. Additionally, swimmers who exhibited amotivation at the first time point had the highest drop-out rate at both 10 and 22 months. Interestingly, introjected regulation was a significant and positive predictor of persistence at 10 months, but not at 22 months. External regulation negatively predicted persistence at 22 months.

A number of studies in physical activity settings have also provided empirical support for the beneficial motivational effects that individuals gain from interacting with autonomy-supportive coaches, instructors and teachers. This work has shown perceptions of autonomy support to positively predict reported levels of self-determined motivation, both directly (e.g. Hagger *et al.*, 2003; Wilson and Rodgers, 2004) and via the satisfaction of autonomy, competence and relatedness (e.g. Standage *et al.*, 2003a, 2006).

Although past research has corroborated the benefits of an autonomy-supportive environment, the percentage of variance explained by autonomy-support alone in satisfying the basic needs of autonomy, competence and relatedness can be small (Standage *et al.*, 2007a). To explain more variance in the need-satisfaction variables, researchers may wish to also explore other social environments alongside autonomy support. In teams, classes and school physical education lessons, there are a number of aspects inherent within the social context that may support participants' basic need satisfaction (e.g. performance outcome, cooperation, competition, etc.). Our focus now shifts to some of these social factors.

Performance outcome and win/loss feedback

When individuals and teams engage in competitive situations, the outcomes of *winning* and *losing* are inevitable. A number of empirical studies have examined the effects of competitive outcome on intrinsic motivation (cf. Vallerand *et al.*, 1987). Much of this work has been grounded in Cognitive Evaluation Theory (CET), which is now a well articulated sub-theory of SDT. Deci (1975) formulated CET to identify and synthesize empirical findings regarding the various *external* events (and later *internal events*; Ryan, 1982) that enhance versus diminish intrinsic motivation (Deci and Ryan, 1985). CET holds that any event that satisfies an individual's innate need for competence and autonomy leads to increases in intrinsic motivation. Empirical work has shown winning to increase competence perceptions and intrinsic interest, whereas losing has been negatively linked to perceptions of competence and intrinsic motivation (Reeve and Deci, 1996; Vallerand *et al.*, 1986; Weinberg and Ragan, 1979).

When considering objective win/loss information, it is important to remember the way in which teams and/or individuals evaluate their performance. Research has demonstrated that individuals who perceive that they have performed well are more likely, even if they have been objectively unsuccessful, to report greater levels of intrinsic motivation than those who perceive failure (McAuley and Tammen, 1989). Such findings suggest that it is the individual's subjective evaluation of success (or lack of) that is key to motivational responses.

In addition to objective win/loss information, past research has shown that by providing athletes with feedback about their strengths and weaknesses, significant others (e.g. coaches, teachers, instructors) can influence participants' reported level of intrinsic motivation (e.g. Vallerand and Reid, 1984, 1988). This work has shown that positive feedback enhances, and negative feedback decreases, reported levels of intrinsic motivation. A study by Thill and Mouanda (1990) found that team handball players who received bogus negative verbal feedback that indicated failure after shooting at targets reported lower levels of intrinsic motivation than players receiving bogus positive verbal feedback that denoted success.

Building on work couched in a CET approach, research has extended the examination of the win-loss distinction to the broader SDT framework (e.g. Blanchard and Vallerand, 1996; Standage *et al.*, 2005b). This work has replicated previous CET-based findings by showing objective outcome and subjective perceptions of performing well to positively correspond to the needs for autonomy, competence and relatedness.

In group settings, team performance and/or perceptions of success may also serve as important antecedents to need satisfaction and motivation. In a study with basketball players, Blanchard and Vallerand (1996) assessed, via their impact on autonomy, competence and relatedness, the effects of both team and individual performance (indexed by perceptions of success and win/loss record) on situational motivation. At the team-level, results revealed perceptions of performance to positively predict reported levels of player relatedness. Such findings suggest that team performance has an influence on a participants' sense of belonging within a collective group. These results are similar to past work that has linked team performance to a group's sense of cohesiveness (see Carron *et al.*, Ch. 7, this volume). While research attention has focused on the benefits of winning a competition, future work may wish to examine the motivational processes associated with losing and how these impact on feelings of 'togetherness'.

Motivational climate

Much work addressing participants' perceptions of the coaching/teaching context created by significant others (e.g. coaches, teachers, etc.) has been steeped in achievement goal frameworks (e.g. Ames, 1992; Nicholls, 1989) (see also Harwood and Beauchamp, Ch. 11, this volume). Research from this perspective suggests that two climates exist that give meaning to achievement settings (see Ames, 1992). These climates are task-involving (or mastery) and ego-involving (or performance). A task-involving climate refers to situations in which ability is evaluated and recognized in a self-referenced fashion (i.e. via improving of one's skill level and putting forth effort to master tasks). In contrast, an ego-involving climate refers to situations in which evaluation and recognition is based on outperforming others and/or demonstrating superior ability (including rivalry among team mates).

Past work conducted in sport and PE settings has documented a positive and direct association between perceptions of a task-involving climate and self-determined forms of motivation (i.e. intrinsic motivation and identified regulation) (e.g. Brunel, 1999; Standage *et al.*, 2003b). In contrast, an ego-involving climate has been shown to be directly associated with external regulation and unrelated to self-determined forms of motivation (e.g. Parish and Treasure, 2003).

Consistent with SDT, it would be expected that the satisfaction of autonomy, competence and relatedness would mediate the effects of task- and/or ego-involving climates on motivation. To this end, Sarrazin *et al.* (2002) tested the influence of task-involving and ego-involving climates on self-determined motivation as mediated by the three needs. Results showed that adolescent handball players who perceived a task-involving environment scored higher on perceived competence, autonomy and relatedness, whereas perceptions of an ego-involving climate predicted lower levels of reported autonomy. In turn, higher perceptions of autonomy, competence and relatedness were found to positively predict self-determined motivation. Further, self-determined motivation was found to be negatively related to intentions to discontinue involvement in one's sport. These behavioral intentions predicted actual drop-out of handball 21 months later.

In addition to the prospective study of Sarrazin and colleagues, support for the inter-relationships among the goal perspective situational dimensions and need-satisfaction has been demonstrated in lab-based work. In a study exploring the differing task and motivational characteristics of the competitive setting on need-satisfaction and indices of subjective well-being, Standage *et al.* (2005b) randomly assigned college-aged PE students to one of four conditions. Specifically, the participants were asked to perform a novel physical coordination task in either a *task-involving individual*, a *task-involving two person team*, an *ego-involving individual*, or an *ego-involving two person team* condition. Win/loss outcome information was also manipulated. Results pertaining to task versus ego-involving climates showed that students who participated in the activity within a task-involving condition reported higher levels of need satisfaction and vitality than those participating in the ego-involving experimental setting. Moreover, losing in an ego-involving condition led to higher levels of negative affect and lower levels of need satisfaction, positive affect and vitality than those who lost in a task-involving setting. Such findings are likely to reside with the fact that when exposed to ego-involving settings individuals are likely to equate success and failure with their self-worth (Ryan, 1982). In contrast, the results for the task-involving condition suggest that a focus on inherent aspects of the task such as trying hard and improving may serve to buffer the negative effects of losing (see Nicholls, 1989, and Ryan, 1982 for related, yet differing discussions of task- and ego-involving structures). To this end, it may be that when an individual loses in a task-involving setting the emphasis on self-referenced criteria conveys to the individual that they need to keep learning rather than that they are lacking in competence. The group-level findings of the Standage *et al.* (2005b) study will be discussed later.

Interpersonal competition

A SDT perspective. SDT also makes hypotheses about the nature of task and ego-involvement. According to Deci and Ryan (1985; Ryan and Deci, 1989) ego-involving environments are controlling as they induce social comparison and create competitive settings in which one's self-esteem hinges on the basis of performing well compared with others (Ryan, 1982). In contrast, task-involving situations support self-referenced gains, the putting forth of effort and provide individuals with choice. As such, task-involving situations are considered to be more supportive of self-determination. Previous work grounded in CET has shown that when participants feel pressured to win (ego-involving) as opposed to being told to just try their best (task-involving), their intrinsic motivation towards the task at hand decreases (Reeve and Deci, 1996; Ryan, 1982; Ryan *et al.*, 1991). Moreover, this effect seems to evolve through the suppression of the participants' reported level of autonomy (Reeve and Deci, 1996).

Cooperative competition

There are many occasions in teams, groups and classes when athletes, exercise participants and students are asked to cooperate towards a common objective. A cooperative structure refers to situations in which separate individuals share and work together towards a common goal (Ames, 1984). Similar to task-involving climates mentioned earlier in this chapter, a cooperative structure emphasizes effort and working with, rather than against, others (Ames and Ames, 1984).

In a recent four-study paper, Tauer and Harackiewicz (2004) assessed the effects of competition, cooperation and intergroup competition on the performance and task enjoyment of children partaking in a basketball free-throw task. Three findings of interest emerged. First, the results replicated the competitive success and failure feedback findings reported in the *performance outcome and win/loss feedback* section of this chapter. Second, in comparing pure competition and pure cooperation the authors found no differences on task enjoyment or performance. Third, intergroup competition was found to consistently lead to the highest levels of task enjoyment and performance (in the two out of three studies that performance was assessed). Tauer and Harackiewicz argued that engaging in intergroup competition leads individuals to be provided with the best overall experience as they derive the benefits available from competition and cooperation. That is, they experience the excitement and challenge of competition as well as the interpersonal enthusiasm and relatedness that come from having a team-mate.

To date, few studies have explored the associations between cooperation and the psychological needs advanced by SDT in physical activity settings. In one of the first studies to examine need satisfaction in school PE, Ntoumanis (2001) found students' perceptions of cooperative learning to positively predict reported levels of relatedness. Such a finding makes conceptual sense, as individuals are more likely to assist, instruct, encourage and facilitate each other's efforts when exposed to cooperative structures (Johnson and Johnson, 1989).

Although it is justifiable and appealing for researchers to propose an association between cooperation and the relatedness need, there are also good reasons to expect associations between a cooperative structure and the needs for autonomy and competence. With respect to autonomy, cooperating and connecting with others may allow the individual to feel supported in their actions and through this 'secure base' facilitate volitional engagement in activities (Ryan *et al.*, 1994). With regard to the competence need, because individuals tend to interact, give feedback and promote each other's success when cooperating, a cooperative structure has been shown to have a positive influence on perceptions of ability (Johnson and Johnson, 1989).

Recent work has provided support for a positive association between cooperation and a composite score of the psychological needs advanced by SDT. Specifically, in the Standage *et al.* (2005b) experimental study that we have previous alluded to, the authors found that participants who cooperated with a partner while working on a competitive task reported higher levels of need satisfaction (as indexed by a composite score of the needs). Although these findings are encouraging as they provide support for a link between cooperation and 'total' need satisfaction, future work would do well to tease out how and under what circumstances do perceptions of cooperation and/ or objective cooperative settings predict each of the need satisfaction variables. Such work would seem important for our understanding of how individuals interact and work together in group/team physical activity settings.

In addition to the significant main effect for working cooperatively with another, Standage *et al.* (2005b) also explored *winning* versus *losing* on participant need satisfaction and subjective well-being. Their findings replicated past CET work by revealing *winning* to result in higher levels of need satisfaction and positive affect and vitality, whereas *losing* led to increased levels of reported negative affect. Interestingly however, results showed that participants who lost alone (i.e. in an individual experimental condition) as opposed to losing in a 2-person team reported significantly higher levels of negative affect and significantly lower levels of need satisfaction, positive affect and vitality. The Standage, Duda and Pensgaard findings suggest that when working in cooperation with another to secure a positive competitive outcome, individuals can still have their needs met and experience subjective well-being (SWB; indexed by positive affect and vitality), despite being objectively unsuccessful. The underpinning mechanisms accounting for this apparent 'buffering' effect merits further investigation. For example, do individuals (a) maintain need satisfaction and resulting feelings of SWB due to sharing the responsibility of the loss (i.e. via the opportunity to offset the potential threat to competence and/or self-worth by attributing unsuccessful performance to their partner/team-mate)? or (b) is it the various positive social aspects embedded within the cooperative exchange that permit adaptive responses in the face of failure?

Peer climate

Adding the relatedness need to SDT, Deci and Ryan (1991) noted that a focus on autonomy and competence neglected the 'intrinsic social need that directs peoples' interest toward the development of relational bonds and toward a concern for interpersonally valued and culturally relevant activities' (p. 242). In a number of descriptive studies in the 1980s, 'affiliation' was identified as a central motive towards participation in youth sports (cf. Weiss and Petlichkoff, 1989). However, it was not until recent years that peers began to be studied in the context of sport. Recent peer-related research has taken a number of avenues and the effort by researchers to ground their work in theory has helped to enhance our understanding of peer-related processes (see Ntoumanis et al., 2007; and Smith, 2007, for reviews).

From an SDT perspective, the social context that peers create represents a promising avenue of work. Indeed, understanding how interactions with others serve to support autonomy, competence and relatedness would provide valuable information that would bear theoretical and practical relevance. Content analytic findings reported by Vazou et al. (2005) from their interviews with British youth athletes, suggest that the climate created by peers encompasses a number of facets that may support (e.g. improvement, relatedness-support, cooperation, autonomy-support) or undermine (e.g. intra-team competition, intra-team conflict) sport participants' needs for autonomy, competence, and relatedness. After developing and validating an assessment of the peer-related climate based on this qualitative work (see Ntoumanis and Vazou, 2005), Vazou et al. (2005) examined the additive and interactive influence of young athletes' perceptions of coach-created and peer-created climates on affective responses (*viz.*, physical self-worth, enjoyment, trait anxiety) and effort as rated by their coach. Results showed a task-involving peer climate to positively predict young athletes' perceptions of physical self-worth and enjoyment. Perceptions of the motivational climate as created by the coach revealed a task-involving climate to positively predict enjoyment and coach ratings of effort, whereas an ego-involving climate positively predicted trait anxiety. Based on their findings, Vazou et al. argued that future research addressing young athletes' self-perceptions and motivation-related variables in sport should consider both coach and peer influences. We would agree with this suggestion, but we would also advocate that other social agents (e.g. mother, father, organizing structures) be considered in unison with these important social influences to allow us to tease out which characteristics of each social agent best supports levels of need-satisfaction (and subsequently indices of motivation and well-being).

Although to date, research has not examined how peer interactions within groups impact on the three innate needs proffered by SDT, past work has provided some support for inter-relationships between peer-related variables and constructs embraced by SDT. For example, Smith *et al.* (2006) found that being accepted by peers and having positive friendship quality was positively related to perceived competence, self-determined motivation and enjoyment. Moreover, cluster analyses revealed that even if a child reported a high conflict with a friend, if they reported relatively high perceptions of quality of friendships and peer acceptance then they were able to preserve their reported levels of perceived competence, self-determined motivation and enjoyment. From an SDT perspective, research would do well to examine how peers may serve as an antecedent to the satisfaction of autonomy, competence and relatedness (i.e. within the sequence outlined in Figure 10.1).

Measurement issues

There are a number of issues pertaining to the measurement of motivational processes in groups that warrant further attention. For example, it is important to consider the differences between individual-level and group-level assessments when attempting to predict outcome variables. If the dependent variable of interest reflects a group-level outcome (e.g. team success) then an aggregate of all the team members' shared perceptions of the group should be a better predictor of group-level outcomes than individual-level indices (Feltz and Lirgg, 1998; see Chow and Feltz, Ch. 12, this volume). Such reasoning is consistent with Bandura's (1997) view that when individuals work on highly interactive tasks their 'collective efficacy' is a better predictor of conjoint outcomes than their individual efficacy beliefs since issues such as interactive and coordinative elements are included in perceptions of the collective group.

Although SDT appropriately assesses the basic needs at an individual-level some support for assessing 'collective' perceptions has emerged. For example, in assessing collective and individual perceptions of competence (in addition to individual perceptions of relatedness and autonomy), Guay *et al.* (2000; study 4) found collegiate basketball players' collective perceptions of competence to be an important predictor of collegiate basketball players' changes in intrinsic motivation scores over a two-game period. Future work may wish to obtain collective perceptions of autonomy, competence and relatedness to see if extending such assessments to the group-level helps to predict team-related outcome variables above and beyond those explained at the individual-level. Akin to Bandura's collective efficacy proposition, such effects should be greatest for highly interactive and interdependent tasks such as those encompassed by soccer, basketball and hockey.

Despite the above proposition departing from SDT, it is important to consider the impact of such reasoning from a practical perspective. In view of the consistent body of work that has shown the need satisfaction variables to positively predict adaptive outcomes, it is plausible to suggest that perceptions of how the group members perceive the collective group to be autonomous, competent and related could provide valuable information needed to develop team efficiency, functioning and as a result, perhaps even performance. We are not alone in thinking that there are occasions when it would be valuable to extend the psychological needs to the group level. For example, Sheldon and Bettencourt (2002) commented that they believe 'SDT's postulates concerning psychological needs could be profitably extended to the group context. This is because individuals may sometimes face restrictive norms and pressures within their groups, just as they do in interpersonal relationships' (p. 33). The application of hierarchical linear modeling (or multilevel modeling) techniques (Goldstein, 1995;

Raudenbush, 1988), which permit the hierarchical and concurrent examination of individual, group and cross-level effects within a hierarchical structure would be most useful in such investigations.

A further issue pertaining to measurement at the group-level resides with a groups' shared perception of the social context. Pulling from Duda's (2001) writings about within-team variation of perceptions of the motivational climate, recent work in the achievement goal theory literature (e.g. Papaioannou *et al.*, 2004) has begun to explore such meaningful lines of inquiry (see Harwood and Beauchamp, Ch. 11, this volume for a discussion on this topic). Clearly, any work examining social factors at the group-level from an SDT perspective needs to tease out individual-level and group-level effects. Not only are such findings interesting from a theoretical perspective, but they also have implications for practice. Indeed, we concur with Duda's appraisal of the same issue facing achievement goal theorists (see also commentary by Harwood and Beauchamp, Ch. 11, this volume) when she commented that '. . . it would be difficult and perhaps even questionable, to intervene with coaches in terms of changing the motivational climate if team members showed no agreement on the nature of that climate' (2001, p. 149). Applying Duda's proposition to SDT and group settings such as sport teams, PE lessons and exercise classes, the question becomes 'how can we best modify various social factors that may support psychological need satisfaction (e.g. cooperation, autonomy-support, etc.) if there is little agreement among the perceptions of group members with regard to these environments?'

In terms of assessing group motivation, Vallerand and Miquelon (2006) have recently started to validate the Group Motivation Scale (GMOS) to assess how group members perceive the motivation of their group or work team to undertake a given team activity. The GMOS was adapted from several motivation inventories including the Work Motivation Inventory (Blais *et al.*, 1993) and the Academic Motivation Scale (AMS; Vallerand *et al.*, 1992, 1993) and measures five types of group motivation. One subscale assess general intrinsic group motivation (e.g. 'Because my team experiences pleasure while learning new things'), three subscales assess types of extrinsic group motivation: identified group motivation (e.g. 'Because this is the kind of work my team has chosen in order to achieve its objectives'), introjected group motivation (e.g. 'Because my team values its work and it does not want to fail'), external group motivation (e.g. 'Because my team wants to be appreciated and recognized by the teacher') and finally, one subscale assesses group amotivation (e.g. 'My team doesn't know why it is getting the work done; it feels like it is wasting its time.'). Each item represents a possible reason for a work team to undertake a given activity. These reasons are scored on a 7-point Likert scale, ranging from 'I do not agree at all' (1) to 'I do extremely agree' (7).

Preliminary results of an on-going research program with a 14 item version of the GMOS are encouraging. Results of a pilot study conducted with 40 academic teams of five members revealed adequate internal consistency, as well as subscale inter-relationships in line with the self-determination continuum (the team served as the unit of analysis in this study). In addition, team cohesion was found to significantly predict a self-determined group motivation index, which in turn predicted team performance as assessed by the teacher. While these findings are preliminary, they are exciting and suggest that it might be possible to assess group motivation independently from individual motivation. Future research is encouraged on this issue.

Practical implications for intervention

In recent years, there have been at least two major types of intervention framed in SDT that hold great promise for maintaining and enhancing the motivational strivings of individuals and teams in sport, exercise and PE settings. The first type seeks to increase the autonomy-supportive behavior displayed by significant others (e.g. coaches, instructors, teachers) toward physical activity participants (e.g. athletes, exercise participants, students). This approach stems from past work in classroom-based education that has shown teaching styles to be malleable (cf. Reeve *et al.*, 2004). For example, field-based work by Reeve (1998) using a sample of pre-service teachers revealed that participants exposed to just an 80-min training session reported significant and enduring changes in their interpersonal teaching style when compared with a control group (i.e. they became more autonomy-supportive). Extending this work to the sporting context, Pelletier *et al.* (2006) recently developed an 18-month intervention program to help swim coaches become more autonomy-supportive and consequently facilitate their athletes' motivation. Results showed that the program was highly effective in leading athletes to perceive their coach as more autonomy-supportive and less controlling and to experience greater levels of perceived competence and intrinsic motivation. Of particular interest is the fact that attendance at practice markedly increased whereas dropout significantly reduced.

A second line of intervention studies takes into consideration that individuals are not intrinsically motivated towards many tasks. That is, similar to almost all life domains, group physical activity settings encompass activities that are desirable but not always intrinsically interesting to team members. Thus, a significant challenge facing coaches, teachers and instructors is how to motivate group members and teams towards tasks that they perceive to be burdensome. SDT sheds light on how this may be achieved via a process labeled *internalization*. Internalization refers to a process by which individuals internalize and integrate socially valued norms, values and rules so as to develop self-representations and to be more effective when dealing with those behaviors deemed to be uninteresting (cf. Deci and Ryan, 2000). Through this process, external regulations are transformed into internal regulations as the person 'takes in' the value and integrates the activity so that initiation of action is believed to originate from a sense of self (Ryan and Deci, 2000). To facilitate the internalization process, Deci and colleagues (e.g. Deci *et al.* 1994; Deci and Ryan, 1991; Deci and Vansteenkiste, 2004; Ryan and Deci, 2002) have identified various social pre-conditions. These pre-requisites and practical implications are discussed below:

- The interpersonal context in which the behavior is performed is required to be supportive of the basic needs for autonomy, competence and relatedness, so as to facilitate autonomous regulation and integration. For example, in sport a coach may enhance autonomy by providing an athlete with the required information regarding a skill or tactic, but then provide choice regarding how he/she executes the task and/or scope regarding tactics/game-plan decisions. Additionally, the coach may establish peer learning groups (i.e. students demonstrate skills to one another, referee games and establish tactics). Perceptions of competence may be facilitated by promoting environments in which self-referenced standards and indicators of improvement are adopted as opposed to competitive situations in which evaluated outcomes are contingent upon the performance of others (Ames,

1992). Finally, the relatedness need may be met if a coach/teacher/instructor uses small group activities and sets reward structures that support cooperation (i.e. group level outcomes).

- A meaningful rationale must be provided, especially when the activity is not interesting to the athlete/student/exerciser. For example, the health benefits of an activity (e.g. circuit training) may be conveyed to an uninterested footballer to allow him/her to understand why self-regulation of the activity would be personally useful (e.g. 'circuit training will improve your fitness and allow you to run for longer during a game'). As discussed below, the way in which the rationale is presented to the individual is crucial. In order to be effective, the rationale should be presented in a non-controlling way, while providing some form of choice and acknowledging the person's feelings (Deci *et al.*, 1994; Koestner *et al.*, 1984).

- There should be some expression of empathy, or acknowledgement of the concerns that the student faces with regard to the requested behavior. For example, a PE teacher may say 'I know that doing press-ups is not much fun', would legitimize the student's perceptions of the activity and allow them to feel understood, accepted and believe that their perceptions are not incongruent with the requested behavior.

- Significant others in physical activity settings should be careful as to how the rationale and acknowledgement of empathy are conveyed to their players/students/exercisers. That is, the significant other (e.g. coach, teacher, instructor) should try to avoid the use of externally controlling vocalizations (e.g. 'you must', 'you have to', 'you should'). Rather, the requesting vocalizations should portray choice and support (e.g. 'you may want to', 'you can try to'), as such communications are likely to convey autonomy support, internalization and facilitate autonomous forms of motivation (cf. Deci *et al.*, 1994). To this end, recent work by Hodgins *et al.* (2006, study 3) showed that priming members of a university rowing team with self-determined words (e.g. choose, freedom) led to faster times on a rowing machine than priming members with non-self-determined (e.g. must, should) and amotivational words (e.g. passive, uncontrollable).

Future research directions

There are many directions to take in future research grounded in SDT. Some of these avenues we have identified already in this chapter. Below, we outline five broad areas of research that we feel represent important agendas for future work.

First, an important direction worthy of further research attention refers to those responsible for creating social contexts. Perhaps the most significant interpersonal social factor in the settings of team sports, exercise classes and school PE lessons are coaches, instructors and teachers, respectively. Past research has shown that these immediate social agents to be germane to the manner in which an individual experiences, behaves and persists in physical activity settings (see Hagger and Chatzisarantis, 2007 for reviews). Similar to work in education (e.g. Vallerand *et al.*, 1997), however, future research would do well to also consider the simultaneous influence of multiple social agents on autonomy, competence and relatedness. The inclusion and study of the social context created by other social agents such as parents, peers and policymakers would provide a more comprehensive insight into how various elements of these environs interact to predict the participants' need satisfaction. If such work involves asking children and adolescents about their parents, researchers should also tease out the unique contributions of mother and father as these socializing agents have been shown to have differing effects on the motivational responses of adolescents (Niemiec *et al.*, 2006; Soenens and Vansteenkiste, 2005).

A second avenue of suggested work pertains to experimental research in group settings. Specifically, while experimental studies examining the needs for autonomy, competence and relatedness in physical activity settings would be most interesting, experimental studies addressing need-satisfaction in real groups would be extremely difficult to conduct and perhaps unethical (Sheldon and Bettencourt, 2002). As Sheldon and Bettencourt propose however, one way of conducting causal relationships in social groups would be via prospective designs. Using this type of approach, researchers interested in motivational processes within sport and exercise groups could assess baseline need-satisfaction when the group is formed and then track changes in dependent variables of interest as a function of changes in group need-satisfaction.

A third direction worthy of research attention refers to the development of measurement tools. Although a number of valid and reliable assessments exist to measure motivation in sport, PE and exercise settings (Vallerand, 2007; Vallerand and Fortier, 1998), a much needed area of research pertains to the development of similar context-specific measures of other SDT constructs (e.g. basic needs and perceptions of an autonomy-supportive climate). Wilson and colleagues' (2006) recent work to create 'The Psychological Need Satisfaction in Exercise Scale' is a promising development, however further work on measurement tools is needed to permit cleaner tests of the SDT model. Researchers taking on this challenge would do well to employ qualitative techniques to better understand the dynamics of teams and classes. In such research, it would be extremely beneficial to involve members of the proposed target sample in all stages of the questionnaire development process (e.g. focus groups, item development, item meaning, etc.) to ensure that measurement items adequately capture accurate accounts of the processes that operate in various physical activity settings. It should also be noted that it is critical that developments and/or refinements of measurement scales are grounded in theory and are not data driven (Mulaik, 1987).

A fourth area of work that deserves mention pertains to linking the motivational processes embraced by SDT to objective performance both individually and within teams. Of course, we would expect the same psychological processes hypothesized by SDT to hold for individuals and groups; however the role of relatedness may be more prominent in team/class settings (e.g. sport teams, exercise classes). As Vallerand (2007) points out, there is much evidence to support the role of self-determined motivation in positively predicting performance on non-sport tasks (see Vallerand, 1997 for a review). However, while there are many consequences that one can examine from a SDT perspective, in some contexts (e.g. elite sport) performance is perhaps the most important outcome variable. To this end and despite some preliminary support for self-determined motivation predicting performance outcomes (e.g. Charbonneau *et al.*, 2001), performance remains somewhat neglected in sport and exercise research (see Vallerand, 2007). Future SDT research using prospective, longitudinal and experimental designs would provide us with a clearer insight of the role that motivation plays on short and long-term performance.

A final, but extremely important avenue of work stems from the fact that around 60 per cent of the world's population is not sufficiently active to derive the known health and well-being benefits offered by physical activity (WHO, 2003). Since past work has shown the most commonly used measures of physical activity (e.g. self-report inventories, pedometers and accelerometers) to be fraught with a number of serious limitations (see Cooper, 2003 for a review), future research examining how motivational processes predict *accurately* assessed physical activity is needed. Recent developments in technology have made such work viable. Indeed, it is now possible, via the use of synchronized accelerometry and heart rate data, to estimate energy 24-hour expenditure at 15 second intervals for a period of up to 10 days or at 60 second epochs for up to 3 weeks (ActiHeart, Cambridge Neuroscience, UK). Work testing the ActiHeart© device has validated its capabilities and research has demonstrated excellent estimates for total energy expenditure against indirect calorimetry during walking and running in healthy young individuals (Brage et al., 2005; Thompson et al., 2006). In preliminary work using this unit, Standage et al. (2007b) found self-determined motivation to positively predict bouts of moderate-intensity exercise behavior. From a public health perspective, the use of these units to assess changes in physical activity level as a function of group interventions grounded in SDT would be an exciting research direction. Ideally, such work would employ cluster randomized controlled trials to provide cleaner tests of the utility of SDT-based work in predicting objective behavior.

Conclusion

Almost 50 years ago, Cartwright and Zander (1960) advanced the argument that 'whether one wishes to understand or to improve human behavior, it is important to know a great deal about the nature of groups' (p. 4). Such a statement is consonant with the theme of the present chapter. We feel that research extending the tenets of SDT to the group-level in physical activity settings is warranted when one considers that much behavior in such settings takes place within social groups. Further, participants have shown a preference to partake in exercise within group settings as opposed to engaging individually (Beauchamp et al., 2007; Burke et al., 2006). Within this chapter, we have reviewed past SDT work that bears significant relevance for teams, classes and lessons in a number of physical activity settings. A number of measurement issues facing researchers considering exploring motivational processes within group settings have been discussed. Further, practical and future research directions have been identified. With the latter in mind, it is hoped that the work reviewed and the identified areas for future work will stimulate some thoughtful contemplation and encourage future SDT research to examine group variables. We hope that this chapter has played a small role in encouraging such needed and meaningful lines of inquiry.

References

Ames, C. (1984). Achievement attributions and self-instructions under competitive and individualistic goal structures. *Journal of Educational Psychology*, 76, 478–487.

Ames, C. (1992). Achievement goals and the classroom motivational climate. In D. H. Schunk and J. L. Meece (Eds), *Student perceptions in the classroom* (pp. 327–348). Hillsdale, NJ: Erlbaum.

Ames, C. and Ames, R. (1984). Goal structures and motivation. *The Elementary School Journal*, 85, 39–52.

Bandura, A. (1997). *Self-efficacy: The exercise of control*. New York: Freeman.

Baumeister, R. F. and Leary, M. R. (1995). The need to belong: Desire for interpersonal attachments as a fundamental human motivation. *Psychological Bulletin*, 117, 497–529.

Beauchamp, M. R., Carron, A. V., McCutcheon, S. and Harper, O. (2007). Older exercisers' preferences for exercising alone versus in groups: Considering contextual congruence. *Annals of Behavioral Medicine, 33,* 200–206.

Blais, M. R., Brière N. M., Lachance, L., Riddle, A. S. and Vallerand, R. J. (1993). L'inventaire des motivations au travail de Blais. *Revue québécoise de psychologie, 14,* 185–215.

Blanchard, C. and Vallerand, R. J. (1996). The mediating effects of perceptions of competence, autonomy and relatedness on the social factors-self-determined situational motivation relationship. (Unpublished manuscript, Université du Québec à Montréal, Canada.)

Brage, S., Brage, N., Franks, P. W., Ekelund, U. and Wareham, N. J. (2005). Reliability and validity of the combined heart rate and movement sensor Actiheart. *European Journal of Clinical Nutrition, 59,* 561–570.

Brunel, P. C. (1999). Relationship between achievement goal orientations and perceived motivational climate on intrinsic motivation. *Scandinavian Journal of Medicine and Sciences in Sports, 9,* 365–374.

Burke, S. M., Carron, A. V. and Eys, M. A. (2006). Physical activity context: Preferences of university students. *Psychology of Sport and Exercise, 7,* 1–13.

Cartwright, D. and Zander, A. (1960). *Group dynamics: Research and theory* (2nd ed.). New York: Harper and Row.

Charbonneau, D., Barling, J. and Kelloway, E. K. (2001). Transformational leadership and sports performance: The mediating role of intrinsic motivation. *Journal of Applied Social Psychology, 31,* 1521–1534.

Chatzisarantis, N. L., Hagger, M. S., Biddle, S. J. H., Smith, B. and Wang, J. C. K. (2003). A meta-analysis of perceived locus of causality in exercise, sport and physical education contexts. *Journal of Sport and Exercise Psychology, 25,* 284–306.

Cooper, A. (2003). Objective measurement of physical activity. In J. McKenna and C. R. Riddoch (Eds), *Perspectives on health and exercise* (pp. 83–108). Basingstoke, England: Palgrave Macmillan.

Deci, E. L. (1975). *Intrinsic motivation.* New York: Academic Press.

Deci, E. L., Eghrari, H., Patrick, B. C. and Leone, D. (1994). Facilitating internalization: The self-determination theory perspective. *Journal of Personality, 62,* 119–142.

Deci, E. L. and Ryan, R. M. (1985). *Intrinsic motivation and self-determination in human behavior.* New York: Plenum.

Deci, E. L. and Ryan, R. M. (1991). A motivational approach to self: Integration in personality. In R. A. Dienstbier (Ed.), *Nebraska symposium on motivation: Perspectives on motivation* (Vol. 38, pp. 237–288). Lincoln: University of Nebraska.

Deci, E. L. and Ryan, R. M. (2000). The 'what' and 'why' of goal pursuits: Human needs and the self-determination of behavior. *Psychological Inquiry, 11,* 227–268.

Deci, E. L. and Vansteenkiste, M. (2004). Self-determination theory and basic need satisfaction: Understanding human development in positive psychology. *Recherché di Psicologia, 27,* 17–34.

deCharms, R. C. (1968). *Personal causation: The internal affective determinants of behavior.* New York: Academic Press.

Donahue, E., Miquelon, P., Valois, P., Goulet, P., Buist, A. and Vallerand, R. J. (2006). A motivational model of performance-enhancing substance use in elite athletes. *Journal of Sport and Exercise Psychology, 28,* 511–520.

Duda, J. L. (2001). Goal perspective research in sport in sport: Pushing the boundaries and clarifying some misunderstandings. In G. C. Roberts (Ed.), *Advances in motivation in sport and exercise* (pp. 129–182). Champaign, IL: Human Kinetics.

Feltz, D. L. and Lirgg, C. D. (1998). Perceived team and player efficacy in hockey. *Journal of Applied Psychology, 83,* 557–564.

Gillison, F., Standage, M. and Skevington, S. M. (2006). Relationships among adolescents' weight perceptions, exercise goals, exercise motivation, quality of life and leisure-time exercise behaviour: A self-determination theory approach. *Health Education Research, 21,* 836–847.

Goldstein, H. (1995). *Multilevel statistical models* (2nd ed.). London: Arnold.

Guay, F., Vallerand, R. J. and Blanchard, C. (2000). On the assessment of state intrinsic and extrinsic motivation: The situational motivation scale (SIMS). *Motivation and Emotion*, 24, 175–213.

Hagger, M. S. and Chatzisarantis, N. L. D. (Eds). (2007). *Self-determination in exercise and sport.* Champaign, IL: Human Kinetics.

Hagger, M. S., Chatzisarantis, N., Culverhouse, T. and Biddle, S. J. H. (2003). The processes by which perceived autonomy support in physical education promotes leisure-time physical activity intentions and behaviour: A trans-contextual model. *Journal of Educational Psychology*, 95, 784–795.

Hodgins, H. S., Yacko, H. A. and Gottlieb, E. (2006). Autonomy and nondefensiveness. *Motivation and Emotion*, 30, 283–293.

Johnson, D. W. and Johnson, R. (1989). *Cooperation and competition: Theory and research*. Edina, MN: Interaction Book Company.

Koestner, R., Ryan, R. M., Bernieri, F. and Holt, K. (1984). Setting limits on children's behavior: The differential effects of controlling versus informational styles on children's intrinsic motivation and creativity. *Journal of Personality*, 54, 233–248.

Kowal, J. and Fortier, M. S. (1999). Motivational determinants of flow: Contributions from self-determination theory. *The Journal of Social Psychology*, 139, 355–368.

Li, F. and Harmer, P. (1996). Testing the simplex assumption underlying the Sport Motivation Scale: A structural equation modeling analysis. *Research Quarterly for Exercise and Sport*, 67, 396–405.

McAuley, E. and Tammen, V. V. (1989). The effects of subjective and objective competitive outcomes on intrinsic motivation. *Journal of Sport and Exercise Psychology*, 11, 84–93.

McClelland, D. M. (1985). *Human motivation*. London: Scott, Foresman and Co.

Mulaik, S. A. (1987). A brief history of philosophical foundations of exploratory factor analysis. *Multivariate Behavioural Research*, 22, 267–305.

Niemiec, C. P., Lynch, M. F., Vansteenkiste, M., Bernstein, J., Deci, E. L. and Ryan, R. M. (2006). The antecedents and consequences of autonomous self-regulation for college: A self-determination theory perspective on socialization. *Journal of Adolescence*, 29, 761–775.

Nicholls, J. G. (1989). *The competitive ethos and democratic education*. Cambridge, MA: Harvard University Press.

Ntoumanis, N. (2001). A self-determination approach to the understanding of motivation in physical education. *British Journal of Educational Psychology*, 71, 225–242.

Ntoumanis, N. (2005). A prospective study of participation in optional physical education using a self-determination theory framework. *Journal of Educational Psychology*, 97, 444–453.

Ntoumanis, N. and Vazou, S. (2005). Peer motivational climate in youth sport: Measurement development. *Journal of Sport and Exercise Psychology*, 27, 432–455.

Ntoumanis, N., Vazou, S. and Duda, J. L. (2007). Towards an understanding of peer motivational climate in youth sport. In S. Jowett and D. Lavallee (Eds), *Social psychology in sport* (pp. 145–156). Champaign, IL: Human Kinetics.

Papaioannou, A., Marsh, H. W. and Theodorakis, Y. (2004). A multilevel approach to motivational climate in physical education and sport settings: An individual or a group level construct? *Journal of Sport and Exercise Psychology*, 26, 90–118.

Parish, L. E. and Treasure, D. C. (2003). Physical activity and situational motivation in physical education: Influence of the motivational climate and perceived ability. *Research Quarterly for Exercise and Sport*, 74, 173–182.

Pelletier, L. G., Fortier, M. S., Vallerand, R. J. and Brière, N. M. (2001). Associations among perceived autonomy support, forms of self-regulation and persistence: A prospective study. *Motivation and Emotion*, 25, 279–306.

Pelletier, L. G., Vallerand, R. J., Brière, N. M. and Blais, M. R. (2006). When coaches become autonomy-supportive: Effects on intrinsic motivation, persistence and performance. Unpublished manuscript, University of Ottawa, Ontario, Canada.

Raudenbush, S. W. (1988). Educational applications of hierarchical linear models: A review. *Journal of Educational Statistics*, 13, 85–116.

Reeve, J. (1998). Autonomy support as an interpersonal motivating style: Is it teachable? *Contemporary Educational Psychology*, 23, 312–330.

Reeve, J. and Deci, E. L. (1996). Elements of the competitive situation that affect intrinsic motivation. *Personality and Social Psychology Bulletin*, 22, 24–33.

Reeve, J., Deci, E. L. and Ryan, R. M. (2004). Self-determination theory: A dialectical framework for understanding socio-cultural influences on student motivation. In S. Van Etten and M. Pressley (Eds), *Big Theories Revisited* (pp. 31–60). Greenwich, CT: Information Age Press.

Ryan, R. M. (1982). Control and information in the intrapersonal sphere: An extension of cognitive evaluation theory. *Journal of Personality and Social Psychology*, 43, 450–461.

Ryan, R. M. and Deci, E. L. (1989). Bridging the research traditions of task/ego involvement and intrinsic/extrinsic motivation: Comment on Butler (1987). *Journal of Educational Psychology*, 81, 265–268

Ryan, R. M. and Deci, E. L. (2000). Intrinsic and extrinsic motivations: Classic definitions and new directions. *Contemporary Educational Psychology*, 25, 54–67.

Ryan, R. M. and Deci, E. L. (2002). An overview of self-determination theory: An organismic-dialectical perspective. In E. L. Deci and R. M. Ryan (Eds), *Handbook of self-determination research* (pp. 3–33). Rochester, NY: University of Rochester Press.

Ryan, R. M., Koestner, R. and Deci, E. L. (1991). Ego-involved persistence: When free-choice behavior is not intrinsically motivated. *Motivation and Emotion*, 15, 185–205.

Ryan, R. M., Stiller, J. D. and Lynch, J. H. (1994). Representations of relationships to teachers, parents and friends as predictors of academic motivation and self-esteem. *Journal of Early Adolescence*, 14, 226–249.

Sarrazin, P., Vallerand, R. J., Guillet, E., Pelletier, L. G. and Cury, F. (2002). Motivation and dropout in female handballers: A 21-month prospective study. *European Journal of Social Psychology*, 32, 395–418.

Sheldon, K. and Bettencourt, B. A. (2002). Psychological need-satisfaction and subjective well-being within social groups. *British Journal of Social Psychology*, 41, 25–38.

Smith, A. L. (2007). Youth peer relationships in sport. In S. Jowett and D. Lavallee (Eds), *Social psychology in sport* (pp. 41–54). Champaign, IL: Human Kinetics.

Smith, A. L., Ullrich-French, S., Walker, E. and Hurley, K. S. (2006). Peer relationship profiles and motivation in youth sport. *Journal of Sport and Exercise Psychology*, 28, 362–382.

Soenens, B. and Vansteenkiste, M. (2005). Antecedents and outcomes of self-determination in 3 life domains: The role of parents' and teachers' autonomy support. *Journal of Youth and Adolescence*, 34, 589–604.

Standage, M., Duda, J. L. and Ntoumanis, N. (2003a). A model of contextual motivation in physical education: Using constructs from self-determination and achievement goal theories to predict physical activity intentions. *Journal of Educational Psychology*, 95, 97–110.

Standage, M., Duda, J. L. and Ntoumanis, N. (2003b). Predicting motivational regulations in physical education: The interplay between dispositional goal orientations, motivational climate and perceived competence. *Journal of Sports Sciences*, 21, 631–647.

Standage, M., Duda, J. L. and Ntoumanis, N. (2005a). A test of self-determination theory in school physical education. *British Journal of Educational Psychology*, 75, 411–433.

Standage, M., Duda, J. L. and Ntoumanis, N. (2006). Students' motivational processes and their relationship to teacher ratings in school physical education: A self-determination theory approach. *Research Quarterly for Exercise and Sport*, 77, 100–110.

Standage M., Duda, J. L. and Pensgaard, A. M. (2005b). The effect of competitive outcome and task-involving, ego-involving and cooperative structures on the psychological well-being of individuals engaged in a coordination task. *Motivation and Emotion*, 29, 41–68.

Standage, M., Gillison, F. and Treasure, D. C. (2007a). Self-determination and motivation in physical education. In M. S. Hagger and N. L. D. Chatzisarantis (Eds), *Self-determination theory in exercise and sport* (pp. 71–85). Champaign, IL: Human Kinetics.

Standage, M., Sebire, S. J. and Loney, T. (2007b). Does an individual's exercise motivation predict their engagement in objectively-assessed bouts of moderate-intensity exercise behavior? A self-determination theory perspective. Manuscript submitted for publication.

Tauer, J. M. and Harackiewicz, J. M. (2004). The effects of cooperation and competition on intrinsic motivation and performance. *Journal of Personality and Social Psychology*, 86, 849–861.

Thill, E. and Mouanda, J. (1990). Autonomy or control in the sports context: Validity of cognitive evaluation theory. *International Journal of Sport Psychology*, 21, 1–20.

Thompson, D., Batterham, A. M., Bock, S., Robson, C. and Stokes, K. (2006). Assessment of low-to-moderate intensity physical activity thermogenesis in young adults using synchronized heart rate and accelerometry with branched-equation modelling. *The Journal of Nutrition*, 136, 1037–1042.

Vallerand, R. J. (1997). Toward a hierarchical model of intrinsic and extrinsic motivation. In M. P. Zanna (Ed.), *Advances in experimental social psychology* (Vol. 29, pp. 271–360). New York: Academic Press.

Vallerand, R. J. (2007). Intrinsic and extrinsic motivation in sport and physical activity: A review and a look at the future. In G. Tenenbaum and E. Eklund (Eds), *Handbook of sport psychology* (3rd ed., pp. 49–83). New York: John Wiley.

Vallerand, R. J., Deci, E. L. and Ryan, R. M. (1987). Intrinsic motivation in sport. In K. Pandolf (Ed.), *Exercise and sport science reviews* (Vol. 15, pp. 389–425). New York: Macmillan.

Vallerand, R. J. and Fortier, M. S. (1998). Measures of intrinsic and extrinsic motivation in sport and physical activity: A review and critique. In J. L. Duda (Ed.), *Advancements in sport and exercise psychology measurement* (pp. 83–100). Morgantown, WV: Fitness Information Technology.

Vallerand, R. J., Fortier, M. S. and Guay, F. (1997). Self-determination and persistence in a real-life setting: Toward a motivational model of high school dropout. *Journal of Personality and Social Psychology*, 72, 1161–1176.

Vallerand, R. J., Gauvin, L. and Halliwell, W. R. (1986). Effects of zero-sum competition on children's intrinsic motivation and perceived competence. *Journal of Social Psychology*, 126, 465–472.

Vallerand, R. J. and Losier, G. F. (1994). Self-determined motivation and sportsmanship orientations: An assessment of their temporal relationship. *Journal of Sport and Exercise Psychology*, 16, 229–245.

Vallerand, R. J. and Losier, G. F. (1999). An integrative analysis of intrinsic and extrinsic motivation in sport. *Journal of Applied Sport Psychology*, 11, 142–169.

Vallerand, R. J. and Miquelon, P. (2006). Preliminary evidence on the Group Motivation Scale. (Unpublished data.)

Vallerand, R. J., Pelletier, L. G., Blais, M. R., Brière, N. M., Senécal, C. and Vallières, E. F. (1992). The academic motivation scale: A measure of intrinsic, extrinsic and amotivation in education. *Educational and Psychological Measurement*, 52, 1003–1019.

Vallerand, R. J., Pelletier, L. G., Blais, M. R., Brière, N. M., Senécal, C. and Vallières, E. F. (1993). On the assessment of intrinsic, extrinsic and amotivation in education: Evidence on the concurrent and construct validity of the academic motivation scale. *Educational and Psychological Measurement*, 53, 159–172.

Vallerand, R. J. and Reid, G. (1984). On the causal effects of perceived competence on intrinsic motivation: A test of cognitive evaluation theory. *Journal of Sport Psychology*, 6, 94–102.

Vallerand, R. J. and Reid, G. (1988). On the relative effects of positive and negative verbal feedback on males and females' intrinsic motivation. *Canadian Journal of Behavioural Sciences*, 20, 239–250.

Vazou, S., Ntoumanis, N. and Duda, J. L. (2005). Peer motivational climate in youth sport: A qualitative inquiry. *Psychology of Sport and Exercise*, 6, 497–516.

Weinberg, R. S. and Ragan, J. (1979). Effects of competition, success/failure and sex on intrinsic motivation. *Research Quarterly*, 50, 503–510.

Weiss, M. R. and Petlichkoff, L. M. (1989). Children's motivation for participation in and withdrawal from sport: Identifying the missing links. *Pediatric Exercise Science*, 1, 195–211.

Wilson, P. M. and Rodgers, W. (2004). The relationship between perceived autonomy support, exercise regulations and behavioural intentions in women. *Psychology of Sport and Exercise*, 5, 229–242.

Wilson, P. M., Rogers, W. T., Rodgers, W. M. and Wild, T. C. (2006). The psychological need satisfaction in exercise scale. *Journal of Sport and Exercise Psychology*, 28, 231–251.

WHO. (2003). *Health and development through physical activity and sport*. Geneva, Switzerland: World Health Organization.

Notes

1   SDT also posits the existence of *integrated regulation* as a type of extrinsic motivation. Integrated regulation refers to when identifications have been incorporated within the self, meaning they have been assessed and brought into congruence with individual's other values and needs (Ryan and Deci, 2000). For example, an individual who says 'I participate in physical activity because it is important to me to be physically healthy' illustrates the principle underlying integrated regulation. Rather than partake in physical activity because social values dictate, individuals high in integrated regulation feel, behave and think in a way congruent with the social values because they have accepted them as their own ('important to me') (Deci and Ryan, 1985). This type of motivation is more often encountered among adults rather than children and most measures of motivation from an SDT perspective do not include an integrated regulation subscale. For these reasons, this construct is not elaborated on further in the present chapter.

2   It is important to note, however, that SDT does not view the self-determination continuum to be a developmental structure, but rather an organizational representation of the regulations (Ryan and Deci, 2002). Indeed, depending on the social context, an individual can adopt a regulation at any stage of the continuum (Ryan and Deci, 2002).

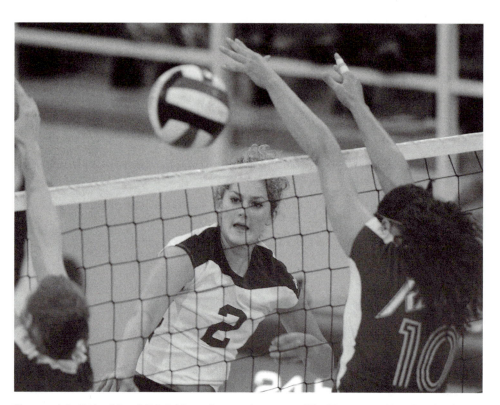

Photograph by Richard Lam/UBC Athletics. Reprinted courtesy of The University of British Columbia.

11 Group functioning through optimal achievement goals

Chris Harwood and Mark R. Beauchamp

Introduction

To many sport psychology graduates the most relevant theories and research topics associated with groups and teams might include areas such as group cohesion, leadership and perhaps collective efficacy. In addition, role theories (e.g. conflict, ambiguity) that have been popularized by recent research efforts might also be viewed as significant to those interested in team or group functioning. However, one major area that certainly has not populated research associated with group dynamics is that of *achievement motivation*. This might seem surprising given that readers with practical and applied experiences of working with or competing in teams will certainly be able to relate to motivational issues and how achievement motivation, as an integral construct that drives team member behavior, can literally make or break seasons.

So why is the theoretical study of achievement motivation, in the context of factors related to the business of teams, somewhat off the radar? Further, what particular research findings from the achievement goal literature are important to note for those interested in team contexts? And, what opportunities exist for researchers to take a different angle to studies of group motivation and team functioning in order to advance knowledge through the lens offered by achievement goal theories? With these questions in mind, the primary purpose of this chapter is to bring achievement goal theory to the attention of researchers interested in team issues, as well as to encourage current achievement goal scholars to consider the uncharted territory that exists in team settings. We begin by introducing the basic tenets of achievement goal theory and review the limited research related to group issues. This is followed by drawing attention to a number of methodological issues in addition to salient research questions that may drive forward our understanding of group functioning in sport settings. When athletes come together to perform in teams, they are by definition interdependent. What this means from a motivation perspective is that athletes will invariably influence and also be influenced by other group members, as well as the prevailing motivational climate. In this chapter, we present a series of conceptual group dynamics considerations that have yet to be applied to the sport achievement motivation literature and demonstrate how research and application might be advanced with regard to both individual and team functioning.

Achievement goal theory in sport

A brief, but very dense history reveals that interest in achievement motivation in sport was rejuvenated in the late 1980s by a cluster of achievement goal theories, largely from the educational domain (Dweck, 1986, 1999; Nicholls, 1984, 1989). These theories focused essentially upon how the 'quality' of an individuals' motivation was reflected in the criteria that was employed to judge his or her competence in a particular achievement task or situation. These criteria, underpinned by one's beliefs about ability, were represented in the qualitative goals of action that the individual adopted for the task. Nicholls (1984, 1989) suggested that an individual's internal sense of ability or competence is a central motivator in achievement situations but proposed that ability could be construed in two different manners. These two conceptions of ability subsequently governed two contrasting achievement goals. Drawing from one of his key publications, he clarified this as follows:

> Achievement behavior is defined as behavior directed at developing or demonstrating high rather than low ability. It is shown that ability can be conceived in two ways. First, ability can be judged high or low with reference to the individual's own past performance or knowledge. In this context, gains in mastery indicate competence. Second, ability can be judged as capacity relative to that of others. In this context, a gain in mastery alone does not indicate high ability. To demonstrate high capacity, one must achieve more with equal effort or use less effort than do others for an equal performance.
>
> (Nicholls, 1984, p. 328)

The two qualitative achievement goal states, regulated by individuals adopting one conception of ability over the other, are known as task involvement and ego involvement. Individuals are task involved when gains in personal mastery of a skill or task enrich them with a sense of competence. In this respect, self-referent improvement or learning on a task is sufficient to generate feelings of personal achievement. In contrast, individuals are ego involved when their sense of competence depends upon demonstrating superior performance to others, or via an equal performance to others but with less effort exhibited. Both achievement goals therefore focus on different aspects of the self; when an individual is in a state of task involvement, his/her main focus is on the *development* of the self irrespective of others. When in a state of ego involvement, the perceived ability of the self and the *demonstration* of its adequacy compared with others, is of primary concern.

One of the critical features of Nicholls' approach with respect to subsequent research in sport is that he promoted the existence of two dispositional goal orientations that reflected 'individual differences in proneness to different types of involvement' (1989, p. 95). As a result of socialization experiences in childhood and adolescence, he suggested that individuals develop a tendency to adopt task and/or ego involved goals in achievement situations. Nicholls viewed these dispositional goals as representative of a worldview or theory about success in a given achievement domain (i.e. education). Early research in education and sport (Duda and Nicholls, 1992) suggested that a task goal orientation was associated with the belief that sport and education provide opportunities for personal growth and mastery and that success stems from working hard, learning and collaboration with others. Conversely, an ego goal orientation was associated with the belief that sport and education provide opportunities for social status, superiority and wealth alongside the view that success stems from outperforming others and even the use of deceptive or illegal tactics.

The assessment of task and ego orientations in sport is typically conducted through one of two self-report scales: the Task and Ego Orientation in Sport Questionnaire (TEOSQ; Duda and Nicholls, 1992); or the Perceptions of Success Questionnaire (POSQ; Roberts *et al.*, 1998). Prompted by the stems 'I feel most successful in sport when' (TEOSQ) or 'When playing sport, I feel successful when' (POSQ), respondents indicate the extent to which they agree or disagree with the subsequent task (e.g. I perform to the best of my ability) or ego statements (e.g. I am the best) being indicative of what makes them feel successful. As goal orientations represent orthogonal, as opposed to a bipolar, cognitive schema (Nicholls, 1989), individuals are capable of being independently high, moderate or low in either or both orientations in combination. In essence, every athlete will possess a goal orientation 'profile' that represents the level of their tendency to be task or ego involved in sport. Recent research in sport has adopted what are termed 'goal profiling' techniques (see Hodge and Petlichkoff, 2000), whereby groups or clusters of athletes with different levels of task and ego orientation are identified and studied (Harwood *et al.*, 2004).

Like Nicholls, Carol Dweck's work on achievement goals has also been applied from education to sport and particularly to physical education settings (see Spray *et al.*, 2006). According to Dweck (1999), attributes of the self, other people, places and the world in general can be conceived as fixed, uncontrollable, or, alternatively, as malleable and controllable factors that are open to development. This former conception has been termed an 'entity theory', the latter as an 'incremental theory' and individuals can be described as entity theorists or incremental theorists depending on their views of human attributes. Related to Nicholls' propositions regarding task and ego goals, Dweck proposed that entity theorists are more likely to endorse performance/ego goals, whereas incremental theorists are more likely to pursue learning/task goals. In sport and PE, it is suggested that performance goals serve to demonstrate or prove the adequacy of one's stable ability (or to avoid displaying the inadequacy of one's stable ability). Learning goals, on the other hand, serve to develop one's unstable, malleable ability. Importantly, individuals can interpret the achievement situation quite differently depending on the nature of their implicit *entity* and *incremental* beliefs for a task and their concern with proving, relative to improving, competence in that setting.

The nature of performance/ego and learning/task goals, along with the predicted consequences of pursuing these two types of goals, are essentially quite similar in Dweck's and Nicholls' theoretical perspectives. Both propose a performance/ego-based achievement goal that is focused on normative perceptions of ability (e.g. winning; superiority) and both argue that the motivational ramifications of pursuing such a normative goal are dependent on perceived competence. If competence perceptions are high, adaptive responses are predicted; if doubts about competence exist, maladaptive/helpless patterns result. In both perspectives, therefore, perceived competence is proposed to moderate the influence of normatively-based achievement goals. Further, both theorists postulate that the self-referenced task/learning goal (e.g. personal improvement, skill development) leads to adaptive cognitions, affective responses and behaviors even if perceived competence is low.

Situational factors and motivational climate

In both Nicholls and Dweck's theories, the achievement situation and the contextual conditions of the task are of significant importance. In essence, the situation or environment may exert a manipulative (or complementary) power over the individual's achievement goal orientations for a specific task or activity. As Dweck and Leggett (1988) note, 'Dispositions are seen as individual difference variables that determine the *a-priori* probability of adopting a particular goal and displaying a particular behavioral pattern and *situational factors* [italics added] are seen as potentially altering these probabilities' (p. 269). Duda (2001) provides an excellent commentary on the interactional (disposition × situation) aspects of these theories, as well as a critical and comprehensive review of sport research in the field. However, for our purposes, it is important to acknowledge that the achievement goals of athletes will likely be influenced by the nature of social and situational cues that exist for the athlete to cognitively process in that setting.

The premise that a team member or athlete's achievement goals are influenced by the evaluative nature of the context and/or behavior of significant others was championed through Carole Ames' work (Ames, 1984, 1992; Ames and Archer, 1988) on competitive, cooperative and individualistic goal structures in classroom settings. Her work investigated the creation of ego-involving (i.e. competitive) versus task-involving (i.e. individualistic) classroom environments, proposing that situational cues (e.g. reward for superior marks; recognition of effort, improvement), chiefly controlled by the teacher, would influence the salience of different achievement goals. In sport, significant others and important social agents were proposed to determine goal salience by the criteria upon which they were perceived to evaluate success and failure, offered recognition and reward, grouped athletes by ability, or responded to mistakes. Ames asserted that it was this *subjective* meaning, or individual's perception of the motivational environment, that was critical in predicting subsequent achievement goals and patterns of behavior in that individual.

Her research principles were translated to sport (similarly to Nicholls and Dweck; see Ames, 1992; Duda 1992, 2001; Seifriz *et al.*, 1992) leading to the proposition and study of two types of *motivational climate* that could be perceived by athletes to exist in a number of settings (e.g. within the team, training, organization, competition, family). When athletes perceive a 'mastery' or task-involving climate, they sense that the criteria for evaluation are self-referenced and that people are viewed as competent when they have made incremental progress, accomplished a task, or learned something new. According to achievement goal theorists, such a climate promotes the activation and adoption of a learning goal or a state of task involvement and this environment is predicted to have positive cognitive, affective and behavioral consequences. Alternatively, a 'performance' or ego-involving climate exists when athletes are evaluated solely on whether they demonstrate superiority relative to their opponents and upon making as few mistakes as possible to prove the adequacy of their ability.

Based on Ames' original Classroom Achievement Goals Questionnaire (Ames and Archer, 1988), a variety of measures subsequently emerged to assess the perceived situational and contextual goal emphases in sport and physical education settings. The most relevant of these to this chapter is the Perceived Motivational Climate in Sport Questionnaire (PMCSQ; Seifriz *et al.*, 1992) and its subsequent revision, the PMCSQ-2 (Newton *et al.*, 2000). The PMCSQ is a team-focused questionnaire and assesses the degree to which each team member perceives two situational factors: a task-involving and ego-involving atmosphere created in the team. It contains items largely focused on the behavior and values of the coach with the task-involving dimension represented by how much the respondent perceives an emphasis to exist upon improving skills, working hard and having an important role on the team. The ego-involving items assess the degree which there is a perceived emphasis on the importance of superior performance over others (i.e. team-mates), intra-team rivalry, behaviors linked to unequal recognition and punishment for mistakes.

The rationale for the revision of the PMCSQ was based on an interest in examining the sub-dimensions of each climate in order to increase the theoretical and practical understanding of how, why and when a particular situational goal structure impacts the dimensions of athletes' motivation (Duda and Whitehead, 1998). In the final version of the PMCSQ-2 (Newton *et al.*, 2000) three lower-order factors emerged for the mastery/task-involving factor (a focus on effort/improvement, important role and cooperative learning). Three lower order factors also reflected the performance/ego-involving scale (unequal recognition, punishment for mistakes and intra-team member rivalry). The PMCSQ-2 therefore provided researchers with an opportunity to examine these sub-dimensions and how such 'circumstances' or conditions perceived in a team may be associated with the cognitive, affective and behavioral responses of team members.

Achievement goals and group-related themes

The introduction of achievement goal theory into sport was followed by a penetrating wave of research into the intrapersonal and environmental influences upon athlete behavior (see Duda, 2001). Our understanding of individual differences in such sub-topics as motivated behaviors (e.g. effort, persistence, task approach versus task avoidance), cognitions and beliefs (e.g. attributions, moral judgments), affective responses (e.g. enjoyment, anxiety) and learning processes/strategy use in athletes has been constructed over twenty years of persistent research effort. During this time, athletes from both individual and team contexts have been investigated with a view to delimiting the antecedents and consequences of task and ego goals in sport. However, the focus of scholars has most definitely been upon understanding achievement goals at the individual level. What emerges from this literature (see Biddle *et al.*, 2003; Duda, 2001; Weiss and Ferrer-Caja, 2002 for extensive reviews) is the positive nature of task orientation, task involvement and task-involving motivational climates. When ego goals or an ego-involving climate prevails, there tends be either a negative or no relationship with motivational, cognitive, affective and performance-related factors at an individual level. However, when perceptions of ability are high or when the individual simultaneously endorses a task goal (i.e. a high task/high ego goal profile; see Hodge and Petlichkoff, 2000), then positive complementary effects of an ego goal are more likely (Harwood *et al.*, 2004).

Over this period, the potential role of achievement goals in optimal group functioning has been touched upon by a number of research strands that have explored links with social psychological processes such as leadership behavior, group cohesion and social loafing. The following sections briefly outline these studies.

Achievement goals and effective leadership

A large proportion of competitive sport takes place within group structures and formal leaders of a team such as the coach are assumed to influence team achievement and the nature of dynamic interactions among team members. Using Chelladurai's (1993) Multidimensional Model of Leadership, Balaguer and colleagues (2002) conducted a detailed study into associations between achievement goals, perceived and preferred leadership style, subjective performance, satisfaction and ratings of the coach among 181 Spanish female handball players competing in a national competition. First, results revealed how the player's perceptions of a task-involving climate corresponded to high training and instruction as well as social support behaviors perceived to be provided by the coach. Players participating in such a climate also reported a preference for their coaches to engage in such behaviors. Conversely, a perceived ego-involving climate correlated negatively with these leadership behaviors suggesting that the greater the perceived emphasis of the coach on winning, favoritism and punishment for mistakes, the less concerned players felt the coach was with respect to their overall welfare or positive training and instruction.

A second set of analyses revealed that perceptions of a task-involving climate positively corresponded to perceived improvement in the tactical, technical, physical, psychological and competitive elements of both individual and team handball performance. In sum, players were more satisfied with their competitive results, level of performance and coach – individually and as a team – when the motivational climate was deemed more task-involving. In contrast, when the motivational environment (largely promoted by the coach in the PMCSQ) was perceived to contain more ego-involving characteristics, lower levels of player satisfaction emerged.

Achievement goals and group cohesion

Within sport psychology, group cohesion has been identified as a major determinant of both individual and collective behavior within teams. Defined as 'a dynamic process which is reflected in the tendency for a group to stick together and remain united in the pursuit of its instrumental objectives and/or for the satisfaction of member affective needs' (Carron *et al.*, 1998, p. 213), group cohesion has been theorized to include task as well as social dimensions. Task cohesion represents a general orientation towards achieving the groups' instrumental objectives and social cohesion represents a general orientation toward developing and maintaining social relationships within the group (see Carron *et al.*, Ch. 7, this volume).

Early research on achievement goals in sport suggested the merit of examining the conceptual relationship between dispositional (i.e. goal orientations) or situationally-emphasized goals (i.e. motivational climate) and group cohesion. However, investigations have been surprisingly sparse in number. From a conceptual standpoint, a task orientation has been associated with cooperation goals (Duda and Nicholls, 1992) as well as the belief that collaborative efforts between team members leads to sport success (Duda and White, 1992). Further, the development and structure of the PMCSQ and PMCSQ-2 reflect how a task-involving climate is one that promotes team member cooperation and important team roles for all, whereas an ego-involving climate supports a sense of intra-team member rivalry and favoritism. With these aspects in mind, a strong task orientation in team members or a prevailing task-involving climate (promoted by coach or team leader) may foster conditions to facilitate greater team cohesion. Conversely, team members with excessive ego orientations and/or a climate that fuels the importance of superiority, rivalry and mistake-contingent punishment represent destructive conditions for achieving optimal team cohesion. Although unpublished, research cited in Duda (2001) by Boone and Duda (1999) and Chi and Lu (1995) corroborated these hypotheses. Within 131 intercollegiate male baseball players, Boone and Duda found that task orientation was positively associated with the extent to which players' were attracted to the team's tasks, as well as the extent to which the team was perceived to be integrated around performing group tasks (i.e. components of task cohesion). Conversely, ego orientation was negatively related to players' attractions to their group's tasks. Chi and Lu (1995) examined the relationships between perceptions of the motivational climate and group cohesion in five men's and five women's university basketball teams from Taiwan. Correlational analyses indicated that a perceived task-involving atmosphere was positively linked to reported task cohesion, while perceptions of an ego-involving environment were negatively related to task and social cohesion. Further, following a median split of the task and ego climate scales to create four motivational climate 'profiles', the high task-involving and low ego-involving climate 'group' reported the highest levels of task and social cohesion.

Achievement goals and social loafing behavior

Few studies in the achievement goal literature have attempted to demonstrate how the behavior and performance of team members may be related to their achievement goals. Swain (1996) however provided a stimulus example of this when he tested the link between achievement motivation and the process of social loafing in a team performance task. As Duda (2001) notes in a fuller review of this literature, *social loafing* occurs when individuals lower their exerted effort when part of a team in contrast to when they are working as individuals on a task. When individuals are predominantly ego-oriented and working on their own, the theory suggests that demonstrations of superior ability would be maximized when paired with as little effort as possible to complete the task. In other words, if an individual could win and expend little effort in doing so, then this would affirm his/her superior level of ability. This 'disregard' for the value of effort may carry over in a different guise when working in a group task. In such a scenario, a highly ego-oriented individual would not be as easily able to demonstrate his or her *individual* superiority at the task. If performance, in terms of achievement relative to others (e.g. team-mates; opponents), is not immediately visible and apparent, then ego-oriented athletes' dispositional disregard for effort means that they may be unlikely to try that hard. After all, in this mindset, such athletes gain nothing from trying apart from wasted effort. In contrast, if success is identifiable to others and athletes can show the quality of their performances relative to others, then it would be in the athletes' best interests to try hard as a means to an end (i.e. the end being to better the opposition or even team-mates). Swain administered the TEOSQ to young adolescent British males who participated in three 30-metre sprints 1 week later. In the first sprint, the boys ran as individuals and recorded a time. In the second sprint – the team identifiable condition – they ran as part of a relay team with each member's performance time identified. In the final dash – the team non-identifiable condition – they ran as a relay team but their personal contribution to the team performance was not identified. Results generally supported hypothesized outcomes. Those athletes with a high task and low ego orientation did not differ across conditions in terms of their times. As expected, they performed (i.e. tried) equally hard as team members in both conditions as they did as individuals. However, high ego and low task oriented athletes were significantly slower in the non-identifiable condition than in the identifiable condition. One might speculate that these individuals conserved effort as a performing team member when they knew they wouldn't be: (a) able to demonstrate how superior they were; and (b) 'found out' for not trying hard (i.e. get away with social loafing). Although limited to a single study of this nature, findings such as these have significant ramifications for appropriate and functional performance-related behaviors in teams and the antecedents thereof. When team members do not appear to be 'pulling their weight' or committing the extra mile for the good of the team, then a pragmatic coach could benefit from an insider's view of team member achievement goals, their perceptions of the motivational climate and how best to manage the delivery of transparent, identifiable performance-related feedback to enhance effortful behavior.

Advancing achievement goal theory: from individual conceptions to interdependent considerations

When drawing together the literature on the study of achievement goals from a team perspective and with optimal team functioning in mind, it is surprising how many unanswered questions or under-explored phenomena exist. A recent systematic review of the correlates of goal orientations (Biddle *et al.*, 2003) in sport revealed that over 21,000 sport participants had been employed in the diversity of achievement goal research. However, few if any of these studies placed the interdependent team environment at the center of the research question. In recent years, from a social psychological perspective, research involving groups has embraced a number of prominent conceptual, methodological and measurement advances that we believe have the potential to substantively contribute to advancing achievement goal theory as well as a practical understanding of motivational processes in sport. In the following section, we highlight some of these advances and present a series of research questions that are broadly concerned with the extent to which individual achievement motives both influence and are influenced by others within their group environment (e.g. coach, team-mates).

Achievement goals: actor and partner effects

Given that achievement goals represent *personal* orientations and motivational states at given points in time, it is entirely logical that researchers would be interested in understanding how achievement goals influence the cognitions, emotions and behaviors of athletes (and coaches) from an *intra-individual* perspective. That is, how do the achievement goals of a given individual affect that same individual? However, when people exist within groups it is also possible, if not likely, that the motivational characteristics of individual group members will influence others. Indeed, it would seem plausible to suggest that achievement goals held by individuals within teams may influence the cognitions, emotions and behaviors of their team-mates.

The intra-individual designs that have pervaded the achievement motivation literature have shed important light on how the task and ego orientations held by athletes are predictive of their enjoyment, interest and satisfaction in sport (e.g. Duda *et al.*, 1995) as well as a host of other factors (see Duda, 2001). Social psychologists refer to such intra-individual outcomes as *actor* effects (Kenny and Cook, 1999; Kenny *et al.*, 2006), whereby a predictor variable is related to the outcome variable for the same person. However, it is also possible that when athletes train or perform with others (e.g. coach, team-mate), as they invariably do in many sport settings, it is also possible that achievement goals and motives held by a given person might also be related to outcomes experienced by one's partner. Social psychologists refer to this as a *partner effect* (Kenny and Cook, 1999; Kenny *et al.*, 2006), which occurs when the independent variable within one person influences the dependent variable within another. To illustrate, Kenny *et al.* (2006) use the example of a spouse who experiences depression, whereby the prevalence of her depression can influence the marital satisfaction for herself as well as the marital satisfaction of her husband. In this case, depression would be said to exhibit both an actor effect (influences wife's marital satisfaction) as well as a partner effect (influences husband's marital satisfaction).

Recent research by Jackson *et al.* (2007) has provided evidence for the simultaneous existence of partner and actor effects within close relationships in sport. Specifically, Jackson *et al.* (2007) used Kenny *et al.*'s (2006) *actor-partner interdependence modelling* (APIM) procedures and found that when athletes (i.e. tennis doubles players) held high perceptions of their own perceived capabilities (i.e. self-efficacy), this was not only related to their own commitment to their partner but was also predictive of their partner's commitment to the relationship. As it relates to inter-relationships within sports teams, it would be useful to know whether task and ego goals have the same transference effects in relation to outcomes experienced by players' team-mates. For example, if a player exhibits particularly high levels of ego orientation (i.e. needs to be better than everyone on the team; desire to be viewed as the 'go-to' player'), does this influence the cognitions of his or her team-mates (e.g. elevated frustration, impatience) and also how s/he interacts with that player? Furthermore, what would be the impact on team members and the team process if this player possessed low as opposed to high perceptions of ability? In terms of actor effects, we would predict a maladaptive pattern of behavior if his/her current confidence was low. Similarly, in this example, one might expect team-mates to display partner effects such as reduced commitment to and social support for this player. To date, APIM procedures have yet to be operationalized within the achievement motivation literature. In our view they represent a potentially invaluable (conceptual, methodological and statistical) framework for understanding achievement goals within interdependent settings.

A recent investigation that did take an intra-partnership perspective towards the study of achievement goals in a team, involved the perceptions of 36 sports acrobat pairs (Harwood and Lacey, 2001). Using adapted versions of the POSQ (Roberts *et al.*, 1998), the authors examined the levels of compatibility and perceptual agreement between each individual's reported goal orientations and their partner's perception of that individual's goal orientations. Each acrobat in the pair completed their self-report perception of achievement goals, as well as their perception of their partner's achievement goals (i.e. meta-perception). In addition, however, the POSQ was adapted to contain a directional subscale that asked acrobats to rate on a scale of +3 'very positive' to −3 'very negative', the degree to which they felt that their response to each POSQ item had a positive or negative effect on their performance as a pair. In this manner, the study gained a view not only of how positive or negative acrobats felt their own achievement goals were to their partnerships, but also a view of how facilitative or debilitative they felt their partners' achievement goals were to the partnerships. Interestingly, in terms of partner-achievement goal similarity, 'bases' (older athletes that form the base of the pair) reported lower levels of ego orientation and higher levels of task orientation than their respective 'tops' (younger athletes that form the top of the pair). In terms of perceived impact of achievement goals, the bases perceived their level of task orientation to be more positive to the performance as a pair than their respective tops.

When analyzing their perceptions of each other's goal orientations, bases perceived their tops to be lower in task orientation than tops' self-reported responses and appraised this level of task orientation to be less positive to performance than tops. In addition, while predictions made by bases about the level of ego orientation of their tops were accurate, they perceived their tops' ego orientation to be less positive to performance than the tops' self-reported perceptions of their ego orientation. These findings illustrated the importance of perceptions (and potential misinterpretation) in team or partnership sport settings, as well as raising the issue of compatible versus incompatible individual-level goals in terms of partner functioning.

Within youth sport contexts, the issue of compatible and incompatible achievement goals is also highly relevant to the *quality of relationships* between peers (Smith, 1999). When athletes differ in their achievement orientations and hold potentially incongruent goal profiles it is possible that the motives and behaviors of certain peers may 'rub off' and influence the motives of others, as well as factors such as friendship quality, team cohesion and social competence (Allen, 2003). In the context of assessing actor-partner interactions, the Peer Motivational Climate in Youth Sport scale (Ntoumanis and Vazou, 2005) may prove to be of use. Essentially, it examines peers' perceptions of the degree to which their team (of peers) promotes a task-involving or ego-involving climate. It would be interesting in future research to examine the extent to which the achievement goals among peers both influence and are influenced by each other to create a setting where improvement is valued and relatedness-support is offered by others compared with a climate characterized by intra-team conflict and negative peer comments.

In summary, while specific actor-partner independence models have not been fully engaged in achievement goal research, their use may provide invaluable information about how dispositional and situational achievement motives held by key actors (e.g. coach, parent, role models, peers) influence the motives and behaviors of others, especially young athletes and team members (Duda and Hom, 1993; Ebbeck and Becker, 1994). At a practical level, it is reasonable to speculate that different leadership and positional roles in teams are suited to individuals with particular achievement goal profiles and that motivational compatibility within a team is an enduring mission. From a consultancy perspective, the optimal functioning of the team may be related to whether (1) team members are educated and aware of achievement goals and what they mean for the team and team-mate behaviors and thus (2) team-mates understand their own and others' achievement goals in a manner that optimizes member-to-member interactions. Indeed, this area of applied intervention research remains completely uncharted.

Understanding intra-team ego-oriented achievement goals

When studying achievement goals in team settings, it pays to give careful attention as to how they might function in manners idiosyncratic to the team context. If one considers that on sports teams, members are not only required to work interdependently (i.e. work cooperatively) with each other to achieve group outcomes such as team success, on occasions they are also required to compete with each other for places on a team. Indeed, in such settings the operational functioning of ego involvement bears closer scrutiny. Specifically, do highly ego-involved team members focus their attention on beating the opposition while cooperating with other members, or do they seek to promote themselves and their ability ahead of other team members (e.g. ball hogging, selfish and incorrect decisions, denying team-mates a chance to shine, making others look incompetent to protect/advance themselves or their status in the team)? Clearly, we would expect major behavioral differences between being highly ego involved with respect to the opposition and being highly ego involved towards your own team-mates and peers (see Ntoumanis and Vazou, 2005). At present, however, we do not know whether these behaviors have their origins in a singular goal orientation, or whether these are two distinct *types* of ego orientation. Items within the TEOSQ and POSQ are unable to provide any insight into these motives, or what might be classed as 'intra-team' ego goal perspectives. Further, no research to our knowledge within achievement goal theory has taken an in-depth qualitative or quantitative look at the specific ramifications for ego involvement in terms of within-team functioning. Notionally, there is a world of difference between a group of players who spark off consistent intra-team member rivalry, egocentric and unsportspersonlike behavior, compared with players who cooperate with their team-mates to achieve normative success over the opposition. Nevertheless, it is possible that ego orientations may pervade intra-team and inter-team contexts and if it comes down to an opportunity for personal glory, a spot on team, or to make a team-mate look less competent than oneself, then such a goal perspective may play out both *within* the confines of the team as it does *between* teams. Such behaviors might include failing to actively support or encourage team members, engaging in negative communication with team-mates and blaming external factors including team-mates. In sum, the last thing that a struggling team needs is a negative player who places a depressing drain on team resources – an energy sapper. Yet if there are multiple team members who respond like this 'when the going gets tough', one can see how 'jumping ship' and creating negative momentum represent viable strategies to protect one's sense of competence.

The 'ME not WE' mindset that reflects within-team ego involvement has not been studied within the sport psychology literature and we have not examined the full scope of behaviors associated with this phenomenon. Furthermore, the role of a team member's task orientation in this case is not precisely clear either. In light of the theorized orthogonal structure of task and ego goals (i.e. athletes can be high or low in both task and ego goals, as well as high in one and low in the other), it is possible that athletes may seek to strive towards personal improvement (high task) and seek to demonstrate superiority over other team members (high *intra-team* ego). Without doubt, this remains one of the most untouched areas of research to aid the practitioner and team coach when it comes to supporting group functioning and team harmony. A more sub-cultural approach to measurement, in this case a qualitative and quantitative assessment of intra-team achievement goals, may open up a more dedicated vein of research into the interplay between Nicholls' theory and important group processes and outcomes.

Understanding inter-team achievement goals

The basic premise of achievement goal theory is that ability can either be judged in reference to an individual's past performance (self-referenced) or in relation to the capabilities of others (norm-referenced). When athletes function and perform within teams, this brings to light the additional dimension of the *team's ability* and how team success and failure is judged by its members. Although the construct of (individual perceptions of) 'competence' forms the centerpiece of achievement goal theories, it would nevertheless be interesting to explore whether team members' perceptions of collective ability have any motivational or behavioral consequences for that individual or team. Ostensibly, team-mates can judge the success of the team relative to their previous performance capabilities (a task goal focus) and conversely relative to other teams (e.g. beating other teams; an ego goal focus). One often hears two well known phrases that emphasize the divergent nature of these two *inter-team* achievement goals. This first is 'winning isn't everything' and implies that taking part and collective improvement are worthy attributes. The second, reflects an inter-team ego orientation and extends the saying by suggesting that 'winning isn't everything: *it's the only thing!'* There is limited, if any research that helps us to understand if and how athletes (at a contextual or situational level) internalize achievement goals for the team beyond (or in addition to) their own individual state of goal involvement. In other words, are certain team achievements necessary for the individual to feel that their needs are being met on the team?

Anecdotal evidence and experience suggests that team members may differ in their cognitive, affective or behavioral responses to positive and negative team outcomes whereby athletes internalize team success or failure (Weiner, 1986) regardless of their own levels of self-referent or norm-referent performance. For example, consider the case of the team member who improves in terms of personal performance in a team competition, yet experiences high negative affect due to team failures. If team members interpret achievement based on norm-based principles of *team* success (i.e. being better than other teams), in accordance with the basic tenets of achievement goal theory, one would expect continued persistence and effort so long as that the team has very high levels of perceived collective competence (Nicholls, 1984). In this case, members who hold ego involved goals for the team are likely to remain motivated and committed as long as they believe the team to have high collective ability and most probably a good win/loss record. However, if team members interpret achievement based on norm-based principles of team success and report low collective competence, one might expect deleterious outcomes to result, such as member drop-out/withdrawal, reduced group cohesion, blaming, decreased persistence intentions and member satisfaction. In simple terms, the thesis would be that inter-team ego involved members do not want to be part of losing teams. Conversely, if team members define success in terms of collective improvement and team mastery, according to theory, one would expect continued persistence and effort intentions regardless of whether the team is high or low in its potential capabilities (collective intra-team ability). For these athletes with high inter-team task involvement, standards of team performance and perceived improvement would be more salient criteria beyond the immediate result or win/loss record.

Although research has yet to investigate inter-team achievement goals in sport and while acknowledging that these are ideas external to traditional individual level goal theory, there is a broad question to be studied here. Namely, what group dynamics and outcomes exist for those teams with members comprising a mix of high inter-team ego and task goals; whereby some judge team success in norm-referent terms, others in self-referent terms, or even in both manners? In this typical team setting, are some members perceived as over-competitive, while others viewed as too developmental and not sufficiently passionate about winning? This type of research may penetrate into the group cohesion domain as a team factor/motivation-based antecedent as well as revealing what other cognitive, affective or behavioral responses play out among team members with conflicting definitions of 'what makes a successful team'.

Motivational climates in teams: multilevel and multidimensional considerations

Beyond individual differences in achievement goals, there are also a number of questions related to the influence of situational factors that remain unanswered or under-explored, in particular with respect to the nature of motivational climates. One such issue relates to the methods by which perceptions of the motivational climate have been measured and subsequently analyzed in physical activity groups such as sports teams or physical education classes. Traditionally, researchers interested in studying motivational climates within physical activity settings have employed a methodology whereby members of multiple sports teams or physical education classes are asked to report their perceptions of the prevailing climate and these responses have been treated as one large group without considering specific within-team factors that may influence participants' responses. On the one hand it may seem reasonable to examine the extent to which a person's perceptions of the environment are predictive of various personal (i.e. individual) outcomes. Unfortunately, taking such an approach fails to account for the fact that when individuals are members of groups, they may be influenced by factors that are specific to one team (or one type of team) that are not evident in others. From a statistical perspective, this also means that such designs do not account for *within-group* and *between-groups* variability. Indeed, when data are nested within a hierarchical structure and analyses do not account for this structural property, standard errors will likely be underestimated which can result in spurious findings (Bryk and Raudenbush, 1992; Rasbash *et al.*, 2000; Raudenbush, 1988).

Recently, a growing number of achievement motivation theorists have recognized that the motivational climate 'construct' is inherently group-like in nature (cf. Duda, 2001; Gano-Overway *et al.*, 2005; Papaioannou *et al.*, 2004) and that researchers need to consider group-level as well as individual-level variability in members' climate perceptions. That is, the very term 'climate' suggests that all members of intact groups are exposed to similar environmental influences, which may have a homogenizing effect on player motivation (they are influenced in a similar way by similar factors). In a particularly interesting study from the physical education domain, Papaioannou *et al.* (2004) examined the effects of the motivational climate on intrinsic motivation, student attitudes, physical self-concept and exercise intentions among children over the course of the school year. This longitudinal multilevel study examined the prospective effects of the motivational climate measured early in the academic year in relation outcomes assessed later in the year and controlled for outcome measures recorded at the first data collection point. As hypothesized, the amount of variance explained at the group-level was substantive (indicating similarity in perceptions within classes) and that the majority of this variance was explained by the influence of the teacher. Furthermore, group-level task-involving climate perceptions were found to be predictive of student intrinsic motivation towards physical education (effort and enjoyment), exercise intentions, as well as perceived behavioral control towards exercise. Interestingly, a combination of high task- and high ego-involving climates were found to have positive effects on students' task orientation and enjoyment. This finding suggests that an ego-involving climate can be harnessed to positively support a task-involving environment. However, when an ego-involving climate was accompanied by a low task-involving climate the effects were negative.

In a study from the sport domain involving rowing crews, Magyar *et al.* (2004) similarly found that crew members' exhibited similarity within their teams (i.e. consensus) in their perceptions of both mastery and performance climates. Their study was designed to examine some of the multilevel determinants of collective efficacy (extent to which team members are confident about their conjoint responsibilities) among rowing crews prior to a regatta and found that average collective efficacy beliefs among crews were found to be predicted by elevated boat-level mastery (or task-involving) climates. Interestingly, group-level performance (or ego-involving) climates were unable to explain any variance in collective efficacy. Gano-Overway *et al.* (2005) found a similar within-team motivational climate consensus in their study of achievement goals and sportspersonship within 25 intact female volleyball teams. Hierarchical linear modeling procedures subsequently revealed that task orientation and team level perceptions of task-involving climate positively predicted team-level pro-social behaviors characterizing respect for the game.

The emergence of studies that belatedly recognize that motivational climates do indeed involve group-like properties is highly encouraging. However, by arguing from a dichotomous perspective regarding whether motivational climate is 'an individual versus group level construct?' (Papaioannou *et al.*, 2004, p. 90), there is also a danger that the proverbial baby is thrown out with the bathwater. In a recent theoretical paper concerning motivational climates within work groups, Dragoni (2005) presented a strong argument to suggest that motivational climate perceptions should *conceptually* be considered at *both* the individual-level as well as at the group-level. Specifically, at the individual-level, Dragoni suggests that 'leaders transmit their achievement priority to individual group members through role modeling, continual guidance and reinforcement for adopting a psychological climate that embodies the leader's favored achievement orientation' (p. 1,086). Indeed, Dragoni suggests that individual members may possess different (unique and individual) motivational climate perceptions to other group members that are shaped by the particular interpersonal relationship with the group's leader. However, Dragoni also recognized that members will invariably interact with each other and will produce 'a shared interpretation of work group routines and rewards' (p. 1,087). Within sport teams these dual motivational mechanisms can be reflected in athletes' perceptions about (1) their direct relationship with the coach and the personal climate that surrounds that relationship and (2) the perceived climate that exists within the team as a whole. Although the athlete's personal climate is clearly embedded within the team climate, the unique relationship that each athlete has with the coach may mean that personal climates may differ somewhat among members of each team. If one accepts Dragoni's thesis that climates conceptually exist at both the individual and group levels, then they should also be operationalized (i.e. *measured*) at *both levels*.

To date, this theory-to-measurement issue has not been considered within the motivational climate literature in sport and exercise psychology. To illustrate, motivational climates in sport have typically been assessed using the Perceived Motivational Climate in Sport Questionnaire-2 (PMCSQ-2; Newton *et al.*, 2000). As noted earlier, this 33-item measure was designed to assess the extent to which athletes perceive the existence of both mastery (task) and performance based (ego) cues and includes items such as 'on this team, players help each other learn' and 'on this team, the coach favors some players more than others.' These items reflect what Chan (1998) refers to as group-level *referent-shift* measures. That is to say, the point of reference being evaluated by each athlete corresponds to the *team as a whole* (i.e. perception held by the individual about the team), rather than the athlete's perception about him or herself (i.e. perception held by the individual about the individual). Specifically, the referent being evaluated shifts *from* the individual *to* the group. However, if we acknowledge Dragoni's (2005) suggestion that motivational climate perceptions can also exist at the individual level, it is important to additionally assess personal perceptions of the environment using the appropriate point of reference. This is not to suggest that the Newton *et al.* (2000) measure is inappropriate. Rather that this instrument is restricted to measuring the group-level *dimension* of the climate and that in order to assess individual-level climate perceptions, an appropriate individual-level measure is required. This would be reflected in such items as 'on this team, my performance is continuously being evaluated in comparison to others' (ego involved individual-level climate) and 'on this team, I am challenged to constantly improve my individual performance (individual-level mastery climate).' Although a multidimensional conceptualization of climate has yet to be considered within the achievement motivation literature, it would be particularly interesting to determine the extent to which both individual- as well as group-level dimensions of climate differentially influence athlete motivation. For example, it would seem plausible to suggest that *personal* and *direct* experiences of task or ego involvement (e.g. 'on this team, the coach favors me over my team-mates'; 'on this team, I am challenged to improve') would be more powerful sources of athlete motivation than any observation that others are subject to such reinforcement (e.g. 'on this team, the coach favors some players more than others'; 'on this team, players are challenged to improve'). This same argument may apply to the peer motivational climate scale (Ntoumanis and Vazou, 2005) that also uses a group-level as opposed to individual-level referent perception. Future research is clearly needed that simultaneously considers individual and group dimensions of the motivational climate and also the antecedents and consequences of those multidimensional perceptions.

Situational assessments of team climate

It was noted earlier how participants in the study by Papaioannou *et al.* (2004) reported greater enjoyment when perceptions of the motivational climate were both task *and* ego-involving. A study by Goudas and Biddle (1994) similarly reported class environments high in *both* mastery and performance cues led to more enjoyment than any other combination (low:high, high:low, low:low). This suggests that an environment with a combination of both task- and ego-involving properties may foster motivated behaviors in a complementary manner. However, this research fails to provide any definitive insights into the exact achievement goals that are adopted 'in situ' when both task and ego-involving cues are supposedly emphasized and perceived within the climate. Achievement goal researchers have debated if and how athletes can be task and ego involved simultaneously in a particular situation at a given moment in time (see Harwood and Hardy, 2001; Harwood et al., 2000; Treasure et al., 2001) without offering an empirically tested answer. The debate extends to measures of motivational climate and whether the two factors represent orthogonal or bi-polar dimensions. That is, can the motivational climate on a sport team really be both task and ego-involving at the same time? By reporting negative correlations ranging from −0.3 to −0.5 of studies using the PMCSQ, Duda (2001) suggested that task and ego-involving perceptions of climate have neither been found to be orthogonal and independent of each other, nor bi-polar constructs. She therefore argues against the technique of 'climate profiling' whereby researchers identify athletes with differing combinations of perceived climate (e.g. high:high; high:low) by allocating them into high and low groups based on perception scores above and below the mean. In essence, it would appear atheoretical to have a group of athletes who were both high in task-involving and high in ego-involving perceptions of the climate.

This current state of ambiguity regarding the structure of task and ego-involving climates can be traced to the level of specificity (i.e. situational versus contextual) that is employed within existing climate measures. The original purpose of assessing the motivational climate was to generate information on the evaluative cues within a situation that may interact with an individual's dispositional goals (e.g. supplant, complement or concede) to determine the athlete's state of task and/or ego involvement in that achievement situation. In reality, current measures of perceived motivational climate do not assess a specific situation at all. They assess an athlete's perception of a context (i.e. being 'on this team' . . .) that reflects the general climate of a sport team regarding what typically goes on. In terms of predicting achievement goals in a competition, measurements at this contextual level may be far different from perceptions taken of the climate in a specific situation or period of time (e.g. pre-match before important games; in training; at half-time). Indeed, if contextual rather than situational measures of climate are employed it should be of little surprise that the existence of both task and ego-involving behaviors should be found. Furthermore, if researchers are interested in understanding the specific outcomes associated with task and ego involvement then climate should clearly be assessed at the situational and not contextual levels.

Researchers are also encouraged to consider the range of agents that are responsible for creating ego- or task-involving climates within teams. Although the PMSCQ-2 has become progressively labeled in academic publications as a measure of coach-created climate, it actually targets perceptions of the team and team-mates behavior as much as it addresses the values, attitudes and behavior of the coach. At least a dozen of the items could be interpreted as having little or nothing to do with the coach. It is not surprising therefore that, with respondents prompted by contextual statements related to the coach, team and team-mates, there are members who might perceive both task and ego-involving cues on the team at different times and prompted by different people. Such a measurement structure may encourage greater within-team variability in the data and an inaccurate representation of the climate in a given situation. In sum, our knowledge of the motivational climate in a team and the effects of its interaction with goal orientation upon goal involvement and motivational outcomes will remain constrained if researchers fail to assess climate at a situational level. It also requires investigators to extrapolate which social agents are most salient in creating the motivational climate for team members and perhaps deciphering the separate and additive effects of the main protagonists (e.g. coach, captain, team-mates, parents).

Conclusion

A number of contentious issues have been discussed in this chapter, especially in the latter sections. We believe that there remain a number of rich veins of research that could contribute to the optimal functioning of sport teams, provided that researchers manage to study intact teams, consider levels of measurement and treat the data appropriately. We also feel that greater research effort may be spent on examining potential constructs (e.g. intra-and inter-team goals) that are highly specific and sensitive to the team context. If such motives do exist in team settings then they may serve to explain variance in team member behavior above and beyond that offered by more traditional higher order constructs.

On reviewing this area, one further issue arose – the lack of targeted intervention research designed to improve sport team functioning or achievement motives in teams via an achievement goal approach. The current authors could not locate an intervention or intra-team based case study that tackled issues of incompatible achievement goal orientations, negative partner effects, role or position-specific variations in achievement goals and variability/incongruence of team members' perceptions of motivational climate. We have only just scratched the surface in understanding the role played by achievement motives in team settings and we need to investigate how and if achievement goals do play an essential role in optimizing group functioning. Carefully constructed intervention research is therefore to be encouraged provided that the exact research question has been well conceived with appropriate instrumentation. The methodological advice in this chapter should hopefully provide new researchers with ideas to go about their work in this area more assiduously.

References

Allen, J. (2003). Social motivation in youth sport. *Journal of Sport and Exercise Psychology*, 25, 551–567.

Ames, C. A. (1984). Competitive, cooperative and individual goal structures: A cognitive-motivational analysis. In R. Ames and C. Ames (Eds), *Research on motivation in education: Student motivation* (pp. 177–207). New York: Academic Press.

Ames, C. (1992). Achievement goals, motivational climate and motivational processes. In G. C. Roberts (Ed.), *Motivation in Sport and Exercise* (pp. 161–176). Champaign, IL: Human Kinetics.

Ames, C. and Archer, J. (1988). Achievement goals in the classroom: Students' learning strategies and motivation processes. *Journal of Educational Psychology*, 80, 260–267.

Balaguer, I., Duda, J. L., Atienza, F. L. and Mayo, C. (2002). Situational and dispositional goals as predictors of perceptions on individual and team improvement, satisfaction and coach ratings among elite female handball teams. *Psychology of Sport and Exercise*, 3, 293–308.

Biddle, S. J. H., Wang, C. K., Kavussanu, M. and Spray, C. (2003). Correlates of achievement goal orientations in physical activity: A systematic review of research. *European Journal of Sport Sciences*, 3, 1–20.

Boone, K. and Duda, J. L. (1999). The relationship of goal orientations to multidimensional cohesion across a baseball season. (Unpublished manuscript.)

Bryk, A. S. and Raudenbush, S. W. (1992). *Hierarchical linear models*. Newbury Park, CA: Sage.

Carron, A. V., Brawley, L. R. and Widmeyer, W. N. (1998). The measurement of cohesiveness in sport groups. In J. L. Duda (Ed.), *Advances in sport and exercise psychology measurement* (pp. 213–229). Morgantown, WV: Fitness Information Technology.

Chan, D. (1998). Functional relations among constructs in the same content domain at different levels of analysis: A typology of composition models. *Journal of Applied Psychology*, 83, 234–246.

Chelladurai, P. (1993). Leadership. In R. Singer, M. Murphey and L. K. Tennant (Eds), *Handbook on research on sport psychology* (pp. 647–671). New York: Macmillan.

Chi, L. and Lu, S. E. (1995, June). The relationships between perceived motivational climates and group cohesiveness in basketball. Paper presented at the annual meetings of the North American Society for the Psychology of Sport and Physical Activity, Asilomar, CA.

Dragoni, L. (2005). Understanding the emergence of state goal orientation in organizational work groups: The role of leadership and multilevel climate perceptions. *Journal of Applied Psychology*, 90, 1084–1095.

Duda, J. L. (1992). Motivation in sport settings: A goal perspective approach. In G. C. Roberts (Ed.), *Motivation and sport and exercise* (pp.57–91). Champaign, IL: Human Kinetics.

Duda, J. L. (2001). Achievement goal research in sport: Pushing the boundaries and clarifying some misunderstandings. In G. C. Roberts (Ed.), *Advances in motivation in sport and exercise* (pp. 129–182). Champaign, IL: Human Kinetics.

Duda, J. L., Chi, L., Newton, M. L., Walling, M. D. and Catley, D. (1995). Task and ego orientation and intrinsic motivation in sport. *International Journal of Sport Psychology*, 26, 40–63.

Duda, J. L. and Hom, H. (1993). Interdependencies between the perceived and self-reported goal orientations of young athletes and their parents. *Pediatric Exercise Science*, 5, 234–241.

Duda, J. L. and Nicholls, J. G. (1992). Dimensions of achievement motivation in schoolwork and sport. *Journal of Educational Psychology*, 84, 290–299.

Duda, J. L. and White, S. A. (1992). Goal orientations and beliefs about the causes of success among elite athletes. *The Sport Psychologist*, 6, 334–343.

Duda, J. L. and Whitehead, J. (1998). Measurement of goal perspectives in the physical domain. In J. L. Duda (Ed.), *Advances in sport and exercise psychology measurement* (pp. 21–48). Morgantown, WV: Fitness Information Technology.

Dweck, C. S. (1986). Motivational processes affecting learning. *American Psychologist*, 41, 1040–1048.

Dweck, C. S. (1999). *Self theories: Their role in motivation, personality and development*. Philadelphia: Psychology Press.

Dweck, C. S. and Leggett, E. L. (1988). A social-cognitive approach to motivation and personality. *Psychological Review*, 95, 256–273.

Ebbeck, V. and Becker, S. L. (1994). Psychosocial predictors of goal orientations in youth soccer. *Research Quarterly for Exercise and Sport*, 65, 355–362.

Gano-Overway, L. A., Guivernau, M., Magyar, T. M., Waldron, J. J. and Ewing, M. E. (2005). Achievement goal perspectives, perceptions of the motivational climate and sportspersonship: Individual and team effects. *Psychology of Sport and Exercise*, 6, 215–232.

Goudas, M. and Biddle, S. (1994). Perceived motivational climate and intrinsic motivation in school physical education classes. *European Journal of Psychology of Education*, 9, 241–250.

Harwood, C. G. and Hardy, L. (2001). Persistence and effort in moving achievement goal research forward: A response to Treasure and colleagues. *Journal of Sport and Exercise Psychology*, 23, 330–345.

Harwood, C. G., Cumming, J. and Fletcher, D. (2004). Motivational profiles and psychological skill use in elite youth sport. *Journal of Applied Sport Psychology*, 16, 318–332.

Harwood, C. G., Hardy, L. and Swain, A. (2000). Achievement goals in competitive sport: A critique of conceptual and measurement issues. *Journal of Sport and Exercise Psychology*, 22, 235–255.

Harwood, C. G. and Lacey, K. (2001, October). Partner perceptions and the intensity and direction of achievement goals in elite sport acrobats. Paper presented at the annual meeting of the Association for the Advancement of Applied Sport Psychology, Orlando, FL.

Hodge, K. and Petlichkoff, L. (2000). Goal profiles in sport motivation: A cluster analysis. *Journal of Sport and Exercise Psychology*, 22, 256–272.

Jackson, B., Beauchamp, M. R. and Knapp, P. R. (2007). Relational efficacy beliefs in athlete dyads: An investigation using actor-partner interdependence models. *Journal of Sport and Exercise Psychology*, 29, 170–189.

Kenny, D. A. and Cook, W. L. (1999). Partner effects in relationship research: Conceptual issues, analytic difficulties and illustrations. *Personal Relationships*, 6, 433–448.

Kenny, D. A., Kashy, D. A. and Cook, W. L. (2006). *Dyadic data analysis*. New York: Guilford.

Magyar, T. M., Feltz, D. L. and Simpson, I. P. (2004). Individual and crew level determinants of collective efficacy in rowing. *Journal of Sport and Exercise Psychology*, 26, 136–153.

Newton, M., Duda, J. L. and Yin, Z. N. (2000). Examination of the psychometric properties of the Perceived Motivational Climate in Sport Questionnaire-2 in a sample of female athletes. *Journal of Sport Sciences*, 18, 275–290.

Nicholls, J. G. (1984). Achievement motivation: Conceptions of ability, subjective experience, task choice and performance. *Psychological Review*, 91, 328–346.

Nicholls, J. G. (1989). *The competitive ethos and democratic education*. Cambridge, MA: Harvard University Press.

Ntoumanis, N. and Vazou, S. (2005). Peer motivational climate in youth sport: Measurement development and validation. *Journal of Sport and Exercise Psychology*, 27, 432–455.

Papaioannou, A., Marsh, H. W. and Theodorakis, Y. (2004). A multilevel approach to motivational climate in physical education and sport settings: An individual or a group level construct? *Journal of Sport and Exercise Psychology*, 26, 90–118.

Rasbash, J., Browne, W., Goldstein, H., Yang, M., Plewis, I., Healy, M., Woodhouse, G., Draper, D., Langford, I. and Lewis, T. (2000). *A user's guide to MLwiN (Version 2.1a): Multilevel models project*. London: Institute of Education, University of London.

Raudenbush, S. W. (1988). Educational applications of hierarchical linear models: A review. *Journal of Educational Statistics*, 13, 85–116.

Roberts, G. C., Treasure, D. C. and Balague, G. (1998). Achievement goals in sport: The development and validation of the Perception of Success Questionnaire. *Journal of Sport Sciences*, 16, 337–347.

Seifriz, J. J., Duda, J. L. and Chi, L. (1992). The relationship of perceived motivational climate to intrinsic motivation and beliefs about success in basketball. *Journal of Sport and Exercise Psychology*, 14, 375–39.

Smith, A. L. (1999). Perceptions of peer relationships and physical activity participation in early adolescence. *Journal of Sport and Exercise Psychology*, 21, 329–350.

Spray, C. M., Wang, C. K. J., Biddle, S. J. H., Chatzisarantis, N. L. D. and Warburton, V. E. (2006). An experimental test of self-theories of ability in youth sport. *Psychology of Sport and Exercise*, 7, 55–267

Swain, A. B. J. (1996). Social loafing and identifiability: The mediating role of achievement goal orientations. *Research Quarterly for Exercise and Sport*, 67, 337–344.

Treasure, D. C., Duda, J. L., Hall, H. K., Roberts, G. C., Ames, C. and Maehr, M. L. (2001). Clarifying misconceptions and misrepresentations in achievement goal research in sport: A response to Harwood, Hardy and Swain. *Journal of Sport and Exercise Psychology*, 23, 317–329.

Weiner, B. (1986). *An attributional theory of motivation and emotion*. New York: Springer-Verlag.

Weiss, M. R. and Ferrer-Caja, E. (2002). Motivational orientations and sport behavior. In T. S. Horn (Ed.), *Advances in sport psychology* (2nd ed., pp. 101–183). Champaign, IL: Human Kinetics.

Photograph by John Stupmanis. Reprinted courtesy of John Stupmanis.

12 Exploring new directions in collective efficacy and sport

Graig M. Chow and Deborah L. Feltz

Introduction

A question that plagues athletes, coaches and even spectators is why are some teams able to consistently perform at high levels, while other teams fail to meet performance expectations? Clearly, the team's amount of relevant resources in terms of abilities and skills is a critical determinant of collective attainments. How is it then that teams with mediocre individual talent can sometimes outperform teams with superior talent during a match, series, or possibly an entire season? Anecdotal and empirical evidence suggests that a team's sense of shared confidence or collective efficacy contributes to optimal team functioning, motivation and perseverance.

While the study of individual efficacy beliefs has been extensively reviewed in sport psychology texts, very little has been written about collective efficacy (Carron *et al.*, 2005; Feltz *et al.*, 2008; Myers and Feltz, 2007), though there has been a meta-analysis of collective efficacy-performance studies that included sports teams (Gully *et al.*, 2002). This chapter is intended to provide a comprehensive review of the existing literature as well as contemporary developments in the area of collective efficacy in sport. We begin by presenting an overview of the theoretical framework which includes adopted definitions, unique characteristics, diverse sources of collective efficacy and team behaviors and cognitions that are influenced by collective efficacy. Next, important conceptual and statistical issues pertaining to measurement are addressed. This is followed by an extensive summary of the supporting empirical research including the behavioral and perceptual determinants and outcomes of collective efficacy. We then focus our attention towards applied techniques that coaches and sport psychologists can employ to enhance perceptions of collective efficacy within teams. Finally, recommendations concerning new directions are advanced in an attempt to stimulate future research and progress this line of inquiry.

Theory and research

Theory development

Bandura (1977) first proposed the concept of self-efficacy to represent an individual's belief in his or her ability to successfully perform the necessary requirements of a given situation. Self-efficacy beliefs are hypothesized to influence the tasks an individual chooses to participate in, the amount of effort an individual will exert in a task and the degree to which an individual will persist in the face of failure. However, many performance arenas including sport are centered on organizational and team contexts where individuals make judgments not only about their own ability, but also judgments related to their team as a whole. Consequently, individual perceptions of team efficacy may differ substantially from beliefs regarding personal efficacy. For instance, an ice hockey player can have a high level of confidence in his offensive skills to pass and shoot effectively, while at the same time experience feelings of diffidence in his team-mates' overall attacking ability. Recognizing that the nature of teams involves members collectively striving to reach common performance objectives and aspirations, Bandura (1986) extended the notion of self-efficacy to include collective efficacy. Collective-efficacy is defined as 'a group's shared belief in its conjoint capabilities to organize and execute the courses of action required to produce given levels of attainments' (Bandura, 1997, p. 477). The consequences of collective efficacy are similar to those of self-efficacy, but extend to the group level. Beliefs in collective efficacy affect the amount of effort members will exert, the degree to which members will remain task-oriented when the team is not performing well and the resiliency of members following difficult defeats.

While Bandura's (1997) definition of collective efficacy has provided the framework for the majority of research on the topic, alternative definitions of the construct have emerged in the literature that deserve attention. One such definition was proposed by Zaccaro et al. (1995) who defined collective efficacy as 'a sense of collective competence shared among individuals when allocating, coordinating and integrating their resources in a successful concerted response to specific situational demands' (p. 309). The detailed description of the interactive tasks required among members of a team signifies the subtle difference between the Zaccaro et al. and Bandura definitions. However, the various conceptualizations of collective efficacy have sparked some controversy as to the correct way of constructing collective efficacy instruments. As described in more detail in the section on measurement, researchers who prefer the Zaccaro et al. defin-ition tend to focus on the interactive factors (allocating, coordinating and integrating) inherent to the definition and suggest that they should be directly measured (e.g. Paskevich et al., 1999). In Bandura's definition, the interactive factors are not as explicitly described, but are implied in that collective efficacy reflects a team's perception in their 'capabilities to organize' effectively.

Nature of collective efficacy

Despite the subtleties between the Bandura (1997) and Zaccaro et al. (1995) conceptual-izations, the two definitions share distinct similarities that characterize the nature of collective efficacy. The first characteristic of collective efficacy is congruent to the notion of self-efficacy in that it signifies confidence that is specific to a certain situation or task. For example, a team can have a heightened sense of confidence about perform-ing in the regular season, but have reduced feelings of confidence in their capabilities to succeed in the playoffs. Likewise, a team can hold strong beliefs in their collective competence when they have the lead, but experience team doubt regarding their ability to come from behind.

The second characteristic of collective efficacy is that it represents a shared belief among members of a team. As perceptions about the team gain consistency, they become part of the group's normative belief structure (Zaccaro et al., 1995). Collect-ive-efficacy beliefs are considered shared if there is a high degree of perceptual consensus between members' judgments of team functioning. However, a shared belief does not mean that every individual holds identical beliefs about the team's abilities (Bandura, 1997). Rather, it implies that there should be less variability in perceptions of collective efficacy within teams than there is between teams. Indeed, researchers have found evidence for the sharing of beliefs primarily among members of highly interdependent teams including volleyball (Paskevich *et al.*, 1999; Vargas-Tonsing *et al.*, 2003), ice hockey (Feltz and Lirgg, 1998; Myers *et al.*, 2004b), basketball (Watson *et al.*, 2001) and American football (Myers *et al.*, 2004a). That is, there was a high level of within team agreement among members' judgments of collective efficacy. While perceptual consensus has also been demonstrated in sports characterized by a low degree of interdependence (Magyar *et al.*, 2004), there appears to be more variation in within team agreement of collective efficacy beliefs in such settings, compared with highly interdependent sports that involve greater levels of interaction and coordination among team-mates.

A third characteristic of collective efficacy is that it not only encompasses perceptions of members' knowledge, abilities and skills, but also judgments about the group's integrative capabilities (Zaccaro *et al.*, 1995). In team sports, confidence in collective processes (e.g. coordination, communication, organization, group decision-making and motivation) may be more important than individual resources. According to Zaccaro *et al.*, 'in a group that has moderate levels of knowledge, skills and abilities among its members, but great coordinative capabilities, members may perceive greater collective efficacy than members of a group with significantly greater resources, but less ability to integrate and coordinate these resources' (p. 311). Thus, teams who possess less individual talent, but believe strongly in their capabilities to function effectively as a unit can outperform teams comprised of superstars who lack togetherness. This occurrence has been observed at the highest levels of competition. For example, during the 2004 National Basketball Association (NBA) Playoffs the Detroit Pistons captured the title by defeating a Los Angeles Lakers team that was considered by many to be considerably more talented.

Finally, the nature of collective efficacy concerns the degree of interdependence that is necessary to achieve performance goals. In sports such as wrestling, track and field and gymnastics that require minimal amounts of interaction and communication among members, team performance is often determined by taking the sum of each individual's performance. Conversely, in highly interdependent sports such as ice hockey, soccer and basketball, team attainments result from the concerted efforts between members. According to Bandura (1997), the degree of system interdependence affects relationships between self- and collective efficacy. When interdependence is low, collective efficacy may be nothing more than the aggregation of each member's personal efficacy. However, in highly interdependent teams, collective - efficacy is best characterized by aggregating individual judgments about the team as a whole. The issue of interdependence in relation to collective efficacy was investigated by Gully *et al.* (2002) in a meta-analysis of 67 empirical studies. Results from the study revealed that interdependence was a significant moderator of the collective efficacy–performance relationship. Perceived collective efficacy was a stronger predictor of team performance with teams characterized by greater levels of interaction and coordination among members than teams with lower system interdependence.

Sources of collective efficacy

How individual team members develop their sense of collective efficacy is similar to how self-efficacy beliefs are formed, that is through sources of efficacy information. Some of these sources are identical to what Bandura (1977, 1997) originally described in his theory of self-efficacy while some are unique to team membership. Bandura hypothesized four major sources of efficacy information that pertain to the self: mastery experiences, vicarious experiences, verbal persuasion and physiological/emotional states. In addition to the determinants of individual efficacy, researchers have suggested that there are unique sources of perceived collective efficacy including leadership, group cohesion, motivational climate and team size (George and Feltz, 1995; Zaccaro *et al.*, 1995).

According to Bandura (1997) and others (George and Feltz, 1995; Zaccaro *et al.*, 1995), the most salient factor contributing to one's beliefs about team functioning is mastery experiences or past performance accomplishments. Teams that experience success in a specific activity have an expectation that they will perform equally well in future tasks of a similar nature. In general, if a team outperforms an opponent during the first meeting, they will have a high level of confidence that they can do the same in future contests against similar competition. Conversely, teams that suffer performance setbacks will lack confidence in their abilities to succeed in subsequent contests. Indeed, Feltz and Lirgg (1998) found that ice hockey players' collective efficacy increased following a team win and decreased after a team loss.

The phenomenon of winning and losing streaks in sport can also be explained in part by past performance accomplishments. When performance success results from the combined coordinative and integrative efforts of members, the accomplishment confirms the team's belief in its abilities to function as a synchronized unit. These increased perceptions of collective efficacy lead to increased performance, which in turn, produces stronger efficacy beliefs about the team. The dynamic reciprocal nature of performance and collective efficacy has been demonstrated in athletic settings (Myers *et al.*, 2004a,b) and is discussed further in the research section of this chapter.

Modeling, or what Bandura (1997) refers to as vicarious experiences, can also provide information that affects collective efficacy beliefs. The degree to which the model will be successful in altering perceptions of efficacy is greatly moderated by actor-observer similarity. Watching a team that is similar in ability perform effectively in a task raises the observant team's level of confidence to succeed in comparable tasks. Likewise, seeing a team with similar attributes struggle undermines the observing team's level of collective efficacy. This type of modeled ineffectiveness is not limited to viewing other teams performing poorly, but can also occur within teams as well. Bandura (1997) contends that the modeling of ineffective performances by key members can create a contagious spread of doubt within the team, which can then spiral into a team slump. Alternatively, the modeling of confidence by coaches in demonstrating their ability to remain task-oriented under stressful conditions can improve team efficacy beliefs. Although recognized as an important source, the influence of vicarious experiences on collective efficacy has rarely been examined in sport. A notable exception was a study conducted by Chase *et al.* (2003) who employed an open-ended measure in order to identify sources of efficacy information. Results confirmed that vicarious experiences were an essential factor that contributed to female basketball players' precompetitive perceptions of collective efficacy.

Although a relatively weak source on its own, verbal persuasion provided by significant others can reinforce and enhance the efficacy beliefs of athletes and teams. A common way in which persuasive messages are delivered in sport is through the motivational speeches of coaches. In terms of facilitating perceptions of team efficacy, precompetitive emotional pleas that produce feelings of group pride and motivation appear to be more effective than speeches that focus purely on game tactics (Vargas-Tonsing and Bartholomew, 2006). Using an experimental design, Vargas-Tonsing and Bartholomew examined the effect of pre-game speeches on collective efficacy with current and former soccer players. Participants were randomly assigned to one of three scenarios conveying different messages: emotionally persuasive information, strategy information and uniform/field information (control). Results indicated that athletes who were in the persuasive speech condition reported higher collective efficacy beliefs than athletes in either the strategy or control conditions.

Another way in which efficacy beliefs are altered through verbal persuasion is feedback. Feedback that conveys information about the team's capabilities will likely have the most influence on collective efficacy beliefs. Such is the case in laboratory studies where teams are provided with bogus comparative feedback in order to manipulate perceptions of collective efficacy (Greenlees *et al.*, 1999a, 2000; Hodges and Carron, 1992; Lichacz and Partington, 1996). In general, teams persuaded into believing that they are superior to their competition develop an increased sense of collective efficacy, whereas teams who are convinced that they are inferior have decreased collective-efficacy beliefs.

A third type of social persuasion that may affect collective efficacy is spectator and media support (George and Feltz, 1995). As George and Feltz noted, team members who hear applause from fans may have more confidence in their teams than those who are jeered. Likewise, reading about team compliments in the newspapers may boost team members' collective efficacy percepts, while harsh criticisms may instill some team doubt.

Consistent with the sources of self-efficacy, physiological states may influence teams' judgments of their capabilities to succeed. While often overlooked as a physiological factor, the physical condition of the team can greatly enhance or hinder team confidence. Some teams pride themselves on their level of fitness. They engage in rigorous training and practice to reduce the susceptibility of fatigue during competition. Teams that are physically fit are confident that they can persist longer than their opponents when the game is on the line. On the other hand, having members who are fatigued or plagued with nagging injuries can severely undermine the level of collective-efficacy within a team.

Besides the factors that extend from self-efficacy theory, researchers have suggested that there are additional sources of collective efficacy that are unique to group dynamics. Within team environments, there are organizational structures, roles and group processes not commonly found in individual performance settings that may contribute to a team's sense of shared confidence. One source that is indicative of the team context is leadership (Zaccaro *et al.*, 1995). Leaders can directly influence collective-efficacy through modeling, encouragement, persuasion, feedback and enhancement of team functioning. Additionally, proscribed and emergent leaders who are confident in their problem solving and decision-making capabilities as well as their ability to motivate and influence their members can increase the sense of collective efficacy within a team (Vargas-Tonsing *et al.*, 2003; Watson *et al.*, 2001). For example, Watson and colleagues explored relationships between leader confidence, leader effectiveness and collective efficacy with 28 female and male Division III basketball teams. Leader confidence was assessed at the beginning of the season, leader effectiveness was assessed near the end of the season and collective efficacy was assessed at both time points. Confident leadership was positively associated with collective efficacy at the beginning of the season, such that teams comprised of leaders who held strong beliefs in their leadership capabilities reported higher perceptions of collective efficacy. At the end of the season, athletes who evaluated their leader positively had higher collective efficacy beliefs than individuals who rated their leader as less effective. Furthermore, the positive influence of effective leadership on collective efficacy was even more pronounced in teams that had not performed well during the previous season.

Zaccaro *et al.* (1995) identified group cohesion as both a source and consequence of collective efficacy, particularly the task dimensions of cohesion. As a determinant, being united around the task objectives of the team provides confirmation that members agree on the salient performance aspects inherent to group membership which increases beliefs in the team's capabilities to coordinate as a unit. As an effect, having confidence in the team's coordinative functioning influences members' feelings of task closeness. The hypothesized reciprocal relationship proposed by Zaccaro and colleagues is expected, considering that the two constructs share similar properties. Whereas collective efficacy represents a team's situation specific integrative performance beliefs, task cohesiveness encompasses a team's general perception of their ability to work together to attain common goals. Accordingly, the group cohesion–collective efficacy relationship has received considerable interest among sport researchers and is discussed in more detail in the research section of this chapter.

The motivational climate in terms of members' evaluations of the goal structures emphasized by coaches has a bearing for informing collective efficacy beliefs. In a performance climate, the coach stresses outcome results, encourages social comparison and praises individual ability. Conversely, a mastery climate promotes effort, learning, improvement and teamwork and thus should be more influential in enhancing teams' judgments of their capabilities (see also Harwood and Beauchamp, Ch. 11, this volume). Magyar *et al.* (2004) investigated the degree to which motivational climate influenced the collective efficacy beliefs of junior rowing teams prior to a championship regatta. They found that teams who perceived a mastery climate held increased beliefs in their ability to successfully perform, whereas no relationship was found between performance climate and collective efficacy.

A final team level source of collective efficacy is team size (Zaccaro *et al.*, 1995), though the exact nature of the relationship remains unclear. One viewpoint suggests that there may be a positive relationship between team size and collective efficacy. Teams that are large may hold stronger perceptions of collective efficacy because they possess greater amounts of resources. By selecting additional members to a team it increases the likelihood that the requisite skills for various roles and positions are met. For example, if a manager was to increase the size of his baseball team, it would enable him to substitute players more effectively to create ideal match ups between his batters and the opponent's pitcher, especially if the team then has greater depth than opposing teams. Conversely, Zaccaro *et al.* (1995) also hypothesized that team size may be negatively related to collective efficacy. As team size increases it becomes more challenging for members to coordinate their efforts in an efficient manner. Moreover, in smaller teams, the prospect of social loafing is minimized as it is easier for leaders to monitor and identify unmotivated players. The social loafing phenomenon represents the reduction in individual effort that occurs when members perform in groups compared with when they perform alone (Latané *et al.*, 1979). In concordance with Zaccaro *et al.*'s (1995) conflicting predictions, results from empirical studies on team size and collective efficacy in sport have been equivocal. Some researchers have discovered a positive relationship (Short, 2005), others have found a negative relationship (Watson *et al.*, 2001) and there has also been evidence that no relationship exists between the variables (Magyar *et al.*, 2004). The equivocal team size findings may be attributed to differences in the normative structures of certain sports. For example, Magyar *et al.* sampled rowing teams that participated in two, four and eight person boats. Because crews only competed against crews of the same size, there was no advantage to having a smaller or larger team. In contrast, Watson *et al.* used basketball teams of various sizes where differences in coordination and motivational processes were apparent and thus more influential to the formation of team efficacy beliefs.

Team variables influenced by collective efficacy

As we mentioned earlier in this chapter, collective efficacy beliefs affect the tasks that teams select to engage in, the level of effort that they will put forth in the activity and the extent to which they will persist when faced with challenges. These are performance-oriented outcomes of collective efficacy and they are the most salient factors associated with collective efficacy. Most of the research on collective efficacy has focused on its relationship to performance. However, just as self-efficacy beliefs are posited to influence motivational behaviors, thought patterns and emotions, beliefs in the team's capabilities also influence collective motivational behaviors, cognitions and affect. For instance, the attributions that teams make following a successful or unsuccessful performance may also be affected by the strength of collective perceptions regarding team functioning. Within the framework of social cognitive theory, Bandura (1986) purported that efficacy beliefs and causal attributions are reciprocal determinants, though the relationship was restricted to individuals and not teams. He stated that perceptions of efficacy provide information that contributes to the formation of causal attributions and, in turn, attributions influence subsequent efficacy beliefs. Highly efficacious teams may ascribe performance setbacks to internal controllable factors such as effort, while lowly efficacious teams may attribute performance decrements to stable factors such as lack of ability (George and Feltz, 1995).

In addition, teams who hold strong judgments of collective efficacy set high performance standards which then contribute to increased team attainments (Bray, 2004). They undertake physical challenges and select team goals that they believe they can master and avoid those that they think exceed their capabilities. In contrast, teams who have low confidence in their collective abilities choose less difficult group goals, especially following performance setbacks (Greenlees *et al.*, 2000). Effective coaches try to influence the challenges that their teams take on so as not to set them up for overwhelming failure while still providing them with reasonably difficult goals. As a result, members are more actively committed towards the pursuit of mutual goals.

Lastly, team emotions can also be affected by collective efficacy beliefs, such as collective worry, team pride and shame and shared joy and sadness. Highly efficacious teams should feel more in control of their performance and have less reason to worry or distress under pressure. Among high collective efficacy teams, the level of precompetitive cognitive anxiety concerning game outcome is diminished as responsibility for both successful and unsuccessful performances are shared throughout members of the group (Greenlees et al., 1999b). Likewise, teams who believe in their coordinative competence should experience more pride in their accomplishments, owing those accomplishments to their collective capabilities. The relationships among the sources and consequences of collective efficacy in terms of team-level variables are illustrated in Figure 12.1.

Measurement

Bandura (2005) has provided guidelines for constructing efficacy measures, both individual and collective. Many of the guidelines are applicable for both self- and collective efficacy scales, such as domain specification, gradations of challenge, content relevance, concordance between the efficacy measure and match performance criteria, minimizing response bias and validation. For instance, Bandura (1997) advocates for the use of efficacy belief measures that are specific to particular domains of functioning rather than ones that assess global expectations of performance that are devoid of context and he recommends that items be challenging enough to avoid ceiling effects. Such guidelines are not reviewed in this chapter. The reader interested in Bandura's recommendations is referred to his 2005 reference or to Feltz et al. (2008) for sport-specific applications. The measurement of collective efficacy is complicated by issues of construct definition, level of analysis, consensus within teams and dimensionality. We focus on these issues specifically in this section of the chapter.

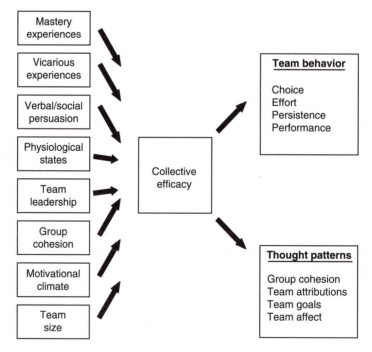

Figure 12.1 Conceptual team-level model of collective efficacy.

Measurement approaches based on construct definition

As we explained earlier, the nature of collective efficacy has been defined in various ways. According to Bandura (1997), collective efficacy is a group level construct that emerges or is composed from individual perceptions. Thus, it is measured at the individual level and aggregated to the team level for analysis. Bandura described two methods for assessing collective efficacy based on his definition. The first involves measuring team members' individual perceptions of their *own* capabilities to perform within the team and aggregating those to obtain a team average, while the second method aggregates team members' perceptions of their *team's* capabilities to perform as a unit. The phrasing of the stem of items in the first method might be, 'Rate your confidence that *you* can . . . (mark your player, make successful serves, run for touchdowns, etc.)'. Using the second method, the stem might be, 'Rate your confidence that *your team* can . . . (keep the opposing team from scoring, make successful serves, score touchdowns in the red zone, etc.).'

Bandura (1997) hypothesized that the 'perceptions of the team' approach is more predictive of team performance when group performance requires a high degree of interdependence (e.g. soccer, basketball, volleyball) than is the method using aggregated perceptions of individual capabilities of team members. Aggregated perceptions of individual efficacy beliefs may be sufficient to predict group performance in tasks that are more additive in nature (e.g. golf, track and field, gymnastics). However, as Feltz *et al.* (2008) have indicated, the majority of studies on collective efficacy in sport have used the second method and also primarily involved sports that were interdependent (Chase *et al.*, 2003; Edmonds, 2003; Feltz and Lirgg, 1998; Greenlees *et al.*, 1999a,b, 2000; Hodges and Carron, 1992; Kozub and McDonnell, 2000; Lichacz and Partington, 1996; Magyar *et al.*, 2004; Myers *et al.*, 2004a,b; Spink, 1990; Vargas-Tonsing *et al.*, 2003).

Zaccaro *et al.*'s (1995) definition is also based on individual perceptions but emphasizes the *coordination*, *interaction* and *integration* components of collective efficacy. Unlike Bandura (1997), they maintain that these three efficacy components should be assessed directly rather than assume that they are encompassed within the perceptions of a team's capability to perform a task. Myers and Feltz (2007) explain that Zaccaro *et al.*'s (1995) sense of shared collective competence has been interpreted by some sport psychology researchers (e.g. Hueze *et al.*, 2006; Paskevich *et al.*, 1999) to mean that individual team-mates should rate *their team's beliefs* in its capabilities rather than rate *their belief in their team's* capabilities. When rating one's *team's* beliefs, the individual team member acts as an *informant* of the team's collective efficacy by cognitively considering what the team believes (Moritz and Watson, 1998). However, Short *et al.* (2002) found no differences between stems that read 'rate your confidence that your team . . .' or 'rate your team's confidence . . .' in a study with American football players. They concluded that either stem was adequate.

A third conceptual approach to measuring collective efficacy requires the team as a whole to make a single response for each item on the questionnaire. This approach is based on the argument that aggregating individual responses is just a surrogate for a team level measure (Prussia and Kinicki, 1996). However, as Bandura (1997) notes, forced consensus of a group's efficacy beliefs may be misleading because the belief is subject to social persuasion and conformity pressures. Thus, team members could consent to a response without truly believing it (Guzzo *et al.*, 1993). There also are impracticalities in using this method in the field where time constraints would make it very difficult to have team members collectively discussing and responding to several items on a questionnaire prior to competitions (Feltz *et al.*, 2008).

Of the three approaches, Myers and Feltz (2007) have argued for using Bandura's 'rate your confidence in your team . . .' approach because they believe that people have better access to their own beliefs about a group's capabilities than they do to a group's beliefs about its capabilities and this approach conforms to how Bandura's original conceptualization of collective efficacy was constructed.

Dimensionality

Most of the measures of collective efficacy in sport have been operationalized as uni-dimensional scales (Myers and Feltz, 2007). When hierarchical scales (i.e. listing the same task in a hierarchical fashion, according to difficulty) are used, unidimensionality can safely be assumed, but that is not the case with nonhierarchical scales where respondents are asked about different aspects of performance within a sport. In such cases, the measure may be multidimensional. Researchers may even favor tapping multidimensional aspects of collective efficacy within a sport based on Bandura's (1997) contention that 'efficacy beliefs involve different types of capabilities, such as management of thought, affect, action and motivation' (p. 45). Myers and Feltz recommend that whenever responses from multiple itemed questionnaires are collapsed into a composite score, that evidence for the imposed measurement model (e.g. factor analysis) be reported to demonstrate its dimensionality.

One collective efficacy questionnaire that was conceptualized as a multidimensional construct is the Collective Efficacy Questionnaire for Sports (CEQS; Short *et al.*, 2005). Short and her colleagues used the 'rate your team's confidence . . .' approach in developing the CEQS in order to match the stem to a correlate team cohesion measure – The Group Environment Questionnaire (GEQ; Widmeyer *et al.*, 1985) – that was used in the study. The CEQS is designed to measure collective efficacy in teams across different sports. Moreover, based on Bandura's conceptualization of efficacy beliefs as state-specific, the CEQS is based on current capabilities, not potential capabilities or expected future capabilities.

Short *et al.* (2005) provided empirical support for a 5-factor instrument containing 20 items (4 items per factor). The five subscales included *Ability* (e.g. play more skillfully than the opponent), *Effort* (e.g. play to its capabilities), *Persistence* (e.g. persist in the face of failure), *Preparation* (e.g. mentally prepare for this competition) and *Unity* (e.g. be united). These findings suggest that aspects of team functioning, in addition to team ability, are salient in defining collective efficacy in sport.

Level of analysis

If collective efficacy is assessed at the level of the individual but aggregated to the team level for analysis, the researcher must deal with level of analysis issues. Rousseau (1985) argues that as long as the team mean is functionally equivalent to the individual perceptions, it can legitimately be used to represent the collective construct. This argument means that there must be some agreement or consensus within the team regarding the efficacy beliefs in the team before the measure can represent collective-efficacy. We discuss the issue of consensus further in the next section. Early research on collective efficacy in sport either avoided aggregation (e.g. Lichacz and Partington, 1996; Spink, 1990) or used team level data without testing for agreement among perceptions within teams (e.g. Hodges and Carron, 1992).

However, Moritz and Watson (1998) argue against just analyzing team level data without also examining the individual within-team perceptions because it ignores potentially informative within-team variability. In addition, Raudenbush and Bryk (2002) in advocating for multilevel modeling, contend that ignoring individual data can also result in a loss of power, inefficient estimation of fixed effects when sample size is unequal within teams and difficulty in interpreting the amount of variance-explained by team level predictors. As Moritz and Watson (1998) and Myers and Feltz (2007) have previously noted, multilevel modeling (e.g. hierarchical linear modeling – HLM) is the optimum framework for analyzing collective efficacy data because it can handle both individual and team level efficacy data, though it has rarely been applied to the study of collective efficacy in sport (exceptions include Magyar *et al.*, 2004; Myers *et al.*, 2004b; Watson *et al.*, 2001). Myers and Feltz provide an in-depth description of the approach that should be used in multilevel modeling of collective efficacy data.

In addition, HLM software programs do not require that a certain consensus estimate exist before computing a weighted average of the individual level responses. As Moritz and Watson (1998) recommend, if there is not a high degree of consensus, there would be more within team variance around the team mean, which could be partitioned and explained in multilevel modeling.

Consensus within teams

Perceptual consensus or inter-rater agreement exists when team members perceive the team or their own abilities to function within the team in the same way (James, 1982; Kozlowski and Hattrup, 1992). In an early review of collective efficacy research, Feltz and Lirgg (1998) argued that researchers need to assess the degree of within group variability of the perceptions of team members' collective efficacy to determine that the beliefs are shared by its members. They advocated James' (1982) concern that failure to consider consensus when aggregating data at the individual level to represent a higher level of analysis may result in aggregation bias. Aggregation bias occurs when individuals' perceptions are aggregated and used to represent the groups' perceptions when the proportion of variance of individuals' perceptions is high within the group. Although James did not offer empirical guidelines for what constituted a sufficient level of consensus for the purpose of aggregating scores to the group level, the use of multilevel modeling has helped to eliminate the concern he once had about aggregation bias because the variance of perceptions within teams can be examined and modeled.

Myers and Feltz (2007) still recommend that consensus estimates be reported in research studies for descriptive purposes and for use as a team level variable within multilevel models to explain variance around an average team level effect. They note that teams that have a low degree of consensus on collective efficacy among team members may show a negligible relationship between collective efficacy and subsequent performance because there is so much within team variance around the mean collective efficacy for these teams. A consensus index would be important in explaining such a finding. Feltz *et al.* (2008) also add that analyzing the relationship between consensus of collective efficacy and other variables (e.g. cohesion, performance, team satisfaction) may be an important research question of its own.

Myers and Feltz (2007) oppose discarding teams from analyses that fail to show an adequate level of consensus, given that there is no clear cut-off value for what is considered 'adequate'. They contend that eliminating teams would limit the population of teams for which one wishes to generalize (i.e. only those teams that consist of athletes who have some level of agreement on what the team's capabilities are). Even when team members disagree on their beliefs about the team's capabilities, Myers and Feltz suggest that a reasonable estimate of collective efficacy at the team level, such as the mean, still exists. The only difference would be that there would be more within team variance around the team mean, which as mentioned previously can be partitioned and explained in multilevel modeling. Myers and Feltz provide a detailed description of how to calculate and report in a manuscript the most commonly used consensus index within sport collective efficacy research – the within group agreement index, r_{wg} (James *et al.*, 1984).

Difference from outcome expectations

The last issue regarding measurement of efficacy beliefs, which has been reported elsewhere (e.g. Feltz and Lirgg, 2001; Feltz *et al.*, 2008; Myers and Feltz, 2007; Myers *et al.*, 2004b), but is worth repeating here, is the confusion that still seems to exist among sport psychology researchers over efficacy and outcome expectations (e.g. Dawson *et al.*, 2001; Eyal *et al.*, 1995; Neiss, 1989). Outcome expectancies are defined as the belief that certain behaviors will lead to certain outcomes (Bandura, 1997). Bandura describes the three major forms that outcome expectations can take: physical effects (e.g. increased heart rate), social effects (e.g. coach's approval) and self-evaluative effects (e.g. self-satisfaction). 'Behavior and the effects it produces are different classes of events' (p. 22). Because the term 'competitive outcome' has been used extensively in the sport psychology literature to mean the final score, rank, or win/loss, the terms can be easily confused. As Feltz and Lirgg (2001) explain however, an athlete's final position at the end of a competition or winning does not fit the class of effects that Bandura (1997) defines as outcomes. Judgments about winning an event, or placing first, second, or third are not outcome expectations; they are expectations about the performance. As Bandura (1997) clearly articulates, 'a performance is an accomplishment; an outcome is something that flows from it. In short, an outcome is the consequence of a performance, not the performance itself' (p. 22–23). Feltz and Lirgg (1998) labeled efficacy beliefs items that pertained to winning or performing better than an opponent as 'competitive' or 'comparative' efficacy. Collective-efficacy measures derived from items of this type are appropriate in a competitive environment.

Research on collective efficacy and performance

The majority of research on collective efficacy in sport has been concerned with its relationship to team performance. Results from both laboratory (Greenlees *et al.*, 1999a, 2000; Hodges and Carron, 1992; Lichacz and Partington, 1996) and field studies (Feltz and Lirgg, 1998; Myers *et al.*, 2004a,b; Watson *et al.*, 2001) have shown that there is a significant positive association between the two variables, such that teams holding strong beliefs about their abilities perform at higher levels and persist longer than teams who lack such beliefs. Furthermore, the relationship between perceived collective efficacy and team functioning appears to be reciprocal in nature (Myers *et al.*,

2004a,b). Collective-efficacy judgments exert an influence on subsequent performance attainments and in turn, previous performance accomplishments influence subsequent collective efficacy.

One of the first studies to examine the effect of collective efficacy on sport-related performance was conducted by Hodges and Carron (1992). A total of 51 *ad hoc* triads competed against a confederate group where the objective was to hold a medicine ball in the air for as long as possible. Collective-efficacy was manipulated through bogus feedback pertaining to relative group strength. Triads who were told that they were stronger than their opponent constituted the high collective efficacy condition, whereas triads who were told that they were weaker than their opponent formed the low coll-ective efficacy condition. To ensure that the experimental groups failed the task, con-federate groups used a foam ball rather than a traditional medicine ball, though this was unbeknownst to the experimental triads. Results indicated that high collective - efficacy groups improved in performance after experiencing failure, while low coll-ective efficacy groups suffered performance decrements. Greenlees *et al.* (1999a, 2000) conducted a series of related studies in which participants performed in triad groups with two confederates on a cycle ergometer. They found that following feedback manipulation, individuals who held decreased beliefs of collective efficacy declined in performance, whereas participants in the high collective efficacy condition maintained performance time (Figure 12.2).

Although laboratory studies like Hodges and Carron (1992) and Greenlees *et al.* (1999a, 2000) provide evidence supporting a positive collective efficacy–performance relationship, the findings are limited in that they used *ad hoc* groups rather than real intact teams. The characteristics of intact sports teams competing in dynamic and complex environments are undoubtedly different from laboratory groups participating in fixed repetitive tasks. Members of intact sports teams develop a collective identity, share common goals, exhibit high degrees of interaction and communication and hold shared organizational perceptions (Carron *et al.*, 2005). Further, laboratory studies have also failed to explore the temporal nature of perceived collective efficacy. Expand-ing on this line of inquiry, Feltz and Lirgg (1998) investigated relationships between self-efficacy, collective efficacy and team performance with six intercollegiate ice hockey teams over the course of a 32 -game season. Teams competed on consecutive days of the week against the same opponent. The collective efficacy measure assessed the degree of confidence athletes had in their team's capabilities to outperform their opponent in seven areas including outskating, outchecking, forcing turnovers, boun-cing back after performing poorly, scoring on power plays, killing penalties, goaltend-ing and winning the competition. Performance indicators included goal differential, game outcome, shot attempts, scoring percentage, powerplay shot attempts, power-play percentage and short-handed defense percentage. As the top part of Figure 12.3 illustrates, they found that aggregated team efficacy was a stronger predictor of team performance than aggregated self-efficacy and that past performance influenced team efficacy to a greater degree than player efficacy. In addition, the bottom half of Figure 12.3 shows that teams who were victorious in their previous competition held higher perceptions of collective efficacy prior to their next game than teams who suffered defeat.

Temporal relationships between collective efficacy and performance were also inves-tigated by Myers *et al.* (2004b) with 12 intercollegiate female ice hockey teams over the course of a competitive season. As was the case in the Feltz and Lirgg (1998) study,

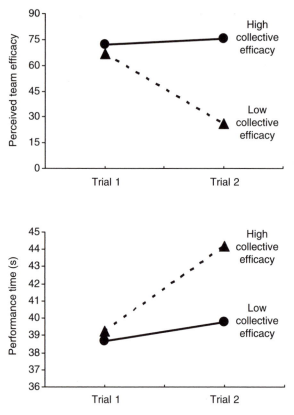

Figure 12.2 Changes in performance after collective efficacy was manipulated through bogus comparative feedback. (After Greenlees *et al.*, 2000.)

teams competed on consecutive days against a constant opponent. However, the methodology was improved upon by statistically controlling for previous performance. The researchers examined the effect of Saturday collective efficacy on Saturday team performance, while controlling for the influence of Friday performance. They also examined the effect of Friday performance on Saturday collective efficacy, after removing the influence of Friday collective efficacy from Friday performance (residualizing past performance). Bandura (1997) has criticized the statistical overcontrol of past performance by using the raw, unadjusted past performance scores along with efficacy as predictors of future performance. He argues that residualizing past performance removes the prior contribution of efficacy that is imbedded in past performance scores. Employing this approach, the authors found that Saturday collective efficacy predicted Saturday performance over and above Friday performance and that residualized Friday performance predicted Saturday collective efficacy. Furthermore, the influence of - collective efficacy on team performance was positive and moderate, whereas the influence of team performance on collective efficacy was positive and small.

In summary, research in sport psychology has consistently shown that a positive association between collective efficacy and team performance exists. The strength of shared efficacy percepts held by members contributes to both subsequent and proximal team performance. Teams with a strong sense of efficacy outperform teams with

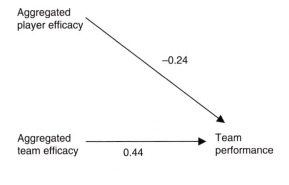

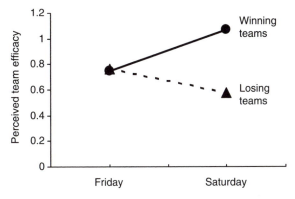

Figure 12.3 The effect of efficacy beliefs on team performance and the influence of game outcome on subsequent perceptions of collective efficacy. (After Feltz and Lirgg, 1998.)

low collective efficacy beliefs. Additionally, after experiencing defeat, teams with high perceptions of collective efficacy mobilize their efforts and persist longer to increase performance attainments. Finally, the relationship between collective efficacy and team performance is not unidirectional, rather the two constructs flow reciprocally. A strong belief in the capabilities of the team leads to successful performance and successful accomplishments bring about increased beliefs in team functioning.

Research on collective efficacy and cognitive variables

The predominance of studies on collective efficacy and behavior (e.g. team performance) has prompted researchers to explore important cognitive variables in concordance with beliefs about a team's ability to succeed. Some of these factors have been analyzed as antecedents of collective efficacy, some have been considered consequences of collective efficacy, while others have been hypothesized as reciprocal determinants. These cognitive variables include self-efficacy, group cohesion and coaching efficacy.

Self-efficacy

Perceived collective efficacy is rooted in self-efficacy beliefs. A group comprised of lowly efficacious members inevitably transitions into a team filled with internal doubts.

Alternatively, if every member is confident in his or her own abilities, members will tend to perceive the confidence in their team's functioning as high. While collective-efficacy differs from self-efficacy in the unit of agency, both share similar sources, consequences and processes (Bandura, 1997). 'Beliefs of personal efficacy are not detached from the larger social system in which members function. In appraising their personal efficacies, individuals inevitably consider group processes that enhance or hinder their efforts' (Bandura, 1997, p. 478). In other words, perceptions of self- and collective efficacy do not function independently of each other. Take for example a goalkeeper on a soccer team. His belief in his abilities to successfully execute the requirements of the position might be affected at least in part by how well his defenders organize, interact and communicate on the pitch. If he holds high perceptions of his defenders capabilities, it is likely that he will be more confident in his goalkeeping skills than if he is skeptical of his defenders' abilities.

Few researchers have explored the relationship between self-efficacy and collective-efficacy among athletic teams. However, it appears that personal beliefs in capabilities contribute to the formation of collective competency perceptions, regardless of interdependence level. For instance, Watson *et al.* (2001) employed a multilevel statistical approach and hypothesized that self-efficacy would be positively related to individual perceptions of collective efficacy among basketball players across two time points: beginning and end of season. Counter to prediction, self-efficacy was negatively associated with collective efficacy at Time 1. Athletes with higher perceptions of personal ability tended to have lower confidence in their team's capabilities to perform successfully. However, the cross-level interaction indicated that self-efficacy was positively related to collective efficacy in teams with high average self-efficacy. On the other hand, when team-mates held relatively weak individual efficacy beliefs on average, players who had high personal efficacy reported lower confidence in their team. At Time 2, the relationship between self- and collective efficacy was positive. Athletes with a strong sense of personal efficacy held similar feelings about their team late in the season. Magyar *et al.* (2004) also investigated whether or not collective efficacy beliefs were rooted in individual efficacy beliefs with rowing teams. Similar to Watson *et al.*, a multilevel approach was utilized to account for the nesting of rowers within crews. The findings replicated those found by Watson *et al.* (2001) in that task self-efficacy was a positive predictor of individual perceptions of collective efficacy. Taken together, the results from these studies indicate that self-efficacy is an important individual level determinant of collective judgments about team performance.

Group cohesion

The group attribute that has received the most attention in relation to collective-efficacy in sport is group cohesion. Studies that have examined the concepts of group cohesion and collective efficacy (Hueze *et al.*, 2006; Kozub and McDonnell, 2000; Paskevich *et al.*, 1999; Spink, 1990) have typically found that perceptions of task cohesiveness relate to efficacy beliefs in the team (see also Carron *et al.*, Ch. 7, this volume). For example, Paskevich *et al.* investigated the collective efficacy-group cohesion association with university and club volleyball teams. What was unique in their study was that they employed a multidimensional measure of collective efficacy that accounted for group processes and interactive skills inherent to volleyball. The questionnaire asked players to rate their team's confidence in their abilities to perform on eight factors: (1) offense, (2) defense, (3) transition, (4) communication, (5) motivation, (6) overcoming the loss of a key player, (7) overcoming obstacles of team-mates and (8) general team functions. Group cohesion was assessed using the GEQ. By employing an extreme groups design, the researchers found that the collective efficacy scales of communication, motivation, overcoming obstacles of team-mates and general team functions differentiated individuals on the group integration-task (GI-T) scale. That is, individuals who perceived that their team was highly confident in communicating, remaining motivated, overcoming obstacles and pursuing normal team functions held stronger feelings about the level of task closeness within the team as a whole than those who perceived team doubt in collective efficacy aspects. In addition, a collective - efficacy composite score was constructed to explore the degree to which the group cohesion scales could distinguish athletes that were either high or low in collective - efficacy. Results showed that both task cohesion dimensions (GI-T and ATG-T) pre- dicted collective efficacy. Athletes who reported stronger levels of task cohesiveness believed that their team was highly efficacious, whereas individuals who scored lower on the task dimensions perceived that their team had a weakened sense of efficacy (Figure 12.4).

Kozub and McDonnell (2000) explored the influence of group cohesion on coll- ective efficacy with seven male rugby teams. The collective efficacy measure employed was a seven-item assessment that was constructed similarly to the one used by Feltz and

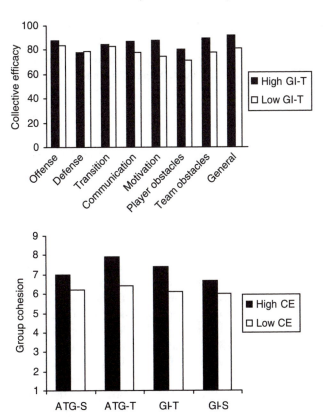

Figure 12.4 Relationships between group cohesion and collective efficacy. (After Paskevich *et al.*, 1999.)

Lirgg (1998) and was consistent with Bandura's (2005) recommendations. The collective efficacy instrument and GEQ were administered toward the end of the season which allowed sufficient time for group processes to develop within the team. Due to the small number of teams, analyses were conducted at the individual level, but standardized around the team mean. They found that only the task dimensions (ATG-T and GI-T) of cohesion were significant predictors of collective efficacy with GI-T emerging as the stronger predictor. In all, task cohesion accounted for 32 per cent of the variance in collective efficacy.

The relationship between collective efficacy and task cohesion may in fact be reciprocal. However, unlike research on collective efficacy and performance, published studies that have explored relationships between collective efficacy and group cohesion have been limited by cross-sectional data. In order to assess the temporal nature of collective efficacy and group cohesion, studies must utilize longitudinal designs with multiple time point measures over the course of several competitions. Zaccaro et al. (1992), as cited in Zaccaro et al. (1995), further suggest that collective efficacy mediates the performance-cohesion relationship. For instance, experiencing successful performances reinforces teams' beliefs about their capabilities to function effectively. As a result, these enhanced efficacy perceptions directly influence the level of togetherness within teams. The mediating nature of collective efficacy has only recently been examined in sport (Hueze et al., 2006), though it involved individual performance rather than team performance. Nevertheless, sport research has consistently found that group cohesion is positively related to judgments of collective efficacy, particularly in highly interdependent intact teams (Kozub and McDonnell, 2000; Paskevich et al., 1999; Spink, 1990). Whether or not cohesion contributes to collective efficacy in coactive sports (e.g. gymnastics, track and field, wrestling) is a topic for future researchers to examine.

Coaching efficacy

The modeling of confidence or ineffectiveness by team leaders has consequences that may affect a team's sense of efficacy (Bandura, 1997). One way collective efficacy can be increased is through coaching efficacy, which refers to coaches' beliefs that they have the capabilities to contribute to the learning and performance of members (Feltz et al., 1999). Coaches who have high levels of efficacy beliefs in their coaching capabilities instill through their actions a sense of collective confidence in their teams (Bandura, 1997). Coaching efficacy, as defined by Feltz et al., comprises four dimensions including *game strategy, motivation, technique* and *character building*, which are hypothesized to predict coaching behavior, athlete satisfaction of coach, individual and team performance and self- and collective efficacy of members. To date, only one study in sport has examined the extent to which coaches' judgments of their own abilities affect their athletes' efficacy percepts. Vargas-Tonsing et al. (2003) administered the Coaching Efficacy Scale (CES) to 12 High School volleyball teams, while their athletes completed both individual and team efficacy questionnaires. They found that the motivation and character building efficacy subscales significantly predicted collective efficacy, but not player efficacy. Coaches who held strong perceptions about their abilities to enhance psychological skills and group motivation led their teams to believe that they possessed the requisite skills to be successful. Interestingly, the relationship between character building and collective efficacy was negative. Teams appear to have less confidence in their collective abilities when coaches perceive that they can positively influence the level of sportspersonship and moral development of their athletes. As Vargas-Tonsing *et al.* concluded, emphasizing character building skills may undermine the value players place on winning in sport.

Practical implications/intervention

Enhancing collective efficacy beliefs

As previously demonstrated, strong empirical evidence supports the notion that increased perceptions of collective efficacy facilitates team performance and group processes. That is, as collective efficacy beliefs are strengthened, teams coordinate, communicate and interact more effectively to attain team goals. However, there has been no systematic intervention research that has attempted to enhance collective - efficacy beliefs within teams. Nevertheless, it is important that athletes, coaches and sport psychologists understand the mechanisms through which these collective judgments can be altered. This section is intended to guide applied practice and focuses on how the theory and research of collective efficacy can be used to enhance confidence within teams. Many of the recommendations that we advocate for are based on the diverse sources of information in which efficacy beliefs are formed, while some are more related to the interactive dynamics that operate within teams.

Mastery experiences

The most powerful factor that determines a team's sense of efficacy is mastery experiences (past performance accomplishments). Teams that have performed well in previous competitions tend to hold strong feelings regarding their ability to be successful, especially when the performance resulted from the combined efforts of all members. Although winning a competition clearly reflects a sort of mastery experience, the absolute and unpredictable nature of winning makes it an unreliable source. Thus, coaches and athletes should be cautious of over interpreting a win when forming judgments about team capabilities and instead opt for instances that are more controllable (Bandura, 1997).

A useful way for coaches to structure mastery experiences is through team simulations in practice. Simulations are often employed as a means of practicing specific situations that occur within competitions using game-like conditions. For example, American football teams often practice the 2-min drill in order to prepare for situations where the offense has the ball in the final moments of the half or end of the game. If a team is to be successful scoring in the allotted time, members must be able to communicate effectively, utilize time management strategies and be aware of their roles on various plays. Simulations such as the 2-min drill can enhance perceptions of collective efficacy by reinforcing beliefs about the team's ability to mobilize their combined resources to produce collective action during strenuous conditions.

Bandura (1997) suggests that coaches can develop team efficacy percepts by creating styles of play that optimizes individual resources. For instance, basketball teams that consist of fast athletic players would benefit more from an uptempo game plan than a more measured style of play. Additionally, 'coaches who are creative in tailoring performance styles to players' particular talents can turn chronic losers into self-efficacious winners within a short time with little change in players' (Bandura, 1997, p. 400). By doing so, coaches capitalize on the unique skills and roles of existing players rather than having to recruit new athletes to satisfy the coach's preferred style. When coaches fail to match existing players to optimal systems, opponents will often exploit team weaknesses causing collective doubt among members.

Team modeling

Watching film clips of other teams with similar attributes performing successfully against a common opponent can dramatically increase perceptions of collective efficacy by providing evidence that a victory is achievable. Indeed, 'filmed testimony is more informative and persuasive than verbalized hype' (Bandura, 1997, p. 406). A great example of team modeling in American football occurred during the 2005 National Football League (NFL) season. The Indianapolis Colts were 13–0 heading into week 15 against the San Diego Chargers and were threatening to become only the second team in NFL history to attain a perfect regular season record. The Colts were led by MVP quarterback Peyton Manning and were recognized for their high powered offense that was averaging just over 30 points per game. Although the Colts were playing in front of their home crowd and appeared to have the momentum heading into the game, the Chargers ended up with the victory. More impressively, they managed to hold the Colts to only 17 points by putting constant pressure on Manning throughout the game. The once invincible Colts had their weaknesses exposed by the Chargers and teams around the league took notice. Future opponents studied videotape of the Colts/Chargers game and devised similar defensive strategies. The Colts lost two more games and were eventually knocked out of the playoffs in their first game. While modeling the defensive schemes the Chargers had employed proved important for future opponents' success, it was watching the way in which the Chargers effectively handled the Colts offense, unlike any of the previous teams, that led to instilled confidence in other teams who began to believe that an upset was possible.

To ensure that the modeled team has a representative array of competencies, a team could utilize self-modeling, in which case they would watch videotape footage of their own performance attainments, particularly instances that resemble high accomplishment (Bandura, 1997). As Bandura contends, viewing oneself performing effectively provides information not only concerning the proper execution of technique, but also increases the observers' beliefs in their capabilities to perform the task successfully. For example, to enhance motivation and confidence when teams have been experiencing setbacks and are conflicted with internal doubt, coaches can play edited video, which highlights exceptional team coordination or achievements from previous competitions. This type of evidence reassures teams that they possess the qualities necessary to combat team slumps or to bounce back from wrenching defeats in a series.

Verbal persuasion

A convenient and accessible form of verbal persuasion that coaches can use to build the efficacy perceptions of their team corresponds to pre-game or halftime speeches (Vargas-Tonsing and Bartholomew, 2006). Motivational speeches that focus on the collective qualities of the team rather than individual attributes espouse feelings of unity and confidence among members. Further, Vargas-Tonsing and Bartholomew suggest that persuasive speeches have an indirect influence on collective efficacy through the affective reactions they provoke. Indeed, Greenlees *et al.* (1999b) found that efficacy beliefs pertaining to team performance were related to perceptions of precompetitive positive affect among male rugby teams. Therefore, in designing and delivering pregame speeches, coaches should consider their team's optimal level of emotion given the strength or importance of their opponent as well as their environmental surroundings.

Related to persuasive messages are the discussions that coaches have with the media following a competition. Given that responses to interview questions posed by newspaper, television and internet personnel are often relayed to members of the team, coaches should be cautious when divulging information to the media, especially after an emotional loss. Diatribes that single out individual members and attribute team failures to internal-stable causes (e.g. lack of ability) may undermine collective efficacy beliefs. Conversely, emphasizing shared accomplishments or blame while attributing losses to controllable factors should at the very least maintain the strength of efficacy within the team.

Team building interventions

We are unaware of any studies that have examined the effect that team building programs have on strengthening the sense of efficacy within a team. Rather, the majority of studies concerning team building in sport have focused on consequences such as group cohesion (Cogan and Petrie, 1995; McClure and Foster, 1991; Prapavessis *et al.*, 1996). In general, findings have indicated that athletes who participate in team building programs hold increased perceptions of cohesiveness compared with their control group counterparts, though some studies have shown a negligible relationship. Because feelings of team togetherness provide information that contributes to the formation of collective efficacy beliefs (Kozub and McDonnell, 2000; Paskevich *et al.*, 1999, Spink, 1990), it stands to reason that increasing cohesion through team building activities that promote role clarity and acceptance may foster teams' judgments of their capabilities to succeed.

Team goal-setting

While it is often a central focus in team building protocols (Yukelson, 1997), team goal-setting is one of the most effective applied techniques that sport psychologists can use to improve team confidence and thus merits specific attention. Setting goals increases the amount of effort put forward in a task, enhances the level of persistence while engaging in a task, improves attentional focus and facilitates the development of new learning strategies (Locke and Latham, 1984). However, research on goal-setting in sport has primarily been confined to the individual level. Widmeyer and DuCharme (1997) have provided recommendations for initiating team goal-setting programs in athletic teams which include establishing long-term goals first, providing a clear path for reaching long-term goals, ensuring that all members are actively involved in the process, monitoring and rewarding goal progress and enhancing collective efficacy regarding goal attainment. They suggested that a team's belief in its capabilities to successfully achieve performance objectives contributes to team functioning. Studies have also shown that during practice, teams tend to emphasize process goals as opposed to outcome goals, whereas in competitions teams emphasize an equal combination between process and outcome goals (Brawley *et al.*, 1992). Because team efficacy has been shown to decrease linearly from midseason until the start of postseason play as a result of increased fatigue, worry and unfulfilled expectations (Feltz and Lirgg, 1998), coaches should especially focus on process-related goals later in the season (Druckman and Bjork, 1994).

Future research directions

Since its initial conception 25 years ago (Bandura, 1982), the field of sport psychology has come a long way toward developing and understating the theory of collective - efficacy in sport. However, there are still many issues surrounding collective efficacy that have not been extensively explored. This section of the chapter is intended to facilitate new research and to further advance the knowledge concerning this line of inquiry. For simplicity, the following suggestions have been organized according to their potential contributions to the literature, which include research development, statistical modeling and applied practice.

Research development

Examining group dynamic consequences of collective efficacy

Previous research has demonstrated that the level of collective efficacy within a team results from a variety of informational sources including but not limited to self-efficacy (Magyar *et al.*, 2004; Watson *et al.*, 2001), group cohesion (Kozub and McDonnell, 2000; Paskevich *et al.*, 1999; Spink, 1990), coaching efficacy (Vargas-Tonsing *et al.*, 2003) and motivational climate (Magyar *et al.*, 2004). While these studies show the diversity of sources from which efficacy judgments are formed, with the exception of team performance, very little research has been conducted to identify the individual or team level consequences of collective efficacy (Figure 12.1). As teams develop a sense of efficacy through complex interaction and coordination patterns, motivational processes emerge that may enhance or hinder team performance. A factor that may be influenced by perceptions of team efficacy is social loafing. As George and Feltz (1995) noted, athletes on high efficacy teams may be more prone to loaf, as they believe their team-mates have the capabilities to overcome motivational losses. Alternatively, athletes on low efficacy teams may try to overcompensate for team doubt by exerting more effort. It is important to note that social loafing is an individual level attribute that is influenced by the team environment, thus making it an ideal variable to examine in multilevel modeling.

As we mentioned earlier, collective efficacy is proposed to influence the attributions that a team makes, but this hypothesized relationship is in need of further research. In one study, Chow and Feltz (2007) explored the relationship between precompetitive efficacy beliefs and post-competitive attributions for team performance with track and field relay athletes. They found that individual perceptions of collective efficacy predicted the team control dimension. That is, athletes who held strong beliefs about the integrative competencies of their team believed that the cause of their team's performance was controllable by the team as a whole. In addition, aggregated collective efficacy emerged as a significant team level predictor of average stability.

Exploring the contagious nature of collective efficacy within teams

Performance ineffectiveness by one key player can quickly spread throughout the team infecting each and every member. Bandura (1997) suggests that there are several ways in which performance decrements become contagious within teams. The first involves the influence of modeling on the efficacy of individual members. Watching someone who is similar in attributes, or more importantly, an individual with higher ability experiencing setbacks plants a seed of internal doubt within the observer. Contagious ineffectiveness can also cause downward team performance spirals by increasing beliefs about the 'overpoweringness' of opponents. At the same time, the modeling of ineffectiveness by star players may result in team-mates taking ill-advised risks, talking negatively and engaging in poor decision-making. Lastly, an injury to a superstar may undermine a team's level of efficacy, particularly if members attribute previous team success to the fallen player. The contagious nature of collective efficacy is an interesting dynamic that can affect team functioning and is uniquely inherent to the team context. Accordingly, future investigators should examine the extent to which the performance of one player contributes to the team's overall sense of efficacy and through which mechanisms it occurs. How to measure this dynamic, however, poses challenges. Fortunately, a fairly recent methodology – agent-based modeling – has been employed to capture contagious phenomena in other spheres of behavior (Epstein and Axtell, 1996).

Collective-efficacy dispersion

Popular knowledge among researchers who study group dynamics in sport would suggest that agreement among members' perceptions of collective efficacy will result in optimal team processes and functioning, at least when perceived efficacy is high. For instance, Zaccaro *et al.* (1995) assert that teams with complete consensus in efficacy beliefs may be more cohesive than teams with dispersed beliefs, especially if the team is highly regarded. Of course, team members who all agree in their lack of ability would not be expected to be task cohesive nor perform well. However, according to Bandura (1997), having some doubt in the preparatory stages of performance may actually increase motivational levels and facilitate the development of skills. Additionally, in order to prevent overconfidence and complacency among members, leaders on highly efficacious teams may attempt to deflate feelings of efficacy by focusing on errors in performance. There are at least two ways that team doubt can exist within teams: (1) all members having similar doubt (shared doubt) or (2) dispersed opinions among team members regarding the team's capabilities. The concept of efficacy dispersion was proposed by DeRue *et al.* (2007) and reflects the team-level variability in the magnitude of team efficacy perceptions within the team. They argue that dispersion enhances preparatory performance by causing teams to reappraise strategies, whereas consensus hinders reappraisal motivation but increases team viability. Future research on collective efficacy in sport could address some of the aforementioned propositions of dispersion as well as questions such as 'for a given level of collective efficacy, do teams with high perceptual consensus in their collective beliefs outperform teams with dispersed efficacy judgments?'

Statistical modeling

Multilevel modeling

The team context provides a unique situation in that each member has individual characteristics (e.g. years of experience, self-efficacy, anxiety), whereas the team as a whole has group characteristics (e.g. level of competition, collective efficacy, motivational climate), though team level variables may simply be an aggregation of individual level variables. Both athlete and team attributes can have differential influences on motivation, persistence and performance. Similarly, these same consequences can affect individual and collective perceptions. In such cases, the observed data are considered hierarchically structured (athletes within teams) and thus should be analyzed using multilevel modeling. As we mentioned earlier, multilevel modeling allows the researcher to pose questions at the individual level, team level and across levels while determining the variation at each level (Raudenbush and Bryk, 2002).

Although multilevel modeling programs such as HLM and MLwiN have been readily available for over 10 years, employing the statistical technique has been considered the exception rather than the rule in group dynamics and collective efficacy research in sport. Instead, researchers have opted to analyze their data only at the individual level which ignores groupings or only at the team level which discards within team information. In addition to the concerns that we described in the measurement section of this chapter, Raudenbush and Bryk (2002) also contend that using the individual as the unit of analysis in team environments violates the assumption of independence, results in misestimated standard errors and increases the risk of Type I errors. Further, using the team as the unit of analysis reduces power, distorts interpretations and produces inefficient and biased fixed effects. We recommend that future investigators interested in the study of collective efficacy employ a multilevel statistical approach to minimize the potential problems associated with single level analyses.

Agent-based modeling

As individuals behave and interact in complex dynamic systems, certain macropatterns emerge that are difficult to analyze using traditional statistical methods. Most of the statistical analyses that have been employed in sport psychology research are based on the assumption of linearity and thus are limited in assessing complicated dynamics that spread within teams such as contagious ineffectiveness. The primary advantage of agent-based modeling is that it captures emergent phenomena from the bottom up by modeling and simulating collective behavior and interactions among members (Epstein and Axtell, 1996). As a result, relationships between individual and team units can be adequately tested. Further, agent-based modeling enables the researcher to analyze complex emergent patterns that cannot be easily observed or understood using linear modeling approaches. Advanced simulated modeling procedures offer promising insight into the psychosocial dynamics that unfold in team contexts.

Applied practice

Designing and evaluating collective efficacy interventions

Although the amount of research on collective efficacy in sport has grown substantially through the years, there is a noticeable exclusion from the literature: collective efficacy intervention studies. This finding is unfortunate considering that a team's belief in its capabilities to successfully execute interactive tasks has been shown to be highly related to team performance, goals, effort and persistence in the face of failure. Great progress in the area of collective efficacy can be made through the development of interventions designed to enhance team efficacy perceptions. Effective intervention studies not only have applied implications for sports teams, but they also allow researchers to test theory. When designing such interventions, a useful starting point may be to focus on the sources of efficacy information as well as the recommendations for enhancing collective efficacy provided in this chapter. Following development, it is imperative that researchers examine the effectiveness of the program's ability to increase judgments of collective abilities. Future research that employs applied methods to bolster the strength of collective - efficacy within teams not only progresses the growing body of literature, but has potential benefits for coaches and sport psychologists concerned with improving team dynamics.

Summary

Collective-efficacy represents an ideal theoretical framework for which to understand team functioning and group motivation in sport. Unfortunately, the concept has received limited attention in sport psychology research compared with other group dynamic variables. Our intent in this chapter, was to discuss the prevalent ideas and concerns related to collective efficacy research in sport and to provide suggestions for advancing conceptual knowledge in this area. The literature that was reviewed in this chapter indicates that a team's sense of efficacy is a key determinant of mutual accomplishments, which develops through diverse sources of efficacy information. Applying the sources of efficacy along with group dynamic intervention strategies can serve as a foundation for enhancing the strength of perceived collective efficacy within teams. While considerable progress has been made, future research that addresses motivational consequences of collective efficacy, examines issues of contagious and dispersed efficacy beliefs, employs advanced statistical methodologies and applies collective efficacy interventions holds promising implications for understanding the efficacy beliefs of sports teams.

References

Bandura, A. (1977). Self-efficacy: Toward a unifying theory of behavioral change. *Psychological Review*, 84, 191–215.

Bandura, A. (1982). Self-efficacy mechanism in human agency. *American Psychologist*, 37, 122–147.

Bandura, A. (1986). *Social foundations of thought and action: A social cognitive theory*. Englewood Cliffs, NJ: Prentice-Hall.

Bandura, A. (1997). *Self-efficacy: The exercise of control*. New York: Freeman.

Bandura, A. (2005). Guide for creating self-efficacy scales. In F. Pajares and T. Urdan (Eds), *Self-efficacy beliefs of adolescents* (pp. 307–337). Greenwich, CT: Information Age Publishing.

Brawley, L. R., Carron, A. V. and Widmeyer, W. N. (1992). The nature of group goals in sport teams: A phenomenological analysis. *The Sport Psychologist*, 6, 323–333.

Bray, S. B. (2004). Collective-efficacy, group goals and group performance of a muscular endurance task. *Small Group Research*, 35, 230–238.

Carron, A. V., Hausenblas, H. A. and Eys, M. A. (2005). *Group dynamics in sport* (3rd ed.). Morgantown, WV: Fitness Information Technology.

Cogan, K. D. and Petrie, T. A. (1995). Sport consultation: An evaluation of a season-long intervention with female collegiate gymnasts. *The Sport Psychologist*, 9, 282–296.

Chase, M. A., Feltz, D. L. and Lirgg, C. D. (2003). Sources of collective efficacy and individual efficacy of collegiate athletes. *International Journal of Sport and Exercise Psychology*, 1, 180–191.

Chow, G. M. and Feltz, D. L. (2007). Exploring relationships between collective efficacy, perceptions of success and team attributions. (Manuscript submitted for publication.)

Dawson, K. A., Gyurcsik, N. C., Culos-Reed, S. N. and Brawley, L. R. (2001). Perceived control: A construct that bridges theories of motivated behavior. In G. C. Roberts (Ed.), *Advances in motivation in sport and exercise*. Champaign, IL: Human Kinetics.

DeRue, D. S., Hollenbeck, J. R., Ilgen, D. R. and Feltz, D. L. (2007). A theory of efficacy dispersion and trajectory in teams: Beyond agreement and aggregation. (Manuscript submitted for publication.)

Druckman, D. and Bjork, R. A. (Eds). (1994). *Learning, remembering, believing*. Washington, DC: National Academy Press.

Edmonds, W. A. (2003). The role of collective efficacy in adventure racing teams. Unpublished doctoral dissertation. Florida State University, Tallahassee.

Epstein, J. M. and Axtell, R. (1996). *Growing artificial societies: Social science from the bottom up*. Cambridge, MA: MIT Press.

Eyal, N., Bar-Eli, M., Tenenbaum, G. and Pie, J. S. (1995). Manipulated outcome expectations and competitive performance in motor tasks with gradually increasing difficulty. *The Sport Psychologist*, 9, 188–200.

Feltz, D. L., Chase, M. A., Moritz, S. E. and Sullivan, P. J. (1999). A conceptual model of coaching efficacy: Preliminary investigation and instrument development. *Journal of Educational Psychology*, 91, 765–776.

Feltz, D. L. and Lirgg, C. D. (1998). Perceived team and player efficacy in hockey. *Journal of Applied Psychology*, 83, 557–564.

Feltz, D. L. and Lirgg, C. D. (2001). Self-efficacy beliefs of athletes, teams and coaches. In R. N. Singer, H. A. Hausenblas and C. Janelle (Eds), *Handbook of sport psychology* (2nd ed., pp. 340–361). New York: Wiley.

Feltz, D. L., Short, S. E. and Sullivan, P. J. (2008). *Self-efficacy theory and application in sport*. Champaign, IL: Human Kinetics.

George, T. R. and Feltz, D. L. (1995). Motivation in sport from a collective efficacy perspective. *International Journal of Sport Psychology*, 26, 98–116.

Greenlees, I. A., Graydon, J. K. and Maynard, I. W. (1999a). The impact of collective efficacy beliefs on effort and persistence in a group task. *Journal of Sport Sciences*, 17, 151–158.

Greenlees, I. A., Graydon, J. K. and Maynard, I. W. (2000). The impact of individual efficacy beliefs on group goal commitment. *Journal of Sport Sciences*, 18, 451–459.

Greenlees, I. A., Nunn, R. L., Graydon, J. K. and Maynard, I. W. (1999b). The relationship between collective efficacy and precompetitive affect in rugby players: Testing Bandura's model of collective efficacy. *Perceptual and Motor Skills*, 89, 431–440.

Gully, S. M., Incalcaterra, K. A., Joshi, A. and Beaubien, J. M. (2002). A meta-analysis of team-efficacy, potency and performance: Interdependence and level of analysis as moderators of observed relationships. *Journal of Applied Psychology*, 87, 819–832.

Guzzo, R. A., Yost, P. R., Campbell, R. J. and Shea, G. P. (1993). Potency in groups: Articulating a construct. *British Journal of Social Psychology*, 32, 87–106.

Hodges, L. and Carron, A. (1992). Collective-efficacy and group performance. *International Journal of Sport Psychology*, 23, 48–59.

Hueze, J. P., Raimbault, N. and Fontayne, P. (2006). Relationships between cohesion, collective - efficacy and performance in professional basketball teams: An examination of mediating effects. *Journal of Sport Sciences*, 24, 59–68.

James, L. R. (1982). Aggregation bias in estimates of perceptual agreement. *Journal of Applied Psychology*, 67, 219–229.

James, L. R., Demaree, R. G. and Wolf, G. (1984). Estimating within-group rater reliability with and without response bias. *Journal of Applied Psychology*, 69, 85–98.

Kozlowski, S. J. and Hattrup, K. (1992). A disagreement about within-group agreement: Disentangling issues of consistency versus consensus. *Journal of Applied Psychology*, 77, 161–167.

Kozub, S. A. and McDonnell, J. F. (2000). Exploring the relationship between cohesion and collective efficacy in rugby teams. *Journal of Sport Behavior*, 23, 120–129.

Latané, B., Williams, K. and Harkins, S. (1979). Many hands make light work: The causes and consequences of social loafing. *Journal of Personality and Social Psychology*, 37, 822–832.

Lichacz, F. M. and Partington, J. T. (1996). Collective-efficacy and true performance. *International Journal of Sport Psychology*, 27, 146–158.

Locke, E. A. and Latham, G. P. (1984). *Goal setting: A motivational technique that works.* Englewood Cliffs, NJ: Prentice-Hall.

Magyar, T. M., Feltz, D. L. and Simpson, I. P. (2004). Individual and crew level determinants of collective efficacy in rowing. *Journal of Sport and Exercise Psychology*, 26, 136–153.

McClure, B. A. and Foster, C. D. (1991). Group work as a method of promoting cohesiveness within a women's gymnastics team. *Perceptual and Motor Skills*, 73, 307–313.

Moritz, S. E. and Watson, C. B. (1998). Levels of analysis issues in group psychology: Using efficacy as an example of a multilevel model. *Group Dynamics: Theory, Research and Practice*, 2, 285–298.

Myers, N. D. and Feltz, D. L. (2007). From self-efficacy to collective efficacy in sport: Transitional issues. In G. Tenenbaum and R. C. Eklund (Eds), *Handbook of sport psychology* (3rd ed., pp. 799–819). New York: Wiley.

Myers, N. D., Feltz, D. L. and Short, S. E. (2004a). Collective-efficacy and team performance: A longitudinal study of collegiate football teams. *Group Dynamics: Theory, Research and Practice*, 8, 126–138.

Myers, N. D., Payment, C. A. and Feltz, D. L. (2004b). Reciprocal relationships between collective efficacy and team performance in women's ice hockey. *Group Dynamics: Theory, Research and Practice*, 8, 182–195 .

Neiss, R. (1989). Expectancy in motor behavior: A crucial element of the psychobiological states that affect performance. *Human Performance*, 2, 273–300.

Paskevich, D. M., Brawley, L. R., Dorsch, K. D. and Widmeyer, W. N. (1999). Relationship between collective efficacy and team cohesion: Conceptual and measurement issues. *Group Dynamics: Theory, Research and Practice*, 3, 210–222.

Prapavessis, H., Carron, A. V. and Spink, K. S. (1996). Team building in sport. *International Journal of Sport Psychology*, 27, 269–285.

Prussia, G. E. and Kinicki, A. J. (1996). A motivational investigation of group effectiveness using social cognitive theory. *Journal of Applied Psychology*, 81, 187–198.

Raudenbush, S. W. and Bryk, A. S. (2002). *Hierarchical linear models: Applications and data analysis methods.* Newbury Park, CA: Sage.

Rousseau, D. M. (1985). Issues of levels in organizational research: Multilevel and cross-level perspectives. *Research in Organizational Behavior*, 7, 1–37.

Short, S. E. (2005). *The effect of team size, type of sport, time of season and gender on collective - efficacy beliefs in sport.* (Manuscript submitted for publication.)

Short, S. E., Apostal, K., Harris, C., Poltavski, D., Young, J., Zostautas, N., Sullivan, P. and Feltz,

D. L. (2002). Assessing collective efficacy: A comparison of two approaches. *Journal of Sport and Exercise Psychology*, 24, S115–S116.

Short, S. E., Sullivan, P. J. and Feltz, D. L. (2005). Development and preliminary validation of the collective efficacy questionnaire for sport. *Measurement in Physical Education and Exercise Science*, 9, 181–202.

Spink, K. S. (1990). Group cohesion and collective efficacy of volleyball teams. *Journal of Sport and Exercise Psychology*, 12, 301–311.

Vargas-Tonsing, T. M. and Bartholomew, J. B. (2006). An exploratory study of the effects of pregame speeches on team-efficacy beliefs. *Journal of Applied Social Psychology*, 36, 918–933.

Vargas-Tonsing, T. M., Warners, A. L. and Feltz, D. L. (2003). The predictability of coaching efficacy on team efficacy and player efficacy in volleyball. *Journal of Sport Behavior*, 26, 396–407.

Watson, C. B., Chemers, M. M. and Preiser, N. (2001). Collective-efficacy: A multilevel analysis. *Personality and Social Psychology Bulletin*, 27, 1056–1068.

Widmeyer, W. N., Brawley, L. R. and Carron, A. V. (1985). *The measurement of cohesion in sport teams: The group environment questionnaire*. London, ON: Sports Dynamics.

Widmeyer, W. N. and DuCharme, K. (1997). Team building through team goal setting. *Journal of Applied Sport Psychology*, 9, 97–113.

Yukelson, D. (1997). Principles of effective team building interventions in sport: A direct services approach at Penn State University. *Journal of Applied Sport Psychology*, 9, 73–96.

Zaccaro, S. J., Blair, V., Peterson, C. and Zazanis, M. (1995). Collective-efficacy. In J. E. Maddux (Ed.), *Self-efficacy, adaptation and adjustment: Theory, research and application* (pp. 308–330). New York: Plenum.

Index

Routledge Sport

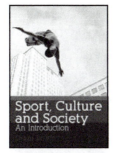

Sport, Culture and Society
Grant Jarvie, Stirling University, UK

An exciting new textbook exploring all of the key themes covered in undergraduate sport studies and introducing students to critical thinking about the complex and symbiotic relationship between sport and its wider social context.

PB :978-0-415-30647-8: **£28.99**

Sports Development, 2e
Kevin Hylton and Peter Bramham, Leeds Metropolitan University, UK

This popular course text examines the roles of those working in and around sports development and explores how professionals can devise better and more effective ways of promoting interest, participation or performance in sport.

PB :978-0-415-42183-6: **£24.99**

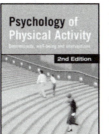

Psychology of Physical Activity, 2e
Stuart J H Biddle, Loughborough University, UK and Nanette Mutrie, Strathclyde University, UK

This text covers the field of exercise psychology in detail. Issues covered include motivation, attitudes, wellbeing, depression and mental illness, clinical populations, interventions and research consensus.

PB :978-0-415-36665-6: **£27.99**

The Sport Studies Reader
Alan Tomlinson, University of Brighton, UK

This reader collects several pieces of valuable, interesting and, in some cases, classic essays and extracts that have been widely recommended over the years, yet which are not always readily available.

PB :978-0-419-26030-1: **£26.99**

This is a selection of our new and bestselling titles. Visit www.routledge.com/sport for more information.

Routledge
Taylor & Francis Group